Teaching Children
with Autism

Teaching Children with Autism

Strategies for Initiating Positive Interactions and Improving Learning Opportunities

edited by

Robert L. Koegel, Ph.D.

Director, Autism Research Center
Professor, Counseling/Clinical/School Psychology
Professor, Special Education, Disability, and Risk Studies

and

Lynn Kern Koegel, Ph.D.

Clinic Director, Autism Research Center

Graduate School of Education
University of California at Santa Barbara

·PAUL·H·
BROOKES
PUBLISHING CO.®

Baltimore • London • Sydney

Paul H. Brookes Publishing Co.
Post Office Box 10624
Baltimore, Maryland 21285-0624
www.brookespublishing.com

Typeset by Brushwood Graphics, Inc., Baltimore, Maryland.
Manufactured in the United States of America by
Victor Graphics, Inc., Baltimore, Maryland.

Second printing, June 1996.
Third printing, June 1998.
Fourth printing, July 1999.
Fifth printing, November 2000.
Sixth printing, August 2003.

Library of Congress Cataloging-in-Publication Data

Teaching children with autism : strategies for initiating positive
    interactions and improving learning opportunities / edited by Robert
    L. Koegel and Lynn Kern Koegel.
        p.   cm.
    Includes bibliographical references and index.
    ISBN 1-55766-180-4
    1. Autistic children—Education.   2. Autism in children.
    I. Koegel, Robert L., 1944–   .   II. Koegel, Lynn Kern.
    LC4717.5.T42   1995
    371.94—dc20   94-45943
                                                                                        CIP

British Library Cataloguing-in-Publication data are available from the British Library.

Contents

Contributors

The Editors

Robert L. Koegel, Ph.D., Director, Autism Research Center; Professor, Counseling/Clinical/School Psychology; and Professor, Special Education, Disability, and Risk Studies, Graduate School of Education, University of California at Santa Barbara.

Lynn Kern Koegel, Ph.D., Clinic Director, Autism Research Center, Graduate School of Education, University of California at Santa Barbara.

The Contributors

Ann Leslie Albanese

Patricia Bloom

William D. Frea

Don Hawkins

Christine M. Hurley-Geffner

Diane Hammon Kellegrew

Douglas Moes

Kimberly B. Mullen

Deborah Rumore Parks

Jennifer Rosenblatt

Stephanie K. San Miguel

Annette E. Smith

Michelle Wood

Preface

The purpose of this book is to provide a useful conceptual and practical guide for teaching children with autism in a way that will maximize their developmental potential. As ever-increasing numbers of children are receiving a diagnosis of autism, we have attempted to provide a guide to understanding the great variability among the children. As the research continues to evolve, it is likely that a more clear knowledge of the early symptoms of infants and toddlers diagnosed with autism will help us define prognostic indicators and discover what early behaviors may need to be taught for the most favorable outcome. We are extremely optimistic about the procedures described in this book, which have been experimentally documented to be more effective than procedures generally used in the past. We are also well aware that, while the course of the disability changes over time and some children are able to reach a functioning level quite similar to that of their typically developing peers, there also are many who are unable to achieve that level. Thus, the need exists for greater understanding of the variability among children with this diagnosis.

The scope of this book is limited primarily to behavioral interventions that have been scientifically documented to be effective and will result in socially significant and durable behavior change. There is particular emphasis on improving communication throughout the book. Existing literature well documents the direct link between communication and behavior. In addition to the scientific literature in general, our own work indicates that improvements in communication are clearly associated with positive behavioral change, and therefore focusing on communication as a pivotal behavior reduces the need for many related interventions. Within the area of communication, emphasis is placed on how to conduct functional analyses that will provide useful diagnostic information for the design of teaching and intervention programs.

Our general approach to intervention is based upon a developmental model. That is, throughout the book we describe ways to normalize the environmental stimulation and interactions that the children receive, so as to maximize their developmental potential. Therefore, we stress the importance of conducting teaching and intervention under naturalistic environmental conditions. We focus on utilizing the benefits of parental involvement and parent education programs, so that the children may learn in their regular community environments. We also focus on interventions that are conducted in full-inclusion environments, in the home, community, and school, where the children are learning among their typically developing peers. We stress the importance of friendships among individuals with and without disabilities and the essential role of friendships in development.

We also emphasize in this book that reaching a child's maximum potential necessitates a coordinated and cooperative effort among professionals. To date, no one individual or group of individuals has unlocked all of the complex variables involved in autism. The key to best helping children with autism involves a group effort. Too often professionals find themselves involved in controversy and perhaps even court cases because those interacting with a particular child cannot agree. At the end of these often-lengthy controversies no one is fully satisfied, and the child has suffered in the meantime. In contrast, a coordinated effort by all involved can greatly enhance the functioning level of the child with autism and concomitantly reduce the tremendous familial stress associated with having a child with a disability.

The intervention procedures described in this book are based upon many years of research and experience interacting with individuals with autism under many different circumstances and conditions. We have come to know individuals with autism as people first and have come to focus more on their abilities than on their disabilities. Doing so has helped us to make many friends among the children and families who have participated in our research programs. Furthermore, this approach has molded research programs that have been meaningful for the individuals involved. We are especially grateful for their assistance.

We also appreciate the assistance of Annette E. Smith, who in addition to working with the children in our center, and contributing to the writing of the initial chapter in this book, also assisted greatly with the editorial process. We are also grateful for the assistance of the funding agencies that have made much of the research described in this book possible. A great deal of the research described in this book was funded by the U.S. Public Health Service, the National Institutes of Health, the National Institute of Mental Health, the U.S. Department of Education, and the National Institute on Disability and Rehabilitation Research.

In general, we have focused our descriptions on research directions that have a strong data base to support their foundations. Every attempt has been made to present thoroughly documented techniques and to focus on future directions that appear to be especially strong. Because of this, we anticipate continued improvements in the prognosis for children diagnosed with autism, and we feel continued optimism about the futures for these children and their families.

Photograph Acknowledgments

The photographs in this book were taken by the following individuals.

Book cover: Cindy M. Carter

Chapter 1:   Eve Helena Davison
                   Lynn Kern Koegel (series)

Chapter 2:   Cindy M. Carter
                   Annette E. Smith (series)

Chapter 3:   Eve Helena Davison
                   Jennifer Rosenblatt (series)

Chapter 4:   Lynn Kern Koegel
                   Annette E. Smith

Chapter 5:   Annette E. Smith

Chapter 6:   Annette E. Smith
                   Sherilyn M. Young
                   Annette E. Smith (series)

Chapter 7:   Annette E. Smith
                   Lynn Kern Koegel (series)

Chapter 8:   Eve Helena Davison

Chapter 9:   Lynn Kern Koegel

Chapter 10:   Mary Baker
                   Mary Baker

Chapter 11:   Mary Baker

Chapter 12:   Mary Baker

Teaching Children
with Autism

Chapter 1

Emerging Interventions for Children with Autism

Longitudinal and Lifestyle Implications

*Robert L. Koegel, Lynn Kern Koegel,
William D. Frea, and Annette E. Smith*

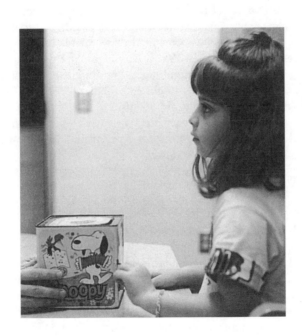

DESCRIBING THE CHARACTERISTICS OF AUTISM

When the label of *autism* was first coined by Leo Kanner in 1943, he was subclassifying a unique group of children who demonstrated relatively common characteristics and who differed from the previous broad classification termed *childhood psychosis*. In his description of 11 case histories, Kanner noted considerable differences in these children compared to the typical child labeled with childhood psychosis. These differences included 1) the degree of the child's disability, 2) the manifestation of specific features, 3) the family constellation, and 4) the step-by-step development in the course of years. Due to the realization of these differences, the number of individuals now diagnosed as having autism or "autistic-like" features has increased geometrically from those original 11 children to include up to as many as 3 or 4 out of every 2,000 children (G. Dunlap, Robbins, Dollman, & Plienis, 1988; Schreibman, 1988). Although these children share the same diagnosis, their behavioral symptoms vary greatly.

In fact, variability may best describe the characteristics of individuals with autism. Whereas all of the children seem to have some difficulties with social communication, the expression of these difficulties differs immensely in both type and severity. Recent interest in the issue of heterogeneity has recognized that children with autism most likely have distinctly different etiologies (Courchesne et al., in press; Damasio & Maurer, 1978; Gillberg & Gillberg, 1983; Ritvo, Ritvo, & Brothers, 1982; Rosenberger-Debiesse & Coleman, 1986). Moreover, specific characteristics such as cognitive ability (Fein, Waterhouse, Lucci, & Snyder, 1985), communication and social skills, and behaviors such as activity level and aggression (Eaves, Ho, & Eaves, 1994) vary greatly across children with autism. Furthermore, the impact of the characteristics of the children changes throughout development (Waterhouse, Fein, Nath, & Snyder, 1987). Thus, the label of autism offers limited communication among professionals and may even enhance misperceptions among those who are unfamiliar with the disorder.

As a result, a number of researchers have attempted to define subtypes of autism. Attempts to delineate subtypes have focused on distinctly different patterns of behavior the children demonstrate, such as perceptual performance, verbal skills, memory, motor skills and asymmetry (Fein et al., 1985), language patterns such as onset of language (Kolvin, 1971), severity and predominance of behavioral characteristics during play (Siegel, Anders, Ciaranello, Bienenstock, & Kraemer, 1986), and social characteristics (Borden & Ollendick, 1994; Wing & Gould, 1979).

The characteristics of autism vary greatly across children, and to be diagnosed with autism does not mean a person must display all of them. The following section describes the most common characteristics of autism.

Characteristics of Autism

Social Communication

As is discussed in depth in Chapters 2 and 5, the one characteristic exhibited in almost all children with autism is their apparent lack of social-communicative gestures and utterances. Very early on, perhaps beginning in the first few months of life, it is evident that children with autism may not engage in simple social behaviors such as eye gaze, smiles, and responses to parents' attempts to prompt vocalizations and play interactions. When vocabulary and language are learned, they are often used instrumentally rather than socially. Such patterns can continue throughout life. Even when language competence is achieved, pragmatic skills such as initiating conversation and responding to the conversation of others (L.K. Koegel, Koegel, Hurley, & Frea, 1992), appropriate turn-taking, prosody, speech detail, perseveration, and attention during conversation may be lacking (Frea, 1990; R.L. Koegel & Frea, 1992). However, researchers are now addressing these issues, and later chapters in this book discuss effective intervention procedures.

Language

Verbal language does not develop in a small percentage of children with autism. Early figures estimated that 50% of children with autism never develop functional expressive language (Prizant, 1983; Rutter, 1978b); however, now that improved language teaching procedures are available, the outlook is considerably brighter. Currently, if language emerges, it is primarily used for requests and desires (Wetherby & Prutting, 1984) and not typically for the purposes of social interaction or social support (newer procedures, discussed in Chapters 2 and 5, attempt to address this). This is most likely due to the social-communicative difficulties of children with autism. A number of authors have recently discussed core underlying problems of communication as the primary disability in autism and other behavioral problems as secondary. Evidence of this has been documented repeatedly. For example, L.K. Koegel, Koegel, Hurley, and Frea (1992) found that, when children are taught to engage in appropriate communicative behaviors, inappropriate behaviors such as aggression, self-injury, and certain types of self-stimulation decrease without special intervention. Other studies have demonstrated this inverse relationship when functionally equivalent communicative responses are taught. Carr and Durand (1985) demonstrated that disruptive behaviors exhibited as attention or escape mechanisms can be reduced or eliminated when functionally equivalent communicative behaviors, such as "Is this right?" (for the teacher's attention) or "I need help" (for the teacher's assistance with a difficult assignment), are taught.

Self-Stimulation

Self-stimulatory behavior, or stereotypic behavior, refers to repetitive behaviors such as hand flapping, twirling objects in front of the eyes, and body rocking that extends for a prolonged period of time and seems to provide sensory or kinesthetic feedback for a child with autism (Lovaas, Litrownik, & Mann, 1971). Self-stimulatory behaviors may be expressed in a variety of ways. Sometimes they are subtle, such as gazing at lights or making inappropriate facial expressions or grimacing. Others are quite obvious, such as body rocking or loud and repetitive vocalizations. Most self-stimulatory behaviors appear to have little or no obvious social meaning to others and appear to interfere with relationships, learning, and neurological development (L.K. Koegel, Valdez-Menchaca, & Koegel, 1994). In addition, these behaviors have an inverse relationship with many appropriate behaviors, and, when they are suppressed, spontaneous increases in academic responding and play are observed; when certain types of play and learning are increased, certain stereotypic behaviors spontaneously decrease (Kern, Koegel, & Dunlap, 1984; Kern, Koegel, Dyer, Blew, & Fenton, 1982; R.L. Koegel, Firestone, Kramme, & Dunlap, 1974).

Self-Injurious and Aggressive Behavior

Occasionally, children with autism display self-injurious and aggressive behaviors. In the past, these behaviors were conceptualized as extremely stigmatizing and potentially harmful, and punitive consequences were administered to treat them. However, a shift in the field has focused on the communicative function of these behaviors, and functionally equivalent replacement behaviors are now being taught. Specifically, analysis of the function of disruptive behaviors has been researched, and behaviors such as self-injury, aggression, and other related disruptive behaviors (e.g., tantrums and property destruction) fall into specific patterns of functions or reasons the individual displays them. Common functions include attention seeking; avoidance of a perceived unpleasant situation; or escape from an undesirable activity, task, or circumstance. If such functions are assessed and appropriate communicative behaviors are taught, self-injury and aggression can be reduced, eliminated, or prevented.

Demand for Sameness and Preoccupation with Objects

Children with autism often develop excessive preoccupations with particular objects, routines, or the preservation of sameness in the environment. They may have particular objects that they interact with in an idiosyncratic fashion, such as lining up small cars by size or color. Attempts to engage the child with other toys or disrupt the order may result in tantrums or aggression. Preservation of routines is displayed when a child insists on unusual patterns of behavior, such as following a specific route to a familiar location or being served foods in a specific order (e.g., requiring milk to be poured into a bowl before the cereal and spoon are placed in the bowl). Again, the child may become upset if such routines are not followed. Desire for sameness can be observed by their apparent distress when specific aspects of their environments are disrupted or changed. For example, some children become troubled if the furniture is rearranged; others may insist on wearing the same clothes daily. Although this behavior is not well understood and few intervention techniques other than response interruption exist, it is a common characteristic of children with autism.

Epidemiology and Etiology

The incidence of autism, *excluding* those children diagnosed as "autistic-like" or with other primary diagnoses, has been estimated to be about 1 out of every 2,000 live births and is four to five times more common in males than females (G. Dunlap et al., 1988; Schreibman, 1988). For a period of time after autism was regarded as its own distinct entity, a parental-causation theory was developed and prevailed for several decades. However, following an emphasis on scientifically based methodologies focusing on etiology, this theory was essentially abandoned. In fact, although the burden and demands of having a child with significant disabilities may result in stress on the family, transactional views suggest that the behaviors a *child* displays may actually *cause* the parents to adjust their style of interaction accordingly (cf. Curcio & Paccia, 1987; Mahoney, 1988a).

Current research and theory regarding etiology are focusing on organic factors, and it is generally accepted that autism is present at birth or shortly thereafter. It is also becoming evident that the behavioral characteristics a child needs to display to be diagnosed as having autism may represent a variety of different causes. It is important to note, in this discussion of the possible physiological correlates, that, although studies have reported the following variables to be significant, *none* has reported any variable to be evident in *all* of the children or families assessed, which again demonstrates the suggestion that the underlying cause may vary across children. Although there is much research to support the various etiologies, it is not the purpose of this book to discuss them in detail; therefore, each one is discussed briefly here.

Some possible causes and signs of autism that have been the focus of research include prenatal, perinatal, and neonatal complications, such as bleedings, pre- and postmaturity, severe infection during pregnancy, generalized edema, medication for more than 1 week during pregnancy, reduced Apgar scores (Gillberg & Gillberg, 1983), and congenital rubella (Chess, 1977).

Neurological and neuroanatomical research has found atypical patterns of cerebral lateralization (Dawson, Finley, Phillips, & Lewy, 1989), differences in brain stem responses (Gillberg, Rosenhall, & Johansson, 1983), abnormal EEGs (Mesibov & Dawson, 1986), and cerebellar asymmetry in specific areas (Courchesne, Lincoln, Yeung-Courchesne, Elmasian, & Grillon, 1989) in children with autism. Because the functioning of the brain structures is not clearly understood, interpretation of these studies is complex and further studies are needed to elucidate these findings.

Neurochemical researchers have noted differences in blood serotonin levels, particularly a tendency toward higher levels (Campbell, Friedman, DeVito, Greenspan, & Collins, 1974), in children with autism. Although results have been varied and some negative side effects have been observed, studies that have administered fenfluramine as a means of reducing blood serotonin levels have sometimes found some positive changes in the behavior of children with autism (Ritvo, Freeman, Geller, & Yuwiler, 1983). Other researchers have hypothesized based on behavioral observations about possible neurochemical factors, such as opioid systems (Sahley & Panksepp, 1987) and beta endorphins and changes in acetylcholine levels (L. Kern, Koegel, Dyer, et al., 1982). Others have discussed possible differences in vitamin metabolism (Rimland, 1994).

Literature addressing chromosomal and genetic patterns has identified a "fragile" site on the X chromosome (fragile X syndrome) in some children with autism; minor physical anomalies (Walker, 1977); and a tendency for relatives of children with autism to have other disabilities, including an increased incidence of autism or related symptoms (Ritvo et al., 1985).

In summary, the physiological data are still inconclusive; however, with the increasing sophistication of medical research and the subclassification of autism based on different behavior topologies, more information on the etiology of autism should be available in the future.

Behavioral Diagnostics

As discussed earlier, the behavioral characteristics of children labeled as having autism vary greatly; therefore, an ongoing assessment that is accurate and reliable regarding the type, amount, environments, and functions of behaviors is essential to develop effective intervention plans.

Description of Behaviors

Researchers and practitioners have long discussed the importance of defining behaviors in an objective, behavioral, and observable manner (Schreibman, 1994) that can be reliably understood and recognized by others. For example, a description of a child as "aggressive" is of little benefit. In contrast, a description such as "pinches adults on the inside of the forearm between the wrist and elbow" provides a clear picture of the aggression the child exhibits.

Degree or Amount of Each Behavior

The strength or degree to which each behavior occurs can be described in terms of amount. This can be accomplished by determining the frequency or duration of the behavior. For example, does pinching occur an average of 10 times a day or once a week? Other behaviors such as self-stimulatory behavior or tantrums may be measured by duration (e.g., length of tantrum) and/or latency (e.g., number of seconds that elapsed between presentation of a task and the child leaving the work table) (Schreibman, 1994).

Environments in Which the Target Behavior Occurs

Behaviors cannot be considered in isolation; they must be viewed as a part of the environment in which they occur. To begin with, to help understand and predict behavior, the environment in which they occur must be analyzed. Specifically, the environment in which a behavior occurs (antecedents) and the actions that usually follow the behavior in that environment (consequences) must be assessed (Baker, Brightman, Heifetz, & Murphy, 1976). This is referred to simply as the A–B–C model—antecedents–behavior–consequences. All comprehensive behavioral diagnostics should include a component that focuses on these complex patterns of behavior so that a proactive approach to intervention can be taken. For example, consider the child described earlier who demonstrated pinching. If antecedents were described as "pinching typically occurs within the 3 seconds following presentation of an academic task," and the consequences were described as "child is taken to the principal's office and parent is called to take child home," we would certainly have a specific idea as to the circumstances surrounding the disruptive behavior.

Perceived Function

Many of the behaviors that a child displays are actually being used as a form of communication; disruptive behavior, in particular, can be a very efficient and effective means of communication. Following the evaluation of the antecedents, behavior, and consequences, an attempt to determine the perceived function of a behavior is important for the development of functionally equivalent behaviors.

Many behaviors can be observed to be maintained by specific functions (this is discussed in detail in Chapter 12). Some of the most common functions or reasons a behavior is exhibited, as discussed by O'Neill, Horner, Albin, Storey, and Sprague (1990), include 1) to obtain attention or a desired item; 2) to escape or avoid a particular demand, request, activity, or person; 3) to avoid specific setting events, such as a difficult task, a transition, or being interrupted from a particular activity; or 4) self-stimulation (described earlier). Consider the A–B–C pattern just described. When an academic task is presented, the child demonstrates aggression and is subsequently taken away from the task. A hypothesis could be made that the likely function of this behavior is avoidance of the academic task. The child's attempt to avoid the task (i.e., the disruptive behavior) is most certainly being rewarded and maintained by the consequence. Understanding the function of a particular behavior can assist with developing and implementing socially appropriate communicative behaviors that meet the same needs as the disruptive behavior.

LONG-TERM IMPLICATIONS OF INTERVENTION STRATEGIES FOR CHILDREN WITH AUTISM

The central theme discussed throughout this book is that normalizing the way children with autism are exposed to and react to environmental stimulation provides a *pivotal* intervention that has widespread, continual, and long-term effects on their subsequent development. Research and data indicating substantial intervention potential are presented in relation to four major areas: 1) motivating the children to respond to social and environmental stimulation; 2) teaching the children to respond to complex multiple cues such as those involved in social, linguistic, and affective learning; 3) instructing the children in self-management and independent responding; and 4) educating the children in full inclusion (regular classroom and community) environments.

Motivating the Children to Respond
to Social and Environmental Stimulation

One critical area of research involves motivating children with autism to interact with their environments similar to the way their typically developing peers interact with social and environmental stimuli. Typical children are usually extremely responsive to their social and physical environments. In fact, parents often have to work to limit their typically developing children's very active levels of responding. However, without intervention, children with autism usually interact with only a very restricted number of stimuli (e.g., repetitive interactions with the same toys) and rarely interact in social and other environmental situations (R.L. Koegel, Koegel, & O'Neill, 1989). This failure to respond appropriately probably begins very early in life, and by the time children with autism reach school age the severity of this problem may be quite significant.

Teaching children with autism to interact with the almost infinite number of stimuli they encounter (as typically developing children do) would be an insurmountable task if each interaction had to be taught individually. Therefore, this book focuses instead on targeting "pivotal behaviors" or behaviors that are likely to affect wide areas of functioning. One of the major pivotal behaviors targeted is to *motivate* the children to interact academically, linguistically, and socially. Motivation was selected because, from a theoretical point of view, the children's behaviors parallel those discussed in the literature on learned helplessness (R.L. Koegel & Egel, 1979; R.L. Koegel & Mentis, 1985). That is, it has been hypothesized that a motivational problem begins very early in life when the children repeatedly experience failure due to (either major or minor) central nervous system dysfunction. This repeated failure causes depressed motivation, impaired performance, and task and social avoidance (Clark & Rutter, 1979; MacMillan, 1971; Rodda, 1977).

Paradoxically, once this cycle starts, efforts to "help" the children can actually create noncontingent reinforcement with respect to the children's own efforts to help themselves. The literature suggests that when individuals experience years of this type of repeated exposure to failure, they appear to learn that responding and reinforcement are independent (Chan & Keogh, 1974; Gruen, Ottinger, & Ollendick, 1974; R.L. Koegel & Egel, 1979; R.L. Koegel & Koegel, 1988; Lewinsohn, Larson, & Munoz, 1982; MacMillan, 1971; Seligman, Klein, & Miller, 1976; Zigler & Butterfield, 1968). Such conditions result in a decrease in the individual's level of responding or a failure to respond altogether. This may have major ramifications for children with autism, who often display difficulty maintaining motivation to attempt tasks in the areas of language, academics, and even self-help or daily living skills. This especially severe lack of motivation has profound implications throughout development.

One of the most significant implications of a child's lack of motivation relates to other individuals' perceptions of the child's competence. That is, persistent lack of motivation to make even feeble attempts at learning new tasks can manifest itself in either extreme lethargy or in active avoidance of teaching or assessment tasks. It is common for such children to exhibit aggression, self-injury, property destruction, and other severe disruptive behaviors in an attempt to escape or avoid such tasks. As a result, brief behavioral observations and standardized assessments used for classroom placement and to develop individualized education programs (IEPs) may considerably underestimate a child's functioning level. In essence, what may actually be tested is the child's motivation to respond, rather than his or her ability to respond.

One can imagine how a cyclical pattern and a self-fulfilling prophecy may occur when a child is inaccurately assessed at a very low functioning level (L.K. Koegel,

Koegel, & Smith, 1995). Because academic planning is directly related to the outcomes on such measures, the child is placed in more restrictive environments and his or her educational goals are developed in accordance with these misinterpreted assessments. Unfortunately, this can exacerbate the problem, because the child's academic activities then functionally consist primarily of maintaining previously learned tasks rather than of learning anything new. This combination of segregation and lack of academic challenges can be devastating to the child's long-term development (cf. L.K. Koegel, Valdez-Menchaca, & Koegel, 1994).

Motivational Intervention Variables

Driven by theory and observations of this apparent lack of motivation and its devastating effects, researchers have developed several techniques to improve responding. A number of individual intervention variables have been identified that have a direct impact on this lack of motivation. When combined into an overall intervention package, the result is extremely powerful, especially for developing language and social-communication skills. Each of the following variables has been shown to have a major effect on motivation, and each is discussed in relation to intervention of the characteristics of autism presented throughout this book (see Chapters 2 and 7).

First, studies have shown when *attempts to communicate* are reinforced, verbal responding progresses very rapidly (R.L. Koegel, O'Dell, & Dunlap, 1988). This is in contrast to more traditional techniques in which only strictly defined, correct, and successive approximations to a target verbalization are reinforced. A second successful technique known to be powerful in influencing motivation is *child choice* of stimulus materials. That is, rather than using stimulus items chosen entirely by the clinician, motivation is greatly improved if the specific stimulus items are highly desirable and chosen by the child. *Task variation* is another variable that improves motivation to respond. Responding seems to be enhanced when the stimulus items are varied, rather than a single stimulus repeatedly presented (Dunlap & Koegel, 1980). Furthermore, certain types of task variation are especially powerful in influencing motivation. For example, if the teacher intersperses *maintenance* trials (tasks the child has already mastered) among new acquisition trials, rather than only presenting new acquisition tasks, the child learns the target behaviors faster (Dunlap, 1984; L.K. Koegel & Koegel, 1986). Finally, using *natural reinforcers* that are directly related to the child's response seems to improve motivation and aid in increasing response acquisition (R.L. Koegel & Williams, 1980; Saunders & Sailor, 1979; Williams, Koegel, & Egel, 1981). Also, when using such natural reinforcers, one can expect an increase in the likelihood of generalization to other environments where the stimulus items are present and where similar types of reinforcers are likely to be available, thus increasing the breadth of the child's responding.

Combined, these variables result in considerably improved levels of appropriate task-related responding (R.L. Koegel, O'Dell, & Koegel, 1987) and significantly lower levels of escape- or avoidance-motivated disruptive behavior (R.L. Koegel, Koegel, & Surratt, 1992). Such teaching strategies are easily implemented by parents (Laski, Charlop, & Schreibman, 1988) and therefore can be carried out on an ongoing basis in the child's home and community environments, which increases the child's level of responding on an extremely widespread scale (Figure 1).

Functional Analysis

In discussing the need to examine the child's motivation to respond over the course of his or her development, the use of functional analysis clearly stands out as a critical device in

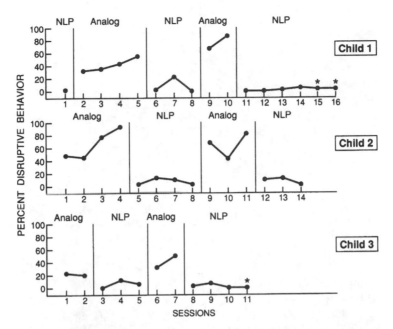

Figure 1.   The figure shows a comparison in the level of disruptive behavior for natural language paradigm versus analog intervention conditions. Percentage of disruptive behaviors is plotted on the ordinate, and sessions are plotted on the abscissa for each child. The asterisks indicate that these final sessions were conducted by the children's parents (who had been trained in the implementation of the NLP intervention procedures). (From Koegel, R.L., Koegel, L.K., & Surratt, A. [1992]. Language intervention and disruptive behavior in preschool children with autism. *Journal of Autism and Developmental Disorders* 22[2], 144–153; reprinted by permission.)

producing behavioral change. This approach assesses the primary motivation or function of the child's behavior and results in the opportunity to provide the child with more appropriate and efficient behaviors that can be used in the place of disruptive or problematic behaviors (Carr & Durand, 1985). Functional analysis has received increasing attention and is now acknowledged as one of the most valuable methods of allowing direct intervention for the behaviors that hinder the child's motivation to respond appropriately in social and academic situations (Horner, Dunlap, & Koegel, 1988) (Figures 2 and 3).

Once thought of as an effective assessment tool, functional analysis is now being researched as an intervention technique. Functional analytic therapy is evolving as a means to tap into the function and motivation of problematic behaviors and produce individualized support programs. A particularly important factor in increasing appropriate developmental gains in children with autism is teaching functional communication. As noted earlier, these children often express their frustration, anger, displeasure, and in some cases their basic needs through disruptive behavior. They are communicating through inefficient and high-energy behaviors such as screaming, tantruming, running away, and physical aggression (Carr & Durand, 1985). By performing a functional analysis and replacing these behaviors with more efficient functionally equivalent communicative behaviors, the child is allowed to appreciate the power of words or other appropriate communication. Teaching children more appropriate communication skills also results in increased acceptance in their natural environments. This in turn results in more positive interactions and more learning opportunities for the child.

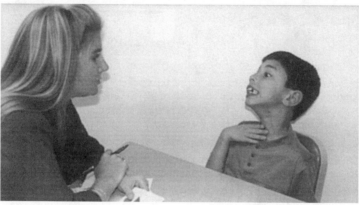

Figure 2.   Here the clinician is conducting the intervention within an analog framework. Notice that the child does not appear to be motivated to
participate in the activity and engages in frequent disruptive behavior.

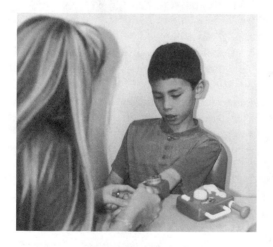 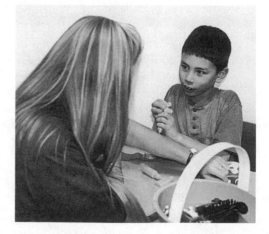

Figure 3.   Here the clinician is using the natural language paradigm, which focuses on variables designed
to increase the child's motivation to learn. In this example, the language intervention is being conducted in
the context of a play situation, where the child is pretending he is a doctor. Notice that he appears highly
motivated to participate in the language session under these conditions.

We are currently exploring parent education in functional analysis as a means to allow the child's primary care provider the ability to assess and intervene with problematic behaviors at an early point as they arise. (Some preliminary results are discussed in depth in Chapter 12.) As with most of the more recently developed interventions, the issue is that the outcome that usually has been studied is the immediate behavioral gain; however, it is hypothesized here that the long-term developmental gains resulting from the child's increased exposure to typical interactions will be far greater. For example, if data from a behavioral assessment show that a child is clearly tantruming as a result of not knowing how to do certain tasks, a clinician may effectively be able to reduce or eliminate these tantrums by teaching functional communication (e.g., "Help me"). Whereas such an intervention has an immediate impact on the child's behavior, it also has long-term implications for the child's development. During an extended number of years, a child who is motivated to remedy difficult problems in learning such as asking for help when a learning task becomes too difficult, instead of screaming, biting, and kicking, is likely to show an entirely different pattern of long-term development.

Teaching the Children to Respond to Multiple Cues

One difference in responding between children with autism and their typically developing peers concerns the way in which they respond to complex environmental stimuli consisting of multiple cues or components. A large body of research now exists suggesting that certain children with autism respond to overly restrictive portions of such complex stimuli (Lovaas, Schreibman, Koegel, & Rehm, 1971). When presented with a complex stimulus (e.g., a human face, a teaching task, a social interaction), the children respond to only a small portion of the total complexity. For example, a child may learn to recognize an adult by a small and irrelevant cue, such as his or her eyeglasses, a necklace, or an incidental hand movement the person makes while talking, but fail to recognize the person if that single cue is absent (Rincover & Koegel, 1975; Schreibman & Lovaas, 1973). This can be contrasted with typically developing children, who usually use three or four cues at a time. Such responding appears to be highly stable over time and not likely to change without intervention. (This topic is covered more in depth in Chapter 3.)

Intervention efforts related to overselectivity have taken two directions. One direction has focused on developing specialized teaching techniques that are effective even if a child remains overselective throughout life. For example, a now widely used technique called *within-stimulus prompting* has been proven to be highly effective (see also R.L. Koegel, Dunlap, Richman, & Dyer, 1981). In *within-stimulus prompting*, children are prompted to respond to a relevant cue by exaggerating the relevant component of the complex stimulus in question (Schreibman, 1975). This is similar to the way in which a cartoonist exaggerates a relevant feature of a celebrity's face to make the person instantly recognizable. Although effective in improving learning, this technique may not alter the fundamental problem of overselective responding—that children are receiving only minimal stimulus input from complex stimuli. Therefore, within-stimulus prompting might be expected to have only a limited effect on subsequent development. Further research on this point is necessary.

In contrast, the second direction of intervention research has broader developmental implications. It is the attempt to normalize the number of cues the children utilize from the environment. Several early studies (e.g., R.L. Koegel & Schreibman, 1977; Schreibman, Koegel, & Craig, 1977) suggested that interventions could gradually and systematically increase the number of cues the children used when they approached a learning task. For example, R.L. Koegel and Schreibman taught conditional discriminations to children with autism in which the children were provided with reinforcement only when they responded to a learning task on the basis of multiple cues. The results showed that the children could learn to use such a strategy and that they would generalize the strategy to novel learning tasks.

In summary, research on overselectivity suggests that children with autism often approach new learning situations by responding to an abnormally restricted number of relevant cues. This restricted responding has been related to the children's atypical social, emotional, and language development. Intervention focused on the pivotal response of responding to multiple cues in complex learning situations has resulted in normalizing the children's subsequent development; however, the research in these areas has been conducted either only during a very short period of time (typically a few weeks or months) or in the context of cross-sectional research. No long-term longitudinal studies have yet been conducted (with the exception of very preliminary data provided by Burke and Koegel in 1982).

Instructing the Children in Self-Management and Independent Responding

Independent responding is directly related to motivation to respond because a child's repeated failure to respond to the environment typically results in an overdependence on others. This relates to the research on motivation in that such extreme dependence on others can exacerbate a cyclical reaction, in which a child learns that his or her own responding is unrelated to the consequences of his or her behavior. This problem can be pervasive and persist into adulthood, such that even simple self-help skills require an inordinate amount of help from others. Although motivational interventions are extremely effective in initiating and improving responding, it is also necessary to produce widespread use of newly learned behaviors in a large variety of natural environments where generalization may not readily occur. Self-management as a pivotal behavior is ideal for this purpose, because it can be used for extended periods of time in the absence of an intervention provider and it is easily adapted for use in a wide variety of natural environments. Thus, self-management increases both responsiveness to the environment and the likelihood that the child will experience natural reinforcers for responding.

Self-management involves first deciding on a specific behavior to target, such as stereotypy, aggression, hygiene, or verbal responses to others. The child is then taught to discriminate the occurrence of an appropriate target behavior (instead of absence of target behavior or occurrence of an undesired behavior). Once this discrimination is learned, the child is taught to monitor brief periods of time or occurrences of the desired behavior. This monitoring is programmed to occur whenever the target behavior is desired in the child's natural environment.

We believe that techniques such as self-management greatly increase children's roles as active participants in the habilitation process and consequently reduce their dependence on their parents and other adults. Preliminary research also suggests that this is an important variable in reducing parental stress and improving family interactions in general (see Chapter 7). That is, mothers of children with autism have been reported to exhibit significantly high levels of stress (R.L. Koegel, Schreibman, et al., 1992) and near diagnosable depression (Moes, Koegel, Schreibman, & Loos, 1992). Frequent underlying causes of this stress relate to specific variables associated with the child's dependency and management, cognitive impairment, limits on family opportunity, and life-span care. The importance of self-management, in relation to these areas, is that it is a technique that creates independent responding and promotes widespread use of desirable behaviors in a variety of community environments. The beneficial implications of creating this widespread independence reaches far beyond the direct benefits for the child—they also involve a reduction in familial stress and a normalization in family and community interactions. As the development of independence is gradual with all children, whether they have disabilities or not, the ramifications of these effects will be clearest in longitudinal studies.

Educating the Children in Full Inclusion Environments

As noted throughout this book, and especially in Chapters 10 and 11, no other time in history has been as crucial as now for the topic of inclusion. The Education for All Handicapped Children Act of 1975 (PL 94-142) and the Individuals with Disabilities Education Act of 1990 (PL 101-476) have resulted in children with disabilities being placed in regular education classrooms, and techniques are now readily available for teaching such children in such classrooms (cf. Russo & Koegel, 1977). This has given researchers the opportunity to study academic progress and social interaction between children with autism and their typically functioning peers during a period of many years. Although additional longitudinal studies are needed to provide information on the impact that increasing social interaction and integration has on the overall development of children with autism, the information that has been collected so far is very promising. There is strong evidence that children with developmental delays can most efficiently learn age-appropriate behavior from an environment of similarly aged typical peer models. Also, it appears that children with severe social impairments can best learn to socialize if they are in an environment that provides a significant number of appropriate opportunities for social interactions (Guralnick & Groom, 1988; Stainback, Stainback, & Forest, 1989).

The implications of integration for long-term development are probably more dramatic than any other factor. Previous concerns regarding the feasibility of educating children with disabilities in a regular education environment are slowly decreasing as new technologies for integration prove to be successful (cf. Brown et al., 1989, 1991). Our experiences have been that children who are integrated into the regular education system form friendships that allow them the opportunity to practice appropriate communication and social skills. They are constantly exposed to appropriate peer models that allow them to shape their behavior accordingly. Also, when in the regular education system and allowed to advance with the same peer group, children with disabilities are more likely to feel accepted; such acceptance can be a significant factor in later typical and successful social development (Asher & Dodge, 1986; Berndt, 1982; Coie & Dodge, 1983; Coie, Lochman, Terry, & Hyman, 1992; Cowen, Pederson, Babigian, Izzo, & Trost, 1973; Hartup & Sancilio, 1986; Ollendick, Green, Francis, & Braum, 1991; Parker & Asher, 1987; Price & Dodge, 1989; Robins, 1966; Roff, Sells, & Golden, 1972; Strayhorn & Strain, 1986). For example, a recent longitudinal study by Ollendick, Weist, Borden, and Green (1992), which followed 267 students for 5 years, revealed that children who are rejected by their peers appear to be significantly more at risk for long-term maladjustment. If acceptance by peers is a critical factor in child development, then segregation from typically developing peers is likely to be a detrimental and further disabling experience for any child.

The vast majority of research in the field of autism has focused on either treating behavior difficulties or increasing language abilities; however, when most people think of autism they see social isolation as the most dominant aspect. Children with autism have a great amount of difficulty with interpersonal interaction, and, as mentioned earlier, many of the behavioral problems seen in children with autism have been found to serve the function of maintaining social avoidance.

The social disability that results from these behavior problems appears to grow at a rapid rate as children with autism mature. Without intervention, the basic component to social interaction—reciprocity—is often not carried out by these children. This characteristic of not taking into account the actions of others, and reciprocating accordingly can be one of the most severe difficulties associated with autism (Rutter, 1983). It is obvious that the subsequent behavioral, communication, and social disabilities that result from a failure to integrate social cues can be devastating in the global development of a child. A child's ability to learn is also seriously influenced by not attending to and processing social information or engaging in social modeling.

A second factor, which is related to reciprocity, is responsivity. Children with autism tend not to respond to verbal or nonverbal initiations from others. Due to the social avoidance that is so characteristic of this disability, these children often fail to understand what is expected of them or what positive outcomes are available from a particular social interaction. Recent research on teaching children with autism to self-manage their responsivity to conversational cues has proven successful (L.K. Koegel, Koegel, Hurley, & Frea, 1992; R.L. Koegel & Frea, 1992). As noted earlier, further longitudinal research is necessary to assess what overall impact this intervention has on the social development of the child. It is clear, however, that increasing the level of responding in the classroom does allow children with autism to focus more on their peers.

The presence of typically functioning peers who increase appropriate social interaction in children with disabilities has proven to be quite successful (e.g., Goldstein, Kaczmarek, Pennington, & Shafer, 1992; Guralnick & Groom, 1988; Odom, Hoyson, Jamieson, & Strain, 1985; Odom & Strain, 1986). These peer-mediated interventions decrease the need for a teacher or therapist to isolate the child with special needs, as well as increase the amount of interaction the child has with classmates and friends. Not only has research found that peers without disabilities can be very beneficial to enhancing social interaction, but the opportunity to interact with children who have disabilities provides special benefits for typically developing peers (Biklen, Corrigan, & Quick, 1989; Peck, Donaldson, & Pezzoli, 1990), which improves the entire classroom interaction pattern.

IMPLICATIONS

One might imagine that if all of the variables discussed in this chapter were taken into consideration in a comprehensive intervention program in which children with autism are 1) motivated to attempt difficult social and academic tasks, 2) taught to respond to complex multiple cues, and 3) included in regular education and community environments, significant long-term developmental improvements would take place. In essence, children with autism would be exposed to stimulus conditions that much more closely approximate those of typically developing children. More specifically, when considering these three major areas, each of the following issues (see box) should be incorporated into the design of a comprehensive intervention program.

We have been attempting such comprehensive interventions with a number of children during the past several years and have noted rather dramatic improvements in the children's functioning. Overall, the preliminary data from these early analyses show a fairly consistent picture of some initial improvement occurring immediately after intervention began (probably as a function of the change to an integrated classroom) and then larger gains beginning to occur after approximately 1 year (probably as a function of the improved motivation and responsivity to multiple cues). These large gains have been

---

Eleven Important Clinical Considerations

1. There is *variability* in symptomatology and responsiveness to intervention across children; therefore, all intervention should be individualized.
2. The earliest possible intervention should be considered to aid in the *prevention* of the emergence of severe problems.
3. Intervention should take place primarily in the *natural environment*.
4. The child's *motivation* to overcome his or her disability needs to be promoted.
5. Analyses of the *functions* of the child's behavior need to be conducted.
6. *Full school and community inclusion* needs to be planned and implemented throughout the life span.
7. *Parental participation* is important.
8. *Generalization and maintenance* of intervention gains need to be planned and evaluated.
9. *Coordination* among intervention providers, educators, and parents enhances the child's progress.
10. The child's *independence* needs to be promoted.
11. The *social significance* of the intervention for the child's and family's quality of life needs to be considered.

---

occurring on standardized verbal and nonverbal intelligence tests, standardized receptive and expressive language tests, standardized academic tests, tests of pragmatic social communication, and direct behavioral observations of the children's linguistic and social behavior. Although these analyses are in preliminary stages, we are extremely optimistic about the pursuit of this avenue of research and foresee the necessity and benefits of longitudinal research in the area of autism as one of the most critical areas for the prevention of the expression of many of the characteristics of the disability.

The subsequent chapters of this book provide in-depth discussions related to intervention procedures for individuals with autism. To date, the cause and cure of autism are unknown, but intervention has improved significantly so that children with autism can often learn to function independently as adults; some who are diagnosed as having "mild autism" may even be difficult to distinguish from their peers after intensive intervention. However, there is not yet enough information about initial intellectual functioning or other characteristics of children who have extremely positive outcomes to point to reliable prognostic indicators (Harris, 1986). Research is now being conducted to attempt to determine specific child and family characteristics and environmental variables that result in most favorable outcomes. However, it is known that with effective behavioral intervention all children with autism will improve.

Chapter 2

Communication
and Language Intervention

—Lynn Kern Koegel

Communication difficulties of one type or another are universally present in individuals with autism, and problems in social communication, such as joint attention (Mundy & Sigman, 1989), are an early sign that a disability is present and may persist (Mundy, Sigman, & Kasari, 1990). This has led many researchers to hypothesize that deficits in social communication or social interaction may be the primary underlying cause of autism (L.K. Koegel, Valdez-Menchaca, & Koegel, 1994; Rutter, 1978b) and that other behavioral problems are secondary as a result of these underlying communication-based difficulties. Even practitioners and researchers who do not speculate on primary causes often refer to the direct correlation between communication and language difficulties and other inappropriate behaviors, such as aggression, self-stimulation, and self-injury. This emphasizes the importance of communication intervention as a primary goal in the habilitation process and suggests that many untreated aberrant behaviors are likely to show concomitant positive changes as communication improves.

Language Characteristics

Generally speaking, the language characteristics of children with autism fall into three categories: 1) nonverbal, 2) delayed verbal, and 3) echolalic. During the mid-1980s, when intervention procedures were still quite primitive, it was estimated that approximately half of the children with autism never develop any functional communication skills and that the other half develop some type of language, whether it is rule governed or echolalic (Prizant, 1983). However, the nonverbal group has been reduced considerably now that children are being diagnosed younger and intervention is being implemented far earlier in life using improved language intervention strategies. In fact, recent data suggest that approximately 70% of the 50% of children with autism who are completely nonverbal can learn at least some expressive language if naturalistic procedures (described later) are commenced before the age of 5. While the focus of this chapter is expressive verbal language, it is also important that one considers the notion of developmental continuity from preverbal to verbal levels. The importance and value of all types of communication cannot be minimized, as communication deficits are correlated with numerous other social and behavioral problems. Thus, for the small group of children who do not develop expressive language, communication should still be a focus of language enhancement efforts, and nonspeech communication may be a legitimate goal in such cases (Prizant & Wetherby, 1989). Increases in the sophistication of communicative intentions can be taught, such as the use of gestures, simple signs, or pictures, in place of physical manipulation to request objects (Prizant & Wetherby, 1989). Existing data also suggest that teaching nonverbal individuals appropriate ways of conveying communicative intent is effective in reducing problem behaviors. That is, procedures such as functional analysis, discussed in detail in Chapter 12, that assess communicative functions of inappropriate behaviors can be especially useful to determine communicative intent. Then, appropriate behaviors that meet the same communicative need (functionally equivalent responses) can be taught to replace the undesired behavior (Day, Horner, & O'Neill, 1994; Frea, Koegel, & Koegel, 1994).

It is also important to consider the intervention needs of children with autism who do have some speech. The subgroup of children that develop rule-governed language often demonstrate marked delays. This may be seen in a variety of areas, including phonology, syntax, and semantics. Even when children with autism use language, their language differs both quantitatively in the number of utterances and qualitatively in the communicative functions of language use when compared to that of typically developing children, which suggests the need for interventions (such as those described later in this chapter).

For example, Wetherby and Prutting (1984) compared the language of children with autism, ages 6–12 years, to control children without disabilities matched for language development (based on grammatical construction abilities and size of lexicon). Samples of communicative behavior were assessed during free play and during a structured communication condition in environments familiar to the children. Items during the free play were the same for all children and included a large variety of toys (e.g., dolls and doll accessories, household objects, plastic airplane, car, clown, blocks, stringing beads). The structured communication consisted of eight communicative situations (e.g., initiating games such as pat-a-cake or peek-a-boo, looking at books, playing with bubbles). Results of the study demonstrated that, in addition to using far fewer verbal communicative acts, children with autism tended to use communication most frequently for requesting objects, requesting actions, and protesting. In contrast, typically developing children's most frequent communicative act was labeling. In addition, typical language developers displayed more variation in their speech acts and developmental changes with age. The children with autism also displayed fewer social responses than the controls (4.5% vs. 24%, respectively).

One can imagine how this limited style of interacting could severely influence the interactions to which children with autism are exposed. First, because of the extremely limited number of utterances emitted, they are likely to be involved in few communicative interactions and, therefore, unlikely to acquire the communicative competence often learned from such interactions. Second, the communicative functions most frequently used by children with autism (requesting and protesting) are more likely to result in needs being met rather than eliciting the social use of language, therefore again limiting the types of interactions to which they are exposed.

This characteristic lack of responsiveness may also influence the children's phonology, syntax, semantics, and pragmatics. That is, failure to use language and in turn receive feedback on the specificity of its use is likely to result in the failure to develop age-appropriate sound use, structure, referential meaning, and related nonverbal aspects of language. Fortunately, a number of newly developed intervention programs deal directly with these issues and are discussed later in this chapter.

The third general language characteristic of children with autism is echolalia. Echolalic utterances refer to the repetition of utterances heard in the immediate or distant past. Whereas imitative repetition is a natural part of typically developing children's language, its persistence past the first few years of language learning is used as one of the diagnostic criteria for autism. In addition, in contrast to typical language learners, children with autism lack clear evidence of communicative intent in their echolalic utterances.

Sometimes echolalic utterances are produced without appropriate prosodic features and may serve some type of self-stimulatory function. This most frequently occurs with delayed echolalia, but occasionally with immediate echolalia. Immediate echolalia, or the repetition of all or part of the utterance just heard, most frequently occurs when the child does not appear to know an appropriate response to the previous utterance or question (Carr, Schreibman, & Lovaas, 1975). The use of a functionally equivalent communicative response, such as teaching children with echolalia to reply "I don't know" or "I don't understand" rather than to echo a previous utterance, has been proven to be an effective generalized strategy to reduce immediate echolalia and provide the child with a socially appropriate response readily applicable to a variety of communicative interactions.

Other echolalic utterances appear to be produced as a method of avoiding appropriate interactions and can be misconceived as appropriate language. For example, if an adult asks a child, "Do you want milk?" and the child responds "milk," the child may appear to be using appropriate language, but in reality the child may be simply repeating a portion of the previous utterances. This can be easily assessed by asking the child a question that has two possible responses. For example, "Do you want the car or the truck?" If the child says "the truck," the order can be reversed so that the question is "Do you want the truck or the car?" If the child then says "car," it is likely that echolalia is occurring. Another way of assessing whether echolalia is occurring is to intersperse a second related question. For example, if the child responds to the question "Do you want to go bye-bye?" by saying "bye-bye," the child can then be asked, "What do you want to do?" If the child says "do," or does not respond, he or she probably was responding with echolalia to the original utterance. This cycle is important to break so that the child actually learns to engage in appropriate social interactions.

Delayed echolalia, or the repetition of sounds, words, phrases, or even entire commercials, songs, or television programs, is usually emitted as self-stimulatory behavior

(Lovaas, Varni, Koegel, & Lorsch, 1977), apparently to provide some sort of sensory input. Such behaviors can also occur to avoid social interactions; however, the exact variables that control and affect delayed echolalia are still poorly understood.

Pragmatics

Another hallmark in the communication intervention needs of children with autism is difficulty with pragmatic skills. Pragmatics can be loosely categorized into four general areas that differ primarily on the basis of degree to which discourse and social interactions are considered and the information they convey. The first two levels (paralinguistic features and extralinguistic or nonverbal features) are typically assessed at the utterance level, the third level (linguistic intent) assesses the utterance but also includes previous and past utterances, and the fourth level (social competence) assesses a broader area inclusive of the utterance and the social context. Each of these levels is discussed on the following pages.

Paralinguistic Features

Paralinguistic aspects of language involve the pragmatic skills to control intelligibility and prosody (R.L. Koegel, Frea, & Surratt, 1994). Paralinguistic features can change the meaning of an utterance entirely. For example, the statement "That is right" can become a question if rising intonation is applied to the utterance. Assessment of paralinguistic skills is primarily concerned with language at the level that analyzes communicative intentions through changes in stress patterns, duration, intonation, pitch, and intensity levels (Spekman & Roth, 1984). Differentiated vocalizations, whether or not they were intended as such, appear to begin prior to 1 year of age (Chapman, 1981). Use of paralinguistic aspects of language are important for both communicative intent and for maintenance of listener engagement. Children with autism are frequently described as speaking in a "monotone"; that is, they lack appropriate paralinguistic features during discourse. This is usually noted in their failure to use appropriate intensity, pitch, and intonation during conversation. Also, echolalic and self-stimulatory verbalizations frequently have unusual stress and intonation patterns.

Extralinguistic or Nonverbal Features

A second level of pragmatic skills concerns the linguistic support an utterance is given. This category involves the use of gestures and a variety of body movements that are nonverbal in nature and aid the communicative intent of an utterance. Assessment of linguistic support can be accomplished at the utterance level within the context of a social interaction. For example, hand movements demonstrating size during conversation give additional communicative information to the listener. Linguistic support features that have been shown to be lacking in individuals with autism include hand and arm movements, facial expressions, and body posturing.

Linguistic Intent

Linguistic intent involves the use of utterances in the context of social discourse and also considers the known, supposed, or presumed knowledge of the listener. For young children, communicative intent can be classified into specific categories such as requesting information, requesting action, responding to requests, stating or commenting, regulating conversational behaviors, and other performatives (cf. Dore, 1974, 1975). Linguistic intent is dependent on the previous knowledge of the listener, and analysis is dependent on both the previous and following utterances and/or actions of the communicative partner. That is, linguistic intent cannot be analyzed at the utterance level; it is dependent on communicative discourse. There are also important interrelationships between linguistic intent and other pragmatic areas. For example, the linguistic intent is supported or aided by paralinguistic and extralinguistic (or nonverbal) cues.

Two areas significantly affect the ability of children with autism to use appropriate linguistic intent. First, they often do not give adequate attention to the communicative partner to be sufficiently able to participate in the dyadic interchange. This may be because they are engaged in self-stimulation, because the communicative interaction is difficult for them or for other reasons. Second, they may not have adequate language skills to appropriately express themselves. As discussed earlier, significant delays in expressive language can cause a myriad of other related difficulties.

Social Competence

The last general category of communication intervention needs discussed here relates to social skills. This level of communication is also dependent on analysis of language at the discourse level. The social level of pragmatic behavior is probably the most widely treated area in individuals with autism. The social level includes both verbal and nonverbal skills the speaker uses during communicative interactions. This area includes several aspects related to 1) topic, such as selection, introduction, maintenance, and change (Prutting & Kirchner, 1987); and 2) turn taking, including initiation, response, pause time, interruption/overlap, feedback to speakers, contingency, quantity, conciseness, and politeness, such as saying "thank you," "please," and so forth.

Nonverbal aspects of this category include such behaviors as eye gaze and distance between speakers. These boundaries are commonly violated by individuals with autism. Tantrums, aggression, and other avoidance, escape, or attention-seeking behaviors displayed by individuals with autism are also included in this category if they are used for communicative purposes. This area can be assessed through analysis of the speaker within an interaction.

Clearly, the communicative difficulties that are common in individuals with autism and the lack of sufficient language development can lead to a significant disability in the area of pragmatic competence. These difficulties are pathognomonic to the syndrome and can persist throughout life unless intervention is provided. Even in Kanner's follow-up study of his original sample approximately 30 years later, he observed that the original clients remained extremely aloof and continued to experience significant difficulties in interpersonal relationships (Kanner, 1971; Kanner, Rodriguez, & Ashenden, 1972). Because discourse regulation involving both verbal and nonverbal cues is necessary for fluent conversation, the conversational partner's ability to monitor the speaker's messages and to provide feedback to the speaker concerning their effectiveness is necessary for the smooth flow of connected discourse (cf. Fey & Leonard, 1983). Most typically developing children learn at a very young age from adult feedback that increased specificity is desirable. For example, a parent may teach the child to verbally request an item rather than cry. Through this feedback, the child is increasingly more effective in social-communicative contexts. However, children with autism who are already burdened with linguistic and behavioral (nonverbal) difficulties may not involve themselves in the adequate number and quality of interactions. Without ongoing feedback, provided through social interactions, they may fall further into social isolation.

INTERVENTION

As a whole, researchers and practitioners have made significant progress over the years in improving language skills in autism and related disabilities with severe language delays. As is described here, researchers have always been concerned with behavior problems in children with severe disabilities, but exactly *how* they are dealt with within the intervention process has shifted. As we continue to move in the direction of conceptualizing language and behavior as interrelated, researchers and practitioners are searching for language teaching strategies that will indirectly affect behavior. These general areas include imitation training procedures, imitation training with generalization strategies incorporated, natural language or milieu teaching, and self-initiation teaching.

Language Intervention: Early Approaches and Their Limitations

Early research demonstrating effective treatment for children with autism who exhibited little or no functional language used principles of reinforcement and punishment to eliminate "psychotic" speech and reinstate appropriate verbal behavior. This operant training technology focused heavily on teaching verbal imitation with the implicit assumption that children learn to speak by attending to and repeating the speech of others and by being rewarded for closer and closer approximations to adult speech (Fay & Schuler, 1980). Central to the effectiveness of the technology was the creation of conditions of maximum stimulus control, whereby the environment was arranged so that all distractions were removed. The general approach was to present a stimulus, such as a question or command (e.g., "What is this?," "Say 'red,'" or "Point to your nose"). Following a correct response, with prompts if necessary, the child was immediately rewarded with edibles, stroking, exaggerated social approval, tokens, or some other desired stimulus. These rewards were gradually delayed as the child improved in an attempt to strengthen the social consequences. Incorrect responses were punished with a loud "no," slaps, attention withdrawal, or other unpleasant consequences (Lovaas, 1977).

Most of these early language programs also had a major component that related to general overall disruptive behavior. That is, such children usually exhibit varying degrees of disruptive and self-stimulatory behavior. Therefore, prior to commencing with language treatment, when the children exhibited aggressive, self-injurious, or disruptive behavior they were contingently presented with some type of aversive stimulation, such as deprivation of lights, rewards, and the presence of others (Hewitt, 1965); time-out; or physical punishment (Lovaas, 1977). This initial emphasis on punishing behavior arose from the philosophy that these types of disruptive behaviors would interfere with teaching and subsequent learning.

The general rationale for this type of teaching was the underlying philosophy that language cannot be separated from any other operant, and therefore "verbal behavior" is subject to the same consequences. Thus, verbal behavior, like any operant, acquires strength and continues to be maintained in strength when responses are frequently followed by reinforcement. Parents begin very early on reinforcing any behavior that is part of the desired final pattern. Eventually, through a series of consequences under suitable conditions, the complex form of the behavior is acquired.

This early theory led some researchers to conceptualize early phonemic behavior (consonants, vowels) as purely a form of imitation, or parroting the utterances of others without meaning. A second event, in order for the vocal output to acquire meaning, occurs when the verbal behavior is emitted within a certain stimulus context. In such a paradigm, the first step was to teach the child to imitate the verbal utterances (phonemes) of others.

During these early attempts to teach language, language was conceptualized outside of its social context so that related behaviors were taught separately. In addition, a nonverbal child's attempts to communicate through nonverbal means were often viewed as disruptive or interfering and were punished before language teaching commenced.

Many children made substantial gains with this type of intervention. Yet because of the highly controlled nature of the language sessions, a large number of the children showed verbal behavior that came under very restricted environmental control, and the children exhibited a general lack of spontaneity in their use of newly learned language skills (Lovaas, 1977). Not only did language fail to be exhibited or generalize to other environments, but most behaviors taught in this type of highly controlled environment also failed to generalize and maintain outside of the clinical setting or be exhibited with items that were not specifically taught. This led researchers to attempt to develop steps in their intervention programs to facilitate generalization.

Three general strategies have been specifically adopted to address generalization problems in children with autism: stimulus generalization, response generalization, and maintenance (for in-depth discussion, refer to Horner, Dunlap, & Koegel, 1988). A few examples of these many attempts include reducing the discriminability of the reinforcement schedules (R.L. Koegel & Rincover, 1974; Rincover & Koegel, 1977), delaying the reinforcer (G. Dunlap, Koegel, Johnson, & O'Neill, 1987), teaching behaviors that are likely to be rewarded in the child's natural environment (Carr, 1980), teaching family members and teachers to provide ongoing intervention (O'Dell, 1974; Russo & Koegel, 1977), fading items or people into the intervention setting (R.L. Koegel & Rincover, 1974), and establishing responses in the clinical setting that are likely to be used in the child's natural environment (Charlop, 1983; Schreibman & Carr, 1978). Whereas these issues still continue to be important theoretically and clinically, in the early attempts they were considered as a second step *after* a new behavior had been instated in a controlled clinical setting.

Schreibman (1988) points out that science is a cumulative process, systematically building on prior knowledge. This is clearly apparent in the literature on generalization of newly learned behaviors in children with autism. Early attempts to teach language that emphasized repetitive practice, carefully controlled instructions, consistent and artificial reinforcers, highly structured and simple training environments, and so forth might have actually retarded the efforts to achieve generalized intervention effects. However, as described in the next section, because of these building blocks that increased the understanding of generalization issues, intervention programs that result in broader treatment gains have been developed and the often complex interactions that are involved in these sophisticated behaviors have been studied (Horner, Dunlap, & Koegel, 1988; Schreibman, 1988).

Nonverbal Children: Natural Language Paradigm Intervention

The newer language intervention programs that evolved as attempts to solve problems of generalization and maintenance explored specific variables that were likely to result in increased "motivation" and responsivity on the part of the child. A major change arose in approaching language intervention that differed in emphasis from the more traditional, highly imitative, and teacher-driven techniques. This change emphasized the reciprocal interactive nature of the communicative interaction and therefore accentuated the child's role as an active communicative partner in the dyad, which represented a shift from the previous techniques that focused almost entirely on adult-initiated interactions. This emphasis on a more social language use led researchers to shift from more traditional instruction in the types of antecedents (shifting from teacher prompt to child interest) and consequences (shifting from those that are merely consistent across trials to those that are functionally related to the response) to instruction procedures that are directly associated with the child's response (Kaiser, Yoder, & Keetz, 1992). Coincidentally, these newer procedures more closely resemble the way typically developing children naturally learn language.

As a group, such naturalistic intervention techniques that focus on teaching functional language skills in a social context have been coined *milieu teaching*. Variations in similar general strategies have been demonstrated in incidental teaching (Hart & Risley, 1968), the mand model (Warren, McQuarter, & Rogers-Warren, 1984), time delay (Halle, Marshall, & Spradlin, 1979), natural language paradigm (NLP) (R.L. Koegel, O'Dell, & Koegel, 1987), and in-context teaching (Camarata & Nelson, 1992). Such milieu procedures described below seem to be especially suitable for children learning their first words. In fact, the procedures were originally developed for use with nonverbal children.

As can be seen in Table 1, specific variables are manipulated in the natural language teaching condition such that 1) stimulus items are functional and varied, 2) natural reinforcers are employed, 3) communicative attempts are rewarded, and 4) trials are conducted within a natural interchange.

There are several underlying philosophies that drive the NLP and other milieu teaching procedures. These techniques build upon arranging the environment to increase children's opportunities to use language. This can be accomplished in the child's home, school, and other natural environments. Initially, the basic motivation for learning language is to gain access to desired items or privileges; however, as is discussed in later sections of this chapter, the responses can then be expanded. The initial verbal responses

Table 1.   Differences between the analog and the natural language paradigm (NLP) conditions

	Analog condition	NLP condition
Stimulus items	a. Chosen by clinician	a. Chosen by child
	b. Repeated until criterion is met	b. Varied every few trials
	c. Phonologically easy to produce, irrespective of whether they were functional in the natural environment	c. Age-appropriate items that can be found in child's natural environment
Prompts	a. Manual (e.g., touch tip of tongue, or hold lips together)	a. Clinician repeats item
Interaction	a. Clinician holds up stimulus item; stimulus item not functional within interaction	a. Clinician and child play with stimulus item (i.e., stimulus item is functional within interaction)
Response	a. Correct responses or successive approximations reinforced	a. Looser shaping contingency so that attempts to respond verbally (except self-stimulation) are also reinforced
Consequences	a. Edible reinforcers paired with social reinforcers	a. Natural reinforcer (e.g., opportunity to play with the item) paired with social reinforcers

being taught serve as mands or requests. These techniques share several common features (as discussed in Kaiser, Yoder, & Keetz, 1992, and in R.L. Koegel, O'Dell, & Koegel, 1987).

Child Choice

First, teaching follows the child's choice, lead, or interest. Following the child's lead, whereby teaching episodes occur only when the child has sustained attention to a target object or intentionally communicates about the target object, results in considerably greater noun acquisition than when the teacher intrusively recruits the child's attention and then teaches (Yoder, Kaiser, Alpert, & Fischer, 1993).

This same effect occurs with morphological and syntactic structures in children exhibiting specific language impairment. That is, Camarata and Nelson (1992) taught grammatical structures to children during natural play interactions. The conditions differed in that the children were presented with the target language structure in the context of the activity *they* were involved in during one condition, as opposed to the activity the clinician had chosen during the other. Their results indicated that, with the exception of very infrequently used targets, the children learned more rapidly when the interventions conformed more closely to the natural language parameters (i.e., using the activity the child had naturally selected) as opposed to the more direct imitation and drill format procedures with the clinician choosing the activities. Children with autism have also been shown to be more successful in learning initial words and language (R.L. Koegel, O'Dell, & Koegel, 1987) and to engage in longer periods of sustained conversational interaction (R.L. Koegel, Dyer, & Bell, 1987) when their interests are considered. As a whole, these studies indicate that a number of different populations of children with language disabilities and targeted linguistic areas could benefit when considering the child's interest and incorporating child-preferred activities in language intervention programs.

Child choice also needs to include a variety of activities and items. That is, children learn more rapidly if a pool of stimulus items are selected and varied from trial to trial according to the child's interest. In addition, interspersing maintenance tasks, or tasks the child has already mastered, results in improvements in responding, as well as affect, such as better behavior, more happiness, and higher interest (Figure 1).

Multiple Examples in Natural Environments

A second component of milieu teaching involves using multiple, naturally occurring examples to teach language. The main reason for teaching multiple exemplars in natural environments is that it provides a means of facilitating generalization. That is, because teaching occurs in the contexts where language is to be used and the cues are similar to those the child will encounter in typical communicative interactions, generalization is more likely (Warren & Kaiser, 1986).

Many effective language intervention programs are implemented entirely in the child's natural environment. For example, Warren, McQuarter, and Rogers-Warren (1984) taught teachers to use milieu (mands and models) during unstructured free-play time with language-delayed preschoolers. In addition to increases in verbal initiations and verbal responses in the first play setting where direct treatment was implemented, the children generalized appropriate verbal skills to a second play setting. Other researchers have emphasized the importance of capitalizing on the child's interests, needs, and desires (described earlier) in naturalistic environments, such as teaching the child to say "want + noun" during free play (Cavallaro & Bambara, 1982) and to request food at mealtime

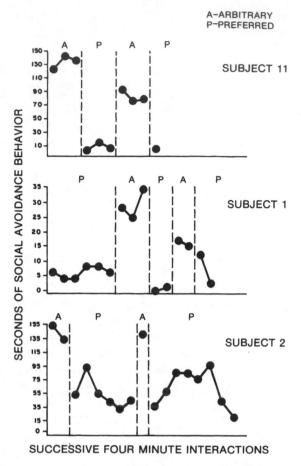

Figure 1.   Results of the repeated reversal analysis measuring the influence of the child-preferred versus arbitrary activities on the amount of social avoidance behaviors exhibited by three individuals with autism. (From Koegel, R.L., Dyer, K., & Bell, L. [1987]. The influence of child-preferred activities on autistic children's social behavior. *Journal of Applied Behavior Analysis, 20*[3], 243–252; reprinted by permission.)

(Halle, Marshall, & Spradlin, 1979) and by teaching parents to provide language intervention at home and in a variety of community environments (R.L. Koegel, Schreibman, Good, Cerniglia, Murphy, & Koegel, 1989).

Explicitly Prompted Language

Next, in milieu teaching paradigms, child production of language is explicitly prompted. For example, many practitioners will provide a delay to give the child opportunities to use language. Other programs use verbal prompting, such as asking the child, "What do you want?" Then, the child is given the requested item immediately after the request. This provides an opportunity for the consequences for child responding to be directly associated with the specific linguistic form. Inherent in this association is that the consequences that follow the child's verbalizations are natural to the context in which the teaching occurs. Thus, the child's language use results in direct natural consequences.

Use of Direct, Natural Consequences

An early example of the importance of providing a direct response–reinforcer relationship was demonstrated with children with autism who were taught to open the lid of a container to obtain a reward that was inside the container as opposed to another condition in which they were taught to open the lid of an empty container and then handed a food reward. In all cases, the children showed rapid acquisition only when the target behavior was a direct and natural part of the chain leading to the reinforcer (cf. R.L. Koegel & Williams, 1980). This has been replicated in expressive language teaching in children with autism with single expressive words or word approximations (R.L. Koegel, O'Dell, & Koegel, 1987) and syntax, such as having the child say, "I want" + a desired object (e.g., cookie) whereby the child receives the item (cookie) following the appropriate request (Charlop, Schreibman, & Thibodeau, 1985).

The significance of ensuring that the child experiences the relationship between his or her behavior and the consequence is particularly pertinent to children with autism who may experience repeated failure as a result of the disability. Researchers have suggested that motivation may be depressed, performance impaired, and task avoidance increased by repeated experiences of failure (Clark & Rutter, 1979; MacMillian, 1971; Rodda, 1977). Therefore, an intrinsically rewarding stimulus item provided contingent on the child's utterance may accelerate the child's learning of the symbolization of language because it may help the child learn the relationship between his or her speech and the consequences of that speech (R.L. Koegel, O'Dell, & Koegel, 1987).

Reinforced Attempts

Research has demonstrated that children with severe communication delays achieve higher percentages of correct speech production and are judged to have more positive affect when they are rewarded for their speech attempts (R.L. Koegel, O'Dell, & Dunlap, 1988). This is in contrast to previous procedures where children were only rewarded when a response was equal to or better than their previous response. For nonverbal children who make few initiations with poor articulation, reinforcing speech attempts is especially important for more rapid and consistent progress in their acquisition of their first expressive words.

Natural Interactions

Finally, the milieu teaching episode is embedded in ongoing interactions between the teacher and the student. As mentioned earlier, this is important in viewing (and therefore attempting to teach) conversational interactions as a reciprocal process in which competence is achieved by regarding both partners as mutually active participants. That is, in contrast to traditional interventions implemented within a repetitive practice paradigm where a drill format with repeated trials was presented, these newer programs place emphasis on turn taking (the exchange between the speaker and listener that takes place in conversation) and shared control (the sharing by both the child and the clinician of the topic and the control over the communicative act) when delivering the stimulus materials. This represents a marked difference from the traditional (analog) techniques that were primarily clinician-controlled to considering both the child and the clinician as active participants in the activity (R.L. Koegel & Mentis, 1985).

This movement toward functional social communication in natural contexts has had widespread effects, not only in demonstrating improvements in speech and language skills over previous (analog) techniques, but also in relation to collateral changes in other related behaviors. For example, in addition to improvements in responding that occur during language sessions that incorporate motivational techniques, disruptive and self-stimulatory behaviors have been shown to occur with a low frequency or to be nonexistent. This is in sharp contrast to the traditional analog intervention sessions where the children display significantly higher levels of disruptive behavior, including self-stimulation, aggression, tantrums, and so forth (R.L. Koegel, Koegel, & Surratt, 1992). Such collateral decreases in disruptive behavior are important as they significantly reduce the need for a major component of the language intervention program that focuses on reducing disruptive behavior, as discussed in the more traditional programs described earlier.

Although there is a general consensus among researchers and teachers that milieu teaching is highly desirable in relation to traditional individualized teaching outside the child's natural environment, and the techniques appear to be especially suited to teaching children in the early stages of language learning, particularly children who do not verbalize frequently and who are learning an initial lexicon, there are several linguistic areas that remain to be addressed before communicative competence is achieved. That is, milieu interventions are heavily based on increasing the child's motivation. As discussed earlier, a common method of achieving this is to instate the use of requests, particularly in populations with significant language disabilities. This is typically accomplished by withholding desired objects, activities, and so forth until the child verbalizes. Although this is highly desirable for demonstrating to the child that verbal behavior can result in positive consequences, and more generally that verbal behavior can have an effect on the environment, there are still additional linguistic skills that the child needs in order to be judged as communicatively competent.

This high degree of clinician control (inherent in withholding a desired item until the child requests it) can result in excessive stimulus control of the interaction. As a result, although the communicative interaction may significantly improve, the child may not be using a wide variety of linguistic forms other than requests. In addition, the child may rely on adult prompting before using the requests. That is, the children often need to be prompted (e.g., withholding a desired item or asking, "What do you want?") before requests are emitted.

Furthermore, many opportunities and prompts for child language use do not occur or occur infrequently if teachers are not specifically taught to provide or increase opportunities for social interaction (Peck, 1985). That is, without specific instruction, adults may not provide the opportunities necessary for significant gains. Also, because the child with a disability may interact with a large number of adults in school, home, and other community environments who may change regularly, it may be unwieldy to attempt to teach all those who interact with the child to provide opportunities for language use. In an attempt to overcome these problems and to make the language-learning environment more like that of typically developing children, researchers have attempted to expand the above procedures so they emphasize child-initiated strategies that result in language learning.

RATIONALE FOR CHILD-INITIATED STRATEGIES

As discussed earlier, the language of children with autism lacks both adequate quantitative *and* qualitative aspects as compared to typical children's language (Wetherby & Prutting, 1984). This may be particularly evident in the more limited range of functions in certain areas of discourse, especially in speaker–listener relations (Tager-Flusberg, 1994) and the lack of self-initiations that children with autism and other language delays display (Paul & Shiffer, 1991). One component of our research is to incorporate milieu procedures to expand the functions of language use. That is, for children who are using language primarily to protest or to gain access to *desired* items, we have begun to teach them a series of self-initiated strategies to expand their functions of language, reciprocal interactions, and initiations.

To do this, researchers have changed the focus of language learning so that it relics on the child's self-initiations. That is, the procedures do not posit the teacher or other adult as the primary source of language learning, but rather teach the child to initiate interactions that will result in language learning from any given environment with any communicative partner. Theoretically, self-learning language strategies would increase the autonomy of the child by providing access to a potentially powerful knowledge base for the child outside of any specific teaching context. With such strategies, a child with significant language delays is more likely to decrease the gaps in language development within a reasonable period of time.

Self-Initiated Queries

One component of research in the area of self-initiations relates to teaching queries. Queries are among the first utterances in typically developing children, and they provide them with a reciprocal interaction that furthers their language development. To be specific, during a child's second year of life "What's that?" (usually emitted as "Dat?" while pointing to an object) emerges and is a specific cue for a parent to label items. Also within the second year "Where" questions develop, and shortly after (usually during the child's third year) questions beginning with "Whose" emerge. These questions are used infrequently in language-delayed children, and children with autism may not use queries at all. However, these structures appear to be important both socially and as a means of accruing additional linguistic information. Without such structures, communicative competence is difficult to achieve. The next sections of this chapter discuss teaching procedures for self-initiated queries (as discussed in L.K. Koegel, 1994).

Teaching "What's That?"

The first question children are taught is "What's that?" to increase their expressive vocabularies of noun labels. To increase the children's motivation and the probability that question asking will occur, the initial steps involve incorporating components of the natural language paradigm. To do this, highly desired items are chosen, such as favorite toys (e.g., puzzle pieces) or foods (e.g., small candies). These items are then placed in an opaque bag and the children are prompted to ask, "What's that?" After a child asks the question, a desired item is removed from the bag, labeled, and shown to the child. The child may then take the item if he or she desires. Gradually, this prompt is faded when the children are emitting the query at a high frequency. Next, a child is prompted to repeat the name of the highly desired item before it is shown to the child. This prompt is also faded gradually. Now, the children are asking the question "What's that?" then labeling the item at a high rate. At this point, the opaque bag is faded so that the items are placed on the table, and new (neutral) items, with unknown labels, that do not appear to be desirable to the children are gradually added. That is, based on pretreatment testing, a number of common, age-appropriate items are selected. To begin, one in four items is a neutral item with an unknown label. These new items are systematically added until the children are asking "What's that?" in response to items with unknown labels. A typical dialogue may resemble the following:

Child: "What's that?" or "What that?"
Adult: "It's a dollar."
Child: "Dollar."
Adult: "Yes, a dollar."

Following this intervention, the children show dramatic increases in vocabulary growth, and, more important, they demonstrate widespread use of the query in their natural environments (e.g., with their mothers at home). Thus, the use of this query provides the children with a tool to access further linguistic information through reciprocal interactions. Such interactions reduce the need for constant and ongoing vigilance by adults to provide teaching and opportunities for language use and improve language growth and appropriate interactions for the children. Again, such self-initiated strategies are common in children with typical language development, but usually need to be taught to children with autism.

Teaching "Where" Questions

The second question taught was "Where is it?" and the acquisition of prepositions was assessed. Intervention for this query is implemented in much the same manner as "What's that?" First, the children's favorite items (e.g., gummy bears) are selected and hidden in *specific* target locations (e.g., in, on, under, on top, behind). A child is then prompted to ask, "Where is it?" The adult then tells the child the location of the item and allows the child to take the item from that location. Once the child is asking the question at a high rate, the child is prompted to repeat the preposition before being allowed to take it. A typical session dialogue resembles the following:

Child: "Where is it?" or "Where cracker?"
Adult: "*Under* the plate."
Child: "Under." (Child looks under the plate and takes the cracker.)
Adult: "Right, under."

As with the first query, the children demonstrate widespread use of the self-initiation and many generalize the question to other situations, such as asking where a specific person is or the location of a lost toy or clothing item.

Teaching "Whose" Questions

The third question focused on teaching the children to ask "Whose is it?" or "Whose + noun?" to learn personal pronouns and third-person possessives. To accomplish this, parents bring a number of items that are clearly associated with a particular family member. In addition, children's desires are incorporated. A child is prompted to ask, "Whose is it?"; then the adult provides the possessive form (e.g., "It's Daddy's") and gives the child the item. Eventually, the child is required to repeat the possessive form. Teaching "yours" and "mine" is implemented in much the same manner. That is, a highly desired object is visible (e.g., a favorite candy or toy), and the child is prompted to ask, "Whose is it?" The adult then responds, "It's yours." However, the child is then prompted to say "mine" before being given the item. This reversal has been noted to be particularly difficult for children with autism, but using a highly desired item greatly facilitates acquisition. A typical session dialogue follows:

Child: "Whose is it?"
Adult: "It's yours."
Child: "Mine." (Child takes desired toy.)

Like the previous questions, the children learned to use "Whose" and as a result of this question, the children rapidly learn a variety of prepositions.

Teaching "What Happened?"

The final linguistic area we attempted to enhance was the children's use of verbs in the past tense. To do this a variety of "pop-up" books are individually selected according to each child's interest. The adult manipulates the pull-tabs so that an action is completed.

Then the child is prompted to ask, "What happened?" The adult then describes the action. Again, eventually the child is prompted to repeat the past tense form of the verb. For example, one child was fascinated by animals, so animal books were selected to teach the regular past tense. A sample dialogue may resemble the following:

Adult: (Manipulates pull-tab so that an alligator appeared to crawl.)

Child: "What happened?"

Adult: "He crawled."

Child: "He crawled."

Again our preliminary research is suggesting that this is an extremely rapid method of teaching. Children who demonstrate some verb use in the present tense (but none in the past) and are able to combine words to form simple sentences seem to especially benefit from this procedure. These children seem to begin learning the past tense after only a few of the reciprocal interactions described here.

In summary, one can see how a child can be taught to systematically progress through grammatical development using self-initiated strategies. These strategies seem to assist with learning reciprocal interactions, and data collected on behavior suggest that these procedures are also associated with positive changes in untreated disruptive behaviors. That is, during baseline, the children demonstrated numerous inappropriate behaviors such as aggression, self-injury, tantrums, and so forth. In sharp contrast, following the implementation of intervention, the children demonstrated appropriate behavior during most of the sessions. That is, their disruptive behavior decreased to negligible levels (L.K. Koegel, 1994).

Overall, we feel these preliminary studies are quite promising in light of the general lack of spontaneous speech, and in particular the lack of question use, in the language patterns of individuals with autism. Although a subgroup of higher-functioning children with autism may develop more diverse language skills that they use in familiar situations (Tager-Flusberg et al., 1990), difficulties in widespread pragmatic use of (sometimes known) grammatical forms persist for most children with autism. This area is deserving of further research with the possibility that by focusing on child-initiated strategies, autonomy and independence are enhanced and natural social interactions can begin to be developed early on (Figure 2).

Figure 2.   This child has learned to ask questions of people in order to expand his language skills. On the left, the child is asking questions about the book. This elicits spontaneous interaction and language instruction from the adult. On the right, the adult is answering the child's question.

SUMMARY

It is now the general consensus that autism is caused by organic factors (L.K. Koegel, Valdez-Menchaca, & Koegel, 1994) and is present at birth. Although recent literature suggests that prior to being labeled as having autism there may be subtle, prelinguistic abnormalities such as a tendency toward isolation, lack of attention and initiation of communication, anomalies of eye contact, deficient variability of emotional expression, poor facial expression, inappropriate body positioning, and the absence of smiles (Adrien et al., 1991), a lack of expressive language development by age 18 months to 2 years is often the time when referrals for intervention of communication delays are made.

This is important in relation to implications for early parent–child social interactions. That is, transactional views of parent–child interaction suggest that particular behaviors displayed by parents of children with autism may be appropriate adjustments to their child's behavior or style of interaction (Curcio & Paccia, 1987; Mahoney, 1988a; Wolchik & Harris, 1982). Children who do not initiate and interact socially with others may not learn further linguistic and social competence that is gained through social interactions. When language emerges, it is often used only for ensuring that needs and desires are met, rather than learning to use a large variety and quantity of linguistic utterances seen in typical language development. In other words, without intervention these children infrequently use language and may never learn the variety of functions of utterances necessary for communicative competence. Therefore, once the child has been taught to use words, as described in the natural language paradigm, providing the child with self-initiated strategies seems especially important to accelerate the progress through grammatical development. Self-initiated strategies promote language learning in a variety of environments and thus encourage independence on the part of the child. Although the preliminary studies described here only dealt with a few of the multitude of behaviors that reduce child dependence, the importance of independence cannot be taken lightly, as it has lifestyle implications both in relation to the individual with the disability and the family. Further research assessing use of communicative functions, the outcome of communicative interactions, other child-initiated language-learning strategies, and the competence of a child in maintaining appropriate dyads and other behaviors that enhance social-communicative interactions are likely to receive increased attention in the future.

Chapter 3

Overselective Responding

Description, Implications, and Intervention

—————————*Jennifer Rosenblatt, Patricia Bloom,*
and Robert L. Koegel

One of the most enigmatic features of children with autism is also a prominent characteristic of typically developing children. *Overselectivity* refers to responding to an overly restricted portion of relevant cues when learning to differentiate components of the environment. It is not uncommon for young children in their initial stages of language acquisition to respond this way when they overgeneralize with their first words. For example, any four-legged animal may be labeled as "doggy" or any bearded man called "daddy." A child who overgeneralizes has recognized the significance of one characteristic of an object but eventually learns to base his or her discriminations on all distinguishing properties (McManis, Stollenwerk, & Zheng-Sheng, 1987). Whereas typically developing children quickly learn to differentiate objects based on more than one salient characteristic, children with autism often demonstrate overselective responding to a much greater extent, which, without intervention, may continue throughout life. Furthermore, whereas typical language learners tend to respond to more relevant components of a stimulus (e.g., anything with four legs is a "doggy"), children with autism frequently respond to an irrelevant component (e.g., a tear or bend in a picture card rather than any component of the picture at all).

This failure to develop responding to the relevant multiple features of objects in the environment can have profound consequences for children with autism and their families. Many prominent characteristics of autism, such as social behavior, language acquisition, and acquisition and generalization of new behaviors, appear to be influenced by this failure to develop responding to multiple relevant cues in the environment.

To illustrate this point, consider the fact that Kanner (1943), in his pioneering research, emphasized that the majority of children with autism demonstrate severe limitations in responding to the environment. He documented the children's general unresponsiveness to people, including their failure to acknowledge parents or peers. One of the most heartbreaking experiences for these parents is their children's seeming lack of recognition of family members. For example, some children with autism frequently fail to acknowledge a parent or sibling, even after a greeting. This failure to respond to or identify family members may be influenced by a child's responding to an irrelevant component of the person (e.g., eyeglasses or article of clothing). This salient phenomenon is discussed further in the section on social behavior later in this chapter, as are other academic difficulties caused by overselectivity.

RESEARCH ON OVERSELECTIVITY

One important line of research addressing overselectivity has focused on children's lack of responding to multiple components in the environment. Instead of responding to multiple pertinent features, certain children with autism tend to respond on the basis of a limited number of often irrelevant components in their surroundings. This characteristic was first reported by Lovaas, Schreibman, Koegel, and Rehm (1971) and was coined *stimulus overselectivity*. In this study, typically developing children and children with autism and mental retardation were taught to press a bar in the presence of a stimulus consisting of simultaneously presented visual, auditory, and tactile cues (e.g., a light, a sound, and pressure to the child's lower leg). They were also taught to refrain from bar pressing in the absence of the stimulus. After the children acquired the task, the researchers assessed their responding to each individual cue by presenting only one component (i.e., either the light *or* the sound *or* the pressure) at a time. The results demonstrated that typically developing children responded equally to each individual component (light, tone, or pressure) of the stimulus, whereas children with autism typically responded to only one of the components and failed to respond to the others. This suggests that children with autism learned to respond to only the visual, auditory, or tactile cue, instead of attending to all three simultaneously.

The findings demonstrating that children with autism often respond to a restricted number of cues in their environment have since been replicated (e.g., K.D. Allen & Fuqua, 1985; Bickel, Stella, & Etzel, 1984; Frankel, Simmons, Fichter, & Freeman, 1984; R.L. Koegel & Schreibman, 1977; Schreibman, Charlop, & Koegel, 1982; Schreibman, Kohlenberg, & Britten, 1986). In addition to the three simultaneous cues described previously, such children also have exhibited overselectivity in studies utilizing only visual and auditory stimuli (Lovaas & Schreibman, 1971), only multiple visual cues (R.L. Koegel &

Rincover, 1976; R.L. Koegel & Wilhelm, 1973; Kovattana & Kraemer, 1974; Schreibman, 1975; Schreibman & Lovaas, 1973), and only multiple auditory cues (Bickel et al., 1984; Reynolds, Newsom, & Lovaas, 1974; Schreibman, 1975).

This same phenomenon of overselectivity evidenced in children with autism and very young children without disabilities (Schover & Newsom, 1976) has also been observed in children with other disabilities, including children with mental retardation (e.g., Allen & Fuqua, 1985; Huguenin, 1985; Litrownik, McInnis, Wetzel-Pritchard, & Filipelli, 1978; Meisel, 1981; Schover & Newsom, 1976) and children with learning disabilities (Bailey, 1981). It has been suggested that overselectivity may be a function of mental age. In a study by Schover and Newsom (1976), mental age was a stronger predictor of whether overselectivity is present than even language acquisition or breadth of learning. Again, this illustrates that the characteristic may reflect a developmental problem—one that to some extent is shared by all other children when they are very young, but one that can lead to severe atypical development if it persists for an extended period of time.

One might ask why the overall development of children with autism does not directly correspond to their mental age. We propose that atypical patterns of development may be attributed to several factors. Although the children may have the equivalent mental age of a much younger child, they are still developing, albeit unevenly. They are attending and responding to some aspects of their environment, thus taking in some information and stimulation. At the same time, other important information is unintentionally disregarded. For instance, if they are responding to the shape of objects, as opposed to all features, they are learning to identify and respond to the shape component but not to the object in its entirety.

IMPLICATIONS OF OVERSELECTIVITY

Reviews of the literature suggest that, without responding to multiple cues in the environment, children may experience difficulties in many areas. There has been a plethora of research indicating the pervasiveness of overselectivity in nearly all aspects of life. It has been hypothesized that overselectivity may play an integral role in the characteristic marked unresponsivity seen in children with autism. Thus, overselectivity has various implications for the development of social behavior, language acquisition, acquisition of new behaviors, generalization, and safety. Each of these is discussed in the following sections.

Social Behavior

Children with autism generally demonstrate significant difficulties with social skills and social relationships. As noted earlier, failure to bond and/or recognize people by a child with autism has been linked to the presence of overselectivity. Schreibman and Lovaas (1973) addressed this issue by conducting an experiment in which children with autism were taught to discriminate gender differences between two lifelike dolls. The children were first taught to discriminate the gender of each doll. Then, to determine the basis of this discrimination, various articles of clothing were switched on the dolls. Results showed that, idiosyncratic to each child, the switching or removal of specific articles had an instrumental effect on responding. For example, if the controlling cue (e.g., the shoes) on the boy doll was switched to the girl doll, the child incorrectly identified the girl as a boy. Also, if the controlling cue (e.g., shoes) was eliminated, responding became random, which suggested that the child no longer recognized the gender difference.

This study suggests that responding to limited portions of social stimuli may relate to atypical social development. A child with autism may recognize a particular adult by responding to irrelevant cues, such as his or her eyeglasses or shirt. If these cues are removed or changed, the child may not be able to recognize the person (Schreibman & Koegel, 1982).

The aforementioned examples may help alleviate some of the distress parents, siblings, and other family members experience by the apparent lack of attachment and recognition by the child with autism. Failure to attach to significant people may be explained, in part, by the child's responding to irrelevant intermittent cues. For example, if a parent consistently wears eyeglasses, a child who attends to the glasses may not recognize his or her parent in the absence of this cue. This suggests that children are not unable to form attachments but rather are inhibited by a failure to repeatedly recognize the constant features of a given person.

In addition, overselective responding may hinder informal and formal social interactions with peers. Even in the most simplistic social games, such as "freeze tag," children may overselect to specific stimuli, inhibiting them from participating appropriately. These authors observed a boy with autism playing tag with his peers by selectively responding to the chasing aspect of the game to the exclusion of the other rules. This failure to play appropriately is often accompanied by a lack of peer acceptance.

Similarly, children's socialization is largely contingent on observational learning, which, in turn, can be hindered by overselectivity. In a study by Varni, Lovaas, Koegel, and Everett (1979), children with autism observed a teacher reinforcing a model for correct responding. Given the opportunity to imitate the model, the children imitated only a portion of the behavior. For example, one child, after observing a model place a square on top of a circle 1,000 times, would consistently pick up and hold the square, never appropriately placing it on the circle. This indicated that she had attended to only that one aspect of the model's behavior. Instead of focusing on the multiple aspects of the behavior, these children with autism only learned the selective aspects to which they attended.

Similarly, a child may only attend to a limited portion of conversation, thereby affecting his or her ability to respond appropriately. If a child with autism is not attending to all of the words in a question or comment, his or her social interactions may be adversely affected. For example, a child may respond to the questions, "How are you?" and "How old are you?" with the same response of "fine." This suggests that he or she was responding to some of the words, such as "how" or "how are you," instead of differentiating the questions by the relevant word "old."

Also, limited responding may impair a child's ability to follow directions. If a teacher gives successive directions, such as "put away your books and line up at the door," a child with autism may only respond to one component of the instruction. For example, the child may put away his or her books but continue sitting at his or her desk while the other children line up at the door. This failure to respond to all the directions can not only frustrate the teacher, but also draw more attention to the child with autism. This may result in ostracism by peers and/or inappropriate punishment for lack of appropriate responding.

Language Acquisition

Another area of development that has been hypothesized as being largely affected by overselectivity is language acquisition (Cook, Anderson, & Rincover, 1982). In language development, children with autism often fail to respond to the multiple cues inherent in speech and language. In Lovaas, Schreibman, Koegel, and Rehm (1971), a child with autism learned to imitate sounds produced by a therapist. After successful imitation, the therapist then produced the same sounds while covering her mouth (eliminating the visual cue). The child was unable to correctly reproduce the previously imitated sounds, which illustrated that the child was responding overselectively to the visual cue instead of the auditory component.

The overselective responding observed in this child may have a tremendous effect on language learning. For instance, it appears that this child may only be able to learn verbal material if it is coupled with the visual cue of the teacher's mouth movements. Therefore, it would be important for this child to be positioned in such a way as to maximize his or her opportunity to observe the teacher (or, as discussed later in this chapter, to eliminate the overselectivity through intervention).

In addition to overselective responding across sensory modalities, research has shown that children with autism can selectively respond within a given modality. Reynolds et al. (1974) suggest that atypical speech may result from a fixation on a specific aspect within the auditory mode (i.e., frequency, duration, or amplitude). In observation of the speech of children with autism, Bagshaw (1978) reported that imitation was based on overselective responding to a limited number of the necessary auditory cues, resulting in an "atonal" or "arrhythmic" replication.

The phenomenon of overselecting in a given modality was observed by the present authors in an 8-year-old boy with autism. When asked to color a bush green, the child was unable to perform the task; however, if the word *green* was printed inside of the bush, he was able to color it appropriately. It seems that this boy was selectively responding to visual cues.

The concept of a preferred modality warrants further research, but it is important to understand whether or not a child operates solely within a given modality in all situations. There are profound implications for education and intervention if consistent patterns are identified. Operating almost solely within a given modality can pose problems in the classroom. If a child operates purely in the visual modality, performance will be contingent on whether or not the child is given oral or written directions. More often than not, it is the parents who first become aware of the modality from which a child with autism operates. If informed of the preferred modality, the teacher can modify directions and/or assignments to accommodate the child's learning style.

Acquisition of New Behaviors

All children need assistance when learning new behaviors. The most common type of assistance involves prompting—a method whereby the teacher points to or otherwise adds stimuli that are supposed to help guide the child's responding (referred to as extra-stimulus prompting). Whereas older children who have had experience with such prompts find this assistance very useful, children with autism can be further confused by extra-stimulus prompting. Therefore, this type of prompting often decreases the likelihood of acquisition of a new behavior if the child selectively responds to the prompt (Cook et al., 1982). Research suggests that prompt fading is ineffective for children with autism because of their lack of responding to the simultaneous multiple cues of the prompt and the target stimulus (Fields, Bruno, & Keller, 1976; Schreibman, Charlop, & Koegel, 1982). For example, if a child with autism is being taught to differentiate "green" from "blue" through the utilization of a pointing prompt, the child may selectively respond to the pointing finger instead of the actual color discrimination.

In addition to learning through prompts, children are taught new behaviors through multiple instructions. For example, when learning to tie shoes, a child is required to attend to simultaneous directions (e.g., hearing "Cross the laces over each other" while watching a manual demonstration of this action at the same time). If a child is only responding to one of these cues, the child may experience difficulty learning the task.

Generalization

In addition to jeopardizing learning across many areas of development, overselectivity may influence generalization of learned behaviors outside of the intervention situation (Carr, 1980). Research has shown that acquired learning is profoundly affected by over-selectivity in relation to behaviors that do not seem to generalize. Often, when a child with autism acquires the ability to imitate a modeled behavior or to reproduce vocalizations, these learned behaviors seem to be situation specific. It appears that stimulus generalization is contingent on the extent to which common controlling stimuli are present in the various environments.

For example, in a study by Rincover and Koegel (1975), children with autism were taught a behavior in an intervention environment. After the behavior was acquired in the given environment, the children were brought to another environment and asked by a different therapist to exhibit the acquired behavior. Some of the children failed to transfer their new behavior due to selective responding to an idiosyncratic stimulus in the intervention room, such as the therapist's hand gesture or a specific prompt. For the children to respond in the new environment, the specific controlling stimulus in the teaching environment needed to be present. This study clearly demonstrates how the tendency to respond to a restricted number of stimuli can severely limit the probability of generalization.

This has major implications for education in that a child may respond to an incidental hand gesture or intonation of a teacher or a specific irrelevant stimulus in the classroom instead of the actual instructions and material being presented. Therefore, the child may not be able to respond appropriately to identical instructions or tasks given by a different teacher, at a different time, and/or in a different environment. Unfortunately, this type of responding is often mistaken for noncompliance when it is actually a documented pattern of attentional behavior in need of intervention.

Safety

Overselectivity can also have serious ramifications for a child's safety. Many stimuli in the environment, from traffic signal colors and locations to subtle social cues, can signal danger or safety to an individual. For example, if a child learns to identify his or her car on the basis of one cue (e.g., color), the child may mistakenly approach any car with this color. In addition, children with autism often fail to recognize dangerous situations due to lack of responding to all environmental components. For example, a child who attends to an interesting stimulus across the street (e.g., a fire hydrant, dog, bike) may run toward the desired object, unaware of the dangerous traffic in his or her pathway. This lack of differentiation can also be observed in very young typically developing children. Children with autism who continue to fail to differentiate require the constant attention and supervision of others.

In summary, the research on overselectivity suggests that effective intervention for remediating overselective responding in children with autism could have widespread implications for their overall functioning (Bickel et al., 1984; Lovaas, Koegel, & Schreibman, 1979; Rincover & Koegel, 1975; Schreibman, 1988).

FEASIBILITY OF INTERVENTION

There have been two major approaches to the intervention of overselectivity. One approach has been to assume that it cannot be modified and that special learning environments might need to be developed (analogous to developing braille for a person with a visual impairment). Another approach has been to try to remediate the problem of overselectivity through directly teaching the children to respond to multiple cues.

Researchers have tried an array of intervention procedures in an effort to reduce and eliminate the problem of overselectivity. In the approach of developing special environments, researchers have tried techniques such as incorporating a prompt (called a within-stimulus prompt by Schreibman, 1988) within the relevant cue (e.g., exaggerating a size cue to teach the concept of size and then gradually reducing the exaggeration). In the example in Figure 1, the length of the stems of the letters *b* and *p* have been exaggerated (elongated) in order to draw the child's attention to the orientation cue. The length of the stems were then gradually reduced to normal proportions. This approach attempts to draw the child's attention to a single relevant cue, in hopes that the child will also learn about other relevant parts of the stimulus complex. The approach has been highly effective in teaching many difficult tasks, as illustrated in the reading example in the figure.

In the other approach, researchers have attempted to eliminate overselectivity by directly teaching the children to respond to multiple cues. R.L. Koegel and Schreibman (1977) investigated the feasibility of teaching children with autism to respond to multiple cues by gradually and systematically teaching them to focus on an increasing number of relevant cues. All of the children in this study acquired the ability to discriminate and respond to complex cues.

Schreibman, Koegel, and Craig (1977) demonstrated that repeated exposure to testing can also have an impact on overselectivity. In this study, children were taught to distinguish between two visual cues through verbal feedback and rewards for correct responses. Following acquisition of this preliminary instruction, discrimination probe trials with the individual component stimuli were introduced but no feedback was given on these probes. The results showed that 13 out of the 16 children in the experiment decreased their level of overselectivity with repeated exposure to testing. The possibility that this effect may have been influenced by the reinforcement schedule was systematically investigated later by R.L. Koegel, Schreibman, Britten, and Laitinen (1979). These researchers found that the children who were rewarded less frequently (i.e., on the average for every third correct response vs. for every correct response) showed significantly less overselectivity. As a whole, these studies demonstrate that one simple method for improving overselectivity is to use a partial reinforcement system, at least following initial acquisition of the discrimination. It is possible that a change to nonreinforced trials (in the variable reinforcement conditions) increases the children's breadth of attention on subsequent trials.

GENERALIZED EFFECTS OF MULTIPLE CUE INTERVENTION

An encouraging outcome of teaching children with autism to respond to multiple cues was demonstrated in a study by Schreibman, Charlop, and Koegel (1982). After the children in the study were exposed to multiple cue instruction, they were able to learn from an extra-stimulus prompt (pointing) that was previously unsuccessful in facilitating discrimination learning. Thus, after intervention, the children were able to learn by using the types of extrastimulus (multiple cue) prompts that teachers and others present to typical children.

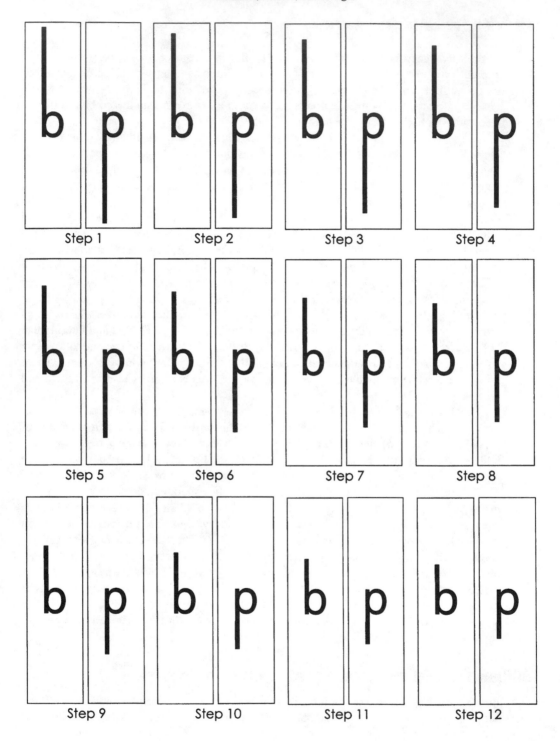

Figure 1.   This figure illustrates the use of within-stimulus prompting to teach the difference between the letters *p* and *b*. The stems of the letters are elongated to draw the child's attention to the relevant cues and then are slowly decreased to natural proportions.

Burke and Cerniglia (1990) wanted to further test the hypothesis that the limitations of children with autism in responding to environmental stimuli increase directly with the number of components contained in the stimuli. Children were asked to respond to verbal instructions that involved both a motor response and a single or multiple component discrimination. Examples of instructions involving one, two, three, and four components, respectively, are as follows: 1) "Hand me the *pencil*," 2) "Hand me the *big pencil*," 3) "Hand me the *big blue cup*," and 4) "Give me the *little red crayon* from the *box*." They found that the degree of difficulty children experienced in responding was related to the increase in the number of components in the instructions. They went on to show that teaching the children to respond to multiple cue instructions would produce a generalized improvement in responding to complex instructions. In Figure 2, an example of teaching a child to respond to two cues is shown. In this example, the child is rewarded for selecting the *large cup*, but not rewarded for selecting the small cup, the small toothbrush, or the large toothbrush (after being asked by someone to hand him or her the large cup). Repeated instruction with similar multiple cue stimuli eventually teaches the child that he or she needs to respond to multiple cues in order to perform tasks correctly.

To test the effects of generalization after children received this type of teaching, the authors examined the children's performance on standardized language tests and observational measures of responding to complex instructions in a social context. Results demonstrated systematic increased levels of correct responding on all tests, as well as improvements in responding to multicomponent social stimuli after intervention.

Burke and Cerniglia (1990) suggest "the degree that a particular child is unresponsive to the environment, in part, may be a function of how frequently the child is required to respond to complex stimuli that contain a certain number of components" (p. 248). In

Figure 2. Procedures for teaching an individual to respond to multiple cues can easily be incorporated in natural environments. Here this youth is being asked to get the large cup (as opposed to the small cup or the large toothbrush).

an attempt to elicit responding and understanding from children with autism, parents and teachers may need to gradually and systematically teach the children to respond to complex multiple cue stimuli in their environment.

The aforementioned studies suggest that increasing children with autism's ability to respond to multiple cues in their environment may be pivotal in increasing their overall functioning. In a study by Burke and Koegel (1982), children were placed in one of two intervention conditions. The first condition involved single cue discriminations and the second condition required multiple cue discriminations (a further explanation of conditions follows). The results suggest that increasing the children's ability to respond to simultaneous multiple cues in their environment was pivotal in increasing their overall functioning. In accordance with Burke and Koegel, we propose the following multiple cue instruction procedure to increase breadth of responding and global functioning.

1. Children can be taught conditional (multiple cue) discriminations through an emphasis on multiple cues utilizing stimuli from standard developmental curricula, such as geometric forms, letters, common objects, eating utensils, clothing, and toys.
2. Tasks can include, but not be limited to, discriminations based on size, shape, and type of object or clothing article.
3. Instead of teaching the tasks one component at a time, multiple components are employed throughout.
4. Children who demonstrate overselective attention should be taught to respond to two relevant cues simultaneously, such as both a specific color and a specific shape. For example, a child could be instructed to "Put on the red sweater" when the stimuli present include a green sweater, a red sweater, green pants, and red pants. To be considered correct the child would need to respond to the stimulus with both the correct color cue (red) and the correct clothing item (sweater). So, instead of instructing the child in single cue color discriminations (e.g., "point to blue" vs. "point to yellow") or single cue object discriminations (e.g., "point to the pants" vs. "point to the shirt"), the child is being taught colors and clothing items simultaneously. Once the child has mastered two cues, the child can be systematically taught to respond to three cues and then four cues.

CONCLUSION

The aforementioned studies have stressed the importance of intervention for exposure to complex stimuli and demonstrated that children with autism are capable of responding to multiple cues when intervention is provided. Overall, the literature suggests that 1) a characteristic lack of responding to multiple components of complex stimuli may relate to broad areas of the children's symptomatology, and 2) intervention that produces generalized responding to multiple cues may produce widespread gains in these broad areas of symptomatology. Specifically, if overselectivity can be remediated, major advances in children's social behavior, language development, and general "responsiveness" to their environment can be anticipated.

Chapter 4

Spontaneous Language Use

—Don Hawkins

The Individuals with Disabilities Education Act of 1990 (PL 101-476) has affirmed the right of all children to fully participate in the life of the community into which they were born (Brown et al., 1989; Rapport & Thomas, 1993). For children with severe disabilities, such as autism, the fulfillment of this right may require intensive intervention for more than one behavioral domain. For maximum effectiveness, such multiple interventions often require coordinated implementation well before a child's school years. A major goal of intervention is to achieve a typical life in the community of a child's birth (Brown et al., 1989); however, the presence of a significant language delay often complicates the realization of this goal.

Children who exhibit language delays are often socially disadvantaged. For example, Halle (1982) has noted that some of these children may become dependent on others for initiating communication. Such dependence may reduce motivation for social interaction and lead to learned helplessness (R.L. Koegel & Mentis, 1985). Thus, the influence exerted by an environment on a skill has profound implications for potential behavioral change in that skill. One skill, language use, is especially critical for accessing the community environment. From the intervention research on this skill, spontaneity of language use has emerged as an important issue.

DEFINITION OF SPONTANEITY

In the research literature, spontaneous language use has received various definitions. The notion that a spontaneous response is controlled by aspects of the environment that are not immediately obvious to the communicative partner has been suggested (Halle, 1987). In other definitions, obvious environmental control is allowed (Carr & Kologinsky, 1983; Cavallaro & Bambara, 1982; Charlop, Schreibman, & Thibodeau, 1985; Charlop & Walsh, 1986). Some examples consider language to be spontaneous if it occurs in the absence of instructional prompts to communicate (Carr & Kologinsky, 1983; Duker & Moonen, 1986; Ingenmey & Van Houten, 1991; Kouri, 1989; Lovaas, Koegel, Simmons, & Long, 1973; Peck, 1985; Reich, 1978), such as when a child says, "thank you" for receiving a gift without a parent prompting, "What do you say?" Spontaneous language use has also been discussed as occurring in response to nonverbal components of the environment (Dyer, 1989; Halle, 1987; L.K. Koegel, 1993; Layton, 1988), such as when a child names objects while riding in a car. Finally, language used in the presence of a conversational partner during a delay in conversation (Mirenda & Donnellan, 1986) has been called spontaneous, such as when a parent pauses in a reprimand (e.g., Mom says, "Who broke the glass?") and the child grasps the opportunity to change the subject ("I love you, Mommy"). Although these examples are quite obvious, they may be considered more subtle than a direct verbal request to communicate, such as when an adult says, "What do you want?"

Other definitions of spontaneity include a specified time since the last verbal response of the communicative partner (Cavallaro & Bambara, 1982; Dyer, 1989; Peck, 1985). Time intervals are important. For example, one child might say, "Let's play soccer!" A peer might echo, "Let's play soccer!" Within the situation, this echoed response might seem natural, yet not truly spontaneous.

Finally, R.L. Koegel, O'Dell, and Koegel (1987) defined spontaneity in terms of two factors: 1) the closeness of the child's communicative responses to the clinician's, and 2) the child's initiated approximations of words that are not the object of instruction. The R.L. Koegel, O'Dell, and Koegel (1987) definition does not eliminate the presence of language cues but does specify their temporal relationship to the spontaneous response.

Table 1 lists specific teaching paradigms that have contributed to our understanding of spontaneity. Examples are provided for each paradigm as well as the manner in which the paradigm evokes language. The examples provided in Table 1 illustrate the varying amounts of support for communication that different procedures provide. The table also highlights the fact that different natural communicative situations actually provide different amounts of support. Thus, different situations in which the child must communicate will make quite different demands on the child's communicative skills. The different instructional paradigms suggest that the unique features of a communicative situation exert an important influence on the child's communicative performance (Figure 1).

This suggestion may be used to propose a definition of spontaneity. A response is considered spontaneous relative to the communicative requirements of a specific situation in which communication is used. Given a specific situation in which communication is used, a spontaneous response is a response that meets the communicative requirements of that situation. As the examples in Table 1 illustrate, different communicative situations naturally provide different communicative support. At snack time, the teacher's approach

Table 1. Examples of spontaneous language used in research

Teaching paradigm	Procedure to evoke language	Examples of spontaneous language
Natural language teaching paradigm	Verbal/nonverbal	Clinician is playing with toy; child labels toy; clinician gives toy to child.
Incidental teaching	Verbal	Child stands and looks at toys out of reach. Teacher asks child, "What do you want?" Child says, "I want the Play-Doh."
General case programming	Verbal	Child approaches supervisor on the playground who is distributing kick balls. Supervisor says, "Do you want a red ball or a blue ball?" Child answers, "A red ball."
General case programming and interrupted chain procedure	Interruption of response sequence	At snack time, child is ready for a second helping of potato chips. Teacher approaches with potato chips and waits. Child says, "More chips please."
Koegel	Nonverbal	Child is shopping with parent; child sees a new product. Child asks parent, "What's that?"

with potato chips and attention to the student are naturally available to the child as cues to communicate. In this situation, instruction needs merely to provide a delay in the teacher's behavior to effectively teach the child to request a second helping of chips. However, in a situation such as shopping where the child encounters a new product, the parent may not be attending to the child and the child will have to obtain the parent's attention to request a label. Thus, these two situations provide quite different communicative challenges to the

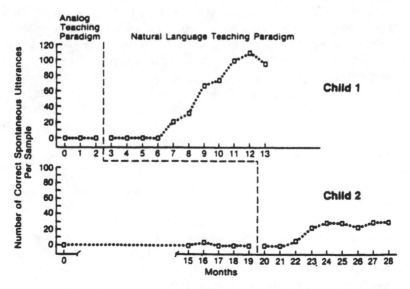

Figure 1. Spontaneous speech generalization results. Probes are plotted by month on the abscissa, and number of correct utterances is plotted on the ordinate. (From Koegel, R.L., O'Dell, M.C., & Koegel, L.K. [1987]. A natural language teaching paradigm for nonverbal autistic children. *Journal of Autism and Developmental Disorders, 17,* 187–200; reprinted by permission.)

child. A child who can request a second helping of potato chips during snack time at school, when the instructor's attention may be immediately available, may not be able to request the name of a new product while shopping when the parent's attention may not always be immediately available.

To assess the appropriateness of spontaneity of language used in a particular situation, one must specify the particular communicative requirements. These requirements include at least the following: when communication should occur, to whom it should occur, acceptable topics of communication, the length of a communicative interaction, the initiation of a communicative interaction, and the rate of communication. It is not suggested that these factors are exhaustive.

According to the definition proposed, the essence of appropriate spontaneous language use is the production of language that functionally relates to the environment (Halle, Chadsey-Rusch, & Collet-Klingenberg, 1993) in which it occurs. Consider the following situation. A child approaches a friend and properly obtains the friend's attention by saying the friend's name. Failing to get a response from the friend, the child says, "Hello." The friend then answers, "Hello." Upon the friend's response, the child then says, "I love you" and continues to repeat this sentence for the next 3 minutes regardless of the friend's further responses.

Although this is spontaneous language, it may not be *appropriate* spontaneous language. This example illustrates the importance of specifying the communicative requirements of the environment in which the response occurs when that response is reported to be spontaneous. From these examples, one might correctly conclude that the natural environment has been an important factor in the emergence of spontaneity as an intervention interest. The next section briefly examines this influence.

ASPECTS OF THE ENVIRONMENT

From their experiences with children who may not use language outside the environment in which it was learned, practitioners have come to appreciate the difference between the natural and analog instructional environments. As intervention research has learned more about natural communicative environments, instructional procedures have responded to the many opportunities for language learning that occur in those environments. Although intervention has tended to occur within the public school environment, the home environment has also been used (Laski, Charlop, & Schreibman, 1988). For example, the motivational characteristics of the child's daily environment have been used by milieu instructional procedures (Hart & Risley, 1974, 1975; Warren & Bambara, 1989) and the natural language paradigm. Instruction has used social settings of varying structure and amounts of social interaction (Charlop & Walsh, 1986; Dyer, 1989; Hargrave & Swisher, 1975). Within social interactions, instruction has been concerned with the initiation of those interactions by distinguishing between procedures that are initiated by the teacher (Campbell & Stremel-Campbell, 1982) and those that are initiated by the child (Duker & van Lent, 1991; Kaczmarek, 1990; L.K. Koegel, 1993; Reich, 1978).

More specifically, intervention instruction has used natural objects and routines of both daily living and play activities (Cavallaro & Bambara, 1982; Chadsey-Rusch, Drasgow, Reinoehl, Halle, & Collet-Klingenberg, 1993; R.L. Koegel, O'Dell, & Koegel, 1987; Laski, Charlop, & Schreibman, 1988). From its experiences with natural activities, intervention has increasingly taken on characteristics of those activities that are important for language use. For example, cuing of language use may be naturally accomplished with indirect questions such as, "What color ball do you want?" More direct cuing is even possible (e.g., "Do you want the red or blue ball?") without violating the natural communicative interactions that would occur in a play environment. Natural routines, whether play or daily living, have been found to be quite flexible in the instruction they will support. For example, the interrupted chain procedure (Gee, Graham, Goetz, Oshima, & Yoshioka, 1991) involves removing an item, such as soap, that is required to complete a natural routine, such as hand washing. The empty soap container cues the child to request soap. Likewise, the time-delay procedure allows the child a few seconds to communicate (Carr & Kologinsky, 1983; Charlop et al., 1985; Gobbi, Cipani, Hudson, & Lapenta-Neudeck, 1986). In particular, this procedure uses a short delay in communication (an event that occurs naturally) for systematic instructional purposes.

The capacity of the natural environment to accommodate instruction may be seen in the use of both distributed and massed instructional trials (Gobbi et al., 1986). For example, snack time at school·naturally presents opportunities for requesting food and drinks. Without disrupting this setting, practitioners may increase the communicative opportunities by controlling the distribution of snack items. Thus, a student may have to request a second or third helping of snacks if the helpings are small. Of interest, natural activities deliver important reinforcers that vary from desired foods, objects, and interactions with preferred persons. These reinforcers are naturally individualized for the child. The influence of the natural environment on the development of intervention procedures may be seen in the fact that attention is now given to the presentation of the reinforcer, whether or not it is visible (Charlop et al., 1985) or partially presented (Duker & Moonen, 1986).

Such details are important in that the natural environment is not uniform in its presentation of reinforcers. For some children, the visibility of a reinforcer may strongly influence communicative performance by distracting the child's attention from the communicative interaction. Intervention work within the natural environment has resulted in instructional procedures that fit into the activities and interactions that occur there. This fit of instruction to the natural environment may be viewed as one important contribution to an understanding of spontaneity (Figure 2).

Figure 2.   Aspects of the natural environment can facilitate spontaneous language. In this picture, capitalizing on the child's interest in pop-up books motivated his spontaneous language use.

PRELIMINARY RECOMMENDATIONS FOR PRACTICE

As children with language disabilities become increasingly involved in the life of their communities, spontaneous language use is increasingly becoming an important focus of their language intervention. Research has not yet achieved a thorough understanding of this important factor. For this reason, any recommendations must necessarily be general and tentative. Nevertheless, the research discussed earlier does provide the practitioner with several suggestions that are well worth consideration. At least three suggestions may currently be offered to those concerned with the language instruction of children with language delays.

1. Focus instruction on aspects of communication involving interaction and the specific demands placed on the requirements for interaction in the environments in which the child actually communicates.
2. Pay attention to changes in the objects and routines that occur within a particular environment in which the child actually communicates. Teach the child to respond to these changes when they are important for using language.
3. In the child's educational focus, include objectives that teach the child to use known language forms as a tool to learn new language.

Each of these important principles is discussed further in the next section.

Focus on Aspects of Communicative Interaction

From a perspective of spontaneity, attention to aspects of communicative interaction involves a close examination of the unique requirements of the specific situations in which the child is actually communicating as they relate to the initiation and continuation of communication. For example, consider the instructional objective that teaches a child to request paper for a copy machine. If we teach a child to request paper when none is available, does this situation often arise for the child in the natural educational environment or does it only arise as an instructional problem? If the child's natural educational environment does frequently run out of paper, what are the actual communicative conditions the child faces? Is there always someone available to ask the child what is needed? Does the child have to report the need by searching for a particular person, acquiring that person's attention, and then stating the problem? Or will the natural environment replace the paper if the child simply waits? After stating to the proper person that paper is needed, will the child also have to state where the paper is needed?

Each of these possible situations places different communicative requirements on the child. If we want the child to request paper in an environment that in actuality replaces it without such communication, then we will have to include self-monitoring in intervention. For example, the child will need to be able to observe that, not only is there no paper in the copier, but for this reason the child will not be able to complete the assigned job. Furthermore, this violation will have to make a difference to the child. Otherwise, the child will likely choose to wait for the environment to replace the paper. Teaching the child to say, "Paper please" when the teacher is present and there is no paper will provide the child with inadequate language skills for environments where the teacher is not present and there is no paper in the copier. In an environment where only specific persons can replace the paper (e.g., public copy machines), the recognition of these individuals will be a critical part of requesting paper. Likewise, we need to consider exactly how access to these individuals changes from day to day. Do the persons who replace paper remain in one location waiting for a request or are they involved in other duties? If so, exactly how complex a search strategy will occasionally be required?

Attention to Change within the Immediate Environment in which Language Is Used

To determine the communicative requirements of any particular environment, one must not only know the where of the environment but also the when of the communication to be considered. For example, ordering food differs according to the restaurant (e.g., a fast-food restaurant compared to a formal restaurant). Accordingly, ordering at different types of restaurants differs in small ways at different times. At a fast-food restaurant, for example, the early morning hours may present a light customer load with immediate service. At noon, however, a 10-minute wait in line may be required. Likewise, a more formal restaurant will work much differently at a noon buffet than at dinner in the evening.

The change in language requirements of a communicative environment that may be observed across time is an important factor for language instruction. The child must learn to recognize these changes and adjust communication accordingly. For children with language delays, these adjustments must be explicitly addressed by instruction. Thus, the child's performance should be observed in order to collect information on at least the following questions:

1. Does the child respond at all to specific changes in the context?
2. If the child does not respond, what exactly are the cues to which the child is not responding?
3. If the child does respond, is the response adequate for the specific situation?
4. If the child's response is inadequate for the specific situation, will the child's present language use interfere with instruction? That is, does the child's language use contain aspects that are incompatible with an adequate response or the instructional procedure?
5. How often do the communicative requirements of a particular communicative environment change?
6. Can the child presently adjust communicative responses at the rate required by the particular environment?
7. Is the child's communication and language adequate for the demands of a particular situation?
8. Given a particular child's communicative history, how novel are the changes presented by a particular environment for this child? Will these changes interfere with the child's language use?

When assessing a specific context with these questions as a guide, the procedure of error analysis that has been developed for general case instruction will offer a valuable assessment tool for the teacher. Through an analysis of the student's response errors, teachers are able to identify aspects of the student's response that may interfere with future instruction on any specific task (Albin & Horner, 1988). Teachers will also recognize the possibility of applying the techniques for partial participation (Baumgart et al., 1982). Partial participation techniques provide the instructor with a means of systematically identifying steps of a task that will require task modification, environmental adaptations, and instructional adjustments. By continuously implementing such an analysis throughout the instructional phase, teachers are able to identify instructional problems before they significantly interfere with learning. Through such means, children may be provided with the optimal conditions for successful educational experiences. Therefore, partial participation techniques are also valuable in providing guidelines for translating the information obtained from the questions asked earlier into actual instructional objectives that are responsive to the requirements of the environment in which children are currently participating.

Teach the Child to Learn How to Learn Language

If we recognize that the natural communicative environment is dynamic, then we agree that no instructional program can encompass the scope of language forms that will be required by such an environment. Essentially, the child's relation to language learning is a lifelong affair. As with all extended relationships, this one must give the child pleasure if it is to be maintained. Therefore, students must become skillful and independent in the task of language learning. It is insufficient that a child merely uses language. Language must be used in such a way that new language use naturally results. For example, asking questions concerning the labels of objects is a natural form of communication that increases a child's vocabulary. Of interest for spontaneous communication are the types of environments and interactions that facilitate such language use (see Chapter 2 for specific steps involved in such teaching). Also, the way instruction is applied to specific tasks may increase or block the development of this skill.

A teacher may instruct a task in such a way as to insert models of information seeking for the student concerning significant aspects of the task. For example, when instructing students to shop, instruction should not be limited to those items that are easily accessible in the store. Shopping for a new product that has just reached the market requires skills not demanded when shopping for products that have been on the market for years. Shopping for products in an unfamiliar store demands communication skills not required when shopping in a familiar store. Such experiences may be overlooked by those who plan the instructional experiences of children. The many small problems that must be solved in children's daily lives provide many language learning opportunities that may be missed. These experiences should be considered as a critical part of children's education. From systematic instruction in experiences such as these, children learn to use language in ways that will increase their access to the opportunities provided by their communities.

CONCLUSION

Research suggests that spontaneity is an important characteristic of language use that can be 1) taught to children with a range of disabilities; 2) effected by a wide variety of instructional procedures; and 3) taught to children who communicate with speech, manual signs or gestures, or a combination of speech and manual signs or gestures. Spontaneity presents itself as a characteristic of language that appears to pervade a large set of language uses. For a behavioral analysis, the problem of spontaneous language use involves a detailed assessment of the environmental influence on language use in light of the particular language requirements of a particular environment. At this early stage of the research, it may be premature to speculate as to the questions that will emerge as we examine this factor; however, the results achieved already suggest the issue of spontaneous language use is relevant to at least one important social problem: the full integration of children with significant disabilities into the communities of their birth. If children with significant disabilities are to achieve independence, they will need to use language in ways that are responsive to a large set of dynamic social environments. Children must learn to use language in ways that are sufficiently flexible to manage the changes presented by the environments in which they will live. Also, they will need to use language in ways that are reinforced by those environments and/or that will increase their access to potential reinforcers provided by those environments (e.g., asking questions to find out how to access reinforcers).

For the problem of community integration, an analysis of spontaneous language use may offer much in determining the role of typical language use in that integration. For example, by examining the influential and reinforcing components of a particular environment in relation to the language use required of that environment, we also may be able to learn much about how language use facilitates or inhibits community acceptance of children with language delays. We may understand better the role of language in such instructional procedures as partial participation (Baumgart et al., 1982; Ferguson & Baumgart, 1991) and self-management (L.K. Koegel, Koegel, Hurley, & Frea, 1992; Skinner, 1989). We may also learn better how to modify social environments to facilitate the independence of children with the most significant disabilities. Society may ultimately find a way for children with even the most significant disabilities to attend the schools of their brothers, their sisters, and their friends (Brown et al., 1989). Beyond the school years, these children may, as adults, enter our lives as legitimate participating members (Lave & Wenger, 1991) of our society and thereby immeasurably enrich us all.

Chapter 5

Social-Communicative Skills in Higher-Functioning Children with Autism

William D. Frea

Effective social interaction and a rich social network are aspects of life that are easily taken for granted. Being accepted as part of a peer-group at school or work is central to the quality of life that many people experience. Such successful social interactions have presented one of the most difficult challenges for individuals with autism. Even higher-functioning children and adults with autism are often reported to have residual social skills difficulties. These difficulties may affect various aspects of the child's development by 1) increasing behavior problems that can preclude skill acquisition, 2) increasing the likelihood for maladaptive behaviors later in life, and 3) decreasing the positive developmental support and learning opportunities found in successful peer relationships. Therefore, it is important to consider variables that might influence the quality of social interactions of individuals with autism.

SOCIAL DIFFICULTIES

It is not surprising that quality of social interaction has been found to be a possible predictor of social acceptance (Asher & Gottman, 1981; Dodge, 1983; Hartup & Sancilio, 1986;
Quay & Jarrett, 1984). Because many higher-functioning individuals with autism have
difficulty with social skills, yet are active in the community, the risk is high for social
rejection.

One factor to be considered in relation to social rejection is the potential for more
serious behavior problems to develop. Recent research on the communicative function of
inappropriate behaviors lends support to the hypothesis that difficulty in using effective
social behaviors may cause a child to use more socially inappropriate means of communication to achieve such goals as seeking attention or avoiding difficult situations (Carr &
Durand, 1985; Day, Horner, & O'Neill, 1994; Hunt, Alwell, & Goetz, 1988). These inappropriate means of social communication that can result from an inadequate repertoire of
skills may serve only to exacerbate a child's social difficulties. For example, Dodge
(1983) performed a short-term longitudinal study in which the interactive behaviors of
children were observed and videotaped. Later sociometric interviews found that the children who were rejected or neglected by their peers were those who engaged in inappropriate behaviors. He also noted that these children engaged in significantly more physical
aggression than their peers.

Peer rejection also has the potential of resulting in later severe depression or other
maladjustment (cf. Roff, Sells, & Golden, 1972). That is, children who experience stigmatization may carry the effects of this peer rejection into adulthood (Robins, 1966). Difficulties in forming and maintaining meaningful social relationships may also continue
throughout life. This is extremely problematic because healthy peer relations play a large
part in a child's or adolescent's social and emotional development (Berndt, 1982; Coie &
Dodge, 1983; Cowen, Pederson, Babigian, Izzo, & Trost, 1973; Hartup & Sancilio, 1986;
Parker & Asher, 1987; Price & Dodge, 1989; Robins, 1966; Roff et al., 1972; Strayhorn &
Strain, 1986), as well as the child's academic achievement (Berndt, 1982).

In contrast, friendships and quality peer interaction may lay the groundwork for later
healthy and satisfying relationships (Amado, 1993) (see Chapter 9). Peer relationships
have the potential for playing significant roles throughout development. Friendships or
regular, close peer interactions can serve such critical functions as providing consensual
validation of interests, hopes, and fears; bolstering feelings of self-worth; providing affection and opportunities for intimate disclosure; promoting the growth of interpersonal sensitivity, serving as a prototype for later romantic and possibly marital and parental
relationships; providing instrumental aid; providing opportunities for nurturing behavior;
promoting a sense of reliable alliance; providing companionship (Amado, 1993; Furman
& Buhrmester, 1985); acting as a cultural institution for transmission of social norms and
knowledge; serving as a staging arena for behavior; serving as a context for the display of
appropriate self-images (Fine, 1981); serving as a context for growth in social competence; providing emotional security and support; and acting as prototypes for later relationships (Hartup & Sancilio, 1986).

Without peer acceptance, the child is at a definite disadvantage, and rejection by
peers can result in limited social learning opportunities. These disadvantages include
restricted access to appropriate behavior models, limited access to spontaneous peer tutor-
ing, and reduced encouragement for doing well (Strain, 1984). In contrast, regular interaction with typically functioning peers can provide valuable social learning opportunities.

Several variables that have a positive impact on programs targeting the social competence of higher-functioning individuals with autism are discussed in this chapter. First,
however, it is helpful to look closer at the types of social difficulties typically encountered.

SOCIAL AND FUNCTIONAL LANGUAGE

Higher-functioning individuals with autism often acquire language structures that seman-
tically and syntactically approach age-appropriate levels. Problems usually exist with the
use of these structures. Although individuals with autism vary greatly, they typically have
significant difficulties with many pragmatic or social aspects of language (Baltaxe & Simmons, 1975; Eales, 1993; R.L. Koegel & Frea, 1993). Several pragmatic areas are frequently discussed in the literature, such as eye gaze, expression of affect, prosody, topic
shifting and maintenance, and nonverbal mannerisms.

Eye Gaze

Abnormal eye contact is probably the most common pragmatic difficulty commented on
in the literature (Rutter, 1978). Children with autism may actively avoid making eye contact (Rimland, 1964), possibly to escape or avoid social-communicative interactions they
perceive as difficult. The amount of eye contact the child makes often relates to the familiarity or complexity of the task at hand (Dawson & Adams, 1984). This difficulty has
many implications for social learning. Many subtle social cues are learned through observation. A child who is not attending to the eyes or facial cues of someone attempting social
interaction will have a difficult time responding to the social initiation and a difficult time
learning to reciprocate or respond in social situations in general. For a child who already
has social-communicative difficulties, a failure to engage in eye contact increases the likelihood of having difficulty acquiring appropriate affect, facial expression, and other
behaviors that require some degree of social engagement. Over time, the results can be
devastating. As more social demands and higher expectations are placed on the maturing
child, social learning can be affected and withdrawal in general may become more
prevalent.

Affect

Inappropriate affect, such as lack of facial expression, is another common characteristic of
autism (Rimland, 1964). Some children will appear to be completely detached from their
social environment and display a seemingly constant, placid expression without emotion.
In some cases, this lack of emotional display may be apparent in the failure to exhibit fear
in dangerous situations, a lack of interest or concern when someone is in pain, the display
of laughter for no apparent reason, or the display of profound irrational fears (Schreibman
& Mills, 1983).

During play, children with autism tend to display less positive affect than typically
developing children (Yirmiya, Kasari, Sigman, & Mundy, 1989). This difference has also
been noted in early interactions in which children with autism smiled less frequently in
response to their mothers' smiles than typically developing children (Dawson, Hill,
Spencer, Galpert, & Watson, 1990). Dawson and Lewy (1989) hypothesized that part of
the difficulty may be associated with a problem experiencing mutual sharing of positive
emotion. This would result in extreme difficulty with learning appropriate affective
expression and responding.

Prosody

Prosody is a speech component closely related to the expression of affect. Dysprosody, and the other paralinguistic properties of speech, is often cited as a difficult problem in the pragmatic aspects of language for children with autism (Baltaxe & Simmons, 1975). Characteristics that make dysprosody a hallmark in the speech characteristics of many children with autism include the following: flat, expressionless speech (Kanner, 1943); rapid, staccato delivery; singsong intonation (Rutter, 1970); errors in stress assignment (Baltaxe, 1984); excessive high pitch without pitch changes (Goldfarb, Braunstein, & Lorge, 1956; Pronvost, Wakstein, & Wakstein, 1966); hoarseness, harshness, and hypernasality (Pronvost et al., 1966); vocal volume at too high or low a level or varying intensity inappropriately (Fay, 1969, 1973; Goldfarb et al., 1956; Pronvost et al., 1966); and incorrect primary sentence stress (Baltaxe & Guthrie, 1987).

Researchers have hypothesized that dysprosody may occur due to a failure to perceive intonation patterns, pitch, and so forth (Simon, 1975), although others have demonstrated that children with autism, like other children, recognize stressed words from memory better than they do nonstressed words (Frith, 1969). Difficulties in attention have also been examined in their relation to prosodic problems in which certain children may fail to attend to all relevant cues necessary for perceiving the entire intonational pattern (Bagshaw, 1978). A physiological basis has also been examined, although it is generally agreed that the problem is not likely a motor impairment in the vocal apparatus (Fay & Schuler, 1980).

Schreibman, Kohlenberg, and Britten (1986) compared nonverbal and echolalic children with autism and found that they responded differently to the content and prosodic components of speech. Echolalic children often had very exaggerated intonation along with fluctuating pitch and intonation, and their speech was contextually inaccurate. They also observed that when children who are nonverbal are taught to speak, their speech lacks appropriate intonation. They also found that, when presented with a complex auditory stimulus, the echolalic children selectively responded to the intonation component and the nonverbal children responded to the content component. In contrast, the typically developing children in this study showed no overselective responding, responding to both components simultaneously. This study suggests that overselectivity, discussed in depth in Chapter 3 by Rosenblatt, Bloom, and Koegel may be at least partially responsible for the children's difficulty in this area.

Detail and Topic Shift

A subgroup of verbal children with autism are characterized as having overly detailed explanations with a refusal to shift topics, regardless of the cues given to them by their conversation partner (Bernard-Opitz, 1982). Individuals who have this difficulty often adhere to their favorite subject throughout a conversation. Perseveration on a preferred topic may continue for years. Ricks and Wing (1975) noted that some individuals with autism have a special interest and are inclined to talk about it persistently without actually being able to discuss and explore any new angles on the subject. This subgroup tends to actively look for opportunities to incorporate their favorite topics into a conversation. This typically results in providing the same information about that topic. Some examples of favorite topics that have been heard include restaurants (specifically the type of furniture found in specific restaurants), Yugoslavia (specifically the different areas that provide swimming opportunities), and Los Angeles (specifically the different freeway connections and alternative streets).

Nonverbal Aspects of Language

Body postures, hand movements, and other nonverbal aspects of language are often found to be inappropriate in many children with autism (McHale, Simeonsson, Marcus, & Olley, 1980; Waterhouse & Fein, 1978). Children with autism have a difficult time both understanding and using nonverbal cues, such as gestures that accompany speech. Success can generally be achieved in teaching the children to understand gestures used by others; however, progress is typically much slower when teaching them the *use* of these gestures (Ricks & Wing, 1975; Wing, 1985). In addition to failing to use appropriate nonverbal language, inappropriate and repetitive movements are often displayed during conversation. One can only speculate whether the inappropriate and repetitive nonverbal behavior of some higher-functioning children is a lesser version of the extreme self-stimulatory behavior evident in children with more severe autism (Kanner, 1943; R.L. Koegel & Covert, 1972). The function of the behavior is a critical focus of assessment for inappropriate nonverbal mannerisms. Also, it is useful in gauging the extent to which certain behaviors are serving the same function within large response classes of behavior. Functional analysis as a means of grouping many social behaviors together, thereby greatly enhancing treatment effectiveness, is discussed later in this chapter (Figures 1 and 2).

FACTORS IN THE TREATMENT OF SOCIAL BEHAVIOR

Fortunately, researchers are now beginning to develop interventions that have the potential to be broadly successful in addressing social competence of children with autism. By following the development of this line of research, one can see how many seemingly insurmountable problems are beginning to yield to new interventions. Drawing from the behavioral literature, many researchers previously treated social skills by decreasing problematic behaviors that interfered with the child's ability to engage in appropriate social behaviors (e.g., Russo & Koegel, 1977) and by teaching behaviors that were not yet in the child's repertoire (e.g., Gaylord-Ross, Haring, Breen, & Pitts-Conway, 1984; McGee, Krantz, & McClannahan, 1984).

One difficulty that has been faced by many researchers in this area is the fact that too often the intervention can only address a small facet of the overall social difficulty, resulting in negligible changes in the child's social networks or quality of social involvement. For example, teaching a child to successfully manage his or her responsivity to questions or eye contact when being spoken to may be quite manageable; however, providing that child with the necessary social competence to create and facilitate an increase in social opportunities that will allow for further development of social skills is a much greater task. In general, there has been difficulty in achieving generalization in the research on social skills (Chandler, Lubek, & Fowler, 1992). For example, much of the work to date has involved teaching the child skills in only one context or with only one treatment provider or peer. This typically does not promote generalization to the myriad of community, school, and group contexts the child will experience (cf. Stokes & Osnes, 1986).

Several variables have been identified in the literature that have a positive impact on the social responsiveness and functioning of children with autism. For example, early inclusion in regular education environments has been found to greatly assist the learning of appropriate social responding and play (Kamps et al., 1992; Strain, 1983). Some specific behavioral interventions have also proven successful in teaching appropriate responding and social behaviors (Goldstein & Cisar, 1992; R.L. Koegel & Frea, 1993; L.K. Koegel, Koegel, Hurley, & Frea, 1992). The use of naturalistic variables within

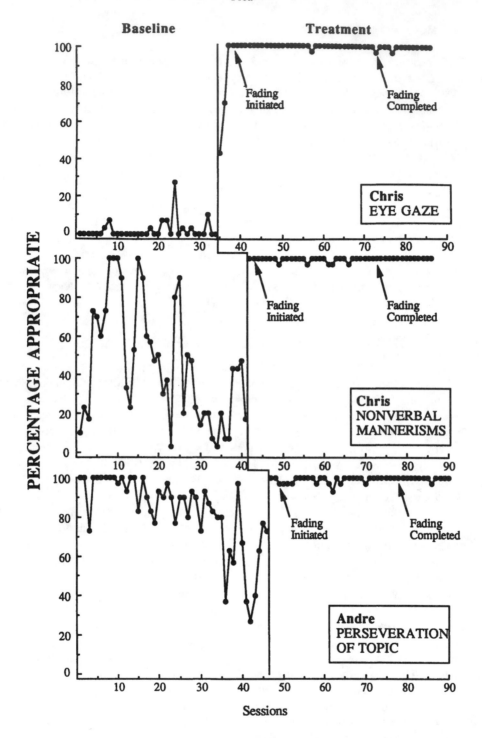

Figure 1.   Intervention data for social-communicative behaviors. Chris received intervention for eye gaze and nonverbal mannerisms; Andre received intervention for perseveration of topic. The arrows indicate the points at which fading (i.e., lengthening of the self-management intervals) was initiated and completed. (From Koegel, R.L., & Frea, W.D. [1979]. Treatment of social behavior in autism through the modification of pivotal pragmatic skills. *Journal of Applied Behavior Analysis, 26,* 369–377; reprinted by permission.)

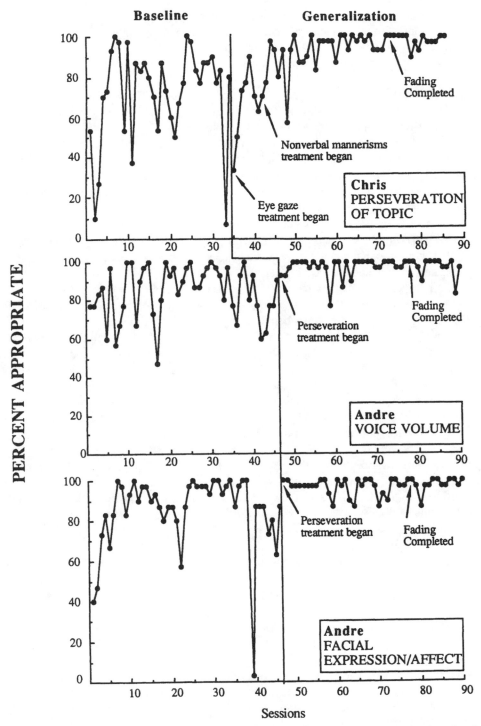

Figure 2. Generalization data for the untreated target behaviors (corresponding to the intervention data in Figure 1). The arrows show the points at which intervention began for each of the behaviors and the points at which fading (i.e., lengthening of the self-management intervals) was completed. (From Koegel, R.L., & Frea, W.D. [1979]. Treatment of social behavior in autism through the modification of pivotal pragmatic skills. *Journal of Applied Behavior Analysis, 26,* 369–377; reprinted by permission.)

behavioral interventions and utilizing peers in integrated environments have also been found to increase the impact and generalizability of the intervention. Following are some intervention variables that have been shown to promote a more effective and generalizable intervention approach for improving social interactions.

Natural Contexts

The intervention for any behavior is best achieved in the environments where it naturally occurs (Breen, Haring, Pitts-Conway, & Gaylord-Ross, 1985; Ford & Mirenda, 1984; Sailor, Goetz, Anderson, Hunt, & Gee, 1988). When addressing social competence, it appears imperative that the individual receive intervention and support in environments where peers and other natural discriminative stimuli are present and where functional reinforcers are plentiful. This has proven very valuable in providing broader treatment gains in social responding (Breen & Haring, 1991; McGee et al., 1984; Strain & Odom, 1986). Beyond the benefits of better generalization to natural environments through treating social behaviors in true contexts (e.g., with peers, at school), the child is able to learn skills faster through meaningful social exchanges and with assistance from classmates that will likely endure and increase in quality.

An important consideration when working with social skills in their natural contexts is the types of stimuli that are typically preferred or reinforcing in those contexts (see Chapter 2). The materials used when teaching interactive behaviors can be a critical variable in the success of the intervention (Quilitch & Risley, 1973). When focusing on social interactions, it is necessary to consider what materials, toys, games, and possibly even clothes are typically viewed by the peers in that environment to be pleasurable. Gaylord-Ross et al. (1984) studied the increases in initiations and duration of social interactions between youths with autism and their typically developing peers as a result of learning to use objects that were preferred by peers at school. They found that learning the behaviors associated with the social use of desirable objects such as video games, portable stereos, and even chewing gum served to increase the number and duration of positive social interactions. Furthermore, these behaviors successfully generalized to unfamiliar peers. Successful generalization of the newly learned behaviors in this study may have been facilitated by the fact that the students with autism were taught these skills within their school environment.

Social Integration

As noted earlier, teaching within integrated environments increases the success that children can achieve in learning appropriate social interaction (Jenkins, Odom, & Speltz, 1989). Placement in a socially integrated environment allows the child access to typical social opportunities and peer models.

It is important to note that the phenomenon of integration is viewed in different ways. For example, some consider that placement in a typical regular education classroom constitutes integration. Although the child may be physically integrated, such a situation is not adequate to assist the individual in developing social competence. A truly socially integrated environment must support the individual's social development by including him or her in the activities and interactions in which the classmates are involved (Sailor et al., 1989). In such a situation, the child is provided with clear social modeling opportunities, as well as opportunities for natural peer assistance and acceptance (Stainback, Stainback, & Forest, 1989).

Specific efforts may need to be made, especially in the initial stages, to help the child take advantage of all the natural benefits that become available in such an environment.

For example, assistance with orienting to peer models whose behavior can serve as valuable prompts may need to be learned. It is helpful to look at the social skills that the individual child is missing in comparison to other children in the classroom and to target those skills that are most likely to be beneficial. For example, Kohler, Strain, and Shearer (1992) looked at four behaviors used by children in an integrated preschool classroom and the social responses received for those behaviors. They found that the children with autism experienced more sharing and play organizing and responded most positively to these behaviors. Requests and offers for assistance from other children occurred less frequently for these children, and they responded less positively to these behaviors. However, when assistance behaviors were provided, they were consistently the longest social interactions. Such data are valuable for the integration process of the individual child. Knowing the types of behaviors the child exhibits and responds to and what social impact these behaviors have allows for more opportunity to increase the frequency and duration of positive social interactions.

Currently there is a strong focus on strategies such as partial participation and teaching more critical alternative skills within the classroom to help children with disabilities in regular education environments (cf. Brown et al., 1989; Sailor et al., 1989). Appropriately, integration is increasingly being seen as a critical goal, but it is important to keep in mind that when a child has an impoverished social network that child may be merely physically integrated and not socially integrated. Haring (1990) compared this phenomenon with some of the older adults in society and demonstrated that it is possible to live a fully physically integrated lifestyle and still be maximally socially segregated. Typically functioning children in regular education classrooms naturally have the opportunity to expand on their social competencies. Children with autism do not share in that opportunity without support and careful planning. Social integration should be an equally important goal for these children and should be worked on separately.

Research on techniques to socially integrate children into their regular education classrooms has explored the use of peers to integrate the child into his or her peers' activities. Haring and Breen (1992) effectively set up support networks to assist two children who were integrated into regular education environments. These small groups of children took part in planning effective integration strategies and even minor intervention programming to produce more appropriate social responding by the target children as well as dramatic increases in the amount of social interactions in which the children were taking part.

Self-Management

Self-management involves incorporating the child as an active participant in the treatment program (L.K. Koegel et al., 1992; R.L. Koegel, Frea, & Surratt, 1994). The self-management package works toward the child's ability to successfully differentiate appropriate from inappropriate behavior by having the child monitor his or her own behavior, then recruit rewards in response to social successes. The success of this approach, particularly with higher-functioning children, has been interpreted as stemming from the independence the child acquires through being able to manage his or her own behavior.

L.K. Koegel et al. (1992) found collateral decreases in untreated disruptive behavior following the implementation of a self-management package for responsivity with four children with autism. Specifically, the children monitored their appropriate responses to adults' questions. It is possible that in this case the ability to independently control their responses to social situations allowed the children to no longer need to use the avoidant behaviors in which they had previously engaged. The following case studies assist in understanding how self-management might be implemented for different behaviors.

An Intervention for Eye Contact

Ron, a 10-year-old boy with autism, was mainstreamed in both a fifth-grade math class and a fifth-grade geography class. Academically, Ron did quite well at school and would most likely have been fully integrated if his school had not been seriously concerned about his social behavior. It was often unclear whether Ron actually heard instructions or feedback and whether he comprehended some of the course material. He never engaged in eye contact and needed to be prompted several times before responding to questions. Ron was a very kind and compliant student who exhibited no severe behavior problems; however, due to his severe social difficulties, school personnel probably inaccurately felt that he would fare poorly without the support of a special education classroom.

Initially Ron was assessed to see whether he could benefit from self-management. He was quickly able to learn to differentiate appropriate eye contact from inappropriate eye contact. He could model after the therapist and eventually, on request, could demonstrate both his method of eye gaze avoidance and his appropriate behavior. Ron enjoyed music and loved to listen to his Walkman. Initially he was able to earn new music when he demonstrated appropriate behavior; for example, he would receive a cassette and be allowed to listen to it after showing good eye contact during conversation. By the end of the first session, he was able to record his occurrence of good eye contact on a sheet of paper. At that point, he was rewarded only for his accurate recording.

A watch with a countdown alarm mode was introduced during the next session, and Ron was instructed to maintain good eye contact until it chimed. When the watch chimed, Ron recorded whether he actually had been demonstrating appropriate eye contact. He began with only 10-second intervals, but this was gradually and systematically increased to 2-minute intervals in the same session. He continued to be reinforced for independent recording of his own behavior. In subsequent sessions, intervals were gradually increased and the number of recordings required for new music was also increased. Eventually he was taught to self-manage at school. Ron received a new cassette at the end of the week whenever he reached the criterion of good eye contact for at least four entire periods each day at school. (Note: Because Ron was providing his own treatment at school, a system was arranged so that his teachers and aides could verify the relative accuracy of recording; see Chapter 6.)

Ron's responsivity to questions was added to his program and he learned to monitor both behaviors simultaneously. (Adding additional behaviors is usually feasible after the self-management structure is in place and successful.) The benefit of self-management is that his program can be carried into any environment where he will spend extended periods of time.

An Intervention for Perseveration

Tarence, a 15-year-old youth with autism required treatment for his conversational skills. He did not discuss other people's topics for longer than 1 or 2 minutes. Instead he continuously reverted to two topics that he particularly enjoyed: trade sanctions and the evils of racial hatred. During the initial assessment, it was clear that all conversations seemed to lead to these topics very quickly. It was decided that first he would need to reduce the amount of speaking he was doing to allow for a more normal exchange. A self-management package was created where he would, after a period of time, ask a question of his speech partner, such as "Did you know that?" "Has that ever happened to you?" or "What do *you* think?" The period of time Tarence was given to talk, prior to needing to ask a question, was increased from an initial rather short and artificial duration to a more natural amount of time. That is, starting with a large interval was not effective because he did not respond to the cue signaling him to ask a question once he was engaged in a lengthy mono-logue. By starting with short intervals of talking then gradually increasing that amount of time, he was able to learn to focus more clearly on the need to ask a question and to release some conversational control to the other person.

To increase the reciprocal exchange, paraphrasing was introduced into Tarence's self-management package. In this stage, he was required to reflect briefly on what the other person just said prior to responding. This was more difficult because he had to listen carefully enough to give a brief summary prior to saying what he wanted. He was taught, through the modeling phase of self-management, to give just brief reflections, such as "You don't get to read as much as you like" or "You like *The Simpsons* a lot." Gradually, after he became more successful, he was able to be prompted to comment a little bit more. This alone contributed to a more natural, reciprocal exchange. The result was that Tarence could give much more relevant responses to the other person's conversational topics because he had already started an appropriate response with the paraphrase.

Utilizing Peers

The use of peer modeling and instruction has grown in recent times to become one of the more valuable lines of research in the area of social functioning (Brady, Shores, McEvoy, Ellis, & Fox, 1987; Goldstein, Kaczmarek, Pennington, & Schafer, 1992; Haring & Breen, 1992; Nientimp & Cole, 1992; Odom & Strain, 1986; Sainato, Goldstein, & Strain, 1992; Shafer, Egel, & Neef, 1984; Strain & Odom, 1986). Peer-mediated interventions help limit the amount of adult contacts, which tend to interfere with children's acquisition of social competence. Although parents, teachers, and professionals are critical in the planning and implementing of programs that teach appropriate social skills, often peers can provide more natural social exemplars that support the generalization and maintenance of the program (Gunter, Fox, Brady, Shores, & Cavenaugh, 1988).

Teacher-mediated and peer-mediated interventions with young children have proven to be very useful in enhancing the social behavior of students with autism (Odom & Strain, 1986). Goldstein and colleagues (1992) were successful in increasing the social interactions between preschool children with autism and their typically developing peers using a peer-mediated strategy. They taught the peers a social facilitative strategy that involved attending to, commenting on, and acknowledging the behavior of the peer with autism. This was thought to be effective because the peers were not using social initia-tions, such as questions or requests that obligated a response and that might have been more likely to result in avoidant behavior from the students with autism. While working with peers to increase social interaction, it is also important to target skill acquisition for the child with autism (Haring & Lovinger, 1989). Oke and Schreibman (1990) found that, although teaching peers to initiate effectively to a higher-functioning child with autism significantly increased social interaction, it was not until the child himself or herself learned to initiate social interactions that the disruptive behavior decreased.

McEvoy and colleagues (1988) studied an alternative to peer instruction or social skills instruction. They proposed that affection activities, rather than more difficult peer-mediated approaches such as initiation instruction, might be an equally valid alternative for young children. In their study, they modified existing group activities in a kindergarten classroom to involve expressions of affection. For example, within a song or a game that the class normally played, they may be asked to give a hug or a pat to their neighbor. They found increases in peer-initiated responding for the children with autism. They also found that two of the three children with autism had subsequent increases in their initiations to the other children in the class.

There is little question that assistance from peers within the teaching context can provide benefit in the development and generalization of social competence and will most certainly receive increased attention in the future; however, how to increase the overall involvement of peers throughout a child's day is yet another issue. Parents, teachers, and professionals alike often experience a considerable amount of frustration when trying to include peers in the programs of children with special needs. The variables involved in making the social interaction reinforcing for all parties need to be identified and utilized. In general, it appears that a situation must be created that naturally brings peers into the context. Also, it appears that the children need to possess a certain amount of control over the situation. They should be given choices and responsibilities, so that the program is seen as their own.

It is important to provide interaction opportunities for children with and without disabilities. Often children without disabilities can provide important assessment information to the teacher and assist with the maintenance of previously learned target behaviors, as in the following example.

An Example of Peer Involvement

Jenny is a sixth grader with autism and mental retardation. She has been taught to manage her excessive physical contact and inappropriate laughter because both were reported to be the most stigmatizing aspects of her behavior. To recruit peer involvement in her program, her teacher created an opportunity for typically functioning children to take on certain responsibilities. Jenny's teacher started a Thursday lunch club in which she had an open classroom at lunch time for anyone to come and play games (e.g., video) as well as other planned activities. She chose three girls who appeared particularly interested. These students were given the opportunity to "assist" Jenny with her new ability to manage her "silly behaviors" and were often provided (thanks to teacher and parent assistance) with privileged activities and events during which they could hang out naturally with Jenny and assist her with "fitting in."

Jenny and her friends met regularly with the teacher for "private" meetings where everyone provided input regarding successful and unsuccessful aspects of their time together. The girls described their friendship with Jenny as an important part of their lives, and they took on more responsibility without being asked or prompted by the teacher or professionals involved. Their time with Jenny increased, and, possibly due to the teacher's support in allowing them to establish their own roles and the activities involved, it became more than simply a project. Jenny was provided with wonderful peer models and was treated with respect. The girls were given enough freedom, responsibility, and encouragement to "fit" Jenny into their lives in a way in which they were not only comfortable but also responsible.

Functional Assessment

Given the complexity involved in approaching social-communicative competence, success may best be achieved when an in-depth functional assessment is performed. As discussed in Chapter 12, the goal is to identify what variables are maintaining the behavior so as to plan an intervention that directly addresses these variables (Carr, 1994; Durand, 1990). Many factors have been shown to relate to disruptive behavior, such as attention, social avoidance, the difficulty or sequence of tasks, and perhaps the individuals involved (Carr, 1994). Similarly, hypothesizing why the individual is using an inappropriate social behavior can lead to interventions that provide assistance in replacing it with more appropriate alternatives (Frea, Koegel, & Koegel, 1994).

It is critical when assessing any behavior that several different contexts be sampled so as to better identify the situations in which these behaviors are occurring (Bailey & Pyles, 1989; O'Neill, Horner, Albin, Storey, & Sprague, 1990). This is especially important when looking at the social-communicative behaviors of higher-functioning individuals with autism because they often do very well within certain social circumstances and can become more inappropriate in others. Different antecedents will be represented across different environments. For example, there may be environments where the individuals experience more frequent or difficult demands than in others. There may be environments where individuals experience social pressure versus environments where they are usually ignored. There may be situations where an individual is quite competent or where assistance is typically provided. Observing the differential responding in these situations may provide critical information for addressing social problems.

Differences in social behavior across situations may provide valuable information for planning an effective intervention. Once it is known why an inappropriate social behavior is occurring, support and teaching can be provided where necessary. This can be done by replacing the inappropriate behavior with an alternative response (Carr & Durand, 1985; O'Neill & Reichle, 1993). Examples of such alternative responses to disruptive behavior might include, "Excuse me, but I'm not very good at that" or "What did you mean by that?" By looking at various different situations, one can also build on the person's strengths.

If functional communication instruction is implemented, it appears important that new social-communicative skills be taught and reinforced in multiple environments that represent different opportunities for the use of the behavior (Day, Horner, & O'Neill, 1994). Providing the individual with a range of stimulus exemplars can also increase the generalization of the new behavior (Stokes & Baer, 1977). By increasing the range of opportunities to practice the new skills, the individual may be more likely to generalize his or her behaviors to new situations (e.g., the mall, a friend's house) and to different functions (e.g., requesting assistance, terminating a difficult topic).

Targeting Response Classes

Response classes represent different behaviors that serve the same function for the individual (Carr, 1988) and can play a major role in the assessment of seemingly minor social difficulties, such as lack of eye contact or perseveration of topic. Different social-communicative behaviors may serve the same function in an individual's daily social interactions. For example, inappropriate affect and lack of eye contact may both be used independently by a single individual to avoid difficult social interactions.

By assessing the response classes that may be present in the person's behavioral repertoire, it may be possible to choose a replacement behavior or self-management strategy that has a pivotal impact on multiple behaviors. R.L. Koegel and Frea (1993) found decreases in untreated social behaviors following social skills instruction with higher-functioning adolescents with autism. In this study, the participants were taught to self-manage specific social difficulties by learning to discriminate between the appropriate and inappropriate use of these behaviors, record the occurrence of appropriate behavior, and recruit a reward for doing so. The authors took data on untreated social behaviors and found generalized improvements in these behaviors that the children were not taught to monitor. This finding suggests that the inappropriate pragmatic behaviors demonstrated by many higher-functioning individuals with autism may exist within response classes that are serving the same functions, such as avoiding difficult social situations or obtaining attention. If this is the case, assessing a broad range of behaviors and utilizing an intervention that provides pivotal skills that address the social difficulties the individual possesses may prove valuable.

CONCLUSION

It is generally accepted that encouraging and facilitating social interaction and friendships for children with autism can have a significant impact on their ability to function socially in society. Although this may be the case, it should be stated that no one is certain of the true impact of social isolation or social skills difficulty on the child's future ability to be successfully integrated in society. Still, most believe that it is important to focus on social integration as much as possible. The goal is not only to teach social skills, but to make these behaviors tools in the person's behavioral repertoire. The specific level of social skills exhibited by a child may not be as important as the effect these skills have for producing positive and reinforcing interactions for all concerned.

It is clear that many interventions in the realm of social functioning have had difficulty with generalization outside of the treatment environment (Strain, Kerr, & Ragland, 1979). This classic problem is an indicator that the tools these children learn, or the changes in their environments, often may not be able to have a broad impact on the way the individuals involved experience reinforcement from their social world. It appears necessary to enhance the children's capacity to independently take part in social interactions that are satisfying; that is, to take the children to a point where they themselves find their social behavior to be useful in enhancing meaningful and reinforcing relationships.

Chapter 6

"Teach the Individual" Model of Generalization

Autonomy Through Self-Management

Robert L. Koegel, Lynn Kern Koegel, and Deborah Rumore Parks

The ultimate goal of most providers for people with autism is to optimize conditions for successful integration into the community. For a person to be successfully integrated into a natural environment, several "minimal" prerequisites must be met: 1) the person must be capable of exhibiting a variety of appropriate behaviors in ever-changing environments, 2) the person must be able to do this for extended periods of time, and 3) the person must do this with minimal feedback from others and often in the absence of a trained intervention provider. In other words, for a person with autism to be integrated into the community, several different types of generalization must occur: generalization across environments, generalization across people and providers, and, ideally, generalization across behaviors and time (Horner, Dunlap, & Koegel, 1988).

Various methods of programming generalization have been discussed and reviewed in great detail (cf. Stokes & Baer, 1977). Many of the most widely used methods of promoting generalization are based on a "teach exemplars" model (see Figure 1). In this model, generalization is programmed to occur in different environments by actually teaching the individual in one environment after another. Generalization across people and providers is programmed by having many different people implement the same intervention program, and generalization across behaviors is programmed by "adding" each behavior to the intervention program, one at a time. Although effective, the extremely time-consuming nature of teaching generalization in this manner (people with autism usually exhibit a large number of behaviors that require modification in a wide range of environments) limits its practical value for facilitating the integration of people with autism.

A widely acclaimed but seldom utilized method of teaching generalization and maintenance is to introduce the child to the positive contingencies that naturally consequate appropriate behavior in integrated environments (Warren & Reichle, 1992). For example, a woman with severe disabilities who masters the language and social skills necessary to buy an ice cream cone is naturally reinforced for using her newly learned skills when she

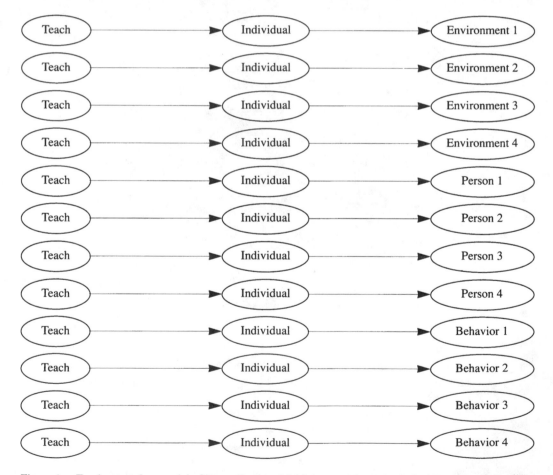

Figure 1. Teach exemplars model of generalization. Multiple exemplars are taught to program generalization across each specific exemplar.

receives the ice cream. Introducing the person to the positive contingencies that naturally consequate appropriate behavior is based on a "teach the individual" model of generalization (see Figure 2). In this model of generalization, the person is taught a skill in a manner such that it spontaneously occurs in numerous environments and in the absence of a trained intervention provider.

Until recently, this model of programming generalization had been rarely documented in research because it was difficult to produce. In order for an individual to receive positive feedback from the environment in a naturally occurring context, the person must first exhibit the appropriate behavior. If this does not occur spontaneously, then the appropriate behavior must be taught to occur in each specific environment and a "teach exemplars" model is functionally in effect.

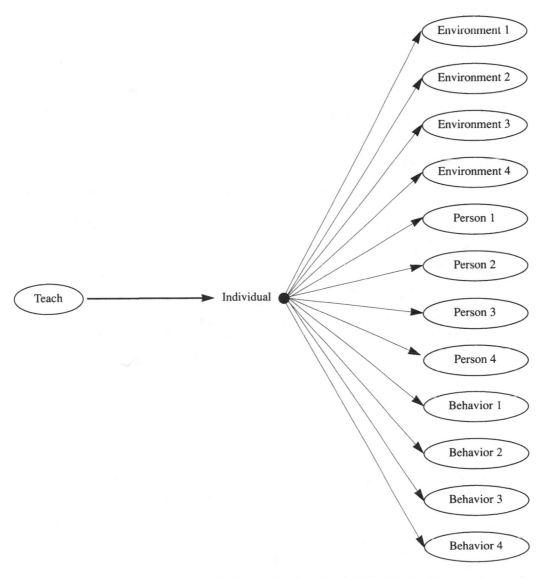

Figure 2. "Teach the individual" model of generalization. The individual is taught to spontaneously exhibit the target behavior in novel contexts.

One way to facilitate the spontaneous occurrence of appropriate behavior in various "novel" contexts is to teach self-management. The term *self-management* generally refers to a procedure in which people are taught to discriminate their own target behavior and record the occurrence or absence of that target behavior (self-monitoring). In addition to self-monitoring, self-management intervention packages often include reinforcers (either self- or other-administered) for engaging in the target behavior (this is described later in this chapter).

Since 1970, when self-monitoring was discovered to be reactive (i.e., to produce behavior change) (McFall, 1970), several major theories have been proposed to explain this reactivity (Kanfer, 1970; Nelson & Hayes, 1981; Rachlin, 1974). Viewpoints differ as to whether self-monitoring is reactive because it triggers covert self-evaluation (Kanfer, 1970) or because it serves as a discriminative stimulus for environmental consequences that ultimately control the behavior (Rachlin, 1974). One published theory (Nelson & Hayes, 1981) postulates that self-monitoring is reactive because it occurs within a self-management "package," which includes such things as "instructions from the service provider, training in self-monitoring, the self-monitoring device, comments by others about the device, the self-monitoring responses if and when they occur, and perhaps other events described as 'self-evaluation' or 'self-consequation' " (p. 7). Nelson and Hayes theorize that this self-management package serves as the discriminative stimulus for environmental consequences that result in behavior change.

SELF-MANAGEMENT AS A PIVOTAL BEHAVIOR

It is interesting to note the evolution of self-management from a technique used only for individuals without disabilities to a technique that also has major advantages for people with multiple disabilities, including autism. Self-management was first developed as an intervention technique for use with adults with typical intelligence (cf. McFall, 1970; McFall & Hammen, 1971) and quickly evolved into a technique frequently used with children of typical intelligence (cf. Broden, Hall, & Mitts, 1971; Drabman, Spitalnik, & O'Leary, 1973; L.K. Dunlap & Dunlap, in press; Glynn, Thomas, & Shee, 1973; O'Brien, Riner, & Budd, 1983; Sagotsky, Patterson, & Lepper, 1978). Subsequent research demonstrated that self-management techniques could also be used successfully with children and adults having mild to moderate retardation (Horner & Brigham, 1979; Knapczyk & Livingston, 1973; Litrownik, Freitas, & Franzini, 1978; Nelson, Lipinski, & Boykin, 1978; Rooney, Hallahan, & Lloyd, 1984; Shapiro & Klein, 1980; Shapiro, McGonigle, & Ollendick, 1980; Sugai & Rowe, 1984; Uhlman & Shook, 1976). In addition, recent studies have reported skills such as self-control of verbal behavior and of self-injurious behavior learned through self-management that now occur for extended periods of time (Gardner, Cole, Berry, & Nowinski, 1983) and in the absence of a trained service provider (Grace, Cowart, & Matson, 1988). Most recently, self-management procedures are being adapted for use with people with severe disabilities such as autism (R.L. Koegel & Frea, 1993; R.L. Koegel & Koegel, 1986; R.L. Koegel & Koegel, 1990; L.K. Koegel, Koegel, Hurley, & Frea, 1992; L.K. Koegel, Koegel, & Parks, 1989; Stahmer & Schreibman, 1992) (Figure 3).

As is illustrated by the "teach the individual" model of generalization (Figure 2), self-management is a "pivotal" behavior (cf. Koegel, Schreibman, et al., 1989). That is, by teaching a person to self-manage behavior, that person learns a skill that will facilitate generalization of an infinite number of behaviors across an infinite number of environments and people. For example, after a student is taught to self-record social interactions in one environment, he or she has learned a general skill (self-management) that may be

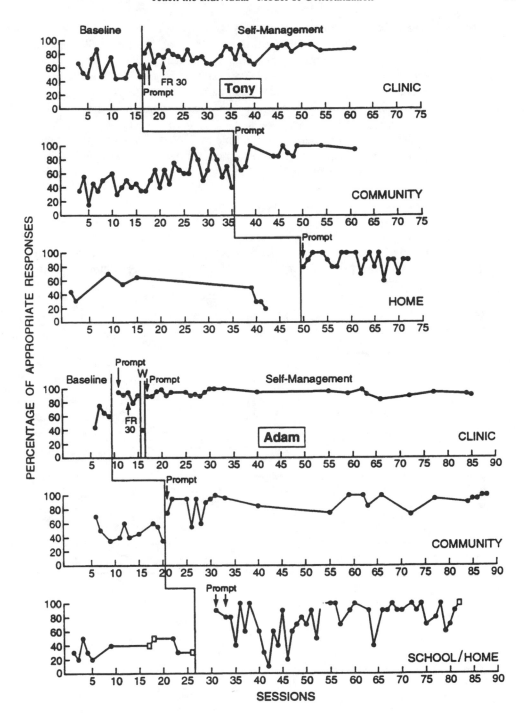

Figure 3. Appropriate verbal responses for Tony and Adam, who each received self-management training in three environments (Adam also had data recorded in his home, indicated by open squares) in a multiple baseline design (with a withdrawal in one environment for Adam). (From Koegel, L.K., Koegel, R.L., Hurley, C., & Frea, W.C. [1992]. Improving social skills and disruptive behavior in children with autism through self-management. *Journal of Applied Behavior Analysis, 25*[2], 341–353; reprinted by permission.)

used to increase the percentage of interactions with others in every environment, regardless of whether a provider is present (R.L. Koegel & Frea, 1993; L.K. Koegel, Koegel, Hurley, & Frea, 1992). In addition, once self-management skills are taught, additional behaviors may be incorporated very easily. For example, the student who is self-recording social interactions may be told, "Now you can earn points for saying things and asking questions, too." Simply stated, by using self-management within a "teach the individual" model, widespread generalization is programmed by teaching one person a pivotal skill rather than teaching an infinite number of multiple exemplars. Obviously, the efficiency of a "teach the individual" model of generalization, and thus self-management, has great practical value for use with people with autism (Figure 4).

SELF-MANAGEMENT INTERVENTION STEPS

The general approach for teaching self-management is outlined here (cf. L.K. Dunlap, Dunlap, Koegel, & Koegel, 1991; L.K. Koegel, Koegel, & Parks, 1989). The steps are discussed in general terms to that the reader may envision how to apply them to a variety of target behaviors.

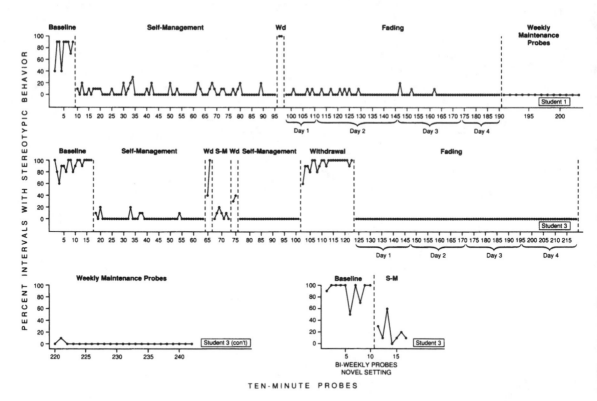

Figure 4.   The percentage of 1-minute intervals that contained stereotypic behavior during the baseline and self-management conditions in novel environments. The fading condition and subsequent maintenance probes (plotted weekly) show the child's behavior in the absence of an interventionist. The park environment for Student 3 represents the environment that was never associated with the interventionist. (From Koegel, R.L., & Koegel, L.K. [1990]. Extended reductions in stereotypic behavior of students with autism through a self-management treatment package. *Journal of Applied Behavior Analysis, 23*[1], 119–127; reprinted by permission.)

Operationally Define the Target Behavior

The initial step in a self-management program is to specify the behavior to be observed. Precise definitions facilitate communication and maintain consistency among observers (Baker, Brightman, Heifetz, & Murphy, 1976; R.L. Koegel & Schreibman, 1982; K.L. Miller, 1980). For example, a certain child's "stereotypic behavior" might be defined as flapping hands at shoulder level for at least 3 seconds, rocking the upper torso forward then backward for at least 3 seconds, and any vocal noise made by the child that can be heard outside the child's room and does not involve recognizable sounds. Target behaviors may be self-managed individually or several behaviors may be self-managed as a group by labeling the behaviors with a term the child understands.

Identify Functional Reinforcers

An effective reinforcer is an event that has been proven through observation to increase the future rate of the behavior that it follows (Axelrod, 1977; K.L. Miller, 1980). To ensure that reinforcers are functional, it is a good idea to allow the child to assist in their selection. If the child appears uninterested in rewards, the rewards may be "discovered" by analyzing the function that the inappropriate behavior is serving for the child (i.e., assessing what consequence usually follows the inappropriate behavior). Once the function of the inappropriate behavior is determined, it is often possible to select an appropriate reinforcer that will serve the same function as the inappropriate behavior (cf. Carr, 1988; Nelson & Hayes, 1981; O'Neill, Horner, Albin, Storey, & Sprague, 1990). For example, if an inappropriate behavior generally results in the termination of a work situation, a functional reinforcer might be a period of free time immediately following appropriate behavior.

Design or Choose a Self-Management Method and Device

Self-management devices depend on the target behavior of the individual. If specific occurrences of a behavior are being monitored, a golfer's wrist counter or a notebook with pencil or stickers enables the child to record each occurrence of the behavior (cf. L.K. Koegel, Koegel, & Parks, 1989). If the person is measuring periods of time with the absence (or presence) of a behavior, a wristwatch with chronograph alarm or a kitchen timer can be used to signal time periods (cf. L.K. Koegel, Koegel, & Parks, 1989).

Teach the Individual to Use the Self-Management Device

A child learns to identify their own target behavior by observing both appropriate and inappropriate behavior modeled by the provider and by receiving reinforcement upon accurate identification of each. Next, the child is prompted to engage in the appropriate behavior and self-record the occurrence (or nonoccurrence) of the behavior. Initially, verbal and tangible reinforcers are provided on a continuous reinforcement schedule for accurate self-recording of the target behavior, whereas only verbal reinforcement is provided for accurate self-recording of inappropriate behavior. As the child's abilities to self-manage behavior improve, the schedule of reinforcement is gradually reduced (Figure 5).

Teach Self-Management Independence

Independent self-management (i.e., without prompts or consequences from others) is taught in a number of ways (Figure 6). Prompts to self-manage behavior (i.e., to engage in the target behavior and self-record when appropriate) are gradually reduced, and the amount of time the child spends self-managing behavior is increased. In addition to requiring that more self-recording responses be made before earning each reinforcer, the sched-

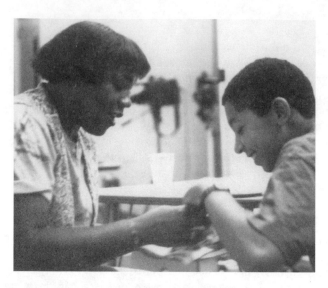

Figure 5.   This student's mother is teaching him to use a pictorial self-management device to guide his behavior. Ultimately, the adult reduces her presence, so that he can use the pictures alone to guide and evaluate his responding.

ule of reinforcement is also reduced by gradually increasing the time period between opportunities to self-record. Finally, the child can be taught to self-administer consequences on completion of the predetermined number of points.

Case Illustration

The self-management program described here was used to teach individuals with autism (chronologically 9–14 years old but functioning in the 2- to 5-year old range according to standardized test scores) to self-manage their stereotypic behaviors (R.L. Koegel & Koegel, 1990). Some of the individuals' stereotypic behaviors were so disruptive and conspicuous that the children were being considered for more restrictive and nonintegrated placements (e.g., one boy's mother was considering a residential placement for her son and another boy's private school teacher was recommending his dismissal). The individuals in this study wore a wristwatch alarm to signal self-recording opportunities. After they

Figure 6.   This figure shows some of the important stages in teaching self-management. In the left-hand picture, the child's mother is prompting him to evaluate and record (by placing a pog in the square) his behavior. In the middle picture, the child is responding independently; and in the right-hand picture he is recruiting reinforcement from his mother after a period of independent responding.

were taught to self-manage their behavior in a controlled environment, dramatic decreases in stereotypic behavior (typically to 0%) occurred. The amount of time between opportunities to self-record was gradually lengthened until each of the participants was able to independently self-manage his or her behavior for several consecutive 15- to 20-minute time periods before exchanging their check cards for a reinforcer.

After the children learned to independently utilize the self-management skills they were taught, self-management was programmed to occur in their natural environments where alternate and more restrictive environments were being considered. To do this, the provider merely needed to enter the second environment for a few minutes to tell the children to begin self-management procedures and then gradually fade out of the environment by leaving for increasingly longer periods of time. The children then continued to self-manage their behaviors in the absence of the provider and without the need for constant vigilance on the part of others, such as parents or a teacher. Most important, appropriate behavior was maintained in future environments simply by allowing the self-management materials to remain with the children in these new environments. For example, after being taught to successfully self-manage stereotypic behavior in his classroom, one student was subsequently told by his classroom teacher (a person not associated with intervention) to take the self-management materials with him to the park where his class ate lunch. Prior to this, stereotypic behavior was occurring at a very high level (typically 100%) in the park. However, after being instructed to take his self-management materials with him, this student's stereotypic behavior decreased to 0%–20% in the park without a provider ever having to enter that environment. In other words, the child was essentially conducting his own intervention, indicating that a "teach the individual" model of generalization had evolved. By the conclusion of the study, all of the children had decreased their levels of stereotypic behavior in their natural environments to such negligible levels that plans for more restrictive placements were terminated.

IMPLICATIONS

By society's standards, individuals with autism require the modification of vast numbers of behaviors. It is unlikely that many individuals with autism will be able to learn enough behaviors to function independently if the behaviors are taught one at a time. However, by teaching self-management directly, it is likely that a high level of independent functioning can be achieved. This has a number of important implications for people with autism.

Learned Helplessness and Motivation

It is hypothesized that the lack of motivation that is so prevalent among people with autism and other developmental disabilities is the result of the phenomenon of learned helplessness (Seligman, Klein, & Miller, 1976; Seligman & Maier, 1967). Learned helplessness occurs when people experience noncontingent consequences and learn that their behavior is not related to the consequences that follow. It is hypothesized that learned helplessness occurs among people with severe disabilities when their disabilities force them to be dependent on others for reinforcement.

Self-management skills allow an individual to take responsibility for his or her own behavior both during and after teaching (cf. Baer, Fowler, & Carden-Smith, 1984; Fowler, 1984; Shapiro, Browder, & D'Huyvetters, 1984), thus strengthening the individual's understanding of the relationship between his or her own behavior and environmental consequences and decreasing the possibility that learned helplessness will occur.

Behavioral and Neurological Development

The widespread responding that occurs when people self-manage their behavior throughout the day may also have behavioral and neurophysiological implications. Because organisms and their environment are involved in mutually influential interactions, a lack of appropriate reciprocal child–environment interactions may have physiological as well as behavioral effects. For example, lack of neuronal growth and complexity has been shown to occur when individuals lack environmental stimulation (cf. R.L. Koegel, Koegel, & O'Neill, 1989). In addition, behaviorally, an individual who does not interact with the environment will not gain skills through environmental feedback or learn through modeling. Thus, a child who is highly dependent on caregivers is likely to make fewer responses and therefore have fewer opportunities for behavioral and neurological development. Once this complex problem occurs, the natural environment does not offer enough consequences to reinforce the child's responses or attempts to respond. With time, the problem worsens so that the individual moves farther behind his or her peers. However, self-management has been shown to result in rapid and widespread gains over time, responses, and environments (cf. R.L. Koegel & Koegel, 1990). Thus, it offers the possibility of providing *enough* responding to alter and improve behavioral and neural development (cf. R.L. Koegel & Koegel, 1988).

Stress Reduction

Another reason for utilizing intervention techniques that promote independent responding of the individuals relates to the psychological issue of stress reduction. One study related to familial stress indicates that parents of children with autism who are living at home feel significantly more stress in the area of life-span care than parents of children without developmental disabilities, as measured by the Questionnaire on Resources and Stress (Antonius, Koegel, & Schreibman, 1988). A main area of stress in families of children with autism seems to center around the question of what will happen to their children after the parents are no longer able to care for them. Parents believe the children will not have the skills necessary to function independently and will be at the mercy of an intolerant society. Certainly self-management is one procedure that increases a child's independence and decreases the need for constant supervision and vigilance. Children who gradually learn to be more responsible for their own behavior are likely to lower the stress experienced by those around them (see Chapter 7) who are responsible almost entirely for their behavior.

SUMMARY AND CONCLUSION

Self-management is a technique that facilitates independence by systematically fading reliance on external control (e.g., service provider's praise, feedback, instructions) and shifting control to the child (Fowler, 1984). Self-management has been effective at improving a variety of behaviors, including appropriate vocational (McNally, Kompik, & Sherman, 1984), academic (Anderson-Inman, Paine, & Deutchman, 1984; L.K. Dunlap & Dunlap, in press), social (Reese, Sherman, & Sheldon, 1984), and recreational (Coleman & Whitman, 1984) skills. In addition, self-management procedures appear to have indirect effects on other nontargeted behaviors (cf. Baer et al., 1984) such as reducing disruptive behavior and increasing motivation to learn, thus resulting in extremely widespread and effective intervention gains.

Although the exact variables that make self-management procedures successful are unknown, its effectiveness can be measured in time efficiency for the service provider (cf. Baer et al., 1984) and in breadth of effectiveness because it can be programmed to occur in virtually any environment, without the presence of a service provider (cf. R.L. Koegel & Koegel, 1990). That is, programming the occurrence of self-management can result in very rapid and widespread gains (cf. L.K. Koegel, Koegel, & Ingham, 1986). The development of intervention programs with these effects is extremely important because in order for individuals with severe disabilities to approximate the knowledge of their peers, or even learn the necessary skills required by society to live independent lives, they will need to engage in interventions that accelerate learning and promote generalization. Procedures such as self-management allow individuals with disabilities to be actively involved in the intervention process and more broadly involved in their environments in general. In turn, a more active involvement with the environment has the potential to improve neurological development, autonomy, and functional independence and therefore results in positive overall lifestyle changes. Finally, it is hoped that when individuals with autism are able to function independently and their lifestyles are improved, stress on parents, teachers, and other concerned individuals will decrease.

Chapter 7

Parent Education and Parenting Stress

— Douglas Moes

WHY FOCUS ON PARENTING STRESS IN AUTISM?

As noted throughout this book, autism is recognized as an unpredictable and pervasive developmental disorder. Numerous studies have documented the stressful effects that raising a child with autism has on the family (e.g., Bristol, 1979; Bristol & Schopler, 1983, 1984; DeMyer, 1979; DeMyer & Goldberg, 1983; Holroyd & McArthur, 1976; Marcus, 1977; Milgram & Atzil, 1988; Moes, Koegel, Schreibman, & Loos, 1992; Schopler & Mesibov, 1984; Wolf, Noh, Fisman, & Speechley, 1989). These stressful effects reflect parents' difficulty meeting the demands associated with raising a child with autism, which often occurs with very little assistance from agencies originally designed to support these children. Indeed, changing educational systems and societal values regarding the roles of individuals with disabilities have also caused confusion for both parents and those involved in professional aspects of these children's lives. Historically, the institutionalization and segregation of children with disabilities limited their interactions with typical children and thus hindered understanding of the unique challenges children with disabilities can present. As a consequence, there is a lack of preparation for families who have children with disabilities and for others who need to provide education, assistance, and social support to meet the demands associated with raising a child with disabilities.

In response to the technical and emotional needs families encounter, parent education evolved to provide parents with specialized and effective procedures to teach their children and reduce maladaptive behaviors (e.g., R.L. Koegel, Glahn, & Nieminen, 1978; R.L. Koegel, Schreibman, Johnson, O'Neill, & Dunlap, 1984; Schreibman, Koegel, Mills, & Burke, 1984). Although immediate and short-term child gains have been well-established in the literature on parent education, the long-term benefits to families are inconsistent with some speculation that the additional responsibilities inherent in some types of parent education programs may exacerbate parenting stress (cf. D.A. Allen & Hudd, 1987; Benson & Turnbull, 1986; Featherstone, 1980; Foster, Berger, & McLean, 1981; Gallagher, Beckman, & Cross, 1983). There is very little systematic research examining the collateral effects of parent education on families to support these claims. Therefore, an important research direction is to combine a more thorough understanding of parenting stress associated with autism with an examination of how various interventions for these children have an impact on parenting stress to provide researchers and practitioners with far greater potential for designing interventions that improve the overall quality of family life.

PARENTING STRESS ASSOCIATED WITH AUTISM

All parents, including parents of typically developing children, experience some degree of stress when attempting to meet the caregiving demands presented by their children (e.g., Belsky, Spanier, & Rovine, 1983; McBride, 1989; B. Miller & Solbie, 1980; Ventura, 1987). As typical children develop and their abilities improve, and as parents gain more experience and expertise in their parenting roles, parents' sense of competency increases and their stress related to child demands diminishes. In contrast, few parents are emotionally and technically prepared to meet the unrelenting demands associated with raising a child with severe disabilities.

A number of early clinical studies in this area show that parents have a variety of concerns related to the challenges they face when parenting children with autism (e.g., Bristol, 1979; Bristol & Schopler, 1983, 1984; DeMyer, 1979; DeMyer & Goldberg, 1983). Most of these early studies examining the impact on parents of raising a child with autism focused predominantly on the mother. However, societal changes (e.g., more women in the work force and more single-parent families) during the past 2 decades have been associated with parental role changes so that many fathers now assume more responsibility for child care than in years past. As a consequence, there has been a growing literature on parenting stress that includes examination of how both mothers and fathers experience raising a child with autism (Milgram & Atzil, 1988; Moes, Koegel, Schreibman, & Loos, 1992; Price-Bonham & Addison, 1978; Rodrigue, Morgan, & Geffken, 1990, 1992; Wolf et al., 1989).

Interestingly, mothers and fathers share several concerns despite historical differences in their assumed parenting roles, such as concerns about the disruption in family planning and social activities a child with autism produces (Morgan, 1988; Rodrigue et al., 1990, 1992). For many parents, family life revolves around their child with autism, with interactions inside and outside the family being altered to accommodate the child's needs. Parents commonly report more problems and tension when taking their child to public places for fear of embarrassment and disappointment. Also, children with autism are reported to be more disruptive of family integration in activities, such as meals, vacations, and family outings, because of their difficult behavioral characteristics (Bristol & Schopler, 1983). In addition, mothers and fathers express similar levels of concern about their child's prospects for future independence and acceptance within the community (Moes et al., 1992; Rodrigue et al., 1992).

Although parents may share some parenting concerns, there are specific areas of stress more pronounced for mothers and for fathers individually. Historically, mothers have commonly served as primary caregivers for their children with disabilities. Consequently, literature on mothers tends to show that they evaluate their children with autism as highly dependent on them for meeting daily needs (DeMyer, 1979). In addition, as primary caregivers, mothers' concerns have typically followed a developmental progression reflecting changing child-related demands (DeMyer, 1979; DeMyer & Goldberg, 1983; Holroyd & McArthur, 1976). For example, DeMyer and Goldberg have shown that mothers of very young children with autism are often consumed with unrelenting caregiving demands and concern for the physical welfare of children who typically show no understanding of danger. Furthermore, as the children grow older, mothers' concerns shift to self-help instruction, management of behavior in public places, and attempts to maintain family cohesion and stability. In some cases, DeMyer and Goldberg have reported that mothers grow increasingly concerned over their ability to manage physical aggression in their children as they reach adolescence and increase in size and strength. The consistency of these maternal concerns led Bristol and Schopler (1983) to speculate that there may be a characteristic profile of stress associated with parenting a child with autism.

Systematic investigation of these parenting concerns in recent years (e.g., Bouma & Schweitzer, 1990; Holroyd & McArthur, 1976; R.L. Koegel, Schreibman, et al., 1992) has shown a consistent pattern of stress among mothers who are primary caregivers. The emerging pattern of stress relates to their child's level of dependency, difficulty managing problem behaviors, cognitive impairment, limits on family opportunity, and life-span care. R.L. Koegel, Schreibman, et al. (1992) have shown that these specific areas of parenting stress remain consistent across geographic location, age, and functioning level of the child. These consistencies provide compelling evidence for the presence of a robust characteristic stress profile that tends to reflect concerns and difficulty meeting the parenting demands ascribed to primary caregivers for their child with autism (Figure 1).

In the past, fathers have traditionally assumed responsibility for the monetary needs of their families. Literature on fathers' parenting concerns has reflected this emphasis (e.g., DeMyer, 1979; Milgram & Atzil, 1988; Price-Bonham & Addison, 1978; Rodrigue et al., 1992). Rodrigue et al. report that fathers tend to be more concerned with the long-term financial responsibilities for their child with autism than mothers. Therefore, fathers are more often stressed by concerns about the availability and adequacy of financial resources to meet current and future child-related expenses (e.g., special schooling, therapy, medical services). As a consequence, fathers often assume more financial responsibility outside of the home and become less available to assume caregiving responsibilities. Milgram and Atzil reported that fathers of children with autism averaged less time in providing parental care than did mothers and that the fathers' contributions to the overall caregiving responsibilities were directly related to their own, as well as their spouse's, life satisfaction.

Moes

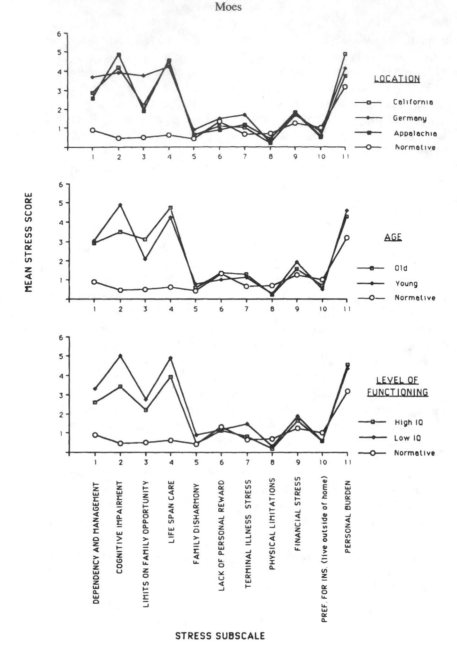

Figure 1.   Stress profiles for mothers of autistic children across geographic location, age, and functioning level of child. The stress profile for the normative comparison families also is plotted. (From Koegel, R.L., Schreibman, L., Loos, L.M., Dirlich-Wilhelm, H., Dunlap, G., Robins, F.R., & Plienis, A.J. [1992]. Consistent stress profiles in mothers of children with autism. *Journal of Autism and Developmental Disorders, 22,* 205–216; reprinted by permission.)

There is some relevant literature on fathers' stress associated with raising children without developmental disabilities (e.g., McBride, 1989; Belsky et al. 1983; B. Miller & Solbie, 1980; Ventura, 1987). McBride, for example, examined the types of stress that fathers of typical children experience in their parental role when they serve as primary caregivers. He found that fathers of younger children and fathers whose spouses were employed tended to report more stress associated with their parental role. Rodrigue et al. (1992) have speculated that the more demanding the child, the less competent fathers feel in their parenting role and, consequently, the more stress they experience. Therefore, future research on parenting stress associated with autism, including mothers and fathers serving in parenting roles that reflect the present shift in parenting role distribution, may be useful to discern if the parenting stress associated with autism is role dependent and can be alleviated by interventions addressing these roles and addressing the strengths of optimally collaborative child-raising practices.

CHARACTERISTICS OF AUTISM CONTRIBUTING TO PARENTING STRESS

To understand how these patterns of stress emerge in parents, it is important to examine the behavioral features of autism that contribute to the specific forms of parenting stress associated with autism. Despite the abundance of behavioral difficulties and excesses that define untreated autism, it is parents' concerns about the 1) inconsistent and/or uneven intellectual development and 2) specific forms of disruptive behavior exhibited by these children (e.g., self-stimulation and self-injury) that contribute most to the characteristic stress profiles previously discussed.

Uneven Intellectual Assessments

Most likely due to delays in communication and behavioral excesses and difficulties that interfere with testing, many children with autism show signs of mental retardation. Early figures estimated that approximately 60% have measured IQs below 50, 20% between 50 and 70, and 20% have IQs of 70 or above (Ritvo & Freeman, 1978). However, with improved testing and teaching procedures, it may be the case that levels of cognitive function will be found to be higher than previously estimated. Although autism and mental retardation are recognized as distinct and independent disabilities, standardized assessment of children with autism, usually using verbal intelligence measures, often leads to a dual diagnosis. Acquiring standardized intellectual assessments for these children can be difficult because many of them are nonverbal, lack motivation, are inattentive, and/or exhibit conflicting disruptive behaviors when excessive demands are placed on them (Schreibman & Charlop, 1987). When assessments are successful, these children consistently show an uneven profile, performing poorly on some tests (typically the verbal tests) and relatively well on others (usually nonverbal measures) (Ritvo & Freeman, 1978).

The presence of isolated skills, uneven performance, and difficulty with assessments often generate confusion among parents about the true intellectual ability of their children. Therefore, it is not surprising that parents of children with autism experience a great deal of stress related to their children's level of cognitive impairment (Bouma & Schweitzer, 1990; Holroyd & McArthur, 1976; R.L. Koegel, Schreibman, et al., 1992). The difficulties of unexpectedly having a child with a disability, as well as indices that the child is functioning relatively higher or even above average in isolated skill areas, can cause even more confusion or distress relating to the expectations that parents should have for their children. Interventions that can effectively teach these children new skills in low-skill areas (e.g., language and adaptive skills), as well as channeling and enhancing the demonstrated skill areas, may help reduce parents' confusion and related stress about their children's cognitive abilities. Unfortunately, the children's lack of motivation and poor responsivity to their environment are central problems in their development that can make assessment of current abilities and teaching new skills extremely difficult unless appropriate technical skills are learned (G. Dunlap & Egel, 1982; G. Dunlap & Koegel, 1980; R.L. Koegel & Egel, 1979; R.L. Koegel & Mentis, 1985; Lovaas, Koegel, & Schreibman, 1979; Schreibman, 1988). Therefore, increasing motivation and attention in children with autism remains a critical focus for successful interventions.

Pervasive Disruptive Behaviors

Many children with autism exhibit specific forms of disruptive behavior that are difficult to control or manage. One form of disruptive behavior is self-stimulation. This is typically repetitive, stereotypic behavior that serves no apparent purpose other than providing the child with sensory input (e.g., kinesthetic, auditory, visual) (Schreibman & Charlop, 1987; Schreibman, Koegel, & Koegel, 1989). Examples include rocking back and forth, hand flapping, repetitive verbalization, and gazing at lights. Some forms of self-stimulatory behavior incorporate objects, such as when the child waves objects in front of his or her eyes, repetitively taps objects, or rapidly flips through the pages of books. Self-stimulatory behavior seems to be excessive in children who lack more typical means of acquiring reinforcement from their environment. Consequently, these children may spend the majority of their waking hours engaged in some form of self-stimulation (Schreibman, Koegel, & Koegel, 1989). That is, it is possible that these children may rely on self-stimulation as a primary source of reinforcement (Baumeister & Forehand, 1973; Collins, 1965; Kern, Koegel, & Dunlap, 1984; Lovaas, Freitag, Gold, & Kassorla, 1965).

Other disruptive behaviors, such as aggression, tantrums, and property destruction, often exist in varying degrees in children with autism. Such behaviors can be extremely disruptive to family life and often result in a family's exclusion from mainstream and integrated school and community environments (Horner, Dunlap, & Koegel, 1988).

Another behavioral excess, and probably the most dramatic form of inappropriate behavior exhibited by a smaller percentage of children with autism, is self-injury. Self-injurious behaviors involve any behavior in which the individual inflicts physical damage to his or her own body (see, for example, Tate & Baroff, 1966). Examples are head banging, self-biting, self-hitting, and, in extreme cases, eye gouging or other forms of self-mutilation. The severity of this behavior can vary, but in its most extreme forms it may result in skull fractures, detached retinas, a broken nose, loss of significant amounts of flesh, or infection (Schreibman, 1988).

These forms of disruptive behavior may stigmatize the child, as well as interfere with the child's responsiveness to his or her environment and impede the acquisition of more adaptive behaviors (R.L. Koegel & Covert, 1972; R.L. Koegel, Firestone, Kramme, & Dunlap, 1974; Lovaas, Litrownik, & Mann, 1971). Clearly, the presence of such pervasive disruptive behaviors would correspond with elevated stress levels of parents related to their children's level of dependency and the parents' and others' difficulty managing these problem behaviors (Bouma & Schweitzer, 1990; Holroyd & McArthur, 1976; R.L. Koegel, Schreibman, et al., 1992).

These specific disruptive behaviors evident in many children with autism have been shown to relate to their lack of appropriate means of communicating (Schreibman, Koegel, & Koegel, 1989). Because of their limited communication skills, they are more likely to avoid demanding social situations (Dyer, 1987). Furthermore, in the absence of an alternative means of communicating their preferences or frustrations, they rely on previously effective and efficient behaviors such as aggression, self-stimulation, and self-injury (Carr, Newsom, & Binkoff, 1976; Durand & Carr, 1987). Research has consistently documented the inverse relationship between lack of appropriate communication skills and disruptive behavior and the fact that disruptive behaviors can be reduced through language acquisition (e.g., R.L. Koegel, Camarata, & Koegel, in press; R.L. Koegel, Koegel, & Surratt, 1992). This relationship suggests that interventions that facilitate language acquisition may help reduce parenting stress related to high levels of disruptive behaviors by children.

PARENT EDUCATION AND PARENTING STRESS

In the area of autism, parent education evolved in response to the pervasive needs of these children and to provide parents with a more effective way of teaching their children and reducing maladaptive behaviors. Given that the uneven intellectual development and excessive disruptive behaviors associated with autism have been identified as major sources of parenting stress, parent education programs have a great deal of potential for alleviating parenting stress associated with autism.

Investigation of parent education programs has shown them to be a cost-effective and efficient form of intervention. In addition, immediate and short-term child gains have been well-established in the literature on parent education programs (Harris, Wolchik, & Milch, 1983; Harris, Wolchik, & Weitz, 1981; Hemsley et al., 1978; Howlin, 1981; R.L. Koegel, Glahn, & Nieminen, 1978; R.L. Koegel, Schreibman, Johnson, O'Neill, & Dunlap, 1984; Schreibman, Koegel, Mills, & Burke, 1984). Despite the success of parent education programs in producing immediate and short-term gains, researchers have identified inconsistencies regarding the long-term effects of these programs in producing generalization and maintenance of intervention gains (see, for example, Dumas & Wahler, 1983; Harris, 1986; O'Dell, 1984). These limitations have been associated with parents' difficulty acquiring a proficient level of skill during instruction and/or problems with their implementation of these skills to a broad range of child behaviors and new environments following intervention. When these limitations are addressed, the potential for parent education programs to alleviate parenting stress associated with autism is greatly increased.

In addressing these problems related to limited generalization and maintenance of intervention gains, researchers have placed considerable emphasis on improving teaching procedures and methods of implementation utilized in parent education programs. Some authors have compared specific parent education approaches to identify those strategies that facilitate skill acquisition and optimize long-term implementation. For example, teaching parents general behavioral principles to give them a basis for developing new interventions as needed has been identified as a more effective approach to improving outcomes related to response generalization than approaches that teach parents specific interventions for a particular problem behavior (Forehand et al., 1979; R.L. Koegel, Glahn, & Nieminen, 1978). Such an approach has been emphasized in parent education programs because the pervasive behavioral excesses and difficulties associated with autism make the need for ongoing intervention highly probable. Because a variety of parent–child interactions involve parental directives, simple compliance instruction procedures have been incorporated into the programs as a way of encouraging response generalization (see, for example, Cataldo, 1984; Forehand & McMahon, 1981; Singer, Singer, & Horner, 1987).

Naturalistic teaching methods (e.g., milieu teaching, incidental teaching, time delay, natural language paradigm, in-context teaching) have been identified as another effective means of facilitating generalization, especially in the area of language development (see, for example, Camarata & Nelson, 1992; Halle, Marshall, & Spradlin, 1979; Hart & Risley, 1974; R.L. Koegel, O'Dell, & Koegel, 1987). These teaching strategies are integrated into naturally occurring interactions with the child, making them ideally suited for use in home and community environments instead of more rigid formalized teaching procedures. For example, Baker (1984) found that parents reported that they continued to utilize teaching skills for incidental (naturally occurring) instruction 17 months after the termination of group parent education classes, rather than highly structured formal teaching.

In addition, teaching pivotal behaviors has been identified as a promising approach for producing broad intervention effects. Pivotal behaviors are those behaviors that seem to be central to wide areas of functioning. Change in pivotal behaviors simultaneously produces changes in many other behaviors and therefore constitutes an efficient way to produce generalized improvements in the behavior of children with disabilities. For example, Carr and Durand (1985) have shown considerable reductions in children's disruptive behavior after teaching them functional communication. As discussed previously, a lack of motivation and responsivity to multiple cues has been identified as a serious impediment to the learning process for children with autism. When targeted for remediation in clinical

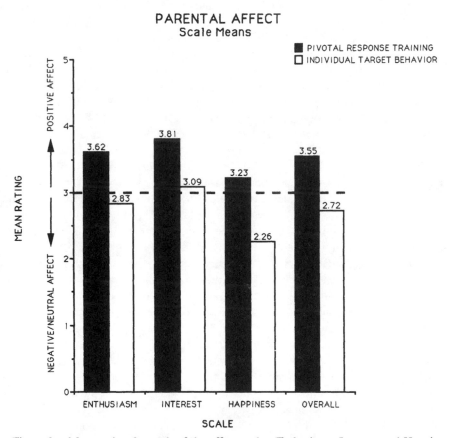

Figure 2.   Mean rating for each of the affect scales (Enthusiasm, Interest, and Happiness) and the overall composite rating for parents in the Pivotal Response Training condition (solid bars) and Individual Target Behavior condition (open bars). (From Schreibman, L., Kaneko, W.M., & Koegel, R.L. [1991]. Positive affect of parents of autistic children: A comparison across two teaching techniques. *Behavior Therapy, 22,* 479–490. Copyright 1991 by the Association for Advancement of Behavior Therapy. Reprinted by permission of the publisher and the author.)

interventions and parent education programs, these pivotal behaviors have been highly effective in facilitating language acquisition (see, for example, Camarata, in press; R.L. Koegel, O'Dell, & Dunlap, 1988; R.L. Koegel, O'Dell, & Koegel, 1987; Laski, Charlop, & Schreibman, 1988) (Figure 2).

Although a variety of teaching procedures and methods of implementation that facilitate intervention generalization have been identified in the literature, further investigation is necessary to determine which combination of these approaches is most efficient for parents to learn and implement in a variety of environments. This emphasis is necessary if parent education programs are expected to improve child functioning and reduce the parenting stress associated with autism.

There is some evidence that parent education programs that combine strategies that facilitate generalization (e.g., teaching parents behavior modification principles or implementation through incidental teaching) produce positive collateral effects for parents raising children with developmental disabilities (e.g., stress reductions, increased self-confidence and ability to handle problems, decreased frustration, improved communication with spouse about child) (e.g., Baker, Heifitz, & Murphy, 1980; Baker, Landen, & Kashima, 1989).

Although comparison studies have typically shown parenting stress to be significantly higher for mothers of children with autism than for mothers of children with mental retardation or physical disabilities (e.g., Bouma & Schwietzer, 1990; Holroyd & McArthur, 1976), there is emerging evidence that parent education programs can produce a broad range of positive collateral effects for families raising children with autism, including reductions in parenting stress. (See the example at the end of this section for a review of a combined parent education program producing a range of child gains and reductions in parenting stress associated with autism.)

Although continued research on teaching procedures and methods of implementation promises to be a highly productive area of investigation for the design of parent education programs that facilitate intervention generalization and produce positive collateral effects to families, numerous investigators have begun to examine a wider range of variables that have considerable influence on the outcome of parent education programs. Some authors have identified contextual variables such as poverty, social isolation, depression, stress, and marital discord as strong predictors for poor parent education outcomes (e.g., poor child progress, parent skill acquisition, follow-through teaching) (see, for example, Baker, 1983, 1984; Dadds, Schwartz, & Sanders, 1987; Dumas & Wahler, 1983; Forehand, Furey, & McMahon, 1984; Plienis, Robbins, & Dunlap, 1988; Robbins, Dunlap, & Plienis, 1991; Wahler, 1980). Given that the outcomes of parent education programs are dependent on a number of variables (e.g., programmatic and contextual) that may vary considerably across families, the focus of parent education programs has been expanded recently to include comprehensive assessment of child and family needs to tailor interventions around those needs (Baker, 1989; Plienis, Robbins, & Dunlap, 1988; Singer, Irvine, & Irvin, 1989).

With the abundance of literature documenting the stressful effects associated with caring for a child with autism, it is not surprising that reducing parenting stress is recognized as a common need by many families. To address this need, some investigators have focused on how parents respond to stress resulting from the accumulation of life events that may or may not be directly related to their child (e.g., child's condition, family development and relationships, family management and decisions, family finances) (see, for example, Patterson & McCubbin, 1983). Interventions changing how parents respond to accumulating stress may provide more immediate relief for distressed families, given that it may take a considerable amount of time to remediate all of the stressful behaviors associated with children with more severe disabilities. This focus has emerged out of advances in family stress theory literature (see, for example, McCubbin & McCubbin, 1987; McCubbin & Patterson, 1983; Patterson, 1988, 1989) that postulate that the interaction among a family's resources, coping skills, and their appraisal of the stressor event determines how families respond to stress. Those families with more resources, effective coping skills, and positive appraisals of the stressor tend to adapt well over time to the various sources of stress they experience raising children with disabilities (Patterson, 1993).

With this conceptualization of family stress, coping skills have become of increasing interest to researchers working with families who raise children with disabilities because they have been successful for many other stress-related problems and can be taught and readily learned by many people (Singer & Irvin, 1989a; Woolfolk & Lehrer, 1984). For example, Intagliata and Doyle (1984) developed an instruction program to improve parents' interpersonal problem-solving skills so that they would be better prepared to deal with the various stressors they experience while raising a child with disabilities. In more recent efforts, Hawkins and Singer (1989) taught parents of children with disabilities specific stress-management approaches (e.g., self-monitoring, relaxation instruction, coping self-statements, modeling) and showed that the approaches can significantly enhance parents' ability to cope with their parenting stress. Although the investigation of coping skills and how they have an impact on families who raise children with disabilities is rapidly expanding, further research is necessary to determine which coping skills are most effective for meeting the needs of families who raise children with autism. The addition of such adjunctive interventions to parent education programs for distressed families may give service providers an optimal approach for ameliorating the parenting stress associated with autism.

PARENT EDUCATION: CASE EXAMPLE

Preliminary results from ongoing research on parent education programs conducted by R.L. Koegel and Schreibman (personal communication, 1995) have shown considerable success with specific types of parent education interventions. In their recent assessment of the effects of two different parenting education models on parenting stress associated with autism, they reported widespread child progress and parenting stress reductions.

The parent education interventions focused on two very different approaches designed to teach receptive and expressive language and decrease the inappropriate behaviors of children with autism. The first group of families participated in an analog-based intervention that focused on teaching individual target behaviors one at a time. Parents in the analog group chose individual behaviors based on a developmental model and spent designated times working on these behaviors with the use of shaping and chaining. Feedback was given for correct and incorrect responses, and when predetermined criteria were met a new behavior was chosen. The second group participated in a naturalistic intervention that focused on teaching pivotal behaviors. The goal of the naturalistic instruction was to teach behaviors that seem to be central to developing wide areas of improved functioning. The basis of the naturalistic approach was to teach skills in the context of natural situations. Pilot data suggested that positive changes in pivotal behaviors would show widespread positive effects on many other behaviors and therefore constitute an efficient way to produce generalized improvements in the behavior of children with autism (R.L. Koegel, Koegel, & Schreibman, 1991). The pivotal target behaviors emphasized were *motivation* and *responsivity to multiple cues*. As described previously, these behaviors have been identified as central problems in the uneven intellectual development of children with autism that impede assessment of child functioning and skill acquisition (e.g., language, social, adaptive skills) as well as contribute to parenting stress (e.g., G. Dunlap & Egel, 1982; G. Dunlap & Koegel, 1980; R.L. Koegel & Egel, 1979; R.L. Koegel & Mentis, 1985; Lovaas, Koegel, & Schreibman, 1979; Schreibman, 1988).

Both interventions included components relating to general behavior modification principles with the use of manuals (e.g., Baker, Brightman, Heifetz, & Murphy, 1976), instructional videotapes, and practice with direct feedback. Ongoing assessments of parents' fidelity of implementation were made to ensure that all parents met proficiency criteria prior to completion of intervention. This required them to demonstrate consistently their ability to utilize the specific behavioral techniques in their interaction with their child. The families attended weekly 1-hour sessions. The length of time for parents to master the techniques typically ranged from 25 to 30 hours of practice with feedback. Despite these similarities, the two interventions differed significantly on stimulus item, prompt, interaction, response, and consequence dimensions. The programmatic differences reflect a combination of empirically derived strategies geared toward facilitating child *motivation* emphasized in the naturalistic pivotal response instruction (see Table 1 in Chapter 2).

Stimulus Item Properties (Child Choice)

The first component differentiating the two instruction interventions was stimulus item selection. R.L. Koegel, Dyer, and Bell (1987) show stimulus item selection to be an important consideration by demonstrating that using child-preferred stimulus items results in decreases in social avoidance behavior during adult–child interactions with a toy. In the parent education project (R.L. Koegel, Koegel, & Schreibman, 1991; Laski et al., 1988), stimulus items in the analog condition were arbitrarily chosen by the parent. Child-preferred stimulus items were selected according to the child's interest in the naturalistic condition. To establish child-preferred items, children in the naturalistic condition were presented with a pool of items. Preferred items were then chosen by observing behaviors such as eye gaze, touching, and pointing that were likely to indicate a strong preference for certain objects.

Another distinction between stimulus item selection for the two intervention conditions related to the age-appropriateness of the stimulus items and whether the items existed in the child's natural environment. For the analog group, stimulus items were chosen by the therapist (parent). Depending on the target behavior, items may or may not have been age-appropriate and available in the child's natural environment. An example of this would be using preprinted pictures of actions to teach a child the -*ing* verb ending. In contrast, in the naturalistic condition only age-appropriate items found in the child's natural environment were employed in teaching the child. For example, the -*ing* verb ending would be taught by actually engaging the child in everyday action activities in play and other age-appropriate contexts. Many authors have suggested that the use of naturally occurring stimulus items provides a more functional experience for children who come in contact with the same, or very similar, stimuli in their everyday life (see, for example, Bloom & Lahey, 1978; Holland, 1975; Muma, 1977; Oldfield, 1966; Stewart & Hamilton, 1976).

A final feature distinguishing stimulus items between the naturalistic and analog intervention conditions was their manner of presentation. More specifically, instead of presenting the stimulus item repetitively until the child learned the appropriate response, as in the analog condition, items in the naturalistic condition were varied from trial to trial according to the child's interests and by interspersing trials with tasks the child had already acquired. Such task variation has been shown to improve responding, maintain gains (e.g., G. Dunlap, 1984; G. Dunlap & Koegel, 1980), and even reduce aberrant behaviors (e.g., Winterling, Dunlap, & O'Neill, 1987) in children with autism.

Prompt Characteristics

A second area of focus differentiating intervention conditions related to the prompts. The analog condition used prompts such as manual manipulation of the lips for speech sounds. In contrast, the naturalistic condition used prompts more likely to occur in natural language interactions, such as modeling the target response. As discussed previously and in detail in Chapter 3, overselectivity has been shown to be a problem limiting the effectiveness of extrastimulus prompts (R.L. Koegel & Rincover, 1976; Schreibman, 1975). Therefore, extrastimulus prompts, such as physical manipulations, were avoided in the naturalistic condition.

Parent–Child Interactions

In contrast to the analog condition, which utilized a timed discrete trial format, the naturalistic condition was more similar to play or other natural interactions where the parent used the stimulus item in a functional manner (e.g., plays with a toy, eats candy) and modeled a response for the child to follow. Teaching language and skill acquisition in this manner has potential benefits for parents and children. This approach may increase the likelihood of generalization and maintenance in other natural situations, and it requires minimal daily activity restructuring by parents in their typical interactions with their other children.

Defining Child Responses Needing Reinforcement

The definition of a correct child response differed for each intervention condition. The analog condition embraced a strict shaping perspective, rewarding successive approximations to improve responding. The criteria for correct responses in the naturalistic sessions were broadened so that the child was rewarded for any clear attempt at a response in addition to correct responses. R.L. Koegel, O'Dell, and Dunlap (1988) demonstrated that reinforcing any obvious attempt to respond rather than only reinforcing successive approximation results in both increased responding and improved motivation in children with autism. These authors speculate that this improvement may relate to the fact that aspects of motivation may be a more important target behavior than are specific behavioral responses (e.g., motor speech production).

Consequences for Correct Responding

The analog condition used praise combined with arbitrary food reinforcers or tokens as consequences for appropriate responding. In contrast, the naturalistic condition reinforced the child with praise combined with natural reinforcers, such as the opportunity to play with (or otherwise appropriately interact with) the stimulus item. Such direct reinforcers most likely integrate the response with the consequences in hopes of illustrating how producing appropriate responses (e.g., language use, social skills) can assist in acquiring desired objects and attention (Hart & Risley, 1974; R.L. Koegel & Williams, 1980; Williams, Koegel, & Egel, 1981).

Increasing Responsivity to Multiple Cues

Another programmatic difference between intervention conditions is the emphasis on facilitating responsivity to multiple cues. As noted in Chapter 3, children with autism frequently respond to limited aspects of complex stimuli (R.L. Koegel, Schreibman, Britten, & Laintinen, 1979; R.L. Koegel & Wilhelm, 1973; Reynolds, Newsom, & Lovaas, 1974), demonstrating "overselective" responding (G. Dunlap, Koegel, & Burke, 1981; Lovaas, Koegel, & Schreibman, 1979; Lovaas, Schreibman, Koegel, & Rehm, 1971). This form of responding is evident when the child responds to one, possibly irrelevant, component of a stimulus. For example, when spoken to, the child might respond on the basis of only the visual cue (e.g., lip movements) and fail to attend to another (e.g., verbal) cue altogether. This overselectivity may impair observational learning, which relies heavily on integrating various relevant multiple cues in the environment. Consequently, overselectivity has been identified as a central problem contributing to the difficulties in intellectual development and skill acquisition (e.g., Lovaas, Koegel, & Schreibman, 1979; Schreibman, 1988).

In the analog condition, the child may or may not have been exposed to multiple cues, depending on the individual target behavior selected. In contrast, a focus of the naturalistic condition was to systematically increase a child's ability to respond to multiple cues. For example, having the child choose a red pen as opposed to a red pencil or blue pen requires the child to respond to more than one cue within the environment. The complexity of multiple cues is determined by the child's functioning level. As the child progresses, the exposure to increasing numbers of cues can be made increasingly more complex. For example, one could request a child to put a glass of juice next to his father's placemat and a glass of milk next to his little sister's placemat while setting the table for dinner. Multiple cue instruction has been demonstrated to improve the child's ability to focus on the multiple relevant environmental cues rather than responding to fewer and sometimes irrelevant cues (Lovaas, Koegel, & Schreibman, 1979).

PRELIMINARY FINDINGS

In light of the empirical evidence supporting the use of strategies that facilitate child motivation and attention to multiple cues, as well as using more natural forms of adult–child interaction as a teaching context, several important issues were addressed comparing the two teaching models. First, as discussed earlier, children with autism demonstrate faster and more generalized gains when taught by their parents as opposed to a clinician. However, an equally important issue relates to parenting stress. Given the increased demands and burdens that confront families when a child with a disability is born, and society's failure to address and provide support for the resulting stress, it is important that parent education programs be designed to encompass family systems, rather than to focus solely on the child's needs. Results from our preliminary analyses showed a number of important results. Although children in both intervention conditions showed improvement in their communication, social, and daily living skills, the gains were more pronounced for children in the naturalistic pivotal response intervention condition (especially in the area of communication). Furthermore, in addition to demonstrating greater child improvements, the naturalistic pivotal response instruction intervention condition reduced mothers' stress related to their children's levels of dependency, management problems, and cognitive impairments. These results suggest that the naturalistic intervention condition provided mothers with more optimism about their ability to facilitate their children's development, reduce their children's dependency, and better manage problem behaviors. There was also an increase in the amount of time mothers in the naturalistic intervention condition spent in teaching-related activities with their children. Postmeasures indicated that the mothers in the naturalistic intervention condition spent an average of 60 minutes a day more than

Figure 3.   Parent education programs, implemented properly, can help to
reduce parent stress.

the mothers in the analog group teaching their children following intervention. This
increase for mothers in the naturalistic pivotal response intervention condition substanti-
ates the ease of implementation and integration of the naturalistic techniques into their
daily routines. The efficiency and ease of implementation of the naturalistic pivotal
response intervention was also evident in mothers' perceptions of time with their children
as less work and less difficult following intervention. These findings are consistent with
previous research on parent education programs showing higher levels of positive affect
while using naturalistic intervention procedures in comparison to the traditional analog
procedures (Schreibman, Kaneko, & Koegel, 1991). These results provide support for
developing parent education interventions that facilitate widespread child progress and
simultaneously help alleviate the parenting stress associated with raising a child with
autism (Figure 3).

SUMMARY

The range and severity of the specific behavioral difficulties and excesses exhibited by
children with autism have proven to be a major challenge for those involved in their analysis and intervention. Contrary to concerns relating to the limitations of former parent
education programs, advances in behavioral technology, as well as the increase in interventions that emphasize the needs of the family system, provide more confidence in the
use of current parent education procedures as a way of producing meaningful changes in
the lives of children with disabilities and their families. As discussed previously, naturalistic interventions that teach parents skills that are easily acquired and applied in parents'
daily routines within home and community environments can simultaneously produce
widespread child progress and reduce parenting stress. Also, in situations where a family
may need more immediate relief from accumulating stress, teaching parents stress-
management procedures and other coping skills appears to be a useful adjunct to parent
education programs.

Additional research designed to further our understanding of the situations leading to stress will enable community service providers to assist families who have children with autism in dealing with their unique concerns. Given an understanding of specific child characteristics, behaviors, and life-span issues associated with elevated stress in parents (e.g., disruptive behavior, uneven intellectual development, long-term planning), it is possible to focus interventions more efficiently and in a manner that may reduce these specific stress areas (e.g., dependency, management, cognitive impairment). Ultimately, understanding and considering such variables when designing parent education interventions will allow service providers to better meet the ongoing needs of families raising children with autism.

Chapter 8

Social Support for Families

Ann Leslie Albanese,
Stephanie K. San Miguel, and Robert L. Koegel

PURPOSE OF SOCIAL SUPPORT INTERVENTIONS

The purpose of interventions targeting social support is to establish and enhance a network of individuals and groups who share an invested relationship with the family. The basic role of these groups and individuals is to provide emotional, psychological, and practical support and to share relevant information and resources (Werth & Oseroff, 1987). A variety of theories have been proposed as underlying the positive effects of social support. Various social supports have been identified by theoreticians and researchers as reducing vulnerability to both internal and external stressors (Gallagher, Beckman, & Cross, 1983). This particular theory appears to be highly relevant to families who have a child with autism.

In her research with families and mothers of children with autism, Bristol (1985) found that the degree of personal social support was negatively related to the amount of stress reported by mothers of children with autism. In other research, Bristol and Schopler (1984) found that adequacy of informal support was also predictive of marital adjustment and quality of parenting (Bristol, 1985). Based on their research and work with families, these authors suggest that the perceived adequacy of social support bears more relevance to the family's ability to adapt than does the severity of the child's disability (Bristol & Schopler, 1984).

Boyce, Behl, Mortensen, and Akers (1991), in a nationwide study of families with children with developmental disabilities, found that social support was negatively correlated, along with family resources and cohesion, with both child-related and parent-related stress. In a longitudinal study of mothers who had a child with a disability, Hanson and Hanline (1990) reported a significant relationship between maternal levels of stress and social support. This last study is particularly interesting in that this finding was consistently significant across data points. Such longitudinal evidence suggests that social support is of central importance to family and individual functioning across the family's life cycle. The studies cited here are only a few of the studies of families who have children with various types of disabilities that indicate that social support is related not only to stress but also to variables such as the functioning of individual family members, parenting experiences, and family adaptation.

Clearly, social support for families who have a child with a disability appears to serve many purposes, some that have been identified, such as the alleviation of stress, and some that remain to be explored. Some of the questions inviting further exploration include a study of which types and combinations of social support are most effective in enhancing family functioning and adaptation and how this varies according to the timing of the intervention in a family's and child's life.

One particularly popular form of social support for families who have a child with a disability is the parent support group. A number of theories have been proposed to explain the positive processes that may occur within the context of support groups. Although support groups are only one specific type of social support, many of these theories appear to be relevant to processes that may be at work in other forms of social support. Therefore, these theories are enumerated for consideration when evaluating in what ways these groups, as well as other types of individual and group support, may be enhancing family, parent, and child well-being. Affiliation and community have been proposed as positive benefits of social support in the support group context, in which participants experience decreased loneliness in coping with their concerns and satisfaction in both giving and receiving support. Advocacy and empowerment are other potential benefits in which parents provide the impetus for advocating changes in the system and experience an accompanying sense of control and power. Coping is a third process that may be activated within this socially supportive context where a salient benefit of the group is seen as gains in information, social reinforcement, modeling, normative identification, attitude change, and other cognitive and behavioral processes (Kurtz, 1990; Stewart, 1990).

Many of these concepts lend themselves readily to hypotheses about the positive processes of other forms of social support. For example, affiliation and community may occur through membership in other community organizations such as churches. Advocacy and empowerment are, of course, salient components of participation in any kind of parent advocacy group. Furthermore, empowerment may be expected to occur in those socially supportive contexts where the parent and/or family is gaining knowledge, skills, and the opportunity to make informed and effective decisions about their child's welfare in the home, school, and community. Parent education programs, such as those described in Chapter 7, are an example of this sort of empowering social support, as is the supportive interaction between a parental advocate and a parent in working with schools to achieve satisfactory educational services for the child. The third beneficial process of support groups, coping, is a complex concept that bears relevance to many, if not all, types of socially supportive interactions. Ideally, the parent who obtains satisfactory information about his or her child's development from a developmental pediatrician, developmental psychologist, or a teacher experiences enhanced ability to cope. Modeling and social reinforcement are inherent components of parent teaching and education, as well as the development of parental advocacy skills. Attitudes and attributions, as two facets of the complex cognitive processes that contribute to coping, are presumably influenced by the social interactions parents encounter with professional and personal as well as group and individually oriented social support systems.

In addition to the exchanges between families and other individuals and groups within the direct contexts of social support, a primary goal is the mobilization of other, new support systems as a result of these current contacts. For example, parents who meet one another in a parent support group may be likely to contact one another outside the group to seek further information and social contact. Also, a parent may learn about resources such as a good developmental pediatrician as a result of his or her contact with a parent education specialist or vice versa. Empirical studies need to be conducted to help validate this association between initial support systems and the development of additional social support. Meanwhile, we base these expectations in part on observations and anecdotal evidence provided by the families with whom we work. Parents report calling other parents for information about services they first became aware of in a casual exchange when picking their child up at school. Parents participating in a support group contact one another outside the group context to seek support and solace when confronting new challenges. These same parents have initiated informal gatherings such as a picnic for their families. In one case, a parent with strong organizational skills turned to other parents she had met through a support group and parent teaching program for help in successfully initiating and securing involvement in a local chapter of the Autism Society of America. Therefore, the purpose of social support is not only to provide immediate support, but to facilitate the expansion of the family's ongoing social network.

Social support has been identified in theoretical and empirical literature as having an important influence on family and individual functioning (Dunst & Trivette, 1986, 1990; Kurtz, 1990; Stewart, 1990). In a review of the literature on the effects of social support, Dunst and Trivette (1990) conclude that social support clearly reduces the probability of emotional and physical distress. In addition, these authors state that social support enhances well-being. Yet a systematic, detailed understanding of how the relationship between social support and psychological and physical health functions may be long forthcoming. Researchers and practitioners increasingly acknowledge that social support is a complex, multifaceted phenomenon that may come in different forms, occur within different contexts, and serve different functions (Dunst, Trivette, & Deal, 1988; Krahn, 1993; Tracy & Whittaker, 1987). Although numerous definitions of social support have been proposed, this chapter utilizes the following description of social support and extrafamily resources offered by Dunst et al. (1988): "emotional, physical, informational, instrumental, and material aid and assistance provided by others to maintain health and well-being, promote adaptations of life events, and foster development in an adaptive manner" (p. 28). This definition is referred to in part due to its comprehensive nature and in part due to its clear relevance to all families as they meet the challenges of providing their children with a healthy present and a promising future.

Despite the strong evidence that social support has a positive impact on families, less is understood about specific characteristics of social support, as these may differ in the degree to which they bear a relationship to individual and family functioning and adaptation. Some of the variables that may be associated with whether or not families find social support helpful are implied or directly identified by existing literature. These variables include the following: the degree to which the family has expressed a need for the type of social support available to them—the match between the identified need and the existing sources of support; the specific expectations family members have regarding the support system in question and the degree to which these expectations are met (e.g., is the parent seeking practical information, emotional support, or both?); the family members' perceived satisfaction with the support; the type, quantity, and quality of other existing sources of support in the family's life; the family members' attributions about the child's disability; and the timing and nature of transitions or critical events within the family as these interact with available support (Dunst & Trivette, 1990; Hanline, 1991; Krahn, 1993; Nixon, 1988).

Clearly, a need exists for ongoing investigation of the nature and value of specific types of social support and how to ensure that the support systems in question will meet the needs of families who have a child with autism. Equally evident is the fact that social support in general has already been established as an important factor in mediating stress and enhancing health. It is our expectation that parents and professionals will continue to pursue development of and access to social support. Therefore, the purpose of this chapter is to identify some of the fundamental issues, questions, and observations that are relevant to establishing and facilitating social support. It is not possible within the scope of this chapter to provide a comprehensive overview of the complex theoretical, empirical, and applied issues that characterize the area of social support for families who have children with disabilities. Rather, it is our intention to alert the reader, whether a parent, student, or professional, to the strong likelihood that attempts to enhance family and child functioning and development will prove most effective when specific attention is paid to the strengths and needs of the family's social support network (Krauss & Jacobs, 1990; Powers, 1991; Singer, Irvine, & Irvin, 1989). The information provided in this chapter is based on questions, hypotheses, and findings addressed by the existing literature, as well as our own experiences working with families who have children with autism.

TYPES OF SOCIAL SUPPORT

The different forms in which social support manifests itself may be distinguished in a variety of ways. In evaluating the value of social support for families who have children with special needs, Dunst and Trivette (1990) differentiate between formal and informal social support. Whereas formal support systems are exemplified by professionals and service agencies, informal support includes individual relationships with family members and friends, as well as affiliations with social groups that are integrated into the daily activities of a family. Examples of formal sources of support include family therapists, parent education experts, professional parent advocates, respite care providers, and estate planners. Informal support may be provided, for example, by family members, friends, neighbors, parent support groups, individual parents who may or may not have a child with autism, and co-workers. Both formal and informal sources of support may comprise an exchange within a group context or a one-on-one interaction. Furthermore, one can interpret the definition of social support provided by Dunst and Trivette (1990) to include assistance that only indirectly involves interaction between two or more people. For example, a parenting education newsletter or a list of community resources may prove to be of invaluable assistance to some parents.

Recent advances in the integration of different sources of support have included the development of what A. Turnbull (1994) refers to as action groups, wherein all individuals who interact with the child and the family work together to create a dynamic and supportive network. In this approach to establishing broad-based social support, both formal and informal sources of support may function as a complementary, integrated whole. As discussed in Chapter 11, the integration of formal and informal sources of support is appealing in that it suggests the building of a communicative bridge between professional and personal social systems. Gallagher (1990) proposes that formal interventions may include as one goal the activation of existing informal social networks and the engagement of informal network members to assist individuals and families in accessing formal support systems. This approach to intervention with and social support for families who have a child with a developmental disability reflects the increasing emphasis placed by researchers, practitioners, and families on the active involvement of family members; friends; professionals from a variety of disciplines; parent and professional advocates; and other relevant personal, community, and professional individuals and groups (Dunst & Trivette, 1986; G.H.S. Singer & Irvin, 1989; A.P. Turnbull, Summers, & Brotherson, 1983; A.P. Turnbull & Turnbull, 1986).

Tracy and Whittaker (1987), in a review of literature regarding social support interventions for families with children who are at risk or who have developmental disabilities, identified some of the primary approaches service providers have taken thus far in the development and enhancement of social support networks. These approaches to social support intervention include family support programs, network facilitation, and support groups. Family support programs as described by Tracy and Whittaker integrate both formal and informal supports that include both one-to-one and group contexts and create linkages between the various support sources. Examples of the services provided within these programs are parent education programs that provide direct or indirect instruction, early intervention, and home visits. Family support programs provide both material and emotional support, and they promote the extension of the family's support system. The second approach, network facilitation, seeks to activate and organize members of the family's informal network to fulfill a variety of supportive roles, including child care and home programming. Finally, support groups provide a context within which parents can discuss common concerns related to parenting a child with a disability. These groups are also intended to increase the parents' access to and utilization of other formal and informal sources of support outside the group. Parents may encounter emotional, informational, and instrumental support as a result of participation in these groups. Although Tracy and Whittaker focus on families whose children are at risk or have developmental disabilities, the social supports they describe are clearly relevant to families who have children with autism.

It is not possible here to provide an exhaustive list of the types of social support one may encounter or the forms of social support interventions or more comprehensive interventions that may be relevant; however, even this brief discussion should begin to illuminate the fact that social support is a multifaceted, complex concept that continues to evolve in its definition and its mobilization. Interestingly, the dynamic, interactive nature of social support networks parallels the dynamic and unique development of each and every family: As the family tasks change and the corresponding tasks of the parents and children within that family change, so will the facets of social support that are most relevant to the family's current needs and progress. Recognition of this changing relationship between the family and its surrounding environment is vital in determining the best approach at any given time to enhancing the family's social support system (Hanline, 1991; A.P. Turnbull et al., 1986; Wikler, 1981).

ASSESSMENT OF FAMILY SUPPORT SYSTEMS

The establishment of appropriate social support should begin with consideration of the following factors:

1. The needs and wishes of the family as identified by family members—a process that may occur informally or in collaboration with professionals
2. Assessment of available support
3. Determination of the degree to which available support and the family's needs match each other
4. Identification of the criteria for adequate and appropriate support (e.g., address questions such as who and how many individuals will constitute each support subsystem, in what environment will the support be offered, how frequently will support be offered and over what period of time)

In considering their own and others' research regarding social support, Dunst and Trivette (1990) enumerate several aspects that they identify as particularly important in the assessment of social support. Network size, as well as the existence of specific types of social relationships and memberships in social organizations, are included in this list. Social relationships and memberships may include, for example, marriage and church membership. The frequency of social contacts as well as the type and amount of support others in the family's informal social network offer are also cited by these authors as important factors to assess. The need for support and the congruences between needs and support systems are additional factors to be considered. Other aspects of social support to assess include the family's utilization of the support, the dependability of the support, and the reciprocity or degree to which the provision of support consists of mutual exchange. Finally, Dunst and Trivette (1990) suggest attention to the family's closeness to and satisfaction with the sources of support.

As with any intervention or attempt by family members and/or professionals to make changes in the family's environment, one should not proceed without first conducting a careful assessment of the existing social support system. Various combinations of the factors identified by Dunst and Trivette (1990) as important to this process have also been identified in other literature that attempts to clarify the nature of social support (Krahn, 1993). Based on current research and practice, reference to these criteria should allow one to establish an understanding of each family's unique support system network that will be relevant to promoting the sustenance and enhancement of that network.

DETERMINING APPROPRIATE
CHARACTERISTICS OF SOCIAL SUPPORT SYSTEMS

We do not intend here to itemize the many variables that one might consider in determining the ideal characteristics of social support systems for individual families; however, we would like to comment on two factors that are frequently identified as important in determining the quality of social support for families. These factors are the diversity and the size of the social support network and the systems that constitute that network.

Diversity

A diverse number and type of sources from which families may derive social support, including professionals, family members, community groups, and parents who may or may not have a child with autism, have already been identified. The diversity of the family's social systems that constitute their current social support network, as well as those systems that are potential sources of support, appears to be one important factor to consider when determining how best to match the family's needs. Diversity within a social system network is important, in part because, any given support system, although it may meet a specific family need, may fail to meet other related needs. Furthermore, as Dunst, Trivette, and Deal (1988) note, from a social system perspective, changes in one social system will influence other social systems within the network. In other words, the support systems that constitute a family's social support network are inevitably interrelated.

G.H.S. Singer et al. (1989) also highlight this interrelationship between various types of supportive interventions for families who have a child with a disability. They recommend a model for effective implementation of behavioral parent education that requires that the intervention plan also address, as necessary, contextual variables such as poverty, social isolation, maternal demoralization, and marital discord. Singer et al. note that a growing body of empirical literature provides evidence that the effectiveness of behavioral parent education is maximized when supportive interventions such as marital therapy or respite care are provided that address these other family concerns when a thorough assessment identifies the need. It is not surprising that families who suffer stress due to challenges other than caring for their children's special needs may experience difficulty committing time and attention to the acquisition and consistent application of parent education skills. Attempting to contend with such issues as the material need of food on the table or the breakdown of the parenting system in the midst of marital conflict is likely to require direct support that specifically matches the difficulty in question. Therefore, specialists in intervention for families who have a child with a disability need to recognize that families have multifaceted needs that require a diverse set of social support systems.

Some degree of diversity across the family's social support system is probably desirable; however, comprehensive guidelines for determining the ideal integration of support systems in a family's social support network have yet to be established empirically. This task is a daunting one because of the unique characteristics of each and every family.

In the absence of specific and conclusive empirical answers about the best composition for a social support network, one may need to rely to some degree on practical factors. For example, the community where the family resides is likely an influential factor. A specific case illustrating this point is the community where, among the families who have a child with autism, only a few parents are able or wish to participate in a parent support group. In this case, one may want to consider a parent support group that includes parents with a variety of concerns, such as a cross-disabilities group (Nixon, 1988). Moreover, the establishment of a support group that includes members whose children do not have disabilities is a feasible option. The current goal of full inclusion for all children may be reflected in parents' wishes to normalize and diversify their own experiences and social relationships in raising children with autism. This is an interesting issue that merits further investigation. Certainly, some studies have identified parents who reported that limiting their support to others who have a child with a disability was at odds with their efforts to normalize their family's identity within the community (e.g., Krauss, Upshur, Shonkoff, & Hauser-Cram, 1993; Nixon, 1988).

Some communities, for example, small, rural communities, may not have clinical resources that offer such sources of support as parent education and consultation. Families and professionals in this case may have to be particularly creative and resourceful in devising socially supportive systems that meet parent and child needs. Collaboration between parents and the community's school psychologist in establishing a parenting skills workshop that relies in part on parents who have prior instruction is one example of responding to limited sources of formal support. Finally, we are cognizant of the likelihood that parents have different needs at different times that may or may not be met by specific support systems, especially if these are not integrated effectively with other, co-existing support systems and interventions (Dunst et al., 1988; Hanline, 1991; G.H.S. Singer et al., 1989; A.P. Turnbull et al., 1986).

Size of the Social Support Network

When identifying the forms of social support on which a family currently relies or that the family would like to develop, several issues arise concerning the size of any given social support system or of the network as a whole. One question to be considered is what number of individuals constitutes a socially supportive system? This may depend in good part on how other systems in the family's social support network are functioning. In the example of spouses who are experiencing serious marital conflict and therefore may find it more, rather than less, stressful to respond to parent instruction (G.H.S. Singer et al., 1989), an increase in the size of the support network that involves the additional support system of behavioral parent instruction may be premature, if well intended. However, an increase in this type of support may be optimal if the parents are functioning well as marital and parenting partners, which in turn allows them to focus on the cooperative effort of effecting progress in their child's functioning.

Furthermore, the size of a single social system within a network can range from interaction between two individuals to involvement in a very large group. The benefits parents experience from either a social support system that comprises one individual or hundreds of individuals (e.g., a nationally based organization) will depend, once again, on the specific needs the family seeks to meet. For example, a one-to-one meeting between a parent and a child development expert may prove particularly supportive if the parent is intent on seeking accurate information about his or her own child's development and functioning. At the other extreme, large groups may develop a greater political impact on societal, legal, and educational processes that will benefit parents and their children. Parents who participate in this type of large advocacy organization may not only perceive themselves as recipients of these long-term benefits but may be at a time in their lives when they experience particular satisfaction in the fact that they are contributing to these global, positive changes. This case exemplifies the process of reciprocity as one important characteristic of an effective support system.

Conclusive evidence across studies has not yet been established that the size of a social support system or the network within which it exists is, by itself, positively related to family functioning and adaptation. Currently, with the obvious exception of clear social isolation and concomitant impaired functioning, one may want to be cautious in assuming that more is invariably better. As always, a detailed assessment that places a strong emphasis on the family's expressed needs for and satisfaction with their support network is perhaps the best approach in determining whether an increase in the size of support systems or networks is advisable. In some cases, for example, one may find that rather than increasing the number of individuals in a system, the focus of change should be on the quality of the supportive interactions.

SOCIAL SUPPORT AND PROFESSIONAL INTERVENTION

The expectation that families will often locate and access the types of social support they need spontaneously, without formal assistance or planning, is a reasonable assumption. Yet one cannot assume that a family's efforts to meet its needs for social support will be automatically successful. Families who have a child with a disability such as autism may encounter a variety of obstacles in their quest for support. The amount of time and energy consumed in attending directly to the child's needs and our society's tendency to stigmatize or exclude people with disabilities are only two examples of these obstacles. Gallagher (1990) observes that families who have a child with a disability may react by reducing their social contacts.

These concerns about the adequacy of the family's social support network are intended to increase an awareness of potential difficulties that the family may confront. Concomitantly, it cannot be emphasized too strongly how critical it is that professionals avoid pathologizing the families with whom they work. One should never make blanket assumptions about the family's vulnerability to stress, crisis, social isolation, or general dysfunction. Yet professionals who intend to embark with the family in pursuit of a strategy that will provide the parents and child with new skills and ways of adapting their behavior to enhance child and family functioning must attend to the adequacy of the family's social support network if they wish to maximize the chances of a successful intervention. Otherwise, they risk disappointing themselves and, far more importantly, disappointing or frustrating the families whom they intend to assist. This chapter has attempted to illustrate why this attention to the family's functioning as it is intertwined with their social support network is so essential. Dunst, Trivette, and Deal (1988) offer a persuasive view of the vital relationship between social support and other aspects of a family's well-being. They observe that social support influences personal health and well-being, which in turn influence family functioning. Personal health and well-being, along with family functioning, are expected, as a trio, to have an impact on styles of parent–child interaction, which then influence child behavior and development. The interrelatedness of these variables as depicted by Dunst et al. identifies social support as a critical, leading factor in the systemic balance of individual family members, relationships between individual members within the family, and the family as a whole. Professionals have many horizons still to explore in understanding how they can assist families in sustaining and enhancing their social support systems. One of the key challenges for those who work professionally with families to enhance family and child functioning is to promote natural support systems that the family can continue to build and sustain in their daily lives that are not replaced by long-term dependence on formal supportive services (Dunst et al., 1988).

CONCLUSION

This chapter has identified social support as an important factor in promoting healthy functioning in families. Social support of various types appears to enhance adaptive processes such as coping, empowerment, a sense of community and affiliation, and overall physical and mental health. In particular, a growing body of evidence indicates that social support mediates the effects of stressful events in an individual's or family's life. Many types of formal and informal social support can play a positive role in families' lives, including exchanges between a parent and a professional, a variety of community gatherings, and parent–parent interactions. Parent support groups, parent education, and the emotional and instrumental support of extended family members are only a few specific examples of social support systems. The benefits of any given type of social support system will depend to some extent on the timing in the family's and child's life and the degree to which they have expressed a need for and satisfaction with available support systems.

Undoubtedly, effective social support should be guided by empirical knowledge about specific types of social support as these interact with specific aspects of family, parent, and child characteristics and functioning. The considerations we offer as relevant to the assessment and development of a social support network are derived from the existing empirical and theoretical literature, as well as our own experiences in working with families. Every family and child is unique. It is imperative to listen attentively to parents' or families' ideas and needs with an awareness that these change over time.

In closing, we would like to offer some brief suggestions of some concrete sources of informational support that the families with whom we work have repeatedly sought and found useful.

- Baby-Sitter List: The first item is an invariably high-demand item—a baby-sitter list that includes the names of individuals who have had experience working with children who have autism. Parents greatly appreciate the option of leaving their child in the care of someone who understands and respects their child's needs.
- Resource List: Another practical item that parents request is a resource list that provides information ranging from books about autism to professionals in the local community and national advocacy groups. Parents who participate in a parent support group contribute and update the information on an ongoing basis. The group's facilitators compile and distribute the resource list to participants and nonparticipants of the group on request.
- Phone/Address List: Support groups can also establish a phone and address list so that participants can easily contact one another outside the context of the group. Parents who are not able to participate in a group can request a copy of this list in order to make contact with others who have a child with autism. Of course, the participants in the group will need to consent to these requests, as one way of sharing their support with others.
- Estate Planning Packets: Estate planning packets are also a high-demand product. Parents who have a child with autism or other disability often have serious concerns about their child's welfare in the event of their deaths. Access to an estate planning packet that provides practical guidelines in this regard can provide parents with considerable relief from this very real anxiety (Dussault, 1994).
- Advocacy Resources: Finally, professional advocacy resources are often a welcome form of informational, instrumental, and emotional support for parents when contending with such challenges as meetings in which they must negotiate their child's individualized education program (IEP).

The practical utility of these resources may be readily apparent. Perhaps the less obvious but remarkable thing about seemingly simple sources of information like these is the power they often give parents in locating and accessing other, multiple forms of support that may be emotional, instrumental, material, or physical in nature. With each small or large avenue of support that a family opts to integrate into its social support network, a new link is created that strengthens the connections between preexisting, new, and future systems of social support.

Chapter 9

Friendships Between Children with and without Developmental Disabilities

Christine M. Hurley-Geffner

The study of the development of friendships between typically developing children and children with disabilities, including autism, is worthy of systematic inquiry in its own right and is long overdue. This line of study is especially relevant at a time when school and community integration is becoming a reality for many children, including children who experience greater cognitive and/or physical challenges, and when typically available resources (e.g., attendant care, transportation) are decreasing every year. Indeed, after nearly 20 years of an emphasis on remediating the skill deficits of children with developmental disabilities (Snell, 1987) and teaching functional academics or functional life skills, parents, to a large extent, and many professionals and researchers are now beginning to see much value and importance in the development of friendships (Amado, 1993;

Guralnick, 1990; Hamre-Nietupski, Hendrickson, Nietupski, & Sasso, 1993; Hamre-Nietupski, Nietupski, & Strathe, 1992; Lutfiyya, 1988; Stainback & Stainback, 1987; Strully & Strully, 1985, 1989; Taylor & Bogdan, 1989). Parents, professionals, and researchers are also beginning to question the extent to which placing a primary emphasis on academics and functional skills, with relatively little emphasis on the development of relationships, has had an impact on the quality of the lives of individuals with developmental disabilities, as well as the lives of their family members and significant others (Guralnick, 1990; Strully & Strully, 1985, 1989).

This is certainly not to say that teaching academics or functional skills to persons with disabilities is not important and should be discontinued; however, to date there is much information about effective teaching and very little about the importance, development, and maintenance of the friendships or relationships of persons with developmental disabilities. The time has come for educators and researchers to take a close look at the development of friendships of persons with disabilities, including autism. Perhaps by examining the literature on friendships of typically developing children, the potential benefits of participation in a relationship for these children will begin to be acknowledged.

THE IMPORTANCE OF FRIENDSHIPS FOR TYPICAL CHILDREN

There is currently an extensive body of research that indicates that participating in meaningful relationships or friendships is an integral part of a typical child's development and well-being. Although some researchers believe that having friends is simply a developmental advantage, as opposed to a necessity (Hartup & Sancilio, 1986), there is a plenitude of research that seems to indicate otherwise. In addition to providing companionship and a context for the development of several different types of skills and support, friendships appear to help protect children from adjustment problems. Given this information, it seems likely that friendships are more important than some would believe and that they deserve a closer look.

Friends provide companionship for one another. When children, ages 6–14, were questioned about characteristics that were important to them in a friend, companionship was listed as an important domain to children older than 6 years of age (Bigelow, 1977; Bigelow & La Gaipa, 1975). Hayes (1978) and Hayes, Gershman, and Bolin (1980) also found companionship to be an important dimension in children's friendships.

Friendships can also create a context for the development of many different social behaviors. Researchers have found that children who are familiar with each other have an increased number of overtures toward their peers, have a greater amount of social interaction, and interact in a way that is cognitively more mature (Doyle, Connolly, & Rivest, 1980). Friendships have also been found to promote social development, including complex forms of play (Gottman & Parkhurst, 1980), social communication, group entry, cooperation, and impulse control (Hartup & Sancilio, 1986).

In addition to facilitating social development, Nelson and Aboud (1985) found that friendship seems to influence reasoning ability. When these researchers placed children in conflict situations with either friends or nonfriends, the level of interaction and discussion was greater between the children who were friends than the children who were not friends. The researchers also found that the discussion between friends was significantly more likely to lead to changes in responses in a positive and more mature direction. In line with this study, research that examines the influence that children have on one another yields similar results. In addition to selecting friends on the basis of similarity (Bigelow, 1977; Bigelow & La Gaipa, 1975; Tesser, Campbell, & Smith, 1984), there is strong evidence that children can become more similar during the course of a friendship as they influence each other's attitudes, social behavior, and academic achievement (Berndt, 1982; Root, 1977).

Within the context of friendship, children have the opportunity to develop the ability to form close relationships with others and to develop social behavior that may promote harmonious social interactions later in life (Crockett, 1984). There is a mutual responsiveness between friends that does not occur between nonfriends (Berndt, 1982; Tesser et al., 1984). This responsiveness allows for the creation of a context for the intimate sharing of thoughts and feelings (Berndt, 1982) and may contribute both to children's understandings of other people and to their understanding of themselves (Crockett, 1984; Hartup & Sancilio, 1986).

Theorists and researchers also believe that a child's interaction with his or her peer group may provide benefits that cannot be provided by adult–child interactions. Perry and Bussey (1984) emphasize that children learn how to dominate, protect, assume responsibility, reciprocate, appreciate another's point of view, and arrive at realistic estimates of their own competencies and other personal attributes through interactions within their peer groups. In addition, Fine (1981) found that friends can provide instruction in important concerns such as managing aggression and sexual relationships, which are often very difficult topics for adolescents to discuss with their parents. Meaningful relationships and friendships have also been found to mediate stress (Cobb, 1976).

Adding more credence to the importance of friendships in a child's life is the well-documented finding that children who have had difficult or negative relations with their peers during childhood are at risk for developing problems related to their mental health later in life. Researchers have found that these children have a greater incidence than their peers of engaging in delinquent behaviors (Robins, 1972; Roff & Sells, 1968; Roff, Sells, & Golden, 1972), having low school achievement (Westman, Rice, & Bermann, 1967), having problems in the armed services (Roff, 1961), and having schizophrenia (Roff, 1970; Roff, Knight, & Wertheim, 1976; Watt, 1978).

Janes, Hesselbrock, Myers, and Penniman (1979) found that teachers' ratings of children's relations with their peers were the best predictor of general mental status. In their study, they found that adults who as children had been rated by their teachers as having problems relating to their peers in school reported having a higher incidence of trouble with the law, arrests, psychiatric hospitalizations, job dismissals caused by behavioral problems, and less success progressing through school.

In an attempt to better understand the continuity and stability of negative peer relations, Coie and Dodge (1983) followed two age-group samples (third-grade and fifth-grade cohorts) of children over a period of 5 years. Their results indicate that children who were identified as rejected in the third-grade and fifth-grade cohorts were significantly likely to remain at that status for 3 and 5 years, respectively. This research supports the findings of "follow-back" studies and indicates that spontaneous recovery of negative peer relations is not likely. Taking into account this research, it appears that difficulty relating to one's peers sets into motion a negative cycle in which further opportunity to have positive relations becomes limited, which only serves to reduce the chances of remediation of the difficulties (Coie & Dodge, 1983; Bierman, Miller, & Stabb, 1987).

The research discussed here clearly supports the importance of childhood friendships for typically developing children. In addition to promoting the development of various abilities and providing a context of support, positive peer relations seem to influence a child's mental health (i.e., children who have had difficult peer relations seem to be at risk for developing a variety of social adjustment difficulties). It is highly likely that children with autism as well as other developmental disabilities would experience similar benefits from participation in meaningful social relationships. In addition, it is likely that friendships of children with developmental disabilities could provide some benefits based on the individual needs of each child. This has yet to be validated experimentally.

FRIENDSHIPS AMONG CHILDREN WITH DISABILITIES

To date, the research on existing benefits and importance of friendships to persons with developmental disabilities is limited at best (Guralnick, 1990). One study examined any existing differences in the play behavior of children with developmental disabilities who have friends versus those who do not have friends. Field (1984) found that the behavior of the two groups was indeed different. The former group of children were more responsive to their peers and spent more time involved in play with their peers. Interestingly, these children also spent more time engaging in negative behaviors, such as taking toys from peers, fussing, and expressing anger. Unfortunately, due to methodological issues, it cannot be determined whether participation in a friendship led to the observed changes or whether the differences observed led this group of children to have friends. In addition, Field's definition for the existence of friendship (i.e., a child who played with a particular child at least 66% of the time) may not have been a valid measure. Nevertheless, the study does yield some interesting findings.

A second study that sought to better understand the behavior of children with developmental disabilities and typically developing children who are friends analyzed the behavior of friendship pairs. Two friendship pairs were compared: In one pair both children were typically developing, and in the other pair one child had a developmental disability and the other child was typically developing. This study yielded several important findings, including the observation that typically developing children were more likely to select as friends other children who were typically developing. However, when typically developing children did select children with disabilities as friends, the latter were usually older than the former. A second finding was that the typically developing children responded positively at an equal level to the initiations of children with and without developmental disabilities. A third important finding of the study was that the behavior of the typically developing children directed toward other typically developing children was different in many ways than the behavior they directed toward children with developmental disabilities. The behavior directed toward typically developing children consisted of more initiations of reward-related activities, verbal compliments, organization of play activities, and sharing; the behavior directed toward children with developmental disabilities consisted of more instances of physical assistance, affection, and conflict resolution. A final finding indicated that the behavior of the typically developing children was more likely to be reciprocated by typically developing children than by children who had a developmental disability (Strain, 1984).

A third study presented information regarding the importance of friendships between typical children and children with developmental disabilities. Peck, Donaldson, and Pezzoli (1990) questioned high school students who had developed relationships with students labeled as having moderate or severe disabilities about any perceived benefits they had experienced based on their interactions. The results of the study indicate that the high school students did perceive benefits from their relationships with their peers who had disabilities. These benefits can be broken down into six different types including 1) improvements in self-concepts, 2) growth in social cognition, 3) increased tolerance of other people, 4) reduced fear of human differences, 5) development of personal principles, and

6) interpersonal acceptance and friendship. These findings are very encouraging, especially in light of the belief held by many that people without disabilities would not enjoy and/or would have nothing to gain from friendships with people with developmental disabilities.

Little is known about the importance or benefits of friendships to persons with developmental disabilities. Yet, after reviewing the literature on the friendships of typically developing children and considering the trends in the field of developmental disabilities, the need for the study of friendships for children with developmental disabilities is especially poignant. Before moving forward, however, it is important to examine and understand how current practices, both in research and application, may affect success in understanding and facilitating relationships. There are likely many such practices that have had and are continuing to have a negative impact. In 1984 one of the first books reporting research conducted on friendships between typically developing peers and children with disabilities was published (see Field, Roopnarine, & Segal, 1984). Around this same time, parents and professionals began advocating strongly for the development of friendships for children with disabilities (Strully & Strully, 1985). Yet, 10 years later, there is still very little known.

There are four practices that seem to particularly limit advancement in this area: 1) limiting the opportunities that children with developmental disabilities have to interact with their typically developing peers; 2) placing too much emphasis on the development of social skills; 3) placing too much emphasis on remediating the "deficits" of the child with the disability; and 4) failing to acknowledge the capabilities of children with developmental disabilities, including those children who are often defined by their social difficulties (e.g., children with autism). To move forward successfully in this area and come to understand the relationships of children with developmental disabilities, each of these four areas must be examined with close scrutiny.

FACTORS ADVERSELY AFFECTING THE DEVELOPMENT OF FRIENDSHIPS

Limited Opportunity

Time and time again, children with developmental disabilities are not given the opportunity to establish and build meaningful relationships with other children. It is this lack of opportunity that creates the largest barrier to the development of friendships between children with disabilities and typical children (Grenot-Scheyer, Coots, & Falvey, 1990). There are two ways that a child's opportunity to form relationships with his or her peers is limited. The first is by limiting the contact children have with one another, and the second is by limiting the support of teachers (i.e., as represented in the curriculum).

The complete lack of opportunity to establish relationships occurs whenever a child with a disability is placed in a segregated school or classroom. After all, children become friends with other children who attend their schools, share their classrooms, live in their neighborhoods, and share their daily experiences (Strully & Strully, 1985). For a child who has no contact with typically developing peers, the chances of establishing friendships or meaningful relationships with those peers is severely limited, if not impossible (Brown et al., 1989a, 1989b).

It is relatively easy to recognize that the complete segregation of children with disabilities (through placement at a segregated school or classroom) from their typically developing peers will greatly reduce any chance they have of establishing and maintaining relationships with those peers. However, when considering the effects of mainstreaming (i.e., the child spending some amount of time in regular education classes instead of all of his or her time in a segregated class) on the development of relationships between children with disabilities and their typically developing peers, the picture becomes more blurred. Currently, there has been no research conducted that examines the effects of limited placement on the development of friendships of children with developmental disabilities. However, an indirect way to determine the effect mainstreaming may have on the development of relationships is to examine the attitudes of typically developing peers toward their mainstreamed peers. Indeed, one of the strongest arguments given for removing children with developmental disabilities from their segregated classes and placing them in regular classes for portions of the day is that doing so will reduce the stigma they face (Gottlieb, Semmel, & Veldman, 1978). Ironically, this has not been found to be the case. Children who are mainstreamed during various times of the day have been found to elicit the negative attitudes of their peers (Gerber, 1977; Gottlieb & Budoff, 1973; Gottlieb & Davis, 1973; Gottlieb & Leyser, 1981; Honig & McCarron, 1988). In addition, some research indicates that children with disabilities are less often rejected when they remain in their self-contained classrooms (Goodman, Gottlieb, & Harrison, 1972; Gottlieb & Budoff, 1973).

These findings have led researchers interested in improving the social status and social relationships of children with disabilities to develop intervention programs and study their effects. A number of these types of studies have indeed reported that the attitudes of the typically developing children can be improved. Voeltz (1982) and Esposito and Peach (1983) both found that interactions specifically structured to be positive between children with disabilities and their typically developing peers led to increased positive attitudes for the typically developing peers. In another study, McHale and Simeonsson (1980) examined the effects of positive interactions on the understanding of autism as well as the attitudes of typically developing peers. Although the researchers found no differences in attitude (i.e., attitudes were positive at both pre- and posttesting), they did find an increase in the understanding of autism after the intervention.

In another study aimed at improving attitudes, Shortridge (1982) attempted to determine the effects of a specific intervention program on the perceptions of typically developing children of the level of intelligence, self-concept, and play capabilities of children with physical disabilities. Shortridge also assessed the typical children's attitudes about having children with physical disabilities mainstreamed into their classrooms. The intervention program consisted of promoting the awareness of disabilities, the acceptance of children with disabilities, and the understanding of similarities and differences between the children. The intervention utilized a storytelling experience to present the material. The results of this study indicated that the intervention was only partially effective. Specifically, significant positive shifts were found in the typically developing children's perception of their peers' play capabilities and self-concept. No significant effects were noted in the typically developing children's perception of level of intelligence or their attitudes toward mainstreaming. Shortridge hypothesized that the lack of improvement in the mainstreaming domain may have been related to the abstract nature of the question used to assess this domain. Because this study dealt with hypothetical situations, some caution should be taken when interpreting the results.

In an attempt to understand how perceived similarity between students influences their attitudes toward one another, Siperstein and Chatillon (1982) studied fifth- and sixth-grade children's attitudes, as assessed by affective feelings and behavioral intentions, toward children with mental retardation. The children with disabilities were presented as either similar to the target children or in neutral terms. The target children were sampled from schools that were either attended by or not attended by children with disabilities. The results indicated that the attitudes of the target children were more favorable toward the children with developmental disabilities who were perceived as similar. However, this result was only found for the children in the school that was attended by children with disabilities, and it was stronger for girls than for boys. Although this study used vignettes to present children with mental retardation and did not assess overt behavior, the findings are interesting and suggest that children may be more accepting of children with developmental disabilities who are seen as having similar interests. More important, the study suggests that these results may only be applicable to children who are exposed to children with disabilities.

Taken as a whole, the findings from the studies discussed here, as well as others, have led researchers to conclude that mainstreaming alone is not likely to improve the attitudes and acceptance toward children with disabilities (Honig & McCarron, 1988; Jenkins, Speltz, & Odom, 1985; Voeltz, 1982). Indeed, it is widely held that systematic programming can be effective and is necessary to facilitate the positive attitudes and understanding of typical children toward their peers with disabilities (Gresham & Reschly, 1986; McHale & Simeonsson, 1980; Voeltz, 1982). The next question that must be considered at this point is whether systematic programming alone is sufficient in improving the attitudes of typical children toward their peers with developmental disabilities. It would certainly be much easier for educators if it were. Unfortunately, the patterns discussed here have not been shown to exist consistently and unequivocally in all situations (Simpson, 1980). For example, Schnorr (1990) found that, even with specific efforts by the teacher to make a mainstreamed student a part of the class, the child was seen as transient and not really belonging to the other children's social structure. For these children, they considered full-time attendance to be the most important variable in determining who belonged to the class and who they were willing to accept.

It would appear then that even when efforts are made to include children with disabilities and facilitate their acceptance, children who are mainstreamed may still be at a disadvantage when considering the development of relationships with their peers. This is supported by three studies that indicate that children who are fully integrated into classrooms attended by typically developing peers, with specific efforts made by the teacher to include and educate all children, can and do develop relationships with their typically developing peers (Biklen, Corrigan, & Quick, 1989; Evans, Salisbury, Palombaro, Berryman, & Hollowood, 1992; Lewis, 1994). These studies are especially encouraging because they do not simply address the attitudes of the typical children, an indirect method of assessing the possibility of developing relationships, but demonstrate the existence of actual relationships and friendships.

In addition to having their contact with typically developing children limited, children with disabilities have not been given the opportunity to learn skills or behaviors that may be important in the development of relationships in their school programs. This is the result of teachers, special education administrators, and professionals placing an emphasis on the acquisition of academic or functional life skills (Hamre-Nietupski et al., 1992; Snell, 1987) for children with disabilities. Unfortunately, when taught under the wrong conditions, the emphasis on teaching academic and functional life skills can be at the expense of teaching skills or behaviors that may help facilitate social relationships (Gresham, 1984).

In an attempt to discover whether teaching social behaviors was emphasized by teachers, Pray, Hall, and Markley (1992) conducted a study that examined the type and frequency of social behaviors that appeared on the individualized education programs (IEPs) of 258 special education students across 2 consecutive years. The researchers examined the children in all grades (kindergarten through 12th). The results of this study indicate that only 34% of the IEPs contained objectives that addressed social behaviors and skills. When examining the 34% of the objectives containing social skills, the researchers found that most of these objectives were academic-related social skills (e.g., "follows teacher's verbal directions" or "works steadily for the required time"). Interpersonal behavior related to peer interaction and teacher–student interaction represented only 10% of the top 22 social skills listed on the IEPs. Perhaps the most surprising finding was that 18% of the IEPs for children with behavioral difficulties contained no social objectives.

In addition to teachers failing to include social behavior objectives on IEPs, a report by Strain (1981) found that the educational curriculum developed to alleviate social withdrawal is, at best, severely lacking. Specifically, of the 60 educational curriculum materials examined, 80% did not specify clear behavioral objectives, 90% had not been shown to produce either immediate- or long-term child behavior changes, 97% contained global curriculum targets that were determined on what appeared to be a "best guess" basis, 80% were concerned with adult–child interactions only, and none provided for systematic programming with the use of peers. It is very easy to see, based on the findings reported here, that children's opportunities to participate in meaningful social relationships with their typically developing peers is limited not only by lack of direct contact with their peers but also by a lack of emphasis on building social behaviors or creating social contexts that would facilitate and support these relationships.

To summarize, the fundamental principles of access, belongingness, and opportunity seem to be met sufficiently only in the context of full inclusion (as opposed to mainstreaming). In addition, the importance of teachers taking responsibility to help children with developmental disabilities and their peers learn to interact with and relate to one another cannot be overstated. When these two conditions are met, children with developmental disabilities, including autism, will finally be receiving the opportunities they need and deserve to establish friendships with their typically developing peers.

Emphasis on Social Skills Development

Fortunately, a number of researchers have addressed the need for focusing on relationships between children with disabilities and their typically developing peers. However, much of this work is somewhat limited by an emphasis placed on the development of individual social skills for children with disabilities. The thinking that guides the emphasis placed on social skills development, simply stated, is that children who do not have friends lack social skills, and children with developmental disabilities often lack social skills; therefore, children with developmental disabilities do not have friends because they lack social skills. This assumption may have partially developed from the literature that examines the peer relations and social behaviors of typically developing children who are unpopular with their peers. Much of this research indicates that children who are unpopular with their peers (i.e., rejected or neglected) have difficulties relating to their peers. Specifically, the research indicates that children who are unpopular are more likely to be aggressive (Bierman et al., 1987; Dodge, 1983; Dodge, Coie, Pettit, & Price, 1990; Ladd, 1983), to engage in behavior that is disruptive to ongoing social interactions (Dodge, 1983; Dodge, Schlundt, Schocken, & Delugach, 1983), to spend time in unoccupied play behaviors (Ladd, 1983), and to be unsuccessful when initiating bids for interactions (Kennedy, 1990).

In addition, observations of behavioral differences between children with developmental disabilities and typically developing children have led researchers to focus on teaching individual social skills. For example, researchers have attempted to teach children with disabilities social skills such as appropriate eye contact (Berler, Gross, & Drabman, 1982; Taras, Matson, & Leary, 1988), greeting responses (Kamps et al., 1992; Stokes, Baer, & Jackson, 1974), delayed imitation (Lancioni, 1982), appropriate sitting skills (Taras et al., 1988), initiation of interactions (Coe, Matson, Fee, Manikam, & Linarello, 1990; Haring & Lovinger, 1989; Kamps et al., 1992; McConnell, Sisson, Cort, & Strain, 1991), responses to intitiations from peers (Coe et al., 1990; Kamps et al., 1992; McConnell et al., 1991), giving and accepting compliments (Kamps et al., 1992), turn taking (Kamps et al., 1992), sharing (Kamps et al., 1992; McConnell et al., 1991), various play or game responses (Coe et al., 1990; Donder & Nietupski, 1981; Gaylord-Ross, Haring, Breen, & Pitts-Conway, 1984; Goldstein, Wickstrom, Hoyson, Jamieson, & Odom, 1988; Haring, 1985; Lancioni, 1982; Stahmer & Schreibman, 1992), and various social language and conversation skills (Berler et al., 1982; Charlop & Milstein, 1989; Downing, 1987; Haring, Roger, Lee, Breen, & Gaylord-Ross, 1986; Hunt, Alwell, & Goetz, 1988; Kamps et al., 1992; L.K. Koegel, Koegel, Hurley, & Frea, 1992; R.L. Koegel & Frea, 1993; Lancioni, 1982; McConnell et al., 1991). There are also a number of studies that have been developed to examine the reduction of negative behaviors (Dougherty, Fowler, & Paine, 1985; Taras et al., 1988).

This type of research has yielded a wealth of information. It is now known that children with developmental disabilities can acquire social skills and can learn to control disruptive behaviors that may interfere with peer interactions. In addition, the types of interventions that are effective in reaching these goals are known. Furthermore, research indicates that peers can be used as intervention agents of social skill development for children with disabilities, including children with autism. There is also new information about the effect of various conditions on the acquisition of social skills (e.g., that a high ratio of teacher involvement may interfere with the development of social skills). Finally, researchers have clarified many factors that relate to the generalization and maintenance of social skills in children with developmental disabilities.

Although the skills learned in these studies may have improved and enhanced interactions between children, the studies are limited in relation to the development of friendships. Specifically, the research cannot tell whether there are any other factors that may lead to the development of friendships. This issue takes on greater significance after reviewing the development of friendships of typically developing children, which demonstrates that a number of factors may be influential to friendship development. Common interests (Hayes et al., 1980), exposure to one another (Bigelow & La Gaipa, 1975; Hayes, 1978), common abilities (Tesser et al., 1984), and gender (Erwin, 1993) may all have an impact on the development of friendships independent of the existence and use of so-called social skills.

In addition to the literature on typically developing children's friendships, a preliminary study by this author that examines the relationships of typically developing adolescents and their peers with disabilities indicates that other variables may influence the development of relationships. This study examined the perceptions of typically developing adolescents who were participating in a club that provided friendship networks for children with disabilities. Each adolescent was questioned about what behaviors or skills might facilitate the acceptance of the peer with whom they and their social network had been matched with and what things might improve their relationship with the peer. Most adolescents did not identify any discrete behaviors that should be learned by their peers

with disabilities, except for increased communication. Instead, a number of the adolescents noted that their relationships could be improved if they were able to spend more time
with their peer (the structure of the club allowed each network to spend one day a week
with the peer with whom they were matched). Taken together, the results of this study and
research conducted on the friendships of typically developing peers indicate that many
factors may lead to the development of friendships. All of these, and any other possible
factors, would expand the data relating to the development of relationships.

Perhaps the strongest argument for the need for more research in the area of friendships is the lack of a clear relationship between social competence (i.e., acquisition and
performance of social skills) and the acceptance of children with disabilities. Few studies
clearly demonstrate that social competence (defined as the acquisition of social skills)
improves their acceptance. In addition, some evidence indicates that the question may be
more complex (Bierman & Furman, 1984; Evans et al., 1992). For example, Evans et al.
examined the behavior and acceptance of children with severe developmental disabilities
who were participating in an inclusive school environment. The researchers observed the
classroom for a period of 7 months. The researchers concluded that social competence was
not related to acceptance. When comparing the acceptance of the children with severe disabilities to the typically developing children, it was found that some of the most challenged children whose formal skills were observed to be very limited were rated as very
popular. The researchers hypothesized that the typically developing children may have
categorized and judged the children whose disabilities were very obvious differently than
they would other children.

In another study that supports the idea that social competence may not be the only
variable related to acceptance, Bierman and Furman (1984) did not target children with
severe developmental disabilities but instead targeted children who were rated at the bot-
tom of their class in terms of acceptance and who exhibited delays in communication-
related behaviors. In this study, the target children were randomly assigned to one of four
intervention conditions: 1) conversational skills instruction, 2) peer involvement under
subordinate goals, 3) conversational skills instruction combined with peer involvement,
and 4) a no-intervention control. The results indicated that children who received only
conversational skills instruction demonstrated increases in the targeted behaviors but did
not improve their level of acceptance, whereas children in the peer involvement group did
not improve their conversational skills but did temporarily improve their acceptance. The
children who seemed to fare the best were the children who received skills instruction and
peer involvement. These children were shown to increase their skills and showed sustained improvements in social status. Taken as a whole, the results of these studies indicate
that improvement in social competence alone may not be enough to improve the social
acceptance of a child with developmental disabilities. At the very least, the results of this
research provide enough support for the importance of closely examining other variables.

Just as it is likely that many factors influence the development of friendships, it is
likely that one of those factors is the development of certain behaviors. After all, children
who are friends relate to and interact with one another. However, rather than call these
behaviors "social skills," it might be helpful to use a less misleading term. The term *social
skill* may refer to any behavior that is used when interacting with another and might be
used in any situation. For example, a certain social skill or set of social skills may be
required as part of a person's job. Although these behaviors might be absolutely critical to
the person's success in that environment, they may have no impact on the development or
maintenance of a person's friendships.

Given that there are probably some "friendship" or "relationship" skills that have an
impact on the development of a relationship, how do we determine what these skills might

be? In terms of research methodology, the only way to understand whether the acquisition or use of certain behaviors affects the development of relationships and friendships among children is by conducting studies in which the behaviors or skills are the independent variable.

This leads to another roadblock that serves to limit understanding of the social relationships of children with disabilities. This is the method by which the skills or behaviors that become the targets of intervention are selected. The social behaviors that have been targeted in interventions have not been empirically demonstrated to lead to meaningful differences in the relationships of children. In addition, it appears that the behaviors that have been selected have been either based on an adult perspective as opposed to a child's perspective or based on observations of children without disabilities (Tremblay, Strain, Hendrickson, & Shores, 1981). Both of these methods of identifying social behavior that is important to a child's relationships may be problematic. When skills or behaviors have been selected based on an adult value system, very few of the studies attempt to teach the child with a disability what children do most—play. Indeed, when examining the literature on the remediation of social difficulties, it is found that only a small number of the studies have attempted to teach play repertoires to children with disabilities (Coe et al., 1990; Donder & Nietupski, 1981; Haring, 1985; Haring & Lovinger, 1989). Unfortunately, only one of these studies attempted to determine the effects of the newly learned play behaviors on the relationships of the children. Donder and Nietupski did indicate that contact between the children with disabilities and their typically developing peers had increased following the intervention, but this was an anecdotal finding.

The selection of social behaviors through the observation of children without disabilities is likely to be more effective in identifying valid targets than reliance on an adult-driven model but must be used cautiously. It is likely that relationships between children with disabilities and their typically developing peers will be different in some ways from the relationships of typically developing peers. Cole (1986), for example, looked at the interactions between typically developing peers and children with physical disabilities and noted that the typically developing children had to do things that they would not have to do when interacting with other typical children (e.g., position toys). There are a number of challenges with which children with disabilities might be faced (e.g., limited verbal communication, cognitive delays) that would require different styles of interaction (e.g., using sign language, less sophisticated play repertoires). To understand the relationships of children with disabilities and their peers, it is important to consider the behaviors and interactions of these children when they are interacting with one another.

Another problem derived from the assumption that acquisition of social skills will lead to friendships for children with developmental disabilities is the translation of this assumption into a prerequisite model. Specifically, many researchers and teachers have drawn the conclusion that friendships are not possible in the absence of social skills (Anastasiow, 1984; Gresham, 1982). This presents a problem for children with developmental disabilities, including autism. Given this line of thinking, other factors important to the development of relationships, such as children sharing common interests, may be overlooked. In addition, given a special education model that strives to teach children in a specialized environment the behaviors or skills they need to advance to the next less restrictive level, children's opportunities to interact with their typically developing peers could be greatly limited. This idea is especially problematic for children who may have a difficult time learning a set of social skills or who may never acquire the social skills that are being required by the researcher/teacher or that are exhibited by typical children. In addition, many skills that may be necessary or important for the development of a relationship may only be acquired (or acquired much more rapidly) within the context of a friendship. By requiring the acquisition of a set of social skills to participate in a friendship, researchers, professionals, and educators may be creating a no-win situation for the child with developmental disabilities.

Emphasis on Changing the Child

Another factor that inhibits the understanding and the facilitation of friendships for children with developmental disabilities is researchers' and clinicians' emphasis on changing the child with the disability without taking into account the importance of the relationship between the child and his or her peers. Many believe that the individual with a developmental disability, especially autism, is deviant (i.e., if the child would only act or become more normal, then he or she would be able to make and be worthy of having friends). Consider, for example, the following quote by Hops (1981):

> The recent proliferation of social skills training and assessment literature is based on the assumption that certain individuals have specific skill deficits that preclude their successful social functioning. The primary goal of assessment is to identify an individual's specific deficits so that appropriate treatment can be planned and carried out. (p. 33)

Also, consider this quote by Anastasiow (1984):

> Developing the social skills demanded by society for such access is an important issue, since, as we have seen, the handicapped child typically has social deficits that need to be remediated. Thus, we return to the essential issue . . . : how to facilitate the handicapped person's social skills early in life so as to enable a larger percentage of these persons to have access to the full range of events in our society when they are adults. (p. 216)

Such statements could be misinterpreted as suggesting that an individual will only be able to participate fully in a range of human experiences and events once he or she has acquired the so-called social behaviors. However, participation in a relationship, whether it be friendship or any other relationship, is a combined effort of the persons involved (Brady, McEvoy, Gunter, Shores, & Fox, 1984; Grenot-Scheyer et al., 1990). Strain, Shores, and Timm (1977) illustrate the importance of studying the relationships between the interacting individuals as opposed to placing emphasis on one individual. Their discussion of the importance of reciprocity is based on the work of Strain and his colleagues, which was conducted with children who exhibited delays in social relations. The work of Strain and Timm (1974) and Strain, Shores, and Kerr (1976) clearly demonstrates that increases in typically developing children's positive social behavior led to the concomitant increases in positive social behavior of the peers with developmental disabilities.

Stainback and Stainback (1987) also agree that, in addition to the child with a disability being required to learn specific skills, the typically developing child must also learn skills. This point is easily made when considering the case of the friendship between a girl with significant disabilities and her peer. This girl does not communicate verbally, but her friend has learned to understand her use of gestures and body language in such a way that they communicate effectively with one another (Strully & Strully, 1985) and enjoy each other's company. Without the peer's willingness to learn and utilize a different form of communication, their friendship would not have been possible.

The idea that the typically developing peer must also learn skills is supported by research that indicates that children without disabilities can have a negative impact on the social behavior of children who exhibit difficulties in peer relations. Strain, Odom, and McConnell (1984) found that regular education students may impede the development of social behaviors of children with disabilities by ignoring or punishing their social behaviors. In a study yielding similar results, Dodge (1983) examined the development of sociometric status in children's peer groups over time. He discovered that boys who became neglected or rejected engaged in inappropriate behavior during their initial contact with their peers. These boys then appeared to gain a reputation such that any initiations they later made were rebuffed by their peers even when their approaches were appropriate.

Another way that typical peers can have a negative effect on the behavior of children with disabilities is by engaging in stereotyping behavior. Miller et al. (1991) demonstrated the detrimental effect that labels and stereotyped expectations can have on peer relations. The researchers had two groups of children (children with disabilities and typical children) talk socially on the phone to children from another school in an attempt to get acquainted. The children from the other school were children who did not have developmental disabilities. The two groups of targeted children were told that the person they were about to talk to either had difficulty learning or did not have trouble learning. The behavior of both partners was analyzed for appropriateness and grade level by two groups of judges who were blind to the study. The results showed that, when questioned before talking on the phone to their partner, children who believed they would be talking to special education students noted that they expected their partners to behave in a stigmatizing fashion (i.e., at a lower level and less appropriately). After their conversations were over, they reported that their partner had behaved in a relatively stigmatizing way. This was despite the fact that the judges' ratings revealed no behavioral differences between partners who supposedly did and did not have learning problems. In addition, the children with disabilities were rated as engaging in more stigmatizing social behavior only when they believed that they were talking to children who were in regular education. Finally, the results indicated that the typical children who believed they were talking to a special education student went to such great lengths to accommodate their partner's supposed lower cognitive abilities that they appeared to be in a lower grade than did the children with disabilities in the same condition. Taken together, the results of this study demonstrate that expectations have observable effects on children with disabilities and typically developing children's social interaction with one another. Placing all the emphasis on changing the children with developmental disabilities to improve their "deficits" will likely feed into this stereotyping behavior.

A necessary consideration is determining and establishing a balance between helping the typically developing peer take responsibility in the relationship without becoming overresponsible. Indeed, it has been found that the style of interaction of typically developing peers can often be characterized as "adult-like" or "older sibling–like." This type of uneven interaction may also have an adverse effect on the development of relationships, especially friendships. It is apparent when examining the results of these studies that the ways children interact with one another is a complex phenomenon. Each child's interactions affects his or her peers' interactions, which in turn affects the child's interaction, and so forth. Researchers and teachers can no longer place all the emphasis on changing the child who has a disability without considering the behavior of his or her peers and the relationship among them.

Viewing the Child as Incapable

Another practice that interferes with the development of friendships between typically developing children and children with developmental disabilities is the belief that some groups of children are simply not capable of participating in meaningful relationships.

Indeed, the inability to establish relationships with others and the lack of appropriate social behaviors have been defining characteristics of autism since the first paper defining autism was written by Kanner in 1943. He included six behavioral categories in this paper—the first of which he called "extreme autistic aloneness." He defined this as the failure during infancy to develop typical relationships with parents, general unresponsiveness to people, failure to interact with peers, and the failure to acknowledge the presence or absence of parents or others. He believed this characteristic to be present from birth. After Kanner's paper appeared, controversy emerged regarding whether autism was a separate entity that could be differentiated from other forms of childhood psychosis. Following this controversy, Kanner reduced his original six defining characteristics to only two. These included extreme autistic aloneness and preoccupation with the preservation of sameness.

Although there continue to be controversy and disagreement about the specific diagnostic criteria to be used when applying a diagnosis of autism, the three main sets of criteria in wide use all include a crtierion that addresses social difficulties and the inability to relate to others. It is commonly held that profound and pervasive difficulties with social attachment and behavior are the hallmarks of autism and are primary to its diagnosis (Schreibman, 1988).

It is probably not surprising, given the emphasis placed on the social difficulties of individuals with autism, that some researchers, teachers, and practitioners believe that it is not possible for these children to establish meaningful relationships with their families and peers. However, this belief alone may serve to further limit or negatively influence the possibility of establishing meaningful relationships. Rosenthal and Jacobson (1968) demonstrated the power of a teacher's expectations of his or her students. In their study, children were given a nonverbal IQ test. Teachers were then led to believe that this test predicted which students would show sudden bursts of intellectual growth during the academic year. Each teacher was given the names of five students who would probably prove to be "rapid bloomers." These so-called rapid bloomers were randomly selected from the class rosters. The only way that these children differed from the other children was that their teachers expected them to achieve at a higher level. When the students were retested 8 months later, the researchers found that, among the children in the lower grades, the so-called rapid bloomers showed significantly greater gains in IQ and reading achievement than the other students in the class. In other words, some of the children who were expected to do well did, in fact, do better than other students of comparable ability.

In an attempt to understand how a teacher's expectations influence a child's performance, Brophy and Good (1970) observed student–teacher interaction in four first-grade classrooms. They found that students who were expected to do better were treated differently from those who were expected to do poorly. Teachers demanded better performance from the "high-expectancy" students and were more likely to praise these children for answering questions correctly. In contrast, "low-expectancy" students were more likely to receive criticism from the teacher when they answered questions incorrectly. On those occasions when high-expectancy students did answer incorrectly, the teacher often responded by rephrasing the question, thus giving these children another opportunity to succeed. Brophy and Good summarize by saying, "teachers do, in fact, communicate different performance expectations to different children through their classroom behavior, and the nature of this differential treatment is such as to encourage the children to begin to respond in ways which would confirm teacher expectancies" (p. 373). If teachers, parents, or practitioners do not expect a child with autism to be able to participate in meaningful social relationships, then they may interfere with this by failing to communicate expectations to participate socially, by failing to structure the environment or activities to encourage social interaction, or by punishing or failing to reward attempts toward social interaction.

To put things into perspective, one should consider that the diagnostic criteria and theories used to describe or explain the social difficulties associated with autism have been largely based on clinical observations rather than empirical investigations (Howlin, 1986). Because of this lack of empirical investigation, little is known about social problems in autism (Schopler & Mesibov, 1986). Without a sound base of empirical investigation, an adequate theory of social relations and behavior in autism cannot be developed.

In the relatively limited situations in which the results of empirical investigations are considered in an explanation of the social behavior of children with autism, a different picture begins to emerge (Howlin, 1986). For example, the attachment behavior of children with autism has been studied empirically by Sigman, Ungerer, Mundy, and Sherman (1987). In this study, the researchers matched a group of 3- to 5-year-old children with autism with groups of typically developing children and children with Down syndrome of similar mental age. As a group, the children with autism showed more social behaviors toward their mothers than toward strangers and interacted significantly more after periods of separation. In addition, the results indicated that the amount of responsiveness toward their mothers was related to the amount of symbolic play shown by the children. This finding, taken with the finding that the children with autism were generally no less responsive than the children with Down syndrome, but that both groups of these children were less responsive than typically developing children, seems to indicate that the differences in attachment behavior may be more a function of cognitive development than autism.

Sigman and her colleagues conducted another study that yielded similar results (Sigman, Mundy, Sherman & Ungerer, 1986). In this study, the researchers observed the play behavior of a group of children with autism and their mothers. As in their previous study, the researchers included two control groups. One group consisted of children with mental retardation who were matched as closely as possible for mental age, chronological age, and mother's level of education, and another consisted of typically developing children matched for mental age and mother's level of education. The researchers found that the group of children with autism looked at their caregivers, touched their caregivers, vocalized, and whined as much as the children in the other two groups.

Another behavioral characteristic that many theories have attempted to explain, with limited understanding, is active physical withdrawal (Howlin, 1986). Strain and Fox (1981) suggest that high rates of stereotyped behaviors emitted by children with autism may give the impression that these children are aloof when they are not actually engaging in active withdrawal from social situations. In addition, R.L. Koegel and Covert (1972) found that children's responsiveness to their environment increased when ritualistic behaviors were reduced. Another study that examined the effects of task variables (activities that were preferred by the child versus those arbitrarily determined by an adult) on social avoidance behavior in children with autism was conducted by R.L. Koegel, Dyer, and Bell (1987). Their results revealed a negative correlation between social avoidance behavior and appropriate child-preferred activities. Adding to the power of this study, the results indicated that social avoidance could be manipulated within a reversal design and would predictably decrease when the child was engaged in child-preferred activities.

There have also been studies conducted to assess different play behaviors of children with autism. Ungerer and Sigman (1981) found that the children with autism in their study displayed a wide range of play behaviors in both unstructured and structured settings, but they spent more time in simple manipulation of objects. A series of studies conducted by McHale and her colleagues (McHale, 1983; McHale, Olley, & Marcus, 1981; McHale, Olley, Marcus, & Simeonsson, 1981) found that children with autism engaged in more cooperative play when playing with typically developing classmates and more stereotyped behaviors and solitary play when interacting with other children with autism. When children with autism were observed in a class exclusively for other children with autism, almost 75% of the behavior of the children was asocial (McHale, Simeonsson, Marcus, & Olley, 1980). Based on these findings, it appears that deliberate attempts to facilitate the interaction between children with autism and their typically developing peers are needed or the isolation of children with autism is likely to continue (Howlin, 1986). This is certainly a different interpretation than the preconception that children with autism are not capable of or motivated to participate in social relationships.

For society to progress in a meaningful way and learn to facilitate the development of relationships of children with autism and their typically developing peers, it needs to replace preconceived notions and theories of social behavior based on simple clinical observations. Instead, theories and understanding should be based on the results of controlled empirical investigation. Any interpretation of observational data collected must be based on the analysis of behavioral systems rather than discrete behaviors, as well as the analysis of behaviors according to the specific social context in which they occur (Howlin, 1986).

LAYING THE FOUNDATION FOR RESEARCH ON FRIENDSHIPS

If researchers are to make meaningful advances in their knowledge of friendships between individuals with developmental disabilities and typically developing persons, a solid methodological foundation should precede all work that is done. The importance of conducting well-planned studies cannot be overstated. There are several factors that should be taken into consideration when building this foundation.

Defining Friendship

The first step to understanding friendships of persons with developmental disabilities is to develop a practical, meaningful, and measurable or observable definition of friendship. Defining friendships has proven to be a challenging endeavor for researchers. Indeed, "there are almost as many definitions of friendship as there are definers" (MacAndrew & Edgerton, 1966, p. 612). One definition that appears pragmatic for educators and researchers is that friendship is a bond between two individuals that can be characterized by mutual preference for one another, a positive affective style, an ability to engage in social interactions, and an ability to last over time (Hartup, 1975; Howes, 1983). Another important characteristic to consider when defining or examining friendships of persons with developmental disabilities is whether the relationship is entered into without obligation (Barber & Hupp, 1993).

Currently, there are two common methods that are used to assess relationships among children: sociometric assessment techniques and behavioral observation. It may be helpful to consider each of the techniques and their ability to assess the existence of friendships of children based on the previous definition. Neither of the techniques is able to assess the existence of all of the characteristics in the definition; however, their combined use certainly comes closer and may be sufficient to cover most characteristics.

Perhaps the most commonly used technique for determining relationships between children is sociometric assessment, which was developed in the 1930s. This procedure is widely used due to its practical and psychometric properties. There are basically four types of sociometric assessment techniques used, each differing slightly in the temporal stability of the scores produced and in the dimensions of social status that they can be used to study. The techniques are the peer nomination method, the rating scale method, the paired comparison method, and the descriptive matching method.

The peer nomination method, which is the most commonly used method of the four, requires children to name classmates who fit a particular sociometric criterion and may be based on positive criteria (e.g., "Name three classmates with whom you like to play") or negative criteria (e.g., "Name three classmates with whom you do not like to play"). A child receives a score based on the number of nominations he or she receives. The number of positive nominations is used as an indicator of acceptance or popularity and the number of negative nominations is used as an indicator of rejection. Children who receive neither positive or negative nominations are generally referred to as neglected (Asher & Taylor, 1981). More recently, another classification called *controversial* has emerged. Children who are considered controversial are those children who receive many positive nominations as well as many negative nominations (Dodge, 1983).

The second type of sociometric technique commonly used is referred to as the rating scale method. For this method, children are given a list of all the students in the class and asked to rate each child on a numerical scale according to a particular sociometric criterion (Singleton & Asher, 1977). This method has been used in various ways, including requiring the children to rate how much they like to play or work with each other on a scale from 1 (do not like to) to 5 (like to a lot) (Hymel & Asher, 1977; Oden & Asher, 1977) or requiring the children to rate each of their classmates on a 6-point scale from their very best friends to children they dislike. In this latter method, the points on the scale correspond to descriptive paragraphs that are read aloud to the pupils (Monroe & Howe, 1971). The rating scale method has some advantages when comparing it to the nomination method. This method obtains information regarding all the members in the class, whereas the nomination method obtains information on only the children who are nominated. It also has superior test–retest reliability (Asher & Taylor, 1981).

The third method used is referred to as the paired comparison method. When using this method, children are presented one at a time with all possible pairings of class members and must select the most preferred classmate for each pairing. The measure is scored by calculating the total number of times each child is selected by classmates for all pairings. Similar to the rating scale method, this technique ensures that each child responds to every other child in the class, but because children make their ratings based on a direct comparison of another child it has the potential to yield more information regarding dyadic relationships. The paired comparison method demonstrates strong temporal stability, but is time consuming and therefore not used as often (Asher & Taylor, 1981).

The fourth method is called the descriptive matching method. This method requires the child to nominate classmates on a variety of attributes or behaviors. An example of this method is called the Revised Class Play (Masten, Morrison, & Pelligrini, 1985). Children are told that they are the director of a class play starring the students in the class and are told to select students to play each role. The children are asked to select children for roles that seem to suit them in real life. This method appears to tap a child's overall reputation in the peer group and has the advantage of not asking children to compile a "hate list." This method also provides more information about a child's social behavior than the nomination technique and generally receives acceptable measures of reliability and validity (Kennedy, 1988).

Although sociometric techniques can yield information about the relationships of children, they were developed and are primarily used to identify groups of children (without developmental disabilities) who are at risk for developing adjustment problems later in life. These techniques measure general acceptance (or lack thereof) within a group rather than individual friendships between children. When considering the earlier definition of friendship, these measures will most likely be able to assess the mutual preference for one another; however, this will only be the case if the assessments are used on an individual basis.

The second way that relationships among children are measured is through direct behavioral observations. Direct observation was the most common method of measurement in child development and educational research during the 1930s and 1940s. With more researchers conducting studies in laboratory settings, direct observation decreased but was reintroduced with the advent of behavior modification and therapy (Hops, 1981). The conclusion that a relationship exists between two children is drawn if the children are seen (through direct observation) interacting together. Interactions can consist of several types of behavior, including playing together, sharing, helping, cooperating, praising, or nurturing one another (Honig & McCarron, 1988). Based on the observation of behavior, judgments are made about the children's relationship. Typically, direct observation has been used to determine the existence or absence of specific "social" behaviors without much attention to the degree of the relationship between the children.

Based on the definition of friendship used earlier, direct behavioral observation could be used to yield information about interaction, length of time of interaction, and affective domain. Caution must be taken, however, as children may interact with one another but not be friends. When combining the use of the two types of techniques for assessing the relationship between children, the only characteristic of the friendship definition that has not been covered is whether the relationship is entered into without obligation. Therefore, it may be necessary to modify the sociometric technique or develop another technique to include this dimension.

Friendship as the Variable of Study

Very little is currently known about the friendships of children with disabilities and their typically developing peers. This is at least partly due to the failure to include the measure of friendship as either the independent or dependent variable of study. Including friendship as either variable will yield precise information about the outcomes and antecedents of friendships (Tesch, 1983). It is not sufficient to use measures of acceptance as a replacement to measure friendship. Acceptance and friendship are likely to be two separate variables. It is also not sufficient to use interaction rate or units of social behavior as the independent or dependent variable of a study and draw conclusions about the existence of friendships.

Research Conducted in the Natural Environment

To the extent possible, analyses conducted on the development of friendships among children with developmental disabilities and their typically developing peers should be conducted in the natural environment. The natural environment is, of course, a richer and more complex environment than could be designed in a laboratory setting. This is especially the case when considering the social behavior among groups of children. Although some control may be lost, there are likely many variables that could never be anticipated or controlled in the lab. In addition, there may exist subtle differences across environments (e.g., playground, home, or class) that have an influence on the children's behaviors.

Another reason for assessing, as well as teaching, in the natural environment for children with developmental disabilities relates to their difficulties in acquiring behavior or skills in settings that differ from this environment. When children with disabilities are taught outside of the natural environment, teachers are often faced with the task of developing ways to ensure the generalization of the newly learned behavior.

Consideration of the Relationship

As discussed earlier, to best understand the friendship of children, the behaviors or interactions of the children need to be viewed in the context of the friendship. Too often, researchers look at the discrete behaviors of the children with disabilities as isolated events. Instead, consideration needs to be given to the behavior of both the child with the developmental disability and the typically developing child and to how the behaviors relate to one another. Consideration of the relationship and viewing both children as cocreators of their relationship will allow researchers to better understand the dynamics of friendship.

QUESTIONS TO BE ANSWERED

Very little is known about the friendships of children with autism and children with developmental disabilities and their typically developing peers. A number of factors have been noted as possible contributors to this lack of knowledge, most of which are based on faulty assumptions or inadequate methodology. Fortunately, there exist solutions for all of these factors. Once consideration has been given to remedying these problems, a number of questions worthy of investigation come to mind. These include the purpose, dimensions, facilitation, and developmental progressions of friendship. Each is discussed in the following paragraphs.

Purpose(s) of Friendship

There are many questions to be answered regarding the purposes or functions of friendships for children with developmental disabilities, including autism, and their typically developing peers. For example, what are the benefits of friendship relationships to both groups of children? Does participation in a friendship facilitate the development of positive social behavior in children with developmental disabilities? In what ways, if at all, do typically developing children provide support or assistance to their friends with developmental disabilities?

Dimensions of Friendship

It is likely that there are different dimensions to the development of friendships between typically developing children and children with developmental disabilities. What is the importance of reciprocity to the development and maintenance of friendships of children with developmental disabilities and their typically developing peers? Are there meaningful gender differences exhibited by typically developing peers? Does the age of the children significantly affect the development or existence of a friendship? Are there different levels of friendship (e.g., best friend, good friend, acquaintance)? If there are different levels, is there a difference in terms of benefits or in terms of behavior emitted?

Facilitation of Friendship

Based on reports of professionals and parents, it is known that it is possible for children with developmental disabilities, including children with autism, and typically developing children to become friends. However, there is much that is not known. For example, how does one successfully facilitate the friendships of children with developmental disabilities and typically developing children? What are the variables that influence the development of friendships? Are there variables that negatively affect the development of friendships? Is it possible for any typically developing child to maintain a friendship with a child with disabilities, or will just a few children be amenable to such a friendship?

Developmental Progression of Friendship

Are there different stages to the development of friendships for exceptional children and their peers? If so, are these stages similar to the stages outlined in the literature of typically developing children? How do friendships change over time? Are there factors that must be considered in the maintenance of friendships of typically developing children and children with developmental disabilities?

SUMMARY

Social relationships and friendships are important to all individuals, including individuals with autism. The absence of meaningful relationships in a person's life can be very detrimental to his or her development as well as quality of life. Unfortunately, individuals with developmental disabilities and autism have an especially difficult time in establishing meaningful relationships. There are several reasons for this.

First, children with developmental disabilities are not often given the opportunity to interact with other typically developing children. Instead, they are placed in segregated, impoverished environments, with no emphasis placed on developing friendships.

Second, children with developmental disabilities, especially children with autism, may need some assistance in acquiring friends. Unfortunately, when assistance is given, an emphasis is placed on teaching the child a set of social skills. The assumption is made that once the child learns these social skills he or she will be worthy of or ready for participation in a relationship. In the worst case scenario, the acquisition of social skills becomes the end product, with no mention of the importance of establishing social relationships. To further complicate this issue, the social skills that are selected as targets appear to be selected based on an adult value system instead of a child value system.

Third, an emphasis is placed on changing the child with the disability or attempting to make him or her "normal" (i.e., if Jimmy acted "normal," he would have friends). It is quite possible that children with developmental disabilities and typically developing children can have meaningful friendships, but these relationships will probably be different in many ways from the friendships of typically developing children—not less important or atypical, just different. An emphasis should be placed on teaching children how to establish a relationship through joint effort. Typically developing children often need to modify their existing attitudes regarding disabilities as well as their behavior and expectations.

Fourth, it is often believed that individuals with certain disabilities (i.e., autism) are not capable of developing meaningful relationships with others. Instead, individuals with autism are described as preferring to be left alone in their own worlds. Unfortunately, many of the descriptions and defining characteristics of autism have been based on clinical observations as opposed to empirical investigation. Recent data suggest that this may be a false assumption. At a minimum, the social behavior of children with autism deserves another look.

Consideration of these four roadblocks to the development of relationships for children with developmental disabilities should assist researchers, teachers, and families in designing studies that will yield important and valid information. The evolution of a theory of the development of friendships of persons with developmental disabilities is long overdue and must proceed based on a strong methodological foundation.

Chapter 10

Integrated School Placements for Children with Disabilities

— Diane Hammon Kellegrew

Since the 1970s, the education of children with autism and other developmental disabilities has become increasingly more integrated with that of typically developing students. The integration of exceptional students into regular education environments has had a significant impact on these students and their families. This chapter explores the historic and social issues that have helped to frame the current practice of integrating children with disabilities into regular education classes. The efficacy of integrated classrooms on the social and academic performance of students with disabilities, as well as the corresponding influence on the parents of these children, is also examined. In addition, the impact of the recent practice of full inclusion is reviewed.

HISTORIC AND SOCIAL BACKGROUND

Prior to 1800, few states had health or educational facilities for children with disabilities because these students were assumed to be "uneducable" (S. Stainback, Stainback, & Forest, 1989). This changed as early as the mid-19th century when the education reform movement advocated that people with disabilities be taught in a protected environment. During this time and continuing into the early 20th century, education reformers such as Horace Mann, Samuel Gridley Howe, Dorothea Dix, and Thomas Hopkins Gallaudet helped establish the first schools for people who were "blind," "deaf," "epileptic," "retarded," or "orphaned." Initially, these schools were formed so that children with disabilities could receive education and more positive intervention; however, by the early 1900s these environments began to evolve into massive public institutions, more focused on custodial care (MacMillan & Hendrick, 1993). This change was in part due to a shift in attitudes regarding people with disabilities. During this time, notions such as the heredity of mental retardation and social Darwinism ("inferior" human beings must be segregated from the general public to prevent "contamination") were common. The isolation of people with disabilities from the mainstream of society served to foster perceptions of people with disabilities as different.

The passage of compulsory education laws in the late 19th and early 20th century stimulated concern regarding the education of students with mild disabilities. At this time, special education environments increased but became a "dumping ground" for recent immigrants as well as students with mild disabilities (H.R. Turnbull, 1992). The criteria used for classification for special education included factors such as native language, religious background, and country of origin. This separate system of education did include some plans for ameliorative intervention of children with mild educational difficulties. People with more significant disabilities continued to be served in institutions, if at all (Sailor et al., 1989).

Civil Rights Movement

At the time of the civil rights movement, special education for children with disabilities was essentially a dual system of education—one track for children enrolled in regular education and another for children identified as needing special education. As a result of the civil rights movement, the dual system of education would be subject to greater scrutiny.

The civil rights movement of the 1950s and 1960s significantly shaped what would later be called the right to education movement. The influence of the civil rights movement was made more profound as, during this time, the country experienced a convergence of political ideology with constitutional doctrines. The political ideology expressed was that of egalitarianism. Egalitarianism, the belief in the equality of people, gave rise to liberties guaranteed by the Constitution of the United States of America. The civil rights movement has been the most powerful manifestation of egalitarian principles expressed in the United States during the 20th century.

The events of the civil rights movement precipitated the *Brown v. Board of Education* (1954) case. In *Brown*, the Supreme Court decision embraced the principle of equal educational opportunity when it held that the school board of Topeka, Kansas, had violated the U.S. Constitution by creating two separate school systems divided solely by race. The Topeka School Board contended that the state-sponsored education was consistent with the constitution because both systems were equal. The U.S. Supreme Court rejected the argument that separate could ever be equal by stating:

Segregation of white and colored children in public schools has a detrimental effect upon the colored children. The impact is greater when it has the sanction of the law; for the policy of separating the races is usually interpreted as denoting the inferiority of the negro group. A sense of inferiority affects the motivation of a child to learn. . . . We conclude that in the field of public education the doctrine of "separate but equal" has no place. Separate educational facilities are inherently unequal. (*Brown v. Board of Education*, 1954, p. 495)

Thus, the impact of the civil rights movement helped lay the foundation for the right to education movement for people with disabilities, building on the principle that separate cannot be equal. With this foundation, the educational practices for children with disabilities came under question by parents and educators alike. In the 1950s, parent movements typified by the formation of groups such as the Association for Retarded Citizens and United Cerebral Palsy had increasing influence on state-sponsored education. In the 1960s, President John F. Kennedy and Senator Hubert Humphrey established the President's Committee on Mental Retardation, which typified the growing interest in services for children with disabilities. Also during this time, educators and researchers working with people with significant disabilities began making progress "training" these students who were previously considered "hopeless" (MacMillan & Hendrick, 1993). Many of these advances came through the use of applied behavior analysis (Kazdin, 1978).

In the 1970s, two conceptual changes regarding the education of the student with disabilities would later influence the movement toward integrated educational environments (Simpson & Sasso, 1992). First, Brown, Nietupski, and Hamre-Nietupski (1976) argued that if children with disabilities were to become competent and independent citizens they would need to learn specific skills dedicated to that goal. Brown and colleagues advocated the "criterion of ultimate functioning" that challenged the developmental model of the time. The developmental model taught readiness skills and used representative materials, rather than actual community environments and events. Brown noted that much of what was taught using this model had no relevance to the students' ability to lead independent lives.

At the same time, the importance of teaching in the natural environment was advocated as a method of increasing skill acquisition and especially skill generalization and maintenance (Stokes & Baer, 1977). In fact, the generalization of teaching frequently did *not* occur in segregated environments (R.L. Koegel & Koegel, 1988). However, the teaching and practice of skills and developmental tasks in the natural environment, whether this be an integrated classroom, community environment, or home, was associated with increased skill achievement, increased skill generalization, and increased skill maintenance (G. Dunlap, Koegel, & Koegel, 1984; Horner, Williams, & Knobbe, 1985; S.J. Miller & Sloane, 1976). These advances fostered new impetus for the education of children with disabilities in integrated environments.

This movement toward integration was also based on the concept of normalization (also referred to as social role valorization), a social value founded as an outgrowth of egalitarianism. Wolfensberger (1972), who coined the term, described normalization as using culturally normative means to teach culturally normative behavior. Nirje (1980) expanded the definition when he described normalization as making available to all persons with disabilities patterns of life and conditions of everyday living that are as close as possible to the regular circumstances and ways of society. In essence, normalization is a process that is shaped by the belief that people with disabilities have the right to as "normal" a life as possible, including full membership in the mainstream of society. The principle of normalization (or social role valorization) has been a paramount value in the right to education movement and a key concept found in the legislation affecting this area.

Despite a growing moral interest in the educational integration of children with disabilities, empirical data to support regular education placements were sparse and inconsistent (Heller, 1982; Odom & McEvoy, 1988). However, there was a growing concern regarding the poor outcomes of students enrolled in special education. The academic achievement of students enrolled in self-contained special education classes was found to be lower than the achievement of children remaining in regular education (Heller, 1982; Kaufman, Gottlieb, Agard, & Kukic, 1975; Kirk, 1964). These findings were particularly unsettling as special education classes at this time had fewer students, yet they also had specially trained teachers and *more* financial resources (Dunn, 1968; Johnson, 1962).

The Education for All Handicapped Children Act (PL 94-142)

In 1966 and again in 1970, Congress enacted laws that attempted to stimulate the states to develop special education resources and personnel. In addition, numerous court cases advocated the right to educational services for children with disabilities (Tremblay & Vanaman, 1979). Confronted with these court decisions and dissatisfied with the states' progress in special education cases, Congress enacted a landmark statute—the Education for All Handicapped Children Act, PL 94-142.

The broad and comprehensive requirements of the Education for All Handicapped Children Act significantly altered public education for children with disabilities between the ages of 3 and 21 years. PL 94-142 addressed six influential principles (H.R. Turnbull, 1992). First, the zero rejection principle ensured that all students, regardless of the significance of their disability, are entitled to a free and appropriate education. Second, the testing, classification, and placement principle sought to accomplish nondiscriminatory evaluations prior to special education placement. The third principle, advancing the notion of an individual and appropriate education, mandated the individualized education program (IEP). The fourth principle mandated that children were to be placed in the least restrictive educational environment. The fifth principle of procedural due process gave children with disabilities avenues for protesting actions taken by the state education agency or the local education agency. The sixth principle gave the parents of children with disabilities rights that they can exercise on behalf of their children. These principles still form the backbone of legislation in this area.

Legislation for Infants and Preschoolers with Disabilities

With the passage of PL 94-142, many people anticipated an expansion of services for younger children with disabilities. It was hypothesized that increased services for school-age exceptional children would have a corresponding impact on the services available for infants and preschoolers. In actuality, a reduction in services to children under the age of 5 years was noted between 1975 and 1980 (Sailor et al., 1989). To correct this situation, the Education for All Handicapped Children Act was amended again in 1986 by PL 99-457. This amendment affected both Title I and Title II of this act. Title II (Section 619), also called Part B, of PL 99-457 required that the services provided for by PL 94-142 also be provided for children between the ages of 3 and 5 years. These provisions removed the necessity of labeling students, provided for instruction to parents, and recognized a range of acceptable preschool programs.

Title I of PL 99-457, written as Part H of PL 94-142, established programs to address the needs of children with disabilities from birth through 3 years of age. The primary goal of this section is to develop the capabilities and skills of infants and toddlers with disabilities by facilitating the family's ability to care for their child. As part of this emphasis on families, Part H mandated the development of the individualized family service plan

(IFSP). The IFSP differs from the IEP used for school-age children in that the family's strengths and needs are incorporated into the child's educational plan. PL 99-457 established grants for states that would define and identify for service 1) children with identified developmental delay, 2) children at high risk for developmental delay, and 3) children at risk for delay for reasons other than those designated as developmental.

Individuals with Disabilities Education Act (IDEA)

In 1990, the Education for All Handicapped Children Act was amended again by PL 101-476 and renamed the Individuals with Disabilities Education Act (IDEA). The changes in the law expanded and clarified the types of students that would be served, clarified the types of related services that could be included in the child's education, and provided for assistive technology as part of the child's education when appropriate. The amendment reiterated the importance of parent involvement in the early education of students with disabilities. Also, the changes in this amendment strengthened the least restrictive doctrine in that participation in regular education environments continued to be promoted for younger and elementary school-age children with disabilities. In addition, for older students, IDEA-mandated transition services that aim toward independent living and full participation in the community after graduation from public education.

Individuals with Disabilities Education Amendments

PL 101-476 was amended in 1991 by the Individuals with Disabilities Education Amendments of 1991 (PL 102-119). This legislation mandates parent involvement in the development of an education program for children with disabilities and requires that states provide services for infants and toddlers with disabilities.

Americans with Disabilities Act (ADA)

Congress ensured the right of people with disabilities to access their communities with the enactment of PL 101-336, the Americans with Disabilities Act (ADA). With this legislation, protection against discrimination of people with disabilities is extended to employment in the private sectors, privately owned accommodations, services provided by state and local governments, public and private transportation, and telecommunication services for people with hearing and visual impairments. In essence, this legislation extends the concept of integration mandated by IDEA to include integration into society.

LEAST RESTRICTIVE ENVIRONMENT (LRE)

Access and participation in integrated public school environments is primarily mandated through the least restrictive environment (LRE) provision of IDEA. There were essentially two major reasons behind the inclusion of this principle in the law. First, because the empirical data to support segregated environments were extremely limited, the decision to mandate integrated educational placements was more in response to the perceived failure of special education.

Second, the LRE provision is based on civil rights issues. This principle is derived from the legal doctrine of least restrictive alternative. In this doctrine, the legitimate legislative actions of the government cannot be pursued by means that stifle personal liberties if these objectives can be achieved by less oppressive means. The personal liberties for a student with disabilities are assumed to be the right to associate with others. The right to associate is guaranteed by the Fifth Amendment of the U.S. Constitution and ensured to all states in the Fourteenth Amendment. This right is seen as a powerful force encompassing the concept of citizenry. Many argue that, through increased participation in the mainstream of society, people with disabilities will become more visible, thus neutralizing discriminatory attitudes and stigmatization (Will, 1989). Through this increased acceptance by the general population, people with disabilities will be better able to contribute and participate fully in society.

As written, the LRE principle presumes that the most integrated environment will be provided for the child with disabilities. Statutory and regulatory language excuses placement in the LRE when a child cannot be educated in this environment even with the use of supplementary aids and services. In addition, the LRE principle may not apply if a child with disabilities may interfere with the education of the students without disabilities.

Despite general widespread support for the notion that students with disabilities should have access to integrated environments, there is controversy around mandating this access with the LRE provision (Peck & Semmel, 1982; Taylor & Knoll, 1989; H.R. Turnbull & Turnbull, 1990). Some suggest that the LRE criterion places more attention on the physical environments rather than the services and supports needed for efficient integration (Aanes & Haagenson, 1978; Gerber & Semmel, 1985; McLean & Hanline, 1990; Semmel, Lieber, & Peck, 1986). Bailey and McWilliams (1990) assert that the greater emphasis should be on the skills related to normalization, such as self-care, communication, motor, and cognitive functioning that allow students to participate in integrated environments. Taylor (1988) takes issue with the continuum model concept underlying the LRE principle.

In the continuum model, a variety of services are available ranging from most restrictive environments, such as institutional placement, to least restrictive environments, such as regular education classes. As part of the services provided, students with autism and other disabilities are progressively prepared for the next step on the continuum. Taylor (1988) asserts that the continuum concept legitimizes restrictive environments. He further asserts that the LRE, progressive for its time, should now be replaced by a commitment to integrate. Taylor states:

> The irony is that the most restrictive placements do not prepare students for least restrictive placements. . . . Institutions do not prepare people for community living, segregated day programs do not prepare students for integrated schooling. . . . [P]rogress through the vocational continuum; that is, from sheltered to integrated settings, is extremely slow; for people with mental retardation in day activity and work activity programs, the probability of movement to competitive employment is nearly nonexistent. (p. 47)

Although the law requires that integrated placements be offered to all students with disabilities, including those with autism, progress toward this goal has been sporadic (Gerber & Levine-Donnerstein, 1989). The way in which state education agencies have allocated fiscal resources has served to reinforce or discourage integration efforts of local schools. Kaufman et al. (1975) describe this situation when they report that some states (e.g., Georgia, Texas) allowed children who were eligible for special education but placed in regular education classes to be included in the funding for both regular and special education. This encouraged the integration of students with special needs because revenues for the school were increased. Other states established either a weighted equivalency formula (Florida) or allowed eligibility for either special education or regular education (New Mexico). As school districts were reimbursed more for special education students, policies that reduced special education funds resulted in limited integration of students with disabilities.

Even for those states that did attempt to comply with the movement toward integration, the actual implementation of the law was inconsistent at the local level. Weatherley and Lipsky (1977) conducted a qualitative study examining the effect of the Comprehensive Education Law of Massachusetts, Chapter 766, on the practices of three local school districts. This law was enacted in response to PL 94-142 and encouraged the integration of students with disabilities in regular education environments. The local school district personnel attempted to comply with the law by developing policies that would balance these new demands against available resources. The authors conclude that as a result

> data obtained from an official of the state department of education indicate that children were actually shifted from less to more restrictive programs during the first year of implementation. In part, this shift probably reflects increased use of resource rooms. Ironically, by providing separate rooms staffed by specialists to provide special-education services, school systems *decreased* the proportion of fully integrated children by sending them out of the regular classrooms for special help. (p. 183)

In reaction to this minimalist approach taken by the judiciary, state government, and local school districts, the passage of the Education for All Handicapped Children Act, at first, resulted in the establishment of new and the expansion of old segregated environments (Sailor, 1991). For example, in Massachusetts between 1974 and 1985 placements in segregated classrooms rose by 234%. Similarly, in California in 1987 55% of the student population labeled as having significant disabilities were served in segregated classrooms (Halvorsen & Sailor, 1990).

After the passage of PL 99-457, similar results were noted for integration of young children with disabilities. It has been estimated that fewer than one third of young children eligible for early intervention are receiving those services in an integrated environment (Lamorey & Bricker, 1993). Many states do not provide public preschools, and fewer still have infant programs for children without disabilities. The lack of public education facilities for young children would require that school districts pay for the private integrated preschool placement of the exceptional child. This type of expanded service requirement has many districts reluctant to participate in implementing the integrated programs called for by Part H of IDEA.

Trends Encouraging the Integration of Students with Disabilities

Although progress toward the LRE has not been consistent, most courts have continued the trend toward integration. In *Hendricks v. Gilhool* (1989), the court considered the quality of the recommended segregated program when determining that 1) separate programs and schools are not comparable to those found in regular education, 2) restrictive environments were routinely and unnecessarily offered to students with mild disabilities, and 3) the relocation of students with disabilities to accommodate students without disabilities was unacceptable. The use of supplementary aids and services has also been challenged and supported in the courts. In one case, *Daniel R. v. State Board of Education* (1982), the court established a two-prong test to determine if placement is appropriate and consistent with the LRE. The test required the court to determine 1) whether placement in the regular classroom, with the use of supplementary aids and services, can be achieved satisfactorily; and 2) if not, and segregated special education is recommended, whether the school placed the student in the least restrictive environment possible. The most recent trends in the legislation continue to support the move toward integration (Rogers, 1993).

Recently increased momentum has been noted for districts experimenting with the full inclusion model in which students with disabilities are placed in regular education environments (Rogers, 1993). Five states currently placed more than 60% of their students in regular education environments. These include Vermont, North Dakota, Nebraska, Massachusetts, and Oregon (The Association for Persons with Severe Handicaps [TASH],

1992). Three states, Colorado, Iowa, and Vermont, have published their intent to move toward a full inclusion delivery model within a short time (Sailor, 1991). This momentum is not shared by all states. Alabama, Georgia, and Texas fully included less than 4% of their students with disabilities.

CHARACTERISTICS OF INTEGRATED ENVIRONMENTS FOR CHILDREN WITH DISABILITIES

Generically, integration describes the process of actively desegregating children with disabilities and their peers without disabilities. Schools practice many forms of integration, most notably mainstreaming, and more recently full inclusion. Typically, the integration of children with autism into regular education classes follows the same criteria used for children with other developmental disabilities. Any differences in classroom placement or goals would be due to the individual differences of the learner.

Following the passage of PL 94-142, the integration of students with disabilities into regular education classes was known as mainstreaming. Early proponents of mainstreaming felt this method of integration would transform special education (Kaufman et al., 1975). For example, Dunn (1968) based his support on the belief that integration of students with disabilities would refocus special education by 1) removing the stigma associated with special education placement; 2) providing a more cognitively stimulating environment; 3) providing a more flexible vehicle from which to deliver educational service; and 4) providing decentralized services, thus avoiding the need to transport a child out of his or her neighborhood. Meyers, MacMillan, and Yoshida (1975) also envisioned mainstreaming as a fairly inclusive practice that would vary from the student spending one half of his or her school hours in a regular class to the student spending all of his or her time in a regular class with no extra assistance.

In the following years, the practice of mainstreaming did not meet the expectations of these early advocates. Kaufman et al. (1975) assert that, "Finally, as a result of the general pressure placed on special education administrators to change the structure of special education, they rapidly began to implement those services they perceived to require only slight modification in orientation or delivery to be considered as mainstreaming" (p. 2). As a result, mainstreaming is now a practice most commonly associated with traditional special education (Odom & McEvoy, 1988).

Characteristics of Mainstreamed Classrooms

Currently, mainstreaming refers to the practice of placing children with autism and other disabilities into an environment with children without disabilities (Buscaglia & Williams, 1979). However, the term *mainstreaming* does little to describe the variation in hours in integrated environments, subjects taught, and support services given (Heller, 1982). For school-age children, mainstreaming most typically refers to the integration of the student with disabilities in one or more places such as regular education classes, as well as nonacademic school and community environments. The primary class placement continues to be the special education class for the mainstreamed student. Students typically "earn" the right to be mainstreamed by performing at a level appropriate for the integrated environment (Rogers, 1993).

Reverse mainstreaming refers to the practice of including students without disabilities in classes and programs primarily geared for students with disabilities. Reverse mainstreamed environments typically have a higher percentage of students with disabilities. This practice has most commonly been used in preschool environments where the students without disabilities are recruited as typical "models" for the students with disabilities (Cole, Mills, Dale, & Jenkins, 1991; Jenkins, Speltz, & Odom, 1985).

Characteristics of Full Inclusion Classrooms

Full inclusion refers to instructional practices that seek to accommodate students with autism and other developmental disabilities in the regular education class such that the student's primary placement is considered the regular education environment. Full inclusion is a relatively new way to describe this integration approach. For example, studies done in the 1970s and early 1980s described full inclusion practices as full mainstreaming. Typically, full inclusion services are provided if the exceptional child exhibits the ability to benefit from the service. Fully included students with disabilities may still receive special education services; however, frequently these services are provided in the regular education classroom (Brown et al., 1989a, 1989b). Although the full inclusion model builds on early full mainstreaming practices, Rogers (1993) describes the differences between mainstreaming and the full inclusion of students with disabilities as a "reconceptualization of special education services." Mainstreamed environments consist of bringing the child to the services. Full inclusion practices bring services to the child.

Many schools are now implementing full inclusion placements on a student-by-student basis, whereas other school districts are moving toward a full inclusion model for all schools served in their jurisdiction (Burrello & Wright, 1993). Sailor (1991) identified six basic components that most full inclusion models incorporate:

1. All students attend the school to which they would go if they had no disability.
2. A natural proportion (i.e., representative of the school district at large) of students with disabilities occurs at any school site.
3. A zero-rejection philosophy exists so that typically no student would be excluded on the basis of type or extent of disability [. . .]
4. School and general education placements are age and grade-appropriate, with no self contained special education classes operative at the school site.
5. Cooperative learning and peer instructional methods receive significant use in general instructional practice at the school site.
6. Special education supports are provided within the context of the general education class and in other integrated environments. (p. 10)

OUTCOMES FOR STUDENTS WITH DISABILITIES PLACED IN INTEGRATED CLASSROOMS

The legal mandate to provide integrated environments for children with autism and other developmental disabilities was established based on the value that these children have a right to participate in regular education classes. The actual effects of these environments on an exceptional child's academic and social skills were frequently hypothesized but rarely examined (Heller, 1982). However, for the momentum toward integration to continue, it was important to assess the value of these educational placements for the child with special needs; without improved outcomes for children with disabilities enrolled in integrated classes, continued momentum toward the least restrictive environment would not be warranted.

Contact Hypothesis

Through the integration of students with disabilities, it was thought that increased contact between these students and their typically developing peers would increase acceptance and reduce stigmatization of children with disabilities (Brewer & Smith, 1989). It was also proposed that children placed in the mainstream would benefit from this placement by proximity to typically developing peers who would model appropriate behavior and skills (Mahoney, Robinson, & Powell, 1992). This contact would then facilitate more mature social, play, and communicative responses from the child with disabilities. Opportunities for observational learning would not be possible in a special education environment due to the limitations of the other special education students (Guralnick, 1990a). In part, mere proximity of students with disabilities and their typically developing peers has produced some positive outcomes for both sets of students; however, more convincing results have been reported when integration is coupled with specific interventions designed to increase the skills of the exceptional student.

Social Outcomes as a Result of Integrated Environments

As discussed in other chapters, social outcomes include communication skills, social competence, and friendships. The vast majority of studies examining the impact of integrated classes focus on the domains of social competence and friendships (Odom & McEvoy, 1988). This perhaps is in response to studies predicting that social isolation may be an outcome of mainstreaming children with disabilities (Heller, 1982; McLean & Hanline, 1990).

Guralnick (1990b) describes social competence as the ability to successfully and appropriately select and carry out interpersonal goals. Social competence is viewed as a dynamic process that allows for individual variation, in that the child must be able to adapt to subtle and varied social cues that take place in a variety of contexts. Social competence is also said to facilitate social interaction. In turn, social interaction can facilitate friendships (Haring, 1993). Friendships differ from popularity because popularity involves being liked by a larger group of peers. Popularity is not a prerequisite for friendship, just as mere social interaction does not guarantee friendship (Sailor et al., 1989). The ability to communicate influences all social interactions and friendships. In addition, communication skills have an impact on other developmental domains, such as cognition, that are needed to function in schools (Notari & Cole, 1993). Social interactions are frequently problematic for children with autism; therefore, classroom placements that enhance social skills are desired.

Although students with autism and other disabilities placed in mainstreamed school environments do demonstrate increased social interaction in comparison to students placed in segregated environments, difficulties in the integrated placement have also been noted. Specifically, in comparison to typically developing students, the students with disabilities placed in integrated classrooms frequently engage in more solitary play as opposed to group play (Burstein, 1986) and exhibit an inability to direct, organize, and use peers as a resource (Guralnick & Groom, 1985). In addition, teachers and the typically developing peers frequently judge the social status of children with disabilities as less socially competent (Ray, 1985). As a consequence, students with disabilities may find it difficult to form reciprocal friendships (Guralnick, 1990b).

However, integrated environments are associated with increased social and communication responses among typical and atypically developing children. This is supported by studies indicating that exceptional children spend proportionately more time interacting with peers in integrated environments than they do in segregated environments (Halvorsen & Sailor, 1990). In addition, children without disabilities are more responsive to the initiations of a child with disabilities (Guralnick & Paul-Brown, 1984) and spontaneously adjust the level of their conversation to the child with a disability (Guralnick & Groom, 1988). These child-to-child responses, called horizontal transactions (Sailor, Goetz, Anderson, Hunt, & Gee, 1988) differ from vertical transactions that involve adult-to-child responses. Interactions among children found in horizontal transactions appear to increase the child's responsiveness to his or her environment (Mahoney et al., 1992).

Outcomes of Intervention Studies Focusing on Social Skills and Friendships

Intervention studies designed to improve social relationships between children with disabilities and typically developing students indicate that the children with disabilities may not be socially integrated if efforts are not made toward this end (Fewell & Oelwein, 1990; Lamorey & Bricker, 1993; McLean & Hanline, 1990; Odom & McEvoy, 1988). Social skills have been successfully facilitated in integrated environments. In addition, success has been noted with increasing communication skills as a method of increasing social interaction (Hunt, Alwell, & Goetz, 1988), improving the social competence of a child with disabilities (Russo & Koegel, 1977; Strain, Odom, & McConnell, 1984), and facilitating friendships between a child with autism and a typically developing peer (Haring, 1993).

A study by Sasso, Simpson, and Novak (1985) examined the impact of three different interventions designed to 1) increase the social skills of children with autism, 2) provide instruction for peers without disabilities, and 3) provide instruction and interaction with students with autism for typically developing children. The study involved 45 regular education students and 6 students with autism, all ranging in age from 8 to 10 years. For the students without disabilities, randomly assigned intervention groups consisted of 1) students who received information about children with autism, 2) students who received the information session as well as structured interaction time with a child with autism, and 3) a control group that did not receive information or contact. The students with autism attended the same school as the typically developing students but were assigned to a self-contained special education class. These students were diagnosed as autistic by a licensed psychologist prior to school entrance. All students were reported to be making excellent progress in their academic placement.

Prior to contact with the typically developing peers, the students with autism participated in an instruction session geared to facilitate acceptable eye contact, response to greeting, and initiation of greeting. Results of this study indicated that 1) typically developing children who had received both information and structured experiences with their classmates with autism were significantly more willing to interact with these children on the playground, and 2) social skills instruction for the students with autism was successful and appeared to be a prerequisite for social interactions.

Studies also suggest that social skills instruction for children with autism may not be effective if the child does *not* participate in an integrated environment. Strain (1983) examined the consequences of integrated environments versus segregated environments on the generalization of social skills instruction. Intervention included contact among a trained typically developing child and four children with autism who were engaged in a session designed to increase participation during play. Data were collected on the generalization of social responses during integrated and segregated recesses. For each child with autism, the generalized sessions resulted in "superior behavior change" (Strain, 1983, p. 30). Interestingly, there was no change in behavior during the segregated sessions.

Strain concludes that children with autism may not produce social responses in a socially unresponsive environment, such as that found in this and other segregated special education environments.

Asher and Taylor (1981) note that increased peer acceptance is one outcome of integrated classroom experiences for children with disabilities. However, this is rarely accompanied by an increase in friendships between the exceptional child and his or her typically developing peers. Despite successes reported in improving the social interactions between students with autism and other disabilities and typically developing pupils, one consideration is worth noting. As discussed in Chapter 9, simply improving social contact and interactions does not ensure that these relationships will result in friendships. Social interactions between children with and without disabilities frequently require direct teacher prompting and reinforcement to maintain results (Haring, 1993). A study by Odom, Hoyson, Jamieson, and Strain (1985) examined a peer initiation intervention in an integrated preschool. Results indicated that the students without disabilities only played with the children with disabilities when prompted and rewarded by the teacher. Guralnick (1990b) suggests that the social competence of a child with disabilities is the key variable, not the disability status. Therefore, he proposes that when the social competence of a child improves, so will the child's social status among peers. This has important implications for social skills programs of children with autism.

Impact of Integrated Environments on Academic and Developmental Outcomes

Academic outcomes refer to achievement in academic subjects for the school-age child. For the younger child and also for the child with more significant disabilities, academic outcomes refer to appropriate developmental gains. Increased skill achievement on both academic and developmental outcomes has been reported as a result of integrated environments for students of all ages (Allen, 1991; Brinker & Thorpe, 1984; Goldstein, Moss, & Jordan, 1982; Ispa & Matz, 1978; Odom & McEvoy, 1988; Wang & Baker, 1986). Skill acquisition has been noted in a variety of environments including community grocery stores for older students (Albin & Horner, 1988) and other community environments for younger students (Peck, Odom, & Bricker, 1993).

Peck, Killen, and Baumgart (1989) examined the IEP goal attainment for young children placed in two community child care programs. This study focused on promoting developmental goals identified on the IEP. The child care staff were instructed by the special educator to independently identify and incorporate specific IEP objectives into regular activities. Although this study was designed to increase teachers' ability to teach the IEP goals, the results indicate that children can successfully attain IEP goals in a community child care program.

In a study with school-age children, Leinhardt (1980) examined the impact of a "transition room" on the reading skills of first graders. Students identified with significantly lower than average academic performance and maturity were randomly placed in either a transition room or a regular first grade with an individualized reading curriculum. The transition room was described as an essentially segregated special education placement, with an adult-to-student ratio three times that of the regular education class. Results at the end of the school year indicated that, despite similar reading levels at the beginning of the school year, the students placed in regular education classes demonstrated reading levels approximately one standard deviation above those students placed in the special education class. This result was partially attributed to the higher expectations of the regular education teacher.

Most studies report academic outcomes for students with autism and developmental disabilities at least equal to, and frequently better than, outcomes reported for students placed in integrated environments (Heller, 1982). However, an analysis of the literature suggests that the quality of the curriculum may be more influential than the classroom placement. Jenkins et al. (1985) examined the impact of integrated placement on the language, motor, and social behavior of 36 preschool students with mild disabilities. In this study, one group was assigned to a segregated classroom while the other group attended a preschool using reverse mainstreaming (approximately 2:1 ratio of exceptional students to typically developing students). The proximity model was used in that the typically developing students were treated in the same way as any relatively higher-functioning child with disabilities. Results suggested that the inclusion of typically developing peers did not detract or enhance the developmental outcomes of the children with disabilities. Therefore, the authors concluded that "acceleration of delayed development by way of integration will require more than proximity" (p. 15).

In addition to the importance of curricular factors, specific child characteristics, most notably the degree of disability, may contribute to the academic outcomes of children with autism and disabilities placed in regular education environments. Although many advocate integrated environments for all students, including those with more significant disabilities (Demchak & Drinkwater, 1992; Ford & Davern, 1989), there are others who report that these students may benefit more from segregated environments (Fewell & Oelwein, 1990; Semmel & Peck, 1986). A study by Cole et al. (1991) examined the impact that the initial level of disability had on the developmental gains of preschoolers with disabilities placed in either integrated or segregated classes. Cole et al. reported that lower-functioning students showed increased gains in the segregated environment, whereas the higher-functioning students made greater gains in the integrated classes. The authors propose that the initial level of functioning may significantly contribute to the outcomes of students with disabilities placed in regular education environments.

Sailor, Gee, Goetz, and Graham (1988) assert that the definition of progress for students with more significant disabilities is subject to debate. As standardized testing is not available for the most involved students, outcome measures are frequently gauged by progress toward the IEP goals; however, the IEP goals are frequently adapted to the environment where services are provided. Therefore, students in segregated environments will have goals obtainable in that environment, whereas students in integrated environments will have different goals. For all students it is important to balance the value of an integrated class against the child's need to achieve skills that will allow him or her to lead a functional and independent life.

In addressing this issue, Brown and colleagues (1991) caution that there is a difference between being "based in" and "being confined to" a regular education class. Children with autism and developmental disabilities who are "based in" a regular education class start their day there and are seen as real members of the class, despite the fact that some portion of the day may be spent elsewhere. To meet the needs of these children, it might be necessary to pull them out of the regular education class for services that cannot effectively be provided in the regular environment. It has also been argued that, as a child with disabilities matures, activities in the community rather than the classroom are better able to prepare him or her for productive work following graduation. Therefore, the primary educational environment of students with autism should include both inclusion in integrated classrooms and inclusion in the community at large (Sailor et al., 1989).

TEMPORAL INTEGRATION: FULL INCLUSION OF CHILDREN WITH DISABILITIES INTO REGULAR EDUCATION CLASSROOMS

Most studies describing integration efforts have focused on some form of mainstreaming. With the recent momentum toward full inclusion, it is important to consider if there are differences in student outcomes as a result of partial mainstreaming versus full inclusion. Many propose that the outcomes of these two types of classroom placements will differ based on the inherent differences in philosophy and implementation between the two integration options. The fully included child with disabilities is seen as "belonging" in the regular education classroom, rather than based in a segregated class and brought into the regular education environment. In addition, the services are brought to the fully included child, rather than the more traditional pull-out type of service, where the child is brought to the service.

Most researchers, educators, and parents support the notion that a child with autism and disabilities can benefit from contact with a typically developing student. Concerns with providing services in fully integrated environments surface when students with disabilities do not fulfill their academic and IEP objectives in the regular education class (Council for Learning Disabilities, 1993; Learning Disabilities Association, 1993; National Joint Committee on Learning Disabilities, 1993). For these students, there is concern that the curriculum advances made through special education services will be difficult to transfer to regular education environments. Many of the interventions practiced in special education environments are provided with resources, such as increased staff, not routinely available in regular education classrooms.

Special education environments offer a different type of service due in part to differences in the way most children with autism and other disabilities are perceived to learn (Semmel, Abernathy, Butera, & Lesar, 1991). It is suggested that one of the difficulties in integrating special education students into regular education environments is implementing the more individualized special education techniques in the regular education class (Gerber & Semmel, 1985). Gerber (1988) asserts that there is a band of "instructional tolerance" that delineates what a teacher is willing to teach. In the typical regular education classroom, the students' needs are relatively homogenous and within this instructional tolerance. Students who require instruction beyond this tolerance can be seen as unteachable by a specific teacher in a specific classroom. This is supported by reports indicating that teachers do not modify large group instruction, as might be needed by the student with disabilities, when the ability levels of the learners are discrepant (Semmel et al., 1986).

Those who advocate for full inclusion conclude that, despite the differences in learning characteristics of students, the basic teaching components that make both special education and regular education effective are very similar (Fleming, Wolery, Weinzierl, Venn, & Schroeder, 1991). Therefore, methods of including the student with autism and other disabilities in the regular education environment can be developed. This is necessary according to these advocates because mainstreaming for only part of the day has not been a successful method of providing both instruction and integration. Wang and Birch (1984b) discuss this when they write that many have argued that the prevailing practice of enrolling exceptional students in regular classes, only to withdraw them for "special" instruction to a resource room staffed by a categorically prepared teacher, might be a primary reason for the scanty and inconsistent results of most efficacy studies of mainstreaming. . . . "Partial mainstreaming" or the inclusion of exceptional students in regular classes for only part of the school day, has resulted in a focus on placement, rather than education, in the "least restrictive environment". . . . Under these conditions, exceptional students are unlikely to be full participants in the school and intellectual life of regular classes, and whatever social and attitudinal benefits might accrue are likely to be diluted. (p. 393)

Thus, because mainstreaming for only parts of the day has not been as successful as was anticipated, current trends point toward full inclusion as the means to facilitate success.

Similar to the early days of mainstreaming, many who advocate for full inclusion of children with autism and disabilities do so primarily on the basis of value judgments because empirical data examining the outcomes of full inclusion are rare (Simpson & Sasso, 1992). However, data are available if one considers the older studies designed to test the impact of full mainstreaming. Wang and Birch (1984a), as part of a larger study, examined the differences between student achievement and classroom behavior for students with disabilities fully mainstreamed in regular education classes versus students partially mainstreamed. Eleven subjects participated in each intervention condition. The pupils with disabilities who were fully mainstreamed in regular education classes received classroom instruction in the morning using a curriculum designed to individualize instruction. The partially mainstreamed group received morning instruction in a resource special education class and afternoon instruction in a regular education environment. Significant increases in independent work and time on task were noted for the fully mainstreamed students. In addition, this group of students generalized these classroom behaviors to the afternoon class session where the individualized curriculum was not used. In contrast, the partially mainstreamed students did not show significantly increased time-on-task behavior in either the resource room or the afternoon mainstreamed environment. These students did show significant improvement in independent work in the resource class, but did not generalize these behaviors to the afternoon mainstreamed environment. Also, fully mainstreamed students initially scored slightly lower on reading and mathematic achievement, but scored significantly higher on these measures than partially mainstreamed students by the end of the study.

The Wang and Birch (1984a) study suggests that students with disabilities who are fully mainstreamed in regular education classes demonstrate increased academic skills, improved classroom behavior, and better generalization of classroom behavior compared to their partially mainstreamed peers. However, it is apparent that the adapted curriculum played an important role in the positive results for the fully included children. Again, one must consider if, as in the studies comparing mainstreamed environments to segregated environments, the impact of curriculum might be as important as that of class placement.

The impact of the curriculum was addressed in a 3-year study by Calhoun and Elliott (1977) that contrasted the impact of a fully mainstreamed class placement versus a segregated special education placement. In this study, the curriculum and materials used for each class placement were similar and the teachers rotated at half year to control for teacher effectiveness. The subjects included 50 students with disabilities and 50 students considered emotionally disturbed. Students placed in regular education environments scored significantly better on the Stanford Achievement Testing as compared to those in the segregated environments. Interestingly, the fully mainstreamed students displayed better self-concept scores than those placed in the segregated environment. This is important due to the well-documented positive relationship between self-concept and achievement.

Impact of Full Inclusion on Social Outcomes

Notably few studies have examined the impact of full inclusion on the social outcomes of students with disabilities. This is surprising because one philosophical premise of full inclusion is that the exceptional student will "belong" in the regular education environment, thereby facilitating increased acceptance and friendships. This issue was addressed by Schnorr (1990) during her enlightening ethnographic study of a mainstreamed first-grade student, Peter, and his typically developing classmates. Peter, who had moderate to significant disabilities, was mainstreamed once daily and for all special classes such as music, physical education, and art. Through participant observation and detailed interviews with the first-grade students, Schnorr identified three themes that defined the first-grade experience for these students. First, the theme of "where you belong" encompassed the concept of grade and teacher. The first-grade students did not see Peter as a member of the class because he had a different teacher and a different room (grade). Second, the theme of "what you do" entailed the kind of classwork completed. The first-grade students were aware that Peter was not doing similar work and was held accountable for different standards. The third theme of "with whom you play" was especially salient for the first-grade students. Of the 23 students in the class, each was mentioned by at least one classmate as a friend, with the exception of Peter, who was not mentioned at all. In addition, first graders tended to play only with other students in their class; therefore, class membership became an important element when forming friends. Peter's part-time participation in the class did not include activities that might allow time for friendships to develop. Schnorr (1990) concluded that

> first, *part-time is different, not just less.* . . . Peter's different class assignment and his "coming and going" were highlighted by a number of students as prominent discrepancies between him and other first graders. In fact, these discrepancies were reported much more frequently than any of Peter's individual characteristics (e.g., academic abilities, or behavior). This study raises questions about part-time placements: Is the difference only quantitative, one that can be measured in hours and minutes? Or, does it in fact redefine the experience for both the individual and the regular class member? (p. 238)

One study has examined the effect of full inclusion on the challenging behaviors of three elementary-age students with severe disabilities (Won, Anderson, & Haring, 1993). In a multiple baseline across subjects design, the authors examined the occurrences of appropriate and inappropriate behavior both in a self-contained special education class (baseline condition) and when fully included in a regular education classroom. The intervention consisted of activities to aid in the transition from the special education class to the regular education class. The activities presented to the fully included students in the regular education class were the same type of activities in which the regular education students participated. The authors note that movement from the segregated class to the integrated class resulted in "immediate decreases in inappropriate behavior for all three students" (p. 10). Furthermore, the authors report the students' success appeared due to differences in the regular education class routines, such as more appropriate toys and increased teacher expectations regarding appropriate behavior.

These studies lend support to the notion that fully integrated environments provide a qualitatively different school experience for the child with autism and other developmental disabilities. This difference appears related to increased expectations and opportunities present in the integrated regular education classes. In addition, differences in typically developing students' perceptions of the pupil with special needs may depend on increased contact. These differences may have the power to substantially alter the school experience, thereby also having an impact on exceptional children's abilities and behavior.

THE IMPACT OF INTEGRATED ENVIRONMENTS ON PARENTS OF CHILDREN WITH DISABILITIES

Integrated environments affect not only children with disabilities, but also their families. This consequence is important as there is a strong relationship between the home environment and the child's school achievement (Bradley, Rock, Whiteside, Caldwell, & Brisby, 1991; Frey, Fewell, & Vadasy, 1988; R.L. Koegel, Schreibman, Johnson, O'Neill, & Dunlap, 1984; Rosenberg, Robinson, & Beckman, 1986). The impact of these environmental factors appears even more salient for children at risk (Mahoney, 1988b; Silber, 1988). For example, family factors account for more than one half the variance in intellectual performance for preterm infants, but only 20% for full-term infants (Crnic & Greenberg, 1987). Therefore, parental support for the school activities of children with autism and other disabilities can be a vital key to the child's progress (Bradley & Caldwell, 1979; Salisbury & Evans, 1988).

The Impact of Parent Participation in Special Education Programs

For parents of children with autism and other developmental disabilities, contact with the school system differs from the contact experienced by parents of children without disabilities. One reason for this difference is that the law, through IDEA, encourages and guarantees parents of exceptional children increased involvement in their children's educational program. Consequently, special education services frequently offer parents increased social support, such as parent groups, and access to social networks that may not be provided in a regular education environment.

Although parents of children with disabilities benefit from these special education support programs (Dunst & Trivette, 1988a; Dunst, Trivette, Hamby, & Pollock, 1990), many studies indicate that the level of service provided for the parent by professionals can actually be detrimental to some families (Brotherson & Goldstein, 1992; LeLaurin, 1992; Winborne, 1991). For example, studies examining the value of parent support groups for families with an exceptional child consistently indicate that parents vary in both satisfaction and perceived benefit as a result of participation (Krauss, Upshur, Shonkoff, & Hauser-Cram, 1993; Yoder, 1990). Affleck, Tennen, Rowe, Roscher, and Walker (1989) suggest that the professional intervention offered through a formal support group had negative findings for mothers of vulnerable infants who had a relatively low need for assistance. Affleck et al. speculated that "some program participants who had little need for support may have experienced threats to their adaptation because the information imparted to them, which they did not actively seek, disrupted their optimistic view of the child's condition and diminished their self-confidence" (p. 501).

Other difficulties associated with parent participation in segregated educational environments and support groups exist when parents of children with disabilities limit their contacts with parents of typically developing children. Research suggests that parents of children with disabilities tend to remain friends with other parents of children with disabilities, even when their child participates in a mainstreamed program (Bailey & McWilliams, 1990).

This issue has additional implications when one considers that parents of children with disabilities do not tend to offer their child the opportunity for contact with typically developing children (Stoneman, 1993). Because children's friendships are influenced by the friendships of their parents (Guralnick, 1990a), children with disabilities may have fewer opportunities to associate with children without disabilities. A study by Goldstein et al. (1965) suggests that children with intellectual disabilities who are placed solely in regular education environments were more likely to interact with neighborhood children than their special education counterparts. Stoneman (1993) states, "It is of little value to facilitate interactions in the classroom if children with disabilities spend their time socially isolated in their homes or neighborhoods. Because parents are important mediators of young children's opportunities for play and social contact with peers, it is important that parental attitudes towards friendships between children with and without disabilities receive more research attention" (p. 242).

Parents' Perception of Integrated Classes for Their Children with Disabilities

Although integrated placements appear to have multiple advantages for both the exceptional child and the family, parents can be reluctant to participate in these programs. Ferrara (1979) surveyed 207 parents of children with disabilities for 1) attitudes toward normalization and mainstreaming for children with disabilities in general, and 2) attitudes toward these activities for their children in particular. Results indicated that, although parents were supportive of normalization and mainstreaming efforts for children with disabilities in general, some were less positive toward these activities when they referred to their own child. This is supported by other studies considering integrated environments. When no special preparation is provided for the integration, parents of children with disabilities have reservations about the regular education teacher's ability to meet the needs of their child, negative comparisons among children, and concerns about the availability of special education support services (Winton, 1986).

Furthermore, attitudes may be developed early on when initial contacts between special education staff and families are made. That is, it is quite possible that school districts that are accustomed to routinely segregating children with disabilities promote this idea as an acceptable alternative, and families unfamiliar with inclusion issues do not consider such options for their children. For example, in a study of this issue, Winton (1986) suggests that the problem with the placement of young children in an integrated environment may not be due to the lack of integrated placement, but rather to an inadequate communication system between service delivery agencies and the families involved. Professionals appear unaware of mainstreamed preschools, thereby reducing the possibility that they will know of integrated facilities to suggest to the families they serve. Winton reports that families who pursue integrated environments for their young children with disabilities frequently do so without the support of the services that are supposed to help them. In addition, families who place their children in integrated environments often find themselves coordinating all additional services for the child because the communication system between agencies is poor. Winton hypothesizes that for "some families, the complications of considering mainstreaming might be so great that automatic enrollment in a specialized preschool might be the best option at that time" (p. 139).

Yet parents of exceptional children who have participated in mainstreamed and fully included environments generally have positive responses about the results (Bailey & Winton, 1987; Peck, Carlson, & Helmstetter, 1992; H.R. Turnbull, Winton, Blacher, & Salkind, 1989). Exposure to the real world, the opportunity for the exceptional child to imitate children who are more advanced, and the opportunity for typically developing children to develop sensitivity to individual differences were all listed by parents as benefits of integrated classroom placements (Winton, Turnbull, & Blacher, 1984).

CONCLUSION

The American civil rights movement of the 1950s and 1960s formed the basis for the current movement to integrate students with disabilities into regular classrooms. The egalitarian social values that have fostered the movement for normalization have also resulted in many laws that mandate equal access to education for students with autism and other disabilities. However, in order for people with disabilities to have equal opportunity in society, equal access to education in and of itself is not enough. An integrated educational environment must foster developmental, academic, and social growth in such a way that each student with disabilities can, within his or her individual capacity, become an independent and productive citizen.

Since the 1970s, various methods of integrating students with autism and developmental disabilities have been implemented and examined. The initial hypothesis for the impact of integrated environments predicted that contact with typically developing students would produce improved outcomes for students with disabilities. This early premise was only partially correct. The curriculum support and intervention provided in the integrated environment appear to have a more powerful impact. Indeed, for most students with autism and other disabilities, inclusion has produced successful academic and social outcomes (Figure 1).

The trend toward the integration of students with autism and other disabilities is to fully include these individuals into regular education classes. It seems probable that

Figure 1.   When procedures for supporting children in full inclusion classrooms have been implemented properly, considerable success can be achieved. The child in the center of the photograph (arrow) was originally provided with a trained support aid and self-management procedures that were subsequently faded. Note his attentiveness to the teacher's instructions and his compatibility with the class.

increased time in integrated environments for the fully included exceptional child will provide a qualitatively different school experience for both the child and his or her family.

The preliminary reports of full inclusion and the long-term consequences appear promising (Russo & Koegel, 1977). However, those involved with children with autism must be concerned that the enthusiasm for integrated placements not take precedence over the more important goal of appropriate education. Without an appropriate education, the child with disabilities will have fewer options available as he or she grows and graduates from school. The challenge now is to identify methods of providing individualized, functional programs to children with disabilities based in regular education classes. The transition to fully integrated environments will require a blending of the best practices from both special education and regular education to provide the exceptional child with the most integrated *and* the most appropriate class.

Chapter 11

Parent–Professional Collaboration and the Efficacy of the IEP Process

Michelle Wood

The Education for All Handicapped Children Act of 1975 (PL 94-142), later amended and renamed in PL 101-476 (1990) as the Individuals with Disabilities Education Act (IDEA), has empowered parents of children with disabilities with critical decision-making rights and responsibilities concerning their children's education. From congressional testimonies given during the fashioning of the law, it appears that Congress intended to empower parents for two important reasons: 1) a belief that parents and educators should work together for their own benefit as well as the benefit of children, and 2) a belief that parents can help ensure that children will receive the full measure of their rights under the law (H.R. Turnbull, Turnbull, & Wheat, 1982). Two major provisions of the law, the individualized education program (IEP) conference and the IEP document itself, are the major means with which parents can exert their decision-making role and hold the schools accountable for appropriate education (A.P. Turnbull & Winton, 1984). Yet even though the requirement for parent–professional collaboration in the IEP has been stipulated, there are no articulated methods within the law to ensure that the programming for special education will proceed in positive, mutually productive ways (Duganne, Ferrara, & Justice, 1986). Consequently, public school educators and parents of children with disabilities may have conflicting expectations of the school system, their professional relationships, and their educational responsibilities in the IEP process.

This chapter examines the historical role of legislation and the efficacy of procedural mandates such as parent participation and IEPs in advancing the quality of education for students with autism. The literature has provided insight into the procedural compliance of typical school districts, the active collaboration of parents and professionals, and the substantive means of IEP implementation. It has also demonstrated educational researchers' and practitioners' attempts to remediate when services and attitudes were counterproductive to the ideology of special education. These issues are perhaps the most critical and complicated in the education of children with autism, not only because of legal and financial implications, but also because of the inherent emotional involvement and ethical responsibility of those invested in the cause.

THE ROOTS OF PARENT–PROFESSIONAL COLLABORATION IN SPECIAL EDUCATION PROGRAMMING

Although the parents of children with autism begin their socialization for the parent role in the same way as parents of children without disabilities, that role diverges from the norm when it becomes inadequate to meet their individual needs (Darling, 1988). According to Bailey and McWilliam (1990), families of children with disabilities inevitably must assume "non-normal" roles and engage in activities not expected of other parents. For example, they must attend program planning meetings and participate in team decision making; they are often expected to implement therapeutic or instructional activities at home and attend parent workshops or support groups; and they must also interact with a variety of specialists and seek out specialized services for the integration of their children.

Lynch and Stein (1982) assert that in no other area of education has the change in parental role expectations been greater than in special education. Active involvement of parents in the assessment, development, and evaluation of their children's public school programs, however, has been a relatively recent development in the dramatic history of special education. The current emphasis on parent participation has two major forces of influence: 1) federal legislation that requires parents of children with disabilities to be involved, and 2) extensive research that demonstrates the powerful role that parents can play in the education and behavior management of their children (Leyser, 1988). Yet, until the passage of PL 94-142, parents had no legal status in the planning, implementation, or appraisal of their child's special education program. The following sections describe the evolution of educational roles invested in parents as a result of legislation and the specific provisions of PL 94-142 affecting the family's involvement in special education.

The Evolving Role of Parents in Special Education

There has been a dramatic shift since the turn of the century with regard to public school policies for involving parents in special education programming and decision making. The eugenics movement of the late 1800s, promoting the notion that disability was caused solely by heredity, resulted in parents being viewed as the sources of their children's problems. Professionals declared that parents were not appropriate providers for their children with disabilities because their weaknesses initially caused or exacerbated the damage, especially in the case of autism (Doyle & Guttierrez, 1988). Therefore, from the early to mid-1900s a common practice was to institutionalize children with severe disabilities based on the premise that their care, nurturance, and education afforded too much of a burden for families and the public school system. The use of segregated care facilities was viewed as a means of promoting more positive outcomes for the community, the family, and the child (A.P. Turnbull & Winton, 1984). Parents were expected to defer and adhere to the recommendations of experts rather than to make their own decisions, and the authority over school policies was jealously guarded against the demands of parents (Cullingford, 1984; A.P. Turnbull & Winton, 1984).

Then, in the mid-1900s, two major forces caused the pendulum to swing in support of integrated public school programs and greater parent participation: 1) the political advocacy of groups such as the National Association of Retarded Citizens (NARC), and 2) the movement for compensatory education programs for economically disadvantaged children (Doyle & Guttierrez, 1988; A.P. Turnbull & Winton, 1984). NARC strongly advocated for more active roles for parents in the decision making, care, and treatment of children with disabilities, and active parent involvement was a primary component of compensatory education programs. Both Head Start (enacted through the Economic Opportunity Act of 1964, PL 88-452) and HCEEAA, the Handicapped Children's Early Education Assistance Act (PL 90-538), which provided funds for innovative early education programs for preschoolers with disabilities, encouraged more extensive services and duties for parents, such as

1. Assistance in understanding and coping with the child's behavior
2. Psychological or social work services
3. Information on child growth and development
4. Information on special education techniques
5. Observation of children in the project
6. Carry-over activities to the home
7. Participation in planning and evaluation of the program (Hocutt & Wiegerink, 1983, p. 213)

Yet, even though the laws appeared to promote active decision-making roles for parents, early implementation actually emphasized more traditional and passive parental roles. Activities such as receiving instruction from professionals to improve their parenting skills and knowledge were stressed over the more collaborative parental roles of assisting in the planning, development, operation, and evaluation of education programs (Hocutt & Wiegerink, 1983; McKinney & Hocutt, 1982). Furthermore, parents were expected to have an unquestioning and grateful attitude for any of the public services available for their children, however limited they may have been (Doyle & Guttierrez, 1988).

The social climate of the 1960s, however, provided a nurturing environment for a renewed special education movement. Following the wake of the civil rights movement, increasing numbers of people with disabilities embraced political activism and demanded integration into the mainstream of society. The quick growth and power of national parents' groups, the Kennedy family's personal and political interest in mental retardation powered by their financial resources, and exposés in the media on the degrading conditions in state institutions made disabilities a topic of national public interest (Sarason & Doris, 1979). Local and statewide special interest coalitions, organized by parents on behalf of their children with disabilities, became increasingly active. They quickly turned to the courts and legislature to demand federal involvement and overdue reform. Attorneys used due process and equal protection guarantees to challenge the dehumanizing conditions of institutions and to attack the constitutionality of segregated classes. Parents played particularly crucial roles in endorsing legislation and in seeing that the intent of the law was achieved and maintained in their schools (Berger, 1991).

As discussed in Chapter 10, congressional reform occurred at a rapid pace. Integration and equality of opportunity mandates were enacted to provide access to public facilities and transportation, and Congress passed legislation that adopted people with disabilities as a class protected by civil rights statutes (Funk, 1987). A powerful precedent that proved influential in advancing the claim of children with disabilities to educational equity was the civil rights case of *Brown v. Board of Education* (1954). This was the first Supreme Court case that focused on the exclusionary practices of the schools and the rights of racial minorities. Justice Warren's decision guaranteed minority children access to equal public education, and this principle was later adopted and applied to students with disabilities as a basis for special education mandates (Baker & Brightman, 1984).

Finally, in 1975, the passage of PL 94-142 empowered parents with the irrevocable roles of decision maker and advocate to ensure that their children's best interests would be protected and their entitled services secured. According to this law, parents are legally entitled to participate in the assessment of their child, the selection of their child's educational services, the challenge of the accuracy of their child's placement, and the implementation and evaluation of their child's program. Such broad parental authority in special education is a radical departure from earlier conventions that implied that parents should remain uninvolved and uninformed about their children's educational program. By increasing the rights of parents and children with disabilities while reducing the school's autonomy in placement decisions, these provisions resulted in a massive redistribution of power in the public education system (A.P. Turnbull & Leonard, 1981; Yoshida & Gottlieb, 1977).

Provisions of PL 94-142 Affecting Parents and Their Children

The mandates of PL 94-142 intend to reverse exclusionary practices of public schools by providing all children with disabilities (ages 3–21 years), regardless of the nature or severity of their disability, with free and appropriate public education. In addition, amendments to the law (PL 99-457) enacted in 1986 extend the rights for full special education services to infants and toddlers with disabilities *and their families*. Through this law children are no longer legally viewed in isolation; attention has finally been focused on understanding their needs from the moment of birth and within the context of the family.

Embodied within PL 94-142 are a variety of requirements that represent the current philosophical stance of special educators relative to the civil and educational rights of children with disabilities. The following sections briefly delineate the provisions of the law that directly affect children with autism and their families in their quests for fair and appropriate education provided by the public school system, including parent participation, due process, and the IEP.

Parent Participation

The stance that PL 94-142 takes on the value of parent participation in the education of children with disabilities is clearly revolutionary. Prior to 1975, parents were often not included in special education placement decisions, and it was difficult for them to have access to academic or placement records. IDEA empowered parents with unprecedented rights; in fact, the opportunity for parent participation in their child's education pervades the law's requirements. According to IDEA, parents are to be key players in the IEP process. In this role, they are expected to act on and provide information; evaluate, accept, or reject proposed educational assessments and placements; advocate and assert their child's interests; collaborate in making instructional and other service provision decisions; and be partners with the school in implementing the IEP (Turnbull & Turnbull, 1982).

Procedural Due Process

Embodied in the Constitution's 14th Amendment, the principle of due process requires that all individuals be treated fairly and afforded the opportunity to contest a governmental decision about themselves. Thus, children with autism, through their parents, have the right to protest actions of the state and local education agencies in order to produce fair and appropriate results. PL 94-142 delineates a range of due process rights to protect both the parents and the child with disabilities. For example, the parents must receive written notification and give their consent before the testing and administration of any service; they must be given opportunities to challenge the evaluations and decisions in nonformal and formal ways; they must have access to and explanations of all records (which must be kept in confidentiality); and they must receive written records of all proceedings. The parents and the school both have a right to an impartial due process hearing on any matter regarding the identification, assessment, placement, or educational program of a child with autism. If the parent or the school is dissatisfied with the decision of the hearing officer, they may also appeal to the state education agency for an impartial review.

Individualized Education Program

It may be safely asserted that the requirement of an IEP for every child with disabilities is the centerpiece of PL 94-142. In the past, students with very different educational needs were often given identical educational programs. Congress felt that IEPs were critical to implement if the intent of the law was to be achieved, namely that all children with disabilities would be provided with an appropriate public education designed to meet their diverse needs (Zettel & Ballard, 1982).

The mandate that all children with disabilities receive individualized plans for their education calls for the development of custom-tailored IEPs by multidisciplinary teams of professionals and periodic reviews of the children's progress toward achieving their goals (H.R. Turnbull, 1993; Zettel & Ballard, 1982). The written content of an IEP must include, among other things, annual goals and short-term objectives, special education services required by the student, and yearly evaluation procedures to determine whether progress has been made (Shore, 1986). Service providers should be held to the requirements of the IEP and should modify students' programs if no progress is seen (Huefner, 1991). Overall, the IEP is intended to act as a document verifying the school's compliance with the law and as a communication instrument to outline students' accepted special education placements and individualized programs to parents and educators.

The passage of detailed and comprehensive legislation, however, may still not be sufficient to realize all of a law's intended academic, social, and political outcomes. Therefore, a more detailed examination of the research regarding whether the policies and procedures defined in PL 94-142 are enacted consistently, effectively, and as intended through individual and group efforts in the IEP process is included in the following sections.

THE ADVANTAGES AND DISADVANTAGES OF PARENT PARTICIPATION

A growing body of evidence has confirmed that parent participation in the education of children without disabilities can contribute not only to academic achievement, but also to the enhancement of parenting skills and family life (Cone, Delawyer, & Wolfe, 1985; Epstein, 1987; Lillie, 1975; Yanok & Derubertis, 1989). According to Epstein (1987), evidence confirms that parental encouragement and interest in school activities affect children's achievement, attitudes, and aspirations, even after student ability and socioeconomic factors are taken into account. Substantial literature also has affirmed the positive impact of parent participation in *special* education, citing parents' abilities to be providers of intervention as well as overseers of their child's educational plan. Karnes, Linnemeyer, and Myles (1983) contend that, if parents are involved in the special education program of their child at an early age, "The child will have a greater likelihood of overcoming the handicap or minimizing its effects" (p. 206). Furthermore, an active parent–school partnership can provide a more meaningful continuity between education at school and at home when both the teacher and the parent use collaborative techniques (D'Alonzo, 1982; Lillie, 1975). Proponents have also argued that when parents become better teachers and decision makers, both the family and the school benefit: Better methods may be developed for dealing with the child's behavior at home and at school, thereby reducing some of the stress of raising or teaching a child with autism (Yoshida & Gottlieb, 1977). Given the important contributions that parents can make, it is imperative that professionals create a variety of ways in which parents can be meaningfully included in their child's education (Salisbury, 1992).

Opponents, however, argue that parent involvement places excessive demands on families and may actually increase the burden of care (Baker, 1989). A child with autism may have an overwhelming effect on the entire family system, increasing the stress, dependency, and disharmony in family relations. Concomitant high expectations of school staff for active parental involvement in the educational process may only cause greater anxiety, guilt, or frustration. Evidence indicates that the demands placed on parents of children with disabilities are indeed different than those placed on the parents of children without disabilities; in terms of the amount, intensity, and duration of involvement, more is expected of them (Allen & Hudd, 1987; Salisbury & Evans, 1988; Yanok & Derubertis, 1989). Furthermore, professionals often overemphasize the educational function of parents, overlooking the fact that it is only one of the many family responsibilities (Winton, 1986). Unfortunately, in their zealousness to create more substantive roles and responsibilities for parents within the special education system, professionals have often forgotten the primary role of parents—being family members (Salisbury, 1992).

Thus, the increase of parent involvement in the special education of children with disabilities has been received with both applause and skepticism. Some see it as a positive step toward increasing professionals' responsiveness to parents and an acknowledgment of their fundamental rights; others question whether the push for involvement causes undue parental guilt and overwhelming obligations for both parents and schools. The following section describes additional factors that may support or impede the successful collaboration of parents and professionals in the educational programming for children with autism and what implications this has to the current system mandated in special education policy.

FACTORS AFFECTING COLLABORATIVE IEP DEVELOPMENT

Parental Choice

Parent participation in the special education process may be a benefit to some parents and a disadvantage to others based on each family's unique characteristics, needs, priorities, obligations, and capabilities (Allen & Hudd, 1987; Leyser, 1988; McKinney & Hocutt, 1982; Winton & Turnbull, 1981). For instance, studies have determined that parent involvement is positively correlated with family income, the mother's education, the father's education, and the child's number of weekly hours in special education; however, it is negatively correlated with the child's grade level (Cone et al., 1985; Pyecha et al., 1980).

Parent involvement mandated in IDEA is based on the assumption that all parents want to be included in the educational decision making and will take advantage of the opportunity for active involvement (A.P. Turnbull & Turnbull, 1986). Some studies of parents of children with disabilities and the IEP process have shown, however, that this idea may be quite presumptuous. In fact, a number of investigators have demonstrated that many parents are more comfortable with assuming a more passive role in the special education system (Lusthaus, Lusthaus, & Gibbs, 1981; Winton & Turnbull, 1981). Based on figures of desired participation along a continuum of options, professionals have come to recognize that a major contribution of the special education system to some parents may be the opportunity to be *un*involved in the program; that is, parents may relegate the educational responsibilities to professionals and give their attention to other family needs (Pyecha et al., 1980; Shore, 1986; A.P. Turnbull & Turnbull, 1986; Winton & Turnbull, 1981; Winton, Turnbull, & Blacher, 1984). Thus, these investigators and parent advocates have encouraged professionals to provide a range of options for parental involvement and to base such opportunities on individual needs and capabilities.

Parents' Legal Knowledge

A considerable amount of knowledge and skill is required by parents to effectively exercise their legal rights with regard to educational decision making and advocacy. In representing their child's interests, parents must have an understanding of their child's educational strengths and weaknesses, the availability of community and school resources, the current laws and district policies, and the ways to exercise sophisticated group decision-making strategies such as conflict resolution. While some parents are exceptionally well versed and comfortable with these responsibilities, it is certainly understandable why a number of parents may feel uneasy, ill prepared, and unfamiliar with the provisions and implications of PL 94-142.

State departments of education have responsibilities under the law to develop and disseminate meaningful information to parents of children with disabilities, and local education agencies must inform parents of their roles and rights in the special education process. These provisions were enacted in the legislation to support parents in making better and more informed educational decisions for their children. However, a number of investigations have demonstrated that schools often fail to sufficiently inform parents about the IEP process, which may circumvent the full exercise of their rights (Goldstein, Strickland, Turnbull, & Curry, 1980; Hoff, Fenton, Yoshida, & Kaufman, 1978). Parents are often unaware of their children's legal entitlements, of the significance of the IEP document, of their expected role, or of the educational alternatives available for their children. They may not know about the formalized channels of appeal, what they should do to prepare for the IEP meeting, and what information may be critical to introduce in the decision-making process.

This deficiency of information occurred frequently in the early years of PL 94-142's implementation. Investigations during that time reported state and national figures indicating that a great number of parents were uninformed about the basic elements of the law: 46.2% of parents reported no knowledge of the IEP conference procedures (Carpenter & Robson, 1979), only one third of the parents were "somewhat familiar" with the contents of their child's IEP, and only one fifth of the parents were "thoroughly familiar" with its contents (Pyecha et al., 1980). More recently, Rose (1990) found that only 48% of the parents surveyed throughout seven states felt well informed about how to work with their schools to support their children with disabilities, and Able-Boone, Sandall, Loughry, and Frederick (1990) reported that only 33% of parents involved in early intervention programs had knowledge of special education laws. These investigations indicate a growing need of the school system to develop more conscientious and aggressive efforts to better inform parents of their roles and resources before their consent is required for any educational assessments or services.

Professionals' Legal Knowledge

Another related area of concern is school professionals' lack of relevant knowledge and preparedness regarding legal mandates and services of the special education process. In an early study, Carpenter and Robson (1979) found that special education teachers generally had a low degree of self-reported understanding of the law—they were familiar with only 7 of the 14 key mandates of PL 94-142 that were surveyed. The teachers reported knowing the least amount of information concerning important elements such as dates of compliance, least restrictive environment (LRE) mandates, due process rights, noncompliance penalties, and funding provisions. Yet, ironically, the parents in this study ranked the child's teacher as their primary source of information about their child's educational program and its procedures. Goldstein et al. (1980) reported that none of eight teachers they asked about an IEP knew what the plan was, although they had children with IEPs in their classrooms for the entire year. Furthermore, even years after the required implementation date of the law, Nevin, Semmel, and McCann (1983) reported that teachers' knowledge of the legislation and special education services available at their school site was still "generally limited"—general education teachers achieved only 56% accuracy in naming the services that were provided in their respective schools. These surveys demonstrate the dearth of information that was provided to crucial players in the educational process and the great need to focus intervention efforts on not only parents but also service providers who may find themselves responsible for filtering information to the families of children with disabilities.

Procedural Compliance

According to law, the IEP must contain the student's present level of performance, annual goals and short-term objectives, prescribed services, degree of mainstreaming, projected dates of service initiation and duration, and evaluation procedures (Schenck & Levy, 1979; Shore, 1986). The program must also proceed without delay; strict deadlines exist regarding IEP implementation and review.

Several studies conducted during the first years of PL 94-142 implementation examined IEP documents to assess their accuracy, efficiency, and legal abiding. The results are staggering in terms of the amount of insufficient and incomplete data. For example, in one of the earliest studies, Alper (1978) found that a majority of IEPs omitted important information (e.g., child characteristics, the rationale for prescribed placement, the degree of mainstreaming, parent consent signatures) and endorsed poorly constructed goals and objectives. Similarly, Schenck and Levy (1979) found that almost two thirds of the examined IEPs did not report children's performance levels, raising serious doubts about the appropriateness of their proposed goals. In fact, about one fifth of the cases did not reveal *any* goals or statement of prescribed services, and one third lacked specific evaluation procedures, thereby denying the assessment of school services and child progress. Furthermore, a significant percentage of the IEPs lacked information regarding the degree of mainstreaming (68%), the time to be spent in special education (37%), the initiation or duration dates (30%), and evidence of parental approval (57%). Wider and more comprehensive analyses verified these statistics on IEP incompleteness (Pyecha et al., 1980; Say,

McCollum, & Brightman, 1980). Pyecha and collaborators reported that only about 40% of IEPs were "reasonably informative and internally consistent," with only one third legally complete. The paucity of substantive, required information in many early IEPs impugned the document's ability to function as a definitive framework for the least restrictive, individualized education program mutually supported and approved by parents and professionals.

Some data, however, support the conclusion that a greater degree of accuracy and completeness of the IEP may be associated with higher degrees of parental involvement in the IEP process. Singer, Bossard, and Watkins (1977) found that, when parents attended the IEP meetings, more school personnel were also present and more recommendations were proposed. This greater staff participation in the planning process may likely affect active involvement in program implementation as well, increasing school accountability and the likelihood of successful services. In addition, Say et al. (1980) found that IEPs of students whose parent either attended the IEP meeting (which occurred 56% of the time) or signed the IEP document (47% of the time) were significantly more accurate than the IEPs developed when parents were not present or did not sign the document. Therefore, parent involvement or final approval of the IEP document may be keys to its quality and efficacy.

The results of these studies indicate that, years after the legislation was enacted, a number of required components were found missing from the education plans of many children with disabilities. These inaccurate and illegitimate practices could seriously compromise the integrity of the system as well as the quality of educational services provided to the students. However, when parents are included in the IEP planning meeting, a greater degree of accuracy and productivity may be seen in the prescribed program. The role of parents as empowered agents to ensure the schools' accountability should not be understated.

IEP Goals and Objectives

An IEP document delineates the specific instructional goals, objectives, and requisite support services approved by both school professionals and parents of a child with autism. By stating desired educational outcomes, the IEP helps to guide service providers toward appropriate methods of instruction (Billingsley, 1984); its content and tone can determine the quality and spirit with which the objectives are implemented. Best educational practices require that students with disabilities be taught desired, functional, and age-appropriate activities that help them to participate actively in the home, school, and community (Downing, 1988; Rainforth, York, & Macdonald, 1992). Therefore, when goals and objectives are proposed for the IEP, they should be chosen with the utmost care and concern for these educational priorities. The following studies, rather than focusing on procedural correctness, have questioned whether IEPs are indeed effective plans for appropriate instruction.

A number of investigations have provided evidence that children's unique needs are not effectively linked to specific IEP goals; consequently, the IEPs fail to effectively guide individualized instruction. For example, in one of the earliest examinations, Andersen, Barner, and Larson (1978) found that a great majority of IEP objectives (75%) were limited to the academic areas of reading, math, or language and neglected the social, emotional, and behavioral needs of the children. Other researchers have demonstrated that a substantial number of goals are either unrelated to the students' needs or inadequate relative to the students' performance levels (Schenck, 1980; Smith, 1990a; Smith & Simpson, 1989). Billingsley (1984) showed that two thirds of the IEP goals for children with severe disabilities were functional but ungeneralizable, and Downing (1988) similarly claimed that about one third of IEP objectives for a similar sample were age-inappropriate and nonfunctional. Therefore, the extent to which IEP goals promote and reflect individualized, functional, and generalizable instruction in all areas of development (social, emotional, behavioral, and cognitive) should be evaluated more critically by each IEP team.

In two well-controlled analyses, researchers found evidence of a positive relationship between the quality of IEP goals and the child's degree of integration. Hunt, Goetz, and Anderson (1986) evaluated IEP objectives for students with severe disabilities on the basis of seven components of best practices (including age-appropriateness, functionality, and generalizability). Results indicated that, with teacher expertise held constant, IEPs written for students at integrated sites scored significantly higher on overall quality than those established for students at segregated sites. Furthermore, the segregated service delivery systems did not typically reflect the child's chronological age, but rather the degree of developmental disability. Subsequently, IEP goals were based on a special education framework striving for the resolution of the impairment; they did not seek to prepare the student for functional independence. In a related study, Fesler (1988) evaluated IEP objectives during a district-wide systems change to determine if the changes were reflected in the IEPs. Results corroborated the finding that IEP objectives written for integrated students were higher in quality than those written for segregated students. In addition, the change to a more community-based instructional program was reflected in IEP modifications—from traditional, developmentally based goals to functional, age-appropriate goals that provided more opportunities for natural interactions with peers without disabilities. Thus, IEPs appear to be framed in the same context as the service delivery system in which they are implemented: If integrated, the written goals more often reflect the philosophy of integration; if segregated, a special education developmental model.

Group Decision-Making Dynamics

A large amount of time and effort is being expended for the mandated team evaluation, placement, and IEP development for each child with disabilities. There are various sources of support for the assertion that collaborative teamwork is essential for special education program design. One of the basic assumptions is that decisions emanating from a *group* of education professionals provide for better placement opportunities, more effective and less fragmented services, and safeguards against arbitrary decisions and errors in judgment (Crisler, 1979; Kehle & Guidubaldi, 1980; Pfeiffer, 1980; Smith, 1990b; Yoshida, Fenton, Kaufman, & Maxwell, 1978). Furthermore, the individual learning characteristics of the heterogeneous population of students with disabilities demand a multidisciplinary resource for knowledge, problem-solving, and support (Gallagher, 1989; Rainforth, York, & Macdonald, 1992). Each team member may bring a unique perspective about a child's strengths and needs: Parents have the greatest information about the student's daily life outside of the school; teachers are the most knowledgeable about the challenges and opportunities in the classroom; and various therapists and parents, if adequately taught, can contribute their knowledge and strategies for improving skill acquisition (Rainforth, York, & Macdonald, 1992). Because of the diversity of the team composition, a wide array of information, skills, and services can provide more consistent attention to the student's needs and synthesized, functional skill acquisition across environments. Therefore, informed parents, trained educators, physical therapists, occupational therapists, speech pathologists, nurses, psychologists, and others have been mandated to work together to design and implement more integrated programs for children with disabilities (Rainforth, York, & Macdonald, 1992).

Although the collective expertise of school professionals would reasonably seem to enhance the successful adaptation and integration of special education students, this assumption is largely based on logic and not empirical validation (Armer & Thomas, 1978; Crisler, 1979; Kehle & Guidubaldi, 1980). In fact, some groups may be dominated by certain members who are especially verbal, authoritarian, and directive, but not particularly well informed about the needs or capabilities of the child (Kehle & Guidubaldi, 1980). Furthermore, differences in professional philosophies and orientations, jargon, and acceptance of the cooperative approach may also result in apathy or sabotage on the part of certain team members (Orelove & Sobsey, 1991; Rainforth, York, & Macdonald, 1992). The professionals who constitute IEP teams have been prepared in different approaches to service provision, and most professional training programs perpetuate unidisciplinary rather than multidisciplinary thinking (Crisler, 1979; Kaye & Aserlind, 1979; Rainforth, York, & Macdonald, 1992). If team members have little or no instruction in the cooperative approach nor individual commitment to collaboration, it is doubtful that teachers, administrators, school psychologists, and parents can integrate all of their diverse knowledge to formulate one comprehensive educational plan.

In addition, research and theory in social and organizational psychology have contributed information about participation in group decision making. Investigators have determined that, in order for the group to be successful, members must share responsibility throughout the entire process including the generation, the evaluation, and the final choice of alternatives (Cooper & Wood, 1974). However, evidence presented in the next section has shown the limited and passive roles extended in practice to parents and other general education personnel in the IEP process. These investigators have thus pointed out the inherent problem of a team approach to the development of an IEP: group variance, multiple interpretations, unequal status, ineffective communication, and individual expectations may subvert the process and cause tension, dissatisfaction, and inefficiency in educational services. As Gerardi, Grohe, Benedict, and Coolidge (1984) so aptly put it, "Anyone who has ever worked on a committee to develop any type of mutually agreed upon written document can easily understand the problems with which this procedure is fraught!" (p. 40).

Parent–Professional Partnership

If school professionals possess negative attitudes on the value of parental participation in the IEP process, they may not provide a supportive environment that encourages parents to exercise their full legal rights and opinions (Yoshida, Fenton, Kaufman, & Maxwell, 1978). A number of studies have shown that, generally, parents give and receive information during IEP meetings, but they may have limited involvement in decisions regarding program development (Goldstein et al., 1980; Lusthaus et al., 1981; Yoshida, Fenton, Kaufman, & Maxwell, 1978). For example, in a study by Goldstein and Turnbull (1982), analyses indicated that a majority of the parental contributions in the IEP meetings were only about family and personal issues, not educational issues of placement, curriculum, and evaluation. Furthermore, Lynch and Stein (1982), in a survey of 400 parents, found that, although 71% of the parents reported "active" participation in IEP development, only 14.6% had expressed opinions and made suggestions in the meeting. McKinney and Hocutt (1982) found that 43% of the parents in their survey felt that they had not participated fully in the development of the IEP; 69% had not helped in writing it. As the preceding sections demonstrate, this passive involvement may be due to a number of factors including parents' conscious decisions to defer responsibilities to school professionals or their inability to influence decisions due to a lack of knowledge related to special education (A.P. Turnbull & Leonard, 1981). However, some evidence indicates that parental passivity may be caused by attitudinal barriers imposed by school personnel due to their feelings of professional superiority. Educators may treat parents "as partially incompetent junior partners" (McAfee & Vergason, 1979, p. 7).

School personnel who may feel "threatened by the prospect of parents usurping their decision-making prerogatives" can "mishandle" parents and view them as "uninformed persons to be tolerated, neutralized, or appeased" (Shore, 1986, p. 99). The existence of such a bias was clearly demonstrated in an early survey of approximately 1,500 IEP team members conducted by Yoshida, Fenton, Kaufman, and Maxwell (1978). A majority of educators indicated that they approved of parental involvement in only 2 out of 24 possible IEP activities: 1) gathering relevant information about their child, and 2) presenting the information to the IEP team. Most of the surveyed members prescribed definite limits as to where parents should influence the decision-making process: Only about 40% agreed that parents should be involved in reviewing their child's progress; only approximately 35% felt that parents should evaluate the appropriateness of their child's educational program and alternatives; and only about 25% believed that parents should be involved in finalizing decisions. School professionals, in the early years of PL 94-142 implementation, appeared to be working from the assumption that parents were generally unqualified and ill-equipped to provide instructional guidance; therefore, they should not contribute as equals in making educational decisions at IEP meetings. Whether this attitude continues to influence parent–professional relationships and the IEP process in the present day remains to be investigated.

A number of investigators have provided evidence that various IEP team members can be ranked in terms of their decision-making power in the meetings (i.e., Gilliam, 1979; Gilliam & Coleman, 1981; Hyman, Carroll, Duffey, Manni, & Winikur, 1973; Yoshida, Fenton, Maxwell, & Kaufman, 1978; Ysseldyke, Algozzine, & Allen, 1982). Generally speaking, a hierarchy of status develops in terms of the members' significant contributions, with special education teachers, administrators, and school psychologists typically receiving the highest rankings in post-meeting surveys. Although parents, general education teachers, and principals were often ranked high in importance *before* the meeting, they appear to have less actual influence in the specific functions of the IEP than other team members. This early research again suggests that parents were not perceived as possessing expertise commensurate with other IEP team members; therefore, they lacked the opportunity to participate on the same level as the other professionals.

The extent of collaboration between parents and professionals in the creation of the IEP document has been investigated throughout the literature. Findings from various sources have indicated that a vast majority of IEPs are prepared exclusively by the special education teacher, with parents and general education personnel either not participating or doing so solely in a superficial manner. For instance, Pyecha and colleagues (1980) found that, in more than half of the cases that they evaluated, the special education teacher personally prepared the IEP, which was later only reviewed by the rest of the team. In addition, Schenck and Levy (1979) found that the referring teacher was involved in the development of the IEP in only 15% of the (total 300) cases, the receiving teacher was involved only 45% of the time, and the school psychologist as well as the parents were involved only 26% of the time. Goldstein et al. (1980) corroborated this evidence by contending that the major objective of most IEP meetings was to simply inform team members of the special educator's prior decisions while obtaining their consenting signatures. In their analyses of IEP meetings for children with mild disabilities, they found that the typical conference was only 36 minutes, that only 25% of the total contributions were provided by parents, and that the meeting typically consisted of a resource teacher describing an already developed and written IEP.

Unfortunately, therefore, most of the responsibility for the development of the IEP has been consigned to the education specialist without taking advantage of group input or collaboration. This may be due to the limitations of the group's ability to function as a cohesive unit (as discussed previously) or limitations of time imposed by the extensive obligations of both the professionals and parents. Thus, whereas parents and other team members typically have little or no real contribution in the educational programming, the special education professionals are inundated with major responsibilities that divert more time away from their direct services to children with disabilities—about 6.5 hours per special education student (Price & Goodman, 1980).

Professionals can often underestimate the importance of involving parents in the special education progress. In fact, in one classic early study, 79% of IEP placement teams were found to be either unaware or unclear that collaboration with parents was a goal of multidisciplinary teams (Fenton, Yoshida, Maxwell, & Kaufman, 1979). Prior research indicates that a great majority of IEP meetings lack the mandated number of professionals for collaboration (Pyecha et al., 1980; Scanlon, Arick, & Phelps, 1981). The limited attendance and passive participation of most of the members of the IEP committees suggest that roles and responsibilities of these participants have not been clearly defined (Goldstein et al., 1980). For the special education process to reflect varied, individualized, and accurate opinions, it is imperative that all participants actively attend and contribute to the IEP goals and objectives, with the home and school working closely together for ideal child outcomes.

This last section has briefly reviewed some of the critical factors that parents and professionals identify as issues influencing the quality of home–school partnerships in special education planning. These include sensitivity to family choice regarding participation; parent and professional knowledge concerning special education provisions; effectiveness of team communication and coordination due to professional language, group dynamics, and interpersonal skills; attitudes toward parent participation in the educational process; and logistical constraints imposed in achieving a cooperative effort among professionals. For the team approach in IEP development to work, the roles and responsibilities of all members need to be more clearly defined, the time restrictions and overburdens of the team players need to be remedied, and greater knowledge and coordination between members need to be communicated.

FACTORS AFFECTING COLLABORATIVE IEP IMPLEMENTATION

Much of the success of PL 94-142 in providing quality education to all children with disabilities lies in the effectiveness of the IEP—how it is conceived, perceived, and carried out (Kaye & Aserlind, 1979). The IEP is the legal nuts and bolts for the education of children with autism for many reasons: It is a reflection of the adequacy of the assessment procedures used to diagnose the needs of a child; it is the means by which an appropriate and individualized education in the least restrictive environment is specified and defined; and it is the major means of involving parents to advocate for their children's rights. For special education, there is no document more significant. The IEP can have an enormous impact in the classroom, on the roles and responsibilities of parents, with educational advocates and administrators, on the school district's organization, on educational goals, and on the acquisition and distribution of resources (Kaye & Aserlind, 1979; Smith, 1990b).

Yet parents and educators have become increasingly aware of the difficulties in translating the detailed and prescriptive policy initiatives of IDEA into practice. As discussed in the previous section, the development of IEPs by multidisciplinary teams may not be met with collaboration or active input of professionals and parents. Concomitantly, a question exists about whether the schools typically offer children with autism programs tailored to their needs or merely programs that are congruent with their existing service models.

Although literature in the preceding section focused on IEP completeness, quality, congruence with child behaviors, and parent involvement, the degree to which services are implemented was not assessed. Great caution must be taken in assuming a direct relationship between children's programs on paper and the actual delivery of these programs in schools, homes, and communities. Most studies evaluating the success of IEP implementation have focused on how well school districts have fulfilled the letter of the law. Perhaps more important is the school districts' success in meeting the spirit of the law, or how acceptable individualized and integrated special education services are at the local level. Just as architectural barriers block the access of persons with physical disabilities, so too may attitudinal barriers block the full participation of children with autism in schools and communities (Stoneman, 1993). Thus, teacher and parent attitudes can make the difference between success and failure of integrative efforts at numerous points during the IEP process: from the initial discussion of placement alternatives to the final evaluation of services (Gickling & Theobald, 1975; Ringlaben & Price, 1981; Stoneman, 1993). The following sections, therefore, discuss how other variables such as parent and professional attitudes and the degree of team collaboration may affect the amount of effort undertaken to reach IEP goals in least restrictive environments (LRE). They also detail how educators and parents rate the usefulness of the IEP in affecting educational equality through mainstreaming efforts and the degree to which the families of children with disabilities themselves are promoting integrated lifestyles.

Attitudes of General Education Teachers

As a direct result of PL 94-142, the composition of the typical elementary school classroom has changed: Children who would have been consigned to segregated special education services by their IEP team in the 1970s are now placed in less restrictive environments with general education teachers and children without disabilities (Carden-Smith & Fowler, 1983). The classroom teachers' attitudes toward mainstreaming and classroom adaptation skills are important factors to the educational and psychological adjustment of these integrated children (Rainforth, York, & Macdonald, 1992; Reynolds, Martin-Reynolds, & Mark, 1982; Stainback & Stainback, 1982b). Their positive responses can affect the behaviors of students without disabilities, help to encourage interactions between children, foster a supportive and respectful home–school relationship, and facilitate service delivery by promoting professional cooperation (W. Stainback & Stainback, 1982). However, the literature has consistently shown that general classroom teachers are often ill prepared, both in knowledge and attitude, to teach children with disabilities (Johnson & Cartwright, 1979; Madden & Slavin, 1983; Nevin et al., 1983). The following paragraphs summarize the investigative surveys of general education teachers that have been launched to better understand their views on mainstreaming and their interpretations of the LRE provision.

In studies assessing teachers' willingness to mainstream, positive attitudes have been shown to be tempered by the children's degree of disability, teachers' perceived degree of professional preparedness, and specific environmental variables. For instance, it was shown in early studies that most elementary and secondary teachers felt capable of assuming major responsibilities for children with mild physical, behavioral, or learning disabilities, but educating children with mental retardation at the moderate level was less acceptable (Hirshoren & Burton, 1979; Moore & Fine, 1978). The inadequacy of training was a common denominator in other teacher surveys: No matter whether investigators found more consistently positive attitudes toward mainstreaming (Reynolds et al., 1982;

Ringlaben & Price, 1981) or more consistently negative attitudes (Childs, 1979; Horne, 1985), a majority of teachers expressed concerns that they had neither the proper training nor the proper knowledge to legally and effectively implement integration. Other teacher-related variables such as perceived past successes with special needs children, access to supportive services, educational background, belief in the schools' obligation to special education students, and self-confidence were highly predictive factors of positive attitudes (Larrivee & Cook, 1979; Stephens & Braun, 1980); perceived degree of stress was negatively related to support of mainstreaming (Bensky et al., 1980). Finally, environment-related variables such as time, class size, grade, and availability of support services were found to differentially affect attitudes; teachers of higher grade levels with less flexibility, time, and supportive services were more resistant to mainstreaming (Larrivee & Cook, 1979). To accommodate children with disabilities in their classrooms, general education teachers expressed a need for additional instruction, more release time to consult with resource people, and smaller class sizes—a remarkably accurate reflection of the adjustments that special education teachers have demanded for years (Salvia & Munson, 1986).

Attitudes are difficult to alter and individuals can remain remarkably fixed in their beliefs, but there is considerable empirical support for the position that positive teacher attitudes can be facilitated through intervention (Horne, 1985). Investigations to determine the relative efficacy of providing educators with information and/or experience in teaching children with disabilities seem contradictory but interesting. Harasymiw and Horne (1976), in the earliest of the studies, found that workshops including instruction, experience, and administrative support helped to modify teachers' intimidation about children with disabilities; Johnson and Cartwright (1979) showed that subjects who received interventions consisting of only information or an information-experience combination had improved attitudes toward mainstreaming; and S. Stainback and Stainback (1982a) demonstrated that experience-only interventions significantly reduced teacher anxieties about integration. However, teachers still felt least responsible for the implementation of integration because it was a mandate externally imposed on them (Harasymiw & Horne, 1976). The authors suggested that programs that involved teachers in decision making would foster greater self-responsibility and ensure more effective transitions into integration. Thus, collaboration in all aspects of the IEP process appears to be key to professional ownership of special education challenges, role satisfaction, and diligence in IEP implementation.

Attitudes of Parents

Generally, lawmakers and professionals in the field of special education have assumed that parents of children with disabilities agree with the principle of integration and would support the implementation of programs leading toward the attainment of this goal for their children (Ferrara, 1979). Yet, in one of the first studies to investigate the attitudes of parents toward mainstreaming, Ferrara found that parents, although supportive of the general concept, did not wholeheartedly endorse its application to their children with mental retardation. Ferrara cautioned that legislation mandating integration could encounter resistance at the grass roots level if policy makers and service providers did not develop effective strategies to minimize this conflict between theory and practice.

Because parents may now be active participants in their child's placement decisions, more systematic information concerning their views and what influences their perceptions about mainstreaming is vital to a program's success (Mlynek, Hannah, & Hamlin, 1982). Therefore, a number of investigators have compared the attitudes of both parents of children with disabilities and those without disabilities involved in integrated public school classes (Bailey & Winton, 1987; Green & Stoneman, 1989; Peck, Carlson, & Helmstetter,

1992; Peck, Hayden, Wandschneider, Peterson, & Richarz, 1989; A.P. Turnbull, Winton, Blacher, & Salkind, 1983). The results of the studies have generally indicated that the two groups hold very similar views about the benefits and drawbacks of mainstreaming. The greatest perceived benefits were described as the social outcomes and opportunities for children with disabilities to be exposed to "real-world" circumstances and to be accepted by their community. Perceived drawbacks related to the issue of instructional effectiveness, teacher preparation, and rejection of children with disabilities by their peers. For instance, Peck et al. (1989), in a qualitative inquiry into the sources of resistance to integrated programs, found that parents were concerned about the availability of teacher time and attention to their child. However, in a later study of the perceptions of parents of children without disabilities enrolled in integrated programs, Peck et al. (1992) found that the parents perceived the overall effects of the mainstreaming as quite positive—they felt that their children exhibited more acceptance of human differences, more awareness of other children's needs, less discomfort with people with disabilities, less prejudice and fewer stereotypes about people who look or behave differently, and more responsiveness and helpfulness to other children. In addition, parents disagreed that their child acquired undesirable behaviors as a result of their integrated contact or that they suffered a loss of teacher attention. These results are notably consistent with previous findings (i.e., Bailey & Winton, 1987; A.P. Turnbull et al., 1983) and suggest that many of the fears reported by parents *before* they experience mainstreaming are often assuaged *after* their children participate in these programs (Peck et al., 1992).

To assess this possible longitudinal effect of integration on parental attitudes, Bailey and Winton (1987) evaluated parents' hopes and concerns about mainstreaming prior to its initiation and again 9 months later. Most parents were generally positive about the potential benefits of mainstreaming and remained so after 9 months, although they were less likely to believe that mainstreaming would help them learn about child development, provide them with more chances to interact with parents of children without disabilities, or help families of children without disabilities understand their situation better. Therefore, whereas most parental concerns are resolved simply by the passage of time, some related to social outcomes might require individualized interventions.

Finally, various investigators have analyzed the influence of particular personal and demographic variables on the attitudes of parents toward integration, and the profiles are dramatically parallel to the teacher data. Green and Stoneman (1989) found that the attitudes of mothers of children without disabilities were related to past positive experiences with persons with disabilities. A.P. Turnbull and Winton (1983) found that the attitudes of parents differed by the preschool service models in which their children were enrolled: Mainstreaming participants extolled the virtues of "real-world" exposure; parents of children in segregated environments praised the respite care and special services that their preschools provided. The following quotations from A.P. Turnbull and Winton (1983) dramatically illustrate these contrasting attitudes:

> (Mother of a child in a mainstreamed program) You need to learn to deal with this world the way it's designed to run right now, which is toward the nonhandicapped. You cannot live in a sheltered environment, whether it be your own home, or a private school for the handicapped, and then all of a sudden become of age and be thrown out into the world and never learn to deal with it. (pp. 63–64)

> (Mother of a child in a segregated program) He's pretty young to be the only one different. He needs to see a lot of people like himself doing a lot of productive things before he can forge out there and be Crusader Rabbit. (p. 64)

In summary, the literature reveals common concerns of parents and teachers, individuals whose support of integrated programs is necessary for their endurance. The foremost concern of all of the individuals involved in the special education system is the adequacy of resources allocated to support least restrictive programs, which includes the adequacy of personnel, instruction, salaries, materials, and information. Parents of both children with and without disabilities are especially concerned that their children's individual needs continue to be met in integrated programs; and educators in both special and regular education are concerned that their teaching strategies remain effective with the structural, procedural, and educational changes required in heterogeneous classrooms. Unfortunately, it appears that most classroom teachers in integrated environments do not perceive children's IEPs as useful instruments for their curriculum planning (Dudley-Marling, 1985; Morgan & Rhode, 1983). Another major source of concern is the degree to which collaboration and mutual support is communicated to all IEP team members. For programs to be effective, parents and professionals must all share in equitable responsibilities for IEP implementation. The following section therefore addresses issues beyond instructional planning to better understand how team planning is translated into team functioning.

Teacher and Parent Ownership of IEP Goals

As was discussed in the previous section, the development of each child's special education plan may hardly be accomplished through collaborative teamwork. Instead, the special education teacher may assume the responsibility for the creation of specific educational strategies. A critical implication of this practice is that, because the other members are not responsible for the design of the plan, they will also accept less responsibility for its implementation. In fact, empirical investigations (i.e., Pugach, 1982; Ysseldyke et al., 1982) have demonstrated that ownership and responsibility for the goals and objectives specified in a child's IEP are often deferred soley to the classroom teacher or education specialist without regard to potential collaboration of all professionals and the parents. When the other IEP team members do participate, they usually generate discipline-focused goals and objectives that result in fragmented services (Rainforth, York, & Macdonald, 1992). Professionals are usually unable or unwilling to integrate the disparate pieces into comprehensive, coordinated programs. Thus, the implementation of the IEP often falls solely on the shoulders of special education personnel, who deliver services congruent with their educational philosophies and practices. This may have a critical impact on the child's ability to generalize and synthesize acquired skills in natural and varied environments.

With the formal act of referral, classroom teachers often transfer the ownership of the problems of a child with disabilities to a team of special education professionals and then assume that they are absolved of further responsibilities (Pugach & Johnson, 1989b; Salvia & Munson, 1986). Yet evidence shows that general education teachers typically continue to be principal providers of instruction to children eligible for special services; many children with disabilities participate in regular programs of science, social studies, reading, and math (Nevin et al., 1983).

Despite these educational responsibilities, general education teachers are relegated to a lower status in the IEP meeting, and a disconcertingly low proportion of IEP goals and objectives are directed toward their efforts (Alper, 1978; Andersen et al., 1978; Goldstein et al., 1980; Nevin et al., 1983; Pugach, 1982; Pugach & Johnson, 1989b; Schenck & Levy, 1979). Andersen et al. (1978) found that the general class teachers were responsible for implementing only 25% of the objectives on IEPs. Schenck and Levy (1979) found that *none* of the 300 IEPs they examined delineated goals, objectives, or instructional strategies to be employed by the general educator. Pugach (1982) corroborated this evidence, finding that the IEP goals and objectives rarely concern the time the student spends in the general classroom, but only the portion of instruction administered directly by special education teachers. As a result, many general education teachers and administrators have admitted to considering the IEP an obsolete and cumbersome tool with no direct bearing on their instructional endeavors or efficacy (Pugach, 1982; Smith & Simpson, 1989). General education teachers seldom use the IEP in planning or monitoring their daily instruction for students with disabilities; in fact, only 12% of Pugach's (1982) research sample even had IEPs on file in their classrooms. Thus, in the end, the IEP may be perceived as simply reflecting special education curriculum objectives developed *by* special educators *for* special educators rather than for the child's multidisciplinary team and total school curriculum (Goldstein et al., 1980).

Repeatedly, despite implicit expectations for parents to actively involve themselves in the special education and intervention efforts for their children, empirical evidence has shown that parents are also not often named as service providers in the goals and objectives of the IEP. McKinney and Hocutt (1982) found that, among parents of children with learning disabilities, almost all of them (93%) had worked with their child at home, yet they did not distinguish between home activities carried out as objectives of the IEP and those generally expected of all parents. Investigators have also found that parents of children in special education desire a greater voice in the development, implementation, and evaluation of their child's program (Rose, 1990; Soffer, 1982). As a result, Crawford (1978) urged parents to demand that the goals of the IEP be specific, clear cut, and "theirs as well as the professionals'" (p. 4); when parents recognize and take advantage of their educational responsibilities, a more consistent and potent educational plan can be maintained for the student. Thus, it appears particularly important that parents be afforded the opportunity to be critical service providers and evaluators of the IEP and that a genuine effort be made to acknowledge them as the foremost authorities on their children.

An interesting contradiction has been shown to occur when families of children with disabilities agree to the implementation of the least restrictive alternative for their children's education. Through studies of parents of mainstreamed preschool children, researchers have gathered evidence regarding the families' quantity and quality of interactions with other parents. The parents of the preschoolers with disabilities have generally named fewer parents with whom they interact and have relied primarily on other parents of children with disabilities for support and assistance (Bailey & Winton, 1989; Blacher & Turnbull, 1983). Interviews and sociometric data also suggest that some parents of children with disabilities still feel isolated and ill at ease around parents of children without disabilities. Thus, parents of children with autism in mainstreamed programs may not themselves be mainstreamed (also see Chapter 10). Guidelines offered by Bailey and McWilliam (1990) suggest methods for enhancing an integrated family focus: Families of children with autism should be accorded the same respect given to parents of typically developing children, and the primary goal of intervention should be to engage in activities designed to promote inclusive community adaptation. If parents are to direct their efforts toward IEP goals such as integration, it is important to practice them in the community in addition to the school environment.

Mere passage of PL 94-142 did not automatically ensure that all children with disabilities would receive an appropriate education in the least restrictive environment. Lamorey and Bricker (1993) have suggested that initiation and maintenance of integrated programs depends largely on the support of the community, the commitment of personnel, and parental attitudes. Thus, variables external to the intervention program greatly influence its success. These preceding sections have delineated some of those external factors that can affect the efforts and intentions of special education policy makers; the next section offers suggestions to improve and ensure appropriate, individualized services to children with autism and their families.

EFFORTS TO PROMOTE COLLABORATIVE
PARTNERSHIPS IN SPECIAL EDUCATION

As a result of both public policy and public outcry, a concerted effort to improve the relationships between parents and education personnel has been undertaken within the last decade (Feldman, Gerstein, & Feldman, 1989). Unfortunately, parents and professionals have a long history of inharmonious relations to reverse. The difficulties between them stem from a variety of sources, including destructive stereotypes; different life experiences and expectations; different levels of knowledge; varied cultural backgrounds; time limitations; unequal levels of interpersonal skills; incompatible values and priorities; and even feelings of competitiveness, superiority, or intimidation (Darling, 1983; Doyle & Guttierrez, 1988; Paget, 1992; Roos, 1978; Sonnenschein, 1984; Turnbull & Turnbull, 1986). Some of the problems seem to lie in the inherent nature of the client–professional relationship, but these problems are intensified by the special vulnerabilities of families of children with disabilities; others evolve from assumptions made by parents and professionals about each other's attitudes, feelings, and skills (Sonnenschein, 1984). The conflicts may not only hinder the development of productive and rewarding relationships, but can also cause pain and grief to families struggling to regain their equilibrium, strength, and self-confidence (Sonnenschein, 1984).

Parents of children with disabilities, despite their passive roles in the IEP meeting and conflicts with school professionals, have generally indicated overall appreciation of the IEP process and its outcomes (Goldstein et al., 1980; Goldstein & Turnbull, 1982; Witt, Miller, McIntyre, & Smith, 1984). Investigators have cited parent satisfaction levels ranging from 85% to 90% in regard to the meeting, the special education program, and related services their children were provided (Leyser, 1988; Say et al., 1980). Many of these parents also expressed appreciation for educators' concern, dedication, and support; they believed IEP meetings kept them in touch with their children's education (Goldstein & Turnbull, 1982). Satisfied parents in a survey by Witt et al. (1984) indicated that they had been encouraged to participate, that their ideas were sought out and used by the school district in developing the IEP, and that the atmosphere of the meeting promoted mutual respect and active involvement of school personnel. Although much of the early literature indicated that the relationships between parents and professionals were often strained and unequal in influence, these contradictory findings indicate that there currently may exist a potentially positive foundation from which to build more collaborative relationships between parents and teachers.

Parent–professional collaboration is a vital element in the accomplishment of special education goals and objectives. If professionals and parents can embark on cooperative team efforts to educate and habilitate children with autism, mutual respect and understanding will grow while misunderstandings and destructive stereotypes diminish. The following sections describe the typical patterns of relationships between the home and the school, the legal alternatives for the resolution of possible conflicts, and proposed intervention efforts to improve the parent–school partnership in special education.

Patterns of Relationships Between Parents and Professionals

A number of investigations have focused on parents' and professionals' perspectives of one another and their roles in the education process to better understand their current relationships and their receptivity to interventions. For example, Ferguson (1984) collected data on parent attitudes toward school professionals and found that parents basically viewed educational personnel as well intentioned but still inept, threatened, defensive, and rejecting. They contended that the schools cover the bases legally, though; they rush through a meeting, get the parent's signature, and breathe a sigh of relief as they go on to the next "case." While they might not intentionally mislead a parent, they will withhold important information because it is safe and easier. . . . Their attitude is that the parent is too protective or over-involved, and just wants an unreasonable amount for the child. (pp. 43–44)

Conversely, in an examination of teachers views, Feldman et al. (1989) found that, regardless of their age, sex, grade level, or years of teaching experience, both special and general education teachers held negative beliefs about parents of children with disabilities. When compared with their views about parents of children without disabilities, the teachers perceived fewer parents of children with disabilities as having trust in them, being competent parents, or undertaking instructional efforts at home. In addition, Cone et al. (1985) found that, overall, parents of children in special education were not seen by their children's teachers as highly involved. Whether teachers are communicating a bias that parents of children with disabilities should participate above and beyond the typical participation of parents of children without disabilities or whether their evaluations accurately reflect a parental passivity in special education is still a question worthy of empirical investigation. However, the findings do suggest the importance of developing strategies for changing unproductive attitudes of teachers and parents in order to facilitate better home–school relationships and the integration of children with autism.

Power and Bartholomew (1987) dramatically characterized the possible outcomes of home–school collaboration:

When the complex, public world of school and the idiosyncratic world of family come together, the kaleidoscope of interactions created can be vibrant, nurturing, explosive, patronizing, or suffocating. Ideally families organize themselves to meet the unique needs of children and attain parents' dreams for them, while schools function to advance a set of societal/communal expectations and values. Schools at times can disregard children's personal needs and place limits on the attainment of parental dreams. Families can become so convoluted as to ignore realistic developmental tasks that children need to face. When family and school meet, many outcomes are possible, which when repeated over and over become relationship patterns that assume a life of their own. (p. 498)

The investigators, in their ecological assessment of family–school relationships, presented five relationship patterns, including *avoidant, competitive, merged, one-way,* and *collaborative,* and illustrated strategies for changing the dysfunctional patterns. Basically, the characterized relationships differ in their patterns of communication, collaboration, and dominance. According to the authors, developing *collaborative* alliances requires the establishment of clear, definable boundaries between the family and school, the reaffirmation the authority of parents and teachers in their respective domains, and the reinforcement of efforts of parents and teachers to share information and voice concerns when they arise.

In summary, the literature characterizing the home–school relationship occasionally presents glimpses of professionals' attempts to be more sensitive to the ordeals of parents of children with disabilities, as well as potential models for the successful coordination of efforts between the home and the school. Too frequently, however, the research also suggests that the typical relationship is clouded in misunderstanding, rivalry, and disrespect as both the school and the family vie for control of educational programs of children with disabilities. To remediate this deleterious cycle of antagonism and opposition, two general options exist in the current special education forum. The following sections describe the available methods of both *conflict resolution* and *conflict prevention:* the legal alternatives to pursue when grievances occur and interventions that have been developed to avoid the disputes from the beginning.

Legal Alternatives for the Resolution of Conflicts

Due process is a procedure that ensures the fairness of educational decisions and the accountability of both the professionals and the parents in making these decisions. Thus, it can be viewed as a system of checks and balances concerning the identification, evaluation, and provision of services for students with disabilities (Strickland & Turnbull, 1990). If, at any time, the parents of a child with disabilities are dissatisfied with the procedures being followed or with the program being planned, they have rights under PL 94-142 to formally challenge the school's recommendations or decisions. Similarly, the school districts are legally entitled to contest the decisions that the parents make about their child's educational program. The primary avenues of conflict resolution include options that vary in their degrees of formality and confrontation from informal mediation meetings to more formal due process hearings (Shore, 1986). Any informal measure to resolve a conflict, such as mediation, may be conducted to alleviate the adversarial nature and emotional stress of a formal hearing, but not to impose a stumbling block to immediate due process. Parents and school districts have the right to be represented by legal counsel in hearings, to have access to all school records concerning the child, to present evidence and cross-examine witnesses, and to prohibit the submission of evidence not revealed to them at least 5 days before the hearing. Congress imposed these and additional procedural safeguards under the assumption that the provisions would secure parental participation vital to the child's educational welfare and achieve accuracy and fairness in hearing decisions (Goldberg & Kuriloff, 1991).

Despite the fact that due process represents an intrusion of the judicial process into the field of special education, little research has actually examined its capacity to produce fair results (Goldberg & Kuriloff, 1991). Investigators have been inhibited by the operational definition of "fairness" in trial outcomes. A "fair" hearing may be determined by the following: the degree to which expected procedures were followed and equal rights were offered by the hearing officer; the range of program alternatives offered as a result of the decision; and/or the participants' emotional investment, financial costs, interpretation of their rights, and temperament (Goldberg & Kuriloff, 1991). Recently, Goldberg and Kuriloff attempted to ascertain parents' and educators' perceptions of both the accuracy and impartiality of their due process hearings. Results indicated that there were large and significant differences between the schools' and the parents' perceptions of the hearings' legality—more than 95% of the school officials, but only 51% of the parents, believed that they had received all or most of their rights. Furthermore, more than 80% of the educators, but only about 40% of the parents, felt that the hearings were fair and accurate. There was also a correlation between perceptions and trial outcomes: The more people won, the more they were satisfied with the decisions (and schools tended to win more often than parents). The authors reported that, because parents are likely to have a greater emotional investment in the outcome of the hearing than are the school officials, they are more apt to judge the fairness by outcome than by procedural safeguards accorded them. In addition, hearings appeared to inflict financial and emotional suffering, as well as create unnecessary antagonisms between parents and professionals. It is ironic that the very provisions of PL 94-142, designed to safeguard the rights of individuals, tend to set up structures and procedures that are confusing and intimidating to the people most needful of the law's protections. Unfortunately, the IEP meetings and the due process formalities exemplify these conflicting outcomes (National Education Association, 1978).

The major belief expressed by parents and special educators is that the legal model is ill-suited to resolving educational disputes. Although both parents and educators firmly believe in each other's right to request a hearing if alternative methods fail to reach agreement, it is critical to find ways to prevent disputes from landing in court in the first place (Goldberg & Kuriloff, 1991). The following section illustrates the attempts of investigators and professionals to intervene in this cycle of conflict and dissatisfaction in order to benefit not only the parents and schools, but, most important, the children with disabilities who deserve competent and effective services in supportive environments.

Interventions for the Prevention of Parent–School Conflict

The pervasive nature of conflict in the parent–professional relationship demands that appropriate strategies be developed for its resolution (Simpson, 1990). Only sensitive, early interventions that involve professionals and parents working together are likely to avoid the costly, emotional battles that erupt once they disagree on the appropriateness of an educational program (Goldberg & Kuriloff, 1991). The facilitation of a collaborative partnership between the school and the home has been approached in five general ways in the literature to date; the interventions have focused on 1) improving teacher and parent attitudes toward collaboration, 2) promoting effective communication techniques, 3) increasing special education knowledge and skills, 4) increasing administrative support, and 5) encouraging more flexibility in roles and more collaborative IEP goals. The following sections describe these methods to improve relationships and gain greater understanding of the needs and capabilities of both parents and professionals. The framework is not from a legal perspective, but rather from a model of collaborative teamwork that has the potential to bridge the idealistic intentions of IDEA with the realities of service provision.

Improving Attitudes

For many years, researchers have expressed their opinions about the proper attitudes with which to approach the formation of parent–professional teams. A number have elucidated recommendations that emphasize the adoption of open, optimistic, and respectful attitudes to enhance coordinated team efforts for consistent and effective services. Parents' and professionals' ability to work effectively together requires leadership, trust, communication, problem-solving abilities, and a commitment to common goals.

Many authors have delineated suggestions for collaboration in the form of prescriptive lists (i.e., Crisler, 1979; Murphy & Della Corte, 1988; Simpson, 1990; Spiegle-Mariska, 1990). The researchers have presented "do's" and "don'ts" that could either be enhancements or detriments to multidisciplinary team functioning. Positive contributions to collaboration include realistic expectations, good listening and communication skills, specifically defined goals and objectives, use of community resources, and an emphasis on positive outcomes. Potential negative contributions to a team include feelings of superiority or absolute authority, judgmental or defensive reactions, individual domination of the proceedings, and pessimistic or patronizing attitudes. These general recommendations for proper special education collaboration were directed toward both parents and professionals in recognition of the reciprocity of the IEP procedures.

However, Comegys (1989) and Winton et al. (1984) have specifically recommended activities and interventions to parents in order for them to assist professionals in the integration process. The authors suggested that parents prepare the classroom teacher with information such as their child's favorite activities, effective discipline strategies, favorite rewards, and special medical needs in order to increase teacher confidence and the consistency of home and school services. They also advocated for parent volunteer programs in the schools and instruction in the community to enhance parents' social relationships, increase their knowledge about the special education system, and encourage their use of community resources. All of these activities focus on positive outlooks, effective communication, individualized education, and the building of networks in the community at the hands of parents.

Recently, Spiegle-Mariska (1990) and Salisbury (1992) focused on the importance of the professionals' role in establishing positive attitudes. Suggestions made specifically for professionals included recognizing the potential strengths of a child with disabilities; helping parents to see that professionals view the child as a person and not as a problem; recognizing and encouraging the valuable role parents play on the multidisciplinary team; and working with the family as an empowering force, helping them to acquire skills and knowledge that will last a lifetime (Spiegle-Mariska, 1990). In addition, teachers were encouraged to carefully examine their attitudes and behaviors toward parents in comparison to their treatment of other professionals. For instance, professionals should recognize that they typically do not take formal action without the input from all of their colleagues, they accept their colleagues' judgments concerning their level of involvement, and they value and respect colleagues' comments; however, parents are seldom consulted before the IEP is written, their commitment to their children is questioned when they are absent from meetings, and their motivations and actions are met with skepticism and judgmental attitudes (Salisbury, 1992). Because most parents have already faced a traumatizing experience in the recognition of their child's disability, the authors have encouraged professionals to take the initiative in establishing coordinated efforts toward nurturing the child's development.

Promoting Effective Communication Techniques

Effective communication is the cornerstone of a meaningful parent–professional relationship (Mori, 1983). But in many cases both the parents and professionals lack the necessary interpersonal skills required to communicate in a productive manner (McNamara, 1986; Sawyer & Sawyer, 1981). Teachers usually receive little or no training in communicating with parents during their preservice years, but they most often bear responsibility for discussing a child's educational program and progress with parents (National Education Association, 1978). In fact, a majority of parents (60%–70%) have identified their child's teacher as the staff member with whom they feel the most comfortable talking about their child's problems (Leyser, 1988; Say et al., 1980). No other group has the frequent and sustained contact with parents that teachers do, nor is any other group so vested with the trust and hope for the success of children with disabilities.

Consequently, a number of investigators have tried to identify some nontraditional ways for teachers to interact with parents in order to enhance communicative effectiveness, build informative partnerships, and increase parental access to meetings (i.e., Goldstein & Turnbull, 1982; Leyser, 1988; McNamara, 1986). The recommendations to teachers have included arranging for transportation to and from school meetings, seeing the parents prior to the IEP conferences in order to gather input from them, arranging meetings in alternative locations such as nearby schools or churches that are closer to the parents' home and/or that provide child care, making the environment as comfortable and nonthreatening as possible, communicating in jargon-free language and in terms of observable child behaviors, giving parents the opportunity to evaluate the IEP conference, and maintaining frequent written and oral communication with the parents to discuss needs and concerns.

In addition, interventions including the representation of parent advocates at IEP meetings and teacher communication instruction have been suggested. For example, Goldstein and Turnbull (1982) found that there was significantly more parental involvement and less parental intimidation in the IEP conference when a parent advocate was in attendance to introduce the parents, direct questions to them, clarify terminology, verbally reinforce their contributions, and summarize the discussion at the end. Sawyer and Sawyer (1981) found that teachers could be assisted in responding appropriately to difficult concerns of parents through a *microcounseling model* in which they used videotapes, role play, and discussions of effective communication skills. Similarly, Simpson (1990) offered educators several helpful recommendations for facilitating active *listening* in parent–professional meetings. He suggested preparation techniques such as outlining an agenda and reviewing a child's progress beforehand, arranging for a private setting, furnishing parents with information to reduce their anxiety, and maintaining a natural demeanor during the meeting while being aware of affective and nonverbal responses. Overall, the researchers appear to be emphasizing the need for parents and professionals to use effective communication techniques, to listen with their ears as well as their hearts, and to be sensitive to each other's feelings as well as to each other's words.

Increasing Knowledge and Skills

State departments of education have a responsibility under PL 94-142 to develop and disseminate information regarding special education to parents of children with disabilities. Investigators have found that the overriding concern of parents is their lack of knowledge about community resources and their children's special needs (Able-Boone et al., 1990). Parents should be given specific and practical information about their children's needs, including lectures and demonstrations on specific instructional strategies, structured and clear-cut goals, and methods of progress evaluation. By increasing parents' knowledge and skills, professionals can empower families to become their children's teachers and advocates, giving parents a sense of control over their lives while strengthening their internal and external supports.

General education teachers and parents of children with autism are at a distinct disadvantage in the amount of information they have access to concerning the special education process. To remedy the disparity, researchers have recommended that both teachers and parents receive instruction on concrete strategies for coping with the individual strengths and needs of children with autism and for adjusting expectations about these children's education (Evans, 1990). For example, Malmberg (1984) advised professionals to develop parent IEP preparation materials containing specific legal roles and responsibilities of each team member, purposes of the IEP, recommendations for things to do before the meeting, procedures during the meeting, and what to do after the meeting. Similarly, A.P. Turnbull and Turnbull (1986) encouraged school psychologists to assist parents in their advocacy roles by instructing them on their children's educational needs, school and community resources, and legal principles. The authors urged professionals to use a variety of formats and instructional strategies, including written documents, radio and public television programs, workshops, and parent-to-parent groups. Madden and Slavin (1983) argued for instructional programs that help general education teachers meet the instructional and social-emotional needs of children with disabilities through cooperative learning or individualized instruction techniques.

Finally, various authors and parent organizations have advocated the use of parent groups to benefit both the family and the school. As a cooperative enterprise, parent support groups can link the needs of both special educators and parents of children with autism. While fulfilling the parents' needs for emotional support, understanding, and information, the groups also are a source of knowledge to the schools. The groups become

cost-effective, preventive conflict-reduction mechanisms that further cooperative relationships, special education knowledge, and positive interactions between the home and the
school. They can assist parents with problems before they grow to crisis proportions and
provide a consistent channel of communication between parents and professionals
(Duganne et al., 1983).

Increasing Administrative Support

Even the most highly motivated teachers and parents cannot fully implement individualized instruction without great personal sacrifice unless carefully planned administrative
support is available at the district level (Safer, Morrissey, Kaufman, & Lewis, 1978). In
fact, an early investigation into the implementation of PL 94-142 showed how administrative support was fundamentally related to the success of special education programs.
When Safer et al. (1978) surveyed teachers' perceptions of the IEP process, two distinct
groups emerged: one group with significant apprehension and negativity toward their new
roles and responsibilities, and another group experiencing confidence and success in parent–professional collaboration. When teachers and directors of special education in the
second group were queried as to why implementation of IEPs had worked so well in their
districts, they overwhelmingly responded with details of their administrative support. The
strategies of the district fell into four general categories: 1) teacher involvement in planning and implementation of the new procedures; 2) in-service instruction on the writing of
behavioral objectives; 3) resource support including assessments, standardized forms,
aides, and consultive assistance; and 4) formal and informal feedback mechanisms. Thus,
administrative support in these districts empowered all teachers with information, skills,
strategies, and assistance while also being responsive to their concerns and opinions about
the programs.

   In recognition of the power of administrative support in determining successful policy implementation, a number of authors have provided principals and administrators with
self-help guides to improve district services to children with disabilities and their families.
In a principal's guide developed by Farkas (1981), administrators are assisted in examining school policies from a family perspective through self-examination, written exercises,
and checklist procedures. Similarly, Wilson (1989) recommended that special education
administrators facilitate integration in the classroom and community by increasing knowledge about service delivery options, opinions of the staff, and current research; involving
teachers and parents in program decisions; gaining the support of principals; and developing an ideal service system that includes a continuum of services, personnel development,
and an appropriate financial plan. In addition, the author encouraged administrators to
engage in continuous self-examination, communication with staff and parents, and a flexible leadership role.

   Although the parent–teacher relationship has been shown to be of utmost concern to
other researchers and professionals in the field of special education, these intervention
strategies recognize the need to secure administrative support for the formation and continued support of this partnership. They also demonstrate the practical and ecological context of the parent–teacher relationship, offering a more clear understanding of how senior
staff, the political system of the district, and community attitudes can also affect the spirit
and tone of the home–school collaborative effort.

Establishing Flexibility in Roles and Collaborative Goals

A number of parent advocates have argued that public policy should tolerate a range of
parent involvement options matched to the needs and capabilities of parents (A.P. Turnbull

& Turnbull, 1982). Specific family variables should be taken into consideration, such as parents' educational priorities and expectations for their children, levels of stress, extent of resources and support, characteristics of parent–child interactions, ecological demands, assertiveness, and desired child outcomes (Allen & Hudd, 1987; Bailey, 1987; Simeonsson & Bailey, 1990; A.P. Turnbull & Summers, 1987; A.P. Turnbull & Turnbull, 1982; Winton, 1993). Furthermore, the means of providing services in the schools and community should promote integration of the child and the parents as *defined by the family* (Winton, 1993). Thereby, the needs, skills, and expectations of the parents would be salient factors in special education programming, increasing the likelihood of their participation in collaborative and individualized efforts.

Recently, Salisbury (1992), with reference to the early work of Yoshida and Gottlieb (1977), claimed that the schools' prior attempts to successfully involve parents in the education of their child with disabilities may have been hampered by the lack of a clear model of alternatives. As a result, schools have not systematically articulated parents' options or the differential degrees of involvement each alternative may offer. So the researchers endorsed strategies for professional teams to obtain information from families about their desired extent of involvement, frequency and type of contact with the program (written, phone, personal), and locations of the meetings. The authors emphasized the importance of assessing the expectations, resources, and interests of families prior to the development of child and family interventions.

Various researchers have also endorsed a focus on *outcomes* of parent participation over its form and frequency. For example, A.P. Turnbull and Turnbull (1982) suggested that instead of simply mandating attendance and participation, public policy should explicate specific and useful criteria for evaluating effective parent involvement in the IEP team. Potential criteria may include improved parent–child–school relationships, improved adaptation of the family and the school to the needs and strengths of the child with disabilities, reduction in the rate of due process hearings, and improved home–school collaboration in IEP implementation. Similarly, Lillie (1975) recommended that four major outcomes be considered when designing parent programs: emotional support of parents; exchange of information with parents about their child's program and development; parent participation in decision making; and improved parent–child interactions to stimulate cognitive, emotional, and social development.

Yet, according to Bailey (1987), parents and professionals often differ in their priorities for educational goals and services to be prescribed to a child with disabilities. Various factors may account for these differences, such as professionals having limited insight into family needs and values; parents lacking motivation because they do not see the relevance of recommended activities; or parents lacking the resources, time, skill, or energy to follow through with their implementation responsibilities (Bailey, 1987). Consequently, the intervention's success will invariably be limited, especially if the service provider attempts to impose values that are not acceptable or important to the family. Bailey argued that a logical approach to resolving these parent–professional value conflicts would be collaborative goal setting, a process by which parents and professionals jointly determine educational objectives. This argument is based on the fact that when parents are not involved in setting goals for themelves and their children, they might only half-heartedly engage in recommended activities and be denied the chance to exert independence in decision making. However, the primary purpose of educational interventions should be to empower parents and children with these self-management responsibilities, guiding them toward the ability to advocate effectively, make decisions, set priorities, and solve their own problems (Bailey, 1987).

Dunst, Trivette, and Deal (1988), in their book *Enabling and Empowering Families,* also delineated principles to enhance the likelihood that relationships between parents and professionals would be proactive and empowering. They strongly encouraged professionals to engage in assistance that would rest the locus of decision making clearly with the family, including decisions about needs, goals, options for implementing interventions, and whether or not to even accept the services offered by the schools. The authors argued that involvement of families in partnerships with the schools is likely to be stronger if this voluntary principle is applied. Furthermore, they suggested that professionals offer services that are congruent with the family's appraisal of their needs and typical in terms of their culture; that promote self-esteem, a sense of control, competence, and adequacy; that can promote an equal partnership and a give-and-take system of service; and that convey a sense of cooperation and joint responsibility in decision making and problem solving.

Therefore, researchers have recently argued that professionals should not attempt to force their values on families of children with disabilities; rather, they should approach the family from a systems perspective and engage in collaborative goal setting to achieve a mutually acceptable educational plan (Bailey, 1987; Paget, 1992). In the process, professionals may need to change their role expectations and compromise strong beliefs about intervention in favor of collaboration. Yet, if parents do not agree with or are not invested in professionals' priorities for their children's education plans, those programs are doomed for failure from their inception. By focusing on family priorities, actively listening to each other, and engaging in continual goal negotiation, parents and professionals can create home–school partnerships in which both feel valued, understood, and respected (Bailey, 1987).

CONCLUSION

How a family functions at home can greatly affect a child's performance at school; thus, if schools expect children to do well, they must also promote the well-being of families through home–school collaboration (Salisbury, 1992). The ability of professionals and parents to create a dynamic, nurturing home environment for the child with autism may make the difference between a future filled with promise and a future filled with uncertainty (Mori, 1983). If professionals and parents can accept the challenge by taking on new roles and expectations, by working creatively and cooperatively with each other, and by establishing an atmosphere of mutual trust and respect, children with diverse needs and capabilities can benefit enormously (Mori, 1983).

Ultimately, the goal of family-centered programs for all parents of children with autism should be that of parental empowerment to control the nature of their own family interventions and agenda regarding their children (Brantlinger, 1991; Dunst et al., 1988; Shea & Bauer, 1991). Schools and professionals should act in ways that foster the self-sufficiency and independence of families. One way to encourage parental potency is to focus on family strengths rather than weaknesses in the intervention. This leads to family (not professional) control in determining the nature of service provisions and more active political voices in the community that can guarantee benefits for all individuals with disabilities (Brantlinger, 1991; Dunst, Johanson, Trivette, & Hamby, 1991). Attempts to work with families of children with autism should be preceded by careful delineation of their individual family needs, an appraisal of the intervention goals, and an examination of the strategies most suited to accomplishing these objectives (Brantlinger, 1991). As Brantlinger (1991) suggested,

There is a need to avoid the patronizing image of the professional expert benevolently guiding the ignorant parent. Similarly, there is a need to be truly open to parental preferences and to build symmetrical home–school relationships. Substantive family involvement recognizes parents' expertise and willingness to advocate for their children and is open to critical examination of school practices. (p. 257)

Similarly, Gargiulo (1985) argued in his book *Working with Parents of Exceptional Children* that parent–professional interactions should not be adversarial. Professionals must recognize that the idea of professional omniscience and omnipotence is merely an age-old adage; in fact, when a parent and educator interact, there are really two specialists involved. For too long the professional–parent relationship has been characterized by a professional superiority and parental inferiority interaction (A.P. Turnbull, 1978). Actions that have devalued single parents, parents whose primary language is not English, parents whose child-raising beliefs are different than the beliefs of the majority, and parents whose jobs compete for time with their family have been counterproductive to the development of collaborative home–school relationships (Salisbury, 1992). Because families, as well as children, represent diverse needs and capacities, it is essential that professionals recognize and accommodate for these differences in the design, development, and implementation of parent involvement opportunities within the special education context.

Two Sculptors

I dreamed I stood in a studio
And watched two sculptors there.
The clay they used was a young child's mind
And they fashioned it with care.
One was a teacher; the tools she used
Were books, music, and art.
One, a parent who worked with a guiding hand
And a gentle, loving heart.

Day after day the teacher toiled
With touch that was deft and sure,
While the parent labored by her side
And polished and smoothed it o'er.
And when at last their task was done,
They were proud of what they had wrought;
For the things they had molded into the child
Could neither be sold nor bought.

And each agreed he would have failed
If he had worked alone,
The parent and the school,
The teacher and the home.

Author Unknown

Chapter 12

A Parent–Professional Consultation Model for Functional Analysis

—————Kimberly B. Mullen and William D. Frea

In the literature on behavioral intervention for children with autism, two factors have begun to stand out as critically important for the success of a behavior program: 1) designing a behavioral support plan that is based on the determination of the function of the target behavior, and 2) developing a collaborative relationship between family members and professionals during the intervention planning and process. With respect to the latter, the current view of autism by the clinical and research communities has moved away from the suggestion that the etiology stems from pathological parent interaction with the child and from the treatment recommendation that parent and child should receive separate individual psychotherapy (e.g., Bettelheim, 1967). Much more common is the view that autism's origins are organic and that the parent–child relationship can in fact facilitate educational and behavioral intervention gains (Baker, 1989). Research studies have indicated that parent involvement in educational and behavioral interventions is associated with an increase in positive behavioral outcomes for the child (Dangel & Polster, 1984; R.L. Koegel, Glahn, & Nieminen, 1978; Kozloff, 1973; Schopler & Reichler, 1971) and a positive impact on the family system (R.L. Koegel, Schreibman, Johnson, O'Neill, & Dunlap, 1984). With a strong body of evidence supporting the value of parental involvement in the interventions of children, many researchers, professionals, and parents have acknowledged that a collaborative relationship between parents and service providers will result in the most effective behavioral support programs (Donnellan & Mirenda, 1984; Schopler, Mesibov, Shigley, & Bashford, 1984).

Although it seems clear that parent involvement in behavior therapy serves to produce broader behavioral gains and generalization, it has been less clear as to what the parents' role should be in the assessment process. It seems peculiar that one of the greatest sources of information about a child has largely been left out of the initial phase of the habilitation process. It is quite possible that the complexity of functional assessment has resulted in the field believing that such in-depth analyses may increase the burden on a parent. Professionals have encouraged the use of behavioral data from parents in the intervention planning process (Vincent, Laten, Salisbury, Brown, & Baumgart, 1981), but the benefits of formally teaching parents to conduct functional assessment has yet to be discussed.

Although there is little question of the potential challenges that may be involved in learning to conduct a functional assessment, perhaps we should not be so quick to decide that it is an inappropriate demand to place on parents. In fact, it could be seen as unethical to deny parents access to these skills because they are ultimately their children's interventionists. Some of the reasons for teaching parents this skill are the following:

1. The understanding that parents are experts on their children and family and thus already possess valuable assessment information
2. The potential for extended assessment in the natural environment
3. The idea that functional analysis is a skill that can be used throughout children's development
4. The potential for more effective communication and collaboration between parents and children's social agents
5. The potential for increased motivation if parents are actively involved in the process and assist with developing goals that fit with their family values and family system

This chapter begins with an introduction to functional assessment, including why it is important and how it is accomplished. Then there is a brief discussion of the historical changing role of parental involvement in children's assessment and intervention process. The remainder of the chapter provides a discussion of the aforementioned benefits of parents learning to functionally assess their children's behavior.

AN OVERVIEW OF FUNCTIONAL ASSESSMENT

Literature of the past decade has furthered the understanding of the importance of designing behavioral interventions that are based on the results of a functional assessment. The concept of functional assessment developed from the belief that, to effectively change a problematic behavior, the function that it is serving needs to be understood. Specifically, it is important to be able to identify the environmental factors that influence the occurrence of target behaviors (Baer, Wolf, & Risley, 1968; Bijou, Peterson, & Ault, 1968). The hypothesis drawn from a functional assessment should result in a prediction of the circumstances under which a target behavior will and will not be exhibited. It is now generally believed that this information is critical to the design of an effective behavioral intervention (Wacker et al., 1990). Information about controlling variables allows us to form hypotheses about the functional relationship between environmental variables and the exhibited target behavior. When an understanding of the function of the behavior is reached, then an intervention can be developed to assist the child in learning appropriate behaviors that have the same function. At the heart of the philosophy that functional analysis is a necessary component of any treatment plan is the belief that learning effective alternative behaviors can result in lasting behavior gains and meaningful lifestyle change.

Iwata, Dorsey, Slifer, Bauman, and Richman (1982) were among the first to perform a systematic experimental analysis of behavior, analyzing the variables that influence self-injurious behavior (SIB). These investigators exposed nine participants with developmental disabilities to four analog conditions that manipulated the antecedent and consequence events to determine the variables that maintained the SIB. In one condition termed *academic demand*, the participants were given difficult academic tasks; when SIB occurred, the demand was removed. In a second condition termed *social disapproval*, positive reinforcement in the form of attention (e.g., "Don't do that") was provided contingent on self-injurious behavior. In a condition termed *alone*, participants were subjected to an environment without toys or activities, demands, or social attention. Any instance of SIB was ignored in this condition. Finally, in an *unstructured play* condition, the participants were provided with social praise and physical contact contingent on appropriate behavior—the absence of disruptive behavior—at least every 30 seconds. This final condition served as a control for the demand and social disapproval condition because no demands were placed on the participant and attention was differentially provided for appropriate behavior. Manipulation of these four conditions was repeated until each subject evidenced a stable SIB pattern. The investigators concluded that if SIB occurred primarily in the social disapproval condition, positive reinforcement was likely to be the maintaining variable. For example, the children who consistently exhibited high rates of SIB in this condition in contrast to the others were apparently using the behavior to recruit attention. In contrast, if SIB occurred most frequently in the academic demand condition, it was likely maintained by negative reinforcement. Thus, for these children, the behavior was serving to allow them escape or removal from an unwanted activity. If it occurred in the alone condition, or across all assessment conditions, it was likely serving as an automatic or self-stimulatory function.

The study reliably yielded identifiable functions for six of the nine participants. Iwata et al. (1982) noted that the significance of the study was that SIB was serving a different function across the different participants. This suggested that for these participants a "generic" intervention designed to address a particular problem behavior would be insufficient to provide clinical gains. The study provided a strong argument for the need to systematically analyze the function a behavior is serving for the individual and for the field to look to designing interventions that specifically address the functions of target behaviors.

Based on the finding that topographically similar behavior can serve different functions in different people, Iwata, Pace, Kalsher, Cowdery, and Cataldo (1990) discuss using the results of a functional analysis to "match" the intervention to the function of behavior. Specifically, identified reinforcers for the problem behavior are withheld upon the occurrence of the target behavior and provided following appropriate behavior. In this study, each participant was exposed to analog conditions to identify maintaining variables for

SIB. It was determined that each of seven participants (persons with developmental disabilities) was engaging in SIB to avoid or escape undesirable activities. Intervention for these individuals involved escape extinction (not allowing the individuals to escape the undesirable activities after self-injurious behavior had occurred) and permitting escape contingent on appropriate behavior (engagement in task demands). Thus, by determining the function of the SIB, an intervention could be designed that prevented the behavior from serving its present function. In addition, these researchers ensured that appropriate behavior was reinforced with the consequence that the inappropriate behavior previously served to obtain.

In a classic study, Carr and Durand (1985) noted that inappropriate behavior may function as a form of communication. These authors investigated whether behavior problems could be reduced by teaching individuals more appropriate methods to communicate their needs and wants. First, an assessment was structured to determine the function that aggressive SIB and tantrumming behavior served. The authors found that either low levels of attention or high levels of task difficulty were discriminative stimuli for disruptive behavior in these children. In the second experiment, the authors used the results of each participant's individual functional assessment to design an alternative communicative behavior that could be taught to replace the specific function of the individual's disruptive behavior. Specifically, during one phase the participants were taught a communicative replacement behavior that elicited the same result that the disruptive behavior provided. For example, if it was determined that a child was engaging in unwanted behaviors to escape a difficult activity, the child was taught to say, "I don't understand." In addition, during a second phase the participants were taught an alternative replacement communication that was irrelevant to the situation that evoked the problem behavior. For example, the child who was engaging in escape-motivated behavior was taught to say, "Am I doing good work?" Results indicated that disruptive behavior was reduced when the participants were taught a relevant communicative replacement, but remained high when an irrelevant response was taught. The authors concluded that, for an appropriate replacement behavior to successfully replace disruptive behavior, it must serve the same function as that of the inappropriate behavior and be made as efficient.

The Carr and Durand study (1985) was an important one because it reflected a developing trend in behavioral intervention—a move away from simple eliminative strategies toward strategies that emphasized targeting adaptive behavior deficits. Traditionally, problem behaviors have been addressed with methods designed to decrease or eliminate them. Examples of such strategies have been procedures such as extinction (Lovaas, Freitag, Gold, & Kassorla, 1965), time-out (Clark, Rowbury, Baer, & Baer, 1973; White, Nielsen, & Johnson, 1972; Zeilberger, Sampen, & Sloane, 1968), restraint (Favell, McGinsey, & Jones, 1978); response-cost (Iwata & Bailey, 1974), overcorrection (Carey & Bucher, 1983; Foxx & Bechtal, 1983), and contingent shock (Carr & Lovaas, 1983) or other aversive stimuli (Dorsey, Iwata, Ong, & McSween, 1980; Singh, Watson, & Winton, 1986). As Carr and Durand (1985) demonstrated, communication skill deficits can maintain disruptive behavior. These authors showed that a behavioral intervention that incorporated remediation of skill deficits (e.g., teaching communicative abilities) could be powerful in reducing the occurrence of unwanted behavior. Thus, for many behavior analysts, the focus of behavioral intervention plans has become the elimination of maintaining contingencies and the teaching and reinforcing of adaptive replacement behaviors (Mace & Roberts, 1993). The ability to determine the function that a problematic behavior is serving assists in the identification of skill deficits and in the design of a behavioral intervention that emphasizes the teaching of positive replacement behaviors. Such proactive interventions, often referred to as behavioral support strategies (Horner et al., 1990), are reflective of a developing movement for creating positive approaches that address global lifestyle concerns of people with disabilities (e.g., Evans & Meyer, 1985) and a move away from simply targeting for elimination unwanted behaviors.

It is apparent that an ability to identify the functional relationships between target behaviors and the variables present in the individual's environment is critical for such proactive intervention strategies. Two general classes of functional relationships have been discussed in the literature (G. Dunlap & Kern, 1993). The most common type of functional relationships identified have been those based on a hypothesis of the contingencies that reinforce or maintain the target behavior. Hypotheses such as "Jeffrey hits his mother because when he does she will start talking to him," or "Mary bites her peers during P.E. because when she does she is allowed to return to the classroom," are representative of hypotheses addressing maintaining contingencies in the child's environment.

A second class of functional relationships, one that identifies the antecedent events and contextual stimuli that are likely to influence behavior, is now beginning to receive attention (e.g., G. Dunlap, Kern-Dunlap, Clark, & Robbins, 1991). Hypotheses that focus on these functional relationships may be more like, "Kristy will push any person who engages in conversation with her mom," or "Henry will begin to whisper to his neighbor after 15 minutes of independent reading." G. Dunlap and Kern (1993) note that hypotheses of this category are useful because they identify the situations in which a target behavior is likely, and *unlikely*, to occur. With this information, a successful intervention may need to involve making ecological changes. For example, in the case of Henry who whispered to his neighbor after 15 minutes of independent reading, it may be that he was unable to focus on the activity for longer than 15 minutes. An ecological manipulation such as varying the assigned task might provide Henry with enough of a break to allow him to return to the reading activity. Consideration of possible environmental changes for the reduction of unwanted behaviors is consistent with the emerging interest in promoting quality lifestyles. The identification that Henry is not disruptive if provided with frequent breaks from particular types of activities and consequently building breaks into his schedule is an example of how a functional assessment and consequent ecological manipulation can facilitate the design of lifestyle-oriented intervention.

METHODS OF FUNCTIONAL ASSESSMENT

There are two parts to be accomplished when performing a functional assessment (G. Dunlap & Kern, 1993; O'Neill, Horner, Albin, Storey, & Sprague, 1990): 1) formulating a hypothesis about the functional relationship between the target behavior and the environment, and 2) testing that hypothesis. Formulating a hypothesis can be accomplished via interview (e.g., O'Neill et al., 1990) and direct observation (e.g., Frea, Koegel, & Koegel, 1993). Hypotheses can be tested indirectly by examining the effect of the intervention on the target behavior, which some researchers say may at times be a sufficient test of the hypothesis (O'Neill et al., 1990), or directly through experimental manipulations, as is considered necessary by other researchers (e.g., Iwata, Pace, et al., 1990). This latter procedure of experimentally testing the hypothesis has been termed *functional analysis* or *experimental analysis*. While sometimes used interchangeably with the term *functional assessment* (e.g., Sasso & Reimers, 1988), the term *functional analysis* has been differentiated from *functional assessment* by whether or not the hypothesis is empirically tested (e.g., Iwata, Pace, et al., 1990).

Formulating Hypotheses

Interview

The structured interview, conducted with the child with autism and significant others in the child's life, is an initial and useful step to narrowing the range of possibilities of controlling variables (O'Neill et al., 1990). Durand and Crimmins (1988) designed the Motivation Assessment Scale (MAS) to be completed by caregivers. This form consists of four statements about the person with autism's behavior corresponding to each of four motivational functions of behavior: 1) positive reinforcement by attention, 2) positive reinforcement by access to objects, 3) negative reinforcement, and 4) sensory reinforcement. Specifically, each of the 16 statements is answered using a Likert Scale format to indicate how frequently a behavior occurs for a particular function. The motivational function that most often corresponds to the occurrence of the target behavior is considered indicative of the function that behavior is serving.

Another interview strategy, the Functional Analysis Interview (FAI), was designed by O'Neill et al. (1990). This structured form helps identify a wide range of antecedent and consequent events that might be influencing the problem behavior. Included in the interview are questions pertaining to the topography of the behavior, the context in which the behavior occurs, the possible functions of the behavior, the efficiency of the behavior, a description of potential reinforcers, and the history of the behavior. Alternatively, Bailey and Pyles (1989) have used a "behavioral diagnosis and treatment information form" that helps provide information about situational variables and environmental events, physiological variables, and operant events that may be influential in maintaining problem behavior.

Direct Observation

The next step in the functional assessment process typically involves direct observation of the individual in his or her natural environments (e.g., O'Neill et al., 1990). G. Dunlap and Kern (1993) suggest that, at minimum, this process should be used to confirm relationships described during the interviews. Ideally, however, this step should include formal data collection. The data should be used to provide a baseline against which to compare data collected during intervention. Several researchers have developed methods for recording observational data. One simple and often used approach has been the A–B–C model (Bijou et al., 1968). In this approach, behavior (B) is operationally described along with its antecedent event (A) and the ensuing consequence (C). Patterns between behavior and particular antecedents and consequences are identified and used to predict the environmental conditions that will maintain a behavior. Touchette, MacDonald, and Langer (1985) designed a scatterplot assessment that uses a grid with time represented along the ordinate. The individuals being assessed are observed throughout their day, with the rate or frequency of the target behavior recorded in intervals across their daily schedule. The result is a visual representation of the target behavior over time, such that the correlation of the behavior with specific environmental variables can be obtained.

O'Neill et al. (1990) designed a Functional Analysis Observational Form (FAOF) that uses the scatterplot idea but provides more specific information about possible controlling variables. Antecedent events are emphasized on the grid-like form. Some common antecedents, such as "left alone," "transitioned," and "demand" are listed, and there are additional spaces for other antecedents to be written on the form. Spaces for the indication of the target behavior's topography follow the antecedent column, which are then followed by a list of common consequences such as "provided attention," "ignored," and "punished." What differentiates this form from other A–B–C analyses is a "perceived function" section, in which the person filling out the form indicates what he or she perceives the function of the behavior to be. This section of the form is useful when trying to develop hypotheses about functional relationships.

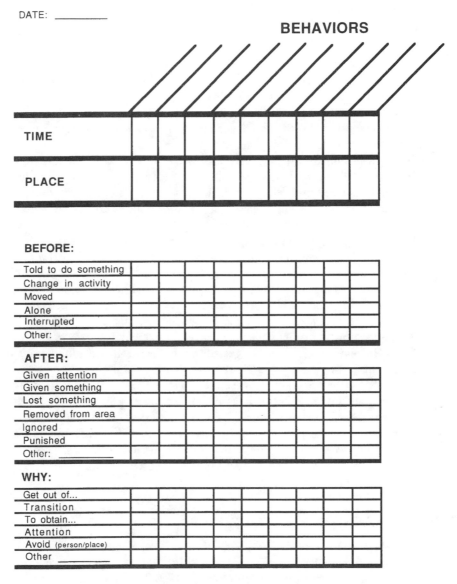

Figure 1. Functional assessment observation form. (From Frea, W., Koegel, L., & Koegel, R. [1993]. *Understanding why problem behaviors occur: A guide for assisting parents in assessing causes of behavior and designing treatment plans.* Santa Barbara: University of California at Santa Barbara; reprinted by permission.)

Frea, Koegel, and Koegel (1993) designed a similar form especially for parents. This functional assessment observation form (see Figure 1) is designed such that the behaviors are listed across the top of the page with space for the time and environment directly below. Beneath that section is a grid of checkboxes and a list of several common antecedents, consequences, and perceived functions. The assessor simply checks the appropriate existing variable and the perceived function for each episode of behavior. Like the O'Neill et al. (1990) form, this form allows for patterns of influencing variables to be identified and for patterns about the perceived function to be noted.

Testing Hypotheses

After completion of the interview and direct observation, it is likely that hypotheses about the function of the behavior can be developed. These suggested functions are based on identified patterns of association between the target behavior and specific environmental variables; however, at this point the functional relationships identified are correlational, not causal. The formulation of hypotheses of functional relationships based on correlational data have been termed *descriptive analysis of function*. In contrast, hypotheses that have been confirmed with *experimental analysis* or *functional analysis* can be considered indicative of true functional relationships.

Until recently, most functional analyses have been conducted in highly controlled analogue conditions (e.g., Carr & Durand, 1985; Iwata et al., 1982). During these conditions, hypothesized maintaining variables (e.g., access to positive or negative reinforcement) are manipulated. High rates of behavior exhibited during a particular condition are considered indicative of the function of the behavior. Some researchers have noted that clinic-based analogue conditions may not reveal all the events maintaining an unwanted behavior in the natural environment (Iwata, Pace, et al., 1990; Mace, Lalli, & Pinter-Lalli, 1991). As a result, several studies have indicated that experimental analysis can be effectively conducted in natural environments (Cooper et al., 1992; Sasso et al., 1992).

Some researchers have used descriptive assessment in natural environments to formulate hypotheses about maintaining variables and then tested the specific hypotheses through systematic manipulations conducted in that environment (e.g., G. Dunlap et al., 1991). However, it has been suggested that the controlled manipulations of functional analysis may not be necessary if sufficient interview and observation strategies are conducted (O'Neill et al., 1990). Furthermore, Durand and Crimmins (1988) point out that functional analysis may not be a reasonable expectation for some intervention providers, such as teachers. For example, G. Dunlap et al. (1991) note that it may be difficult for teachers to conduct experimental manipulations with sufficient control or to systematically collect the data needed for a functional analysis. In these instances, a descriptive analysis, in which hypothesized functional relations are tested indirectly by the effects of the intervention, may prove more practical.

THE CHANGING ROLE OF THE PARENT

The role of the parent in the treatment of autism, as perceived by professionals, has evolved from one of a causal factor (Bettelheim, 1967) to one that is often considered critical in the goal of effective change. Until the 1960s, psychodynamic theory dominated the field's conceptualization of the etiology of autism. Researchers and theorists believed that young children experienced threats from their mothers and fled within themselves as a means of defending themselves (Ward, 1970). At that time, the child was typically removed from the parent so that a more nurturing and safe environment could be provided.

The parents were seen as cold and themselves in need of intervention. It was not until the publication of Rimland's (1964) landmark book, *Infantile Autism,* and Wing's (1972) major contribution, *Autistic Children: A Guide for Parents,* that society was provided with a more logical and sensitive view of the disability. Although such materials for parents were available, most parents were unaware of these resources; therefore, it was under-standable why many parents of children with autism felt somewhat helpless and guilty while searching for a means of obtaining help for their children.

As noted in Chapters 10 and 11, parents of children with disabilities were given a significant amount of control over the education of their children with the passage of PL 94-142 (Education for All Handicapped Children Act) in 1975. The individualized edu-cation program (IEP) process that resulted required that parents not only be informed of the goals and procedures being set for their children, but provided them with the right to be part of the planning process and to sign the final decision. Parents of children with dis-abilities were increasingly seen as critical sources of information about what was best for their children.

In addition, around this time research studies began to appear that investigated the need to include parent involvement in behavioral interventions of children with autism. For example, Lovaas, Koegel, Simmons, and Long (1973) compared two groups of chil-dren during a 1-year follow-up to intervention. One group had received 1 year of interven-tion in an inpatient facility where the parents were not instructed to provide behavioral intervention when the children returned to the family. The second group received 1 year of intervention on an outpatient basis, and the parents were taught to provide behavioral intervention at home. At follow-ups, which ranged from 1 to 4 years later, the children who returned to homes where the parents were not educated in the principles of behavioral intervention had lost many of the gains they had obtained during treatment. In contrast, the children who lived in homes where their parents had learned the procedures maintained their gains, and some continued to show improvements. Schreibman, Koegel, and Britten (1982) offered further support for these results with a study that was conducted during a 5-year period and involved more than 50 parents of children with autism. The children of trained parents showed maintenance of clinical gains in a variety of different environ-ments, whereas the children whose parents were not trained did not. These early studies lent support to the emerging belief that parents could be considered a valuable resource in the treatment of their children.

The 1980s saw a dramatic increase in the number of articles addressing the role of parents in the habilitation process (e.g., R.L. Koegel, Schreibman, Johnson, O'Neill, & Dunlap, 1984; McClannahan, Krantz, & McGee, 1982). Parent participation was explored across many different behaviors, such as adaptive skills (Allen, Bryant, & Bailey, 1986); behavior problems (Cipani, 1988; Lovaas, Koegel, Simmons, & Long, 1973; Lovaas & Newsom, 1976; Van Hasselt, Sisson, & Aach, 1987); play behavior (Lowry & Whitman, 1989); social skills (Chen, Hanline, & Friedman, 1989; Harrold, Lutzker, Campbell, & Touchette, 1992); and use of speech (Hanrahan & Langlois, 1988; Hart & Risley, 1978; Laski, Charlop, & Schreibman, 1988). It was clear at this time that the field was becoming aware of the need to tap into the myriad benefits that parent-delivered therapy provided over traditional clinic-delivered therapy. For example, there was a growing understanding of the significant benefits that parents, who spend more time with their children than any-one else, can contribute in contrast to clinicians who typically spend only a few hours a day with the child (Schreibman, Koegel, Mills, & Burke, 1984).

Another critical issue being discussed at this time was the difficulty of achieving gen-eralization and maintenance of intervention outcomes (R.L. Koegel, Egel, & Williams,

1980; Stokes & Baer, 1977). Professionals who had investigated the incorporation of parent involvement in therapy found that use of these natural therapists facilitated the generalization and maintenance of treatment gains (Rincover & Koegel, 1975). It was
acknowledged that parents provided a natural medium for incorporating some of the critical generalization programming variables (Horner, Dunlap, & Koegel, 1988) into the therapy. For example, parents have access to more opportunities to naturally reinforce
unprompted use of appropriate behavior by their child. Furthermore, they are able to
incorporate a wide range of environments into the therapy process. Parents were no longer
seen as insensitive and in need of help themselves. Now they were more often viewed as a
necessary factor in treatment planning and implementation. A natural continuation of this
trend toward parent–professional collaboration is to include parents in the assessment
process. Although parent education has often resulted in parents learning to effectively
address serious behavior problems as therapists, they have not yet been given the skill to
formally determine why a behavior is occurring. Functional assessment is thought to be an
effective component of identifying appropriate interventions for the child with autism. To
guarantee that parents truly are supported in their role as primary therapists for their children, they should be provided with the necessary means of assessing the function of their
child's behavior. Furthermore, the involvement of parents as primary assessors of their
child's behavior is bound to facilitate the accuracy and efficiency of the assessment
outcome.

PARENTS AS FUNCTIONAL ASSESSORS

Now that the importance of determining the function of a target behavior when designing
a behavioral intervention has been discussed, and the developing role of parent involvement in service delivery examined, it is possible to consider the potential benefits of parents becoming involved in the assessment process. Specifically, it is suggested that parents
may be ideal candidates to take an active role in conducting their children's functional
assessment.

Parents as Experts on Their Child and Family

There is a growing acknowledgment among professionals that parents possess in-depth
and unique information about their child that would take an "outside" professional longer
to access. Researchers are beginning to recognize the usefulness of this information in the
assessment process (Vincent et al., 1981). Powers and Handleman (1984) note that parents, siblings, grandparents, and peers have all been effective contributors to the behavioral assessment process. These researchers point out that when significant others in the
individual's natural environments can be taught to accurately conduct a reliable and valid
assessment, there exists the possibility for an ongoing, systematic study of behavior. An
understanding of the function of the target behavior, they note, will facilitate intervention
gains and may increase the assessor's feelings of competence and self-efficacy.

As addressed in Chapters 7 and 8, another topic also emerging in the developmental
disabilities literature is a concern for addressing the needs of the entire family system.
Currently there is an evolving shift from intervention packages that target the needs of just
the child to ones that consider the needs of each family member (Foster, Berger, &
McLean, 1981). This concept stems from family systems theory, which assumes that
members of a family are highly interrelated, each having an impact on and responding to
the whole family structure. An influence on one member is likely to influence other members in the system (Minuchin, 1974; Powell & Ogle, 1985). As a result, many profession-

als now agree that information about family relationships (e.g., specific members' interrelationships and subsystems), values (e.g., parenting philosophies and family intervention beliefs and priorities), and circumstances (e.g., economic, cultural, or religious standings) ought to be identified in the assessment process and considered during the design of an individualized support plan (Marcus & Schopler, 1989).

Parents typically provide the most comprehensive information about the values and circumstances and interactive relationships of the family. It also seems certain that parent involvement will contribute to a more comprehensive and thus efficient assessment. For example, parents may have the greatest amount of information about the antecedent, consequent, and contextual variables that affect their family.

Consider the example of a clinician who observes 7-year-old Betsy ask her father for help with her homework while he is talking to her brother. She receives no response and proceeds to engage in disruptive behavior. It might be concluded that, upon being ignored when asking for help, Betsy will respond with disruption. Thus, one hypothesized function of the aggression for Betsy may be to obtain assistance. However, Betsy's mother might know that Betsy frequently attempts to interrupt conversations between her parents and sibling and will usually engage in disruptive behavior if a verbal interruption behavior is not successful. The final hypothesis of the function of the behavior then changes: Betsy will act in a disruptive manner when not able to successfully remove the parent's attention from another family member. It is clear that the intervention strategy designed to target Betsy's disruption would be different, assuming each of the decided functions of the behavior. For example, if the behavior serves the first (incorrect) function, Betsy might be taught to approach another family member for assistance. This would clearly not address the more likely function of the behavior (to end her father's attention to her brother) and would probably not result in a decrease of the behavior. If the correct function of the behavior is determined, Betsy might be taught to ask her father if he will have a conversation with her when he is through. This method of ensuring that she will have her own turn may be reinforcing enough to decrease Betsy's need to behave aggressively.

This example illustrates that parents have a degree of understanding of the dynamics of their family as a whole that would take a professional longer to achieve. Although it is likely that a clinician experienced in functional assessment would eventually arrive at an accurate determination of the function of Betsy's disruptive behavior (with an extended cost of time, stress, and money for the family), the facilitative effect of parents' unique knowledge cannot be ignored. They are, in fact, experts on their families and possess information that should be utilized to accomplish an accurate, timely behavioral assessment.

Extended Assessment in the Natural Environment

As has been discussed in the literature on the benefits of parents as intervention providers, one benefit of parent involvement is the possibility of "round-the-clock" intervention (R.L. Koegel, Schreibman, Britten, Burke, & O'Neill, 1982). Although a family systems perspective acknowledges that continuous attention provided to one family member is usually incompatible with a healthy family system's existence, disruptive behavior from one member can be a constant source of stress for the family system as well. It has been demonstrated that parents in many families have a greater opportunity to provide intervention than the outside professional (R.L. Koegel et al., 1982). Similarly, due to the proximal nature of the parent–child and parent–family relationship, the parent may be able to produce a greater quantity of assessment data than the professional who visits the home less frequently.

Related to the benefit of parents being able to conduct an extended assessment is the opportunity for the functional assessment to be conducted in the child's natural environment. It has been suggested that functional analyses conducted in highly controlled environments, such as the typical clinic environment, may be limited by the fact that the precision and control required for experimental analysis may not reveal all of the maintaining variables found in a child's natural environment (Iwata, Vollmer, & Zarcone, 1990). Because parents are caregivers, their responsibilities often include duties such as going to the grocery store with the children, entertaining their children with trips to the park, going to grandma's house, and taking the children to the dentist. Each of these environments contains complex variables (often ones that cannot be replicated in a clinic environment) that may or may not serve to maintain the target behavior. Therefore, it is important to accurately determine the functions that the target behaviors serve by assessment in each of these natural environments.

In addition, it has been demonstrated that problem behavior may be maintained by more than one variable and that a successful intervention package needs to include multiple components to address all functions of the target behavior (Carr & Carlson, 1993). A functional assessment conducted across community environments may reveal that a behavior is serving different functions across environments. This information then will aid in the design of a comprehensive intervention package.

Finally, the literature has shown that topographically different behaviors may be functionally related (Parrish, Cataldo, Kolko, Neef, & Egel, 1986). In such cases, separate interventions for each behavior may not be necessary, but instead a single intervention that addresses the common function of the co-varying behaviors would be effective. It is apparent that a functional assessment conducted across natural environments would be an important part of identifying co-varying behaviors that serve the same function.

In conclusion, several studies have indicated the importance of performing functional assessments in natural contexts (Mace & Lalli, 1991; Michael, 1982). The many opportunities parents have to observe their children in natural environments makes them ideal candidates to capitalize on these occasions as forums to conduct functional assessments. Although it may not be reasonable to expect parents to conduct a continuous functional assessment in all the environments in which their child participates, it is possible that consultation with a professional experienced in functional assessment might provide parents with the skills they need to be able to formally examine their child's behavior in its natural context.

Acquisition of a Skill to Be Used Across the Life Span

Teaching parents to functionally assess behavior provides them with a skill that they can use to further their understanding of the many behavior problems they may encounter during their child's development. As a child experiences changes and transitions throughout life, one can be certain that many different variables will have an impact on his or her behavior. Parents can benefit from a tool to assess these variables and their individual effects.

Currently there is an evolving interest in considering the antecedent events (e.g., ecological, curricular, or physiological variables) that influence problem behavior (Bailey & Pyles, 1989; G. Dunlap, Kern-Dunlap, Clark, & Robbins, 1991; Evans & Meyer, 1985). Antecedent variables are often subject to change across the life span. For example, a curriculum or teacher may change from one year to the next, or physiological changes during puberty or a transition from the family home environment to a supported living environment might occur. Matson and Marchetti (1988) note that life-span transitional periods, such as entry into the public school system, emergence into adolescence, transition from public school to adult services, postparental care, and retirement, are all critical times in the life of a person with autism and may have a significant impact on the individual and family. With each of these transitions, there is the possibility for inappropriate behavior to become functional for the person with autism. As changing life events influence behavior, it may be useful for a family member to be skilled in identifying the functions of exhibited behavior. With these skills, parents may also be better able to prevent initial behaviors from developing into complex and problematic behavioral patterns that may eventually require more intensive and intrusive interventions.

Facilitation of Collaborative Parent–Professional Relationships

A final implication of parents becoming able to accurately identify the maintaining variables of problem behavior is a potentially decreased dependency on outside professionals. Parents who do not have this skill typically rely on professionals to assess their child's behavior and make subsequent intervention recommendations. In contrast, parents who are able to conduct the assessment themselves can then provide the bulk of the necessary assessment information to the professional. This has two advantages. First, the parent can be sure that the assessment accurately indicates the dynamics, circumstances, and values of the child and family. Second, the parent can take a more active role in the habilitation of their child. The parent, in fact, may be able to assume the role of "consultant" on his or her own child's behavior. The relationship between parent and professional then becomes one of collaboration, where each contributes his or her own area of specialization in a consultation format. For the parents, this is their unique understanding of their family system and child; for the professionals, this is their general experience with autism and basic behavioral therapy techniques.

Dougherty (1990) notes that a characteristic of consultation is the delivery of indirect service to the client (the child) through the provision of direct service to the consultee (the parent). In this case, both the parent and the professional can at times assume the role of consultee. When the parent is providing the professional with relevant assessment information for assistance in the development of a support strategy, the parent is acting as consultant and the professional as consultee. Similarly, when the professional is providing assistance with the development of potential interventions, the professional is now engaging in consultation while the parent is assuming the role of consultee. Such mutually collaborative relationships, in which both parties, the parent and the professional, provide each other with relevant information for the design of the child's intervention program are likely to result in the most comprehensive behavioral support package.

Finally, it is possible that parents will show increased motivation for carrying out an intervention if they have been active participants in the development of its methods and goals. For example, if a communication deficit is identified following a functional assessment that the parents have conducted, it is likely that the parents would then have an understanding of why teaching and reinforcing the use of replacement behaviors is important. By becoming involved in the identification of necessary intervention strategies, and ensuring the "fit" of these strategies with the family, parents may be more motivated to implement the suggestions recommended by the professional.

CONCLUSION

Teaching parents to understand the function that their children's behaviors are serving may be the missing step in the field's growing commitment to assist parents in becoming active participants in the habilitation of their children. As discussed earlier, potential bene-fits of parent involvement in the intervention process have been well established. Yet often parents are encouraged to utilize intensive behavioral intervention without the missing piece of information that would make the choice of treatment strategies clear—the func-tion of the target behavior. By the nature of their relationship with their children, parents have the potential to become highly effective assessors of behavior. As primary partici-pants in this critical component of the behavior change process, parents may obtain a more comprehensive involvement in the behavioral support strategies for their children and have a positive impact on the outcome of the assessment.

References

Aanes, D., & Haagenson, L. (1978, February). Normalization: Attention to a conceptual disaster. *Mental Retardation*, pp. 55–56.

Able-Boone, H., Sandall, S.R., Loughry, A., & Frederick, L. L. (1990). An informed, family-centered approach to Public Law 99-457: Parental views. *Topics in Early Childhood Special Education, 10*(1), 100–111.

Adrien, J.L., Faure, M., Perrot, A., Hameury, L., Garreau, B., Barthelemy, C., & Sauvage, D. (1991). Autism and family home movies: Preliminary findings. *Journal of Autism and Developmental Disabilities, 2,* 43–50.

Affleck, G., Tennen, H., Rowe, J., Roscher, B., & Walker, L. (1989). Effects of formal support on mothers' adaptation to the hospital-to-home transition of high-risk infants: The benefits and costs of helping. *Child Development, 60,* 488–501.

Albin, R.W., & Horner, R.H. (1988). Generalization with precision. In R.H. Horner, G. Dunlap, & R.L. Koegel (Eds.), *Generalization and maintenance: Life-style changes in applied settings* (pp. 99–120). Baltimore: Paul H. Brookes Publishing Co.

Allen, D.A. (1991). *Evaluating the effects of implementing the Moorpark collaborative model.* Unpublished doctoral dissertation, University of California at Santa Barbara.

Allen, D.A., & Hudd, S.S. (1987). Are we professionalizing parents? Weighing the benefits and pitfalls. *Mental Retardation, 25,* 133–139.

Allen, D.L., Bryant, M.C., & Bailey, J.S. (1986). Facilitating generalization: The effectiveness of improved parental report procedures. *Behavior Modification, 10,* 415–434.

Allen, K.D., & Fuqua, R.W. (1985). Eliminating selective stimulus control: A comparison of two procedures for teaching mentally retarded children to respond to compound stimuli. *Journal of Experimental Child Psychology, 39,* 55–71.

Alper, T.G. (1978). *Individualized educational plans: How well do they work?* Sacramento, CA: California State Department of Education. (ERIC Document Reproduction Service No. ED 161–235)

Amado, A.N. (Ed.). (1993). *Friendship and community connections between people with and without developmental disabilities.* Baltimore: Paul H. Brookes Publishing Co.

American Psychiatric Association. (1987). *Diagnostic and statistical manual of mental disorders* (3rd ed., rev. ed.). Washington, DC: Author.

Anastasiow, N.J. (1984). Handicapped preschool children: Peer contacts, relationships, or friendships? In T. Field, J.L. Roopnarine, & M. Segal (Eds.), *Friendships in normal and handicapped children* (pp. 209–217). Norwood, NJ: Ablex.

Andersen, L.H., Barner, S.L., & Larson, H.J. (1978). Evaluation of written individualized education programs. *Exceptional Children, 45*(3), 207–208.

Anderson-Inman, L., Paine, S., & Deutchman, L. (1984). Neatness counts: Effects of direct instruction and self-monitoring on the transfer of neat-paper skills to nontraining settings. *Analysis and Intervention in Developmental Disabilities, 4,* 137–155.

Antonius, T., Koegel, R.L., & Schreibman, L. (1988, May). *Targeting specific versus general areas of stress in families of children with autism.* Paper presented at the meeting of the Association for Behavior Analysis, Philadelphia.

Armer, B., & Thomas, B.K. (1978). Attitudes toward interdisciplinary collaboration in pupil personnel services teams. *Journal of School Psychology, 16*(2), 167–176.

Asher, S.R., & Dodge, K.A. (1986). Identifying children who are rejected by their peers. *Developmental Psychology, 22*, 444–449.

Asher, S.R., & Gottman, J.M. (Eds.). *The development of children's friendships.* Cambridge, MA: Cambridge University Press.

Asher, S.R., & Taylor, A.R. (1981). Social outcomes of mainstreaming: Sociometric assessment and beyond. *Exceptional Education Quarterly, 1*, 13–30.

Asher, S.R., & Taylor, A.R. (1983). Social skill training with children: Evaluating processes and outcomes. *Studies in Educational Evaluation, 8*, 237–245.

Axelrod, S. (1977). *Behavior modification for the classroom teacher.* New York: McGraw-Hill.

Baer, D.M., Wolf, M.M., & Risley, R.R. (1968). Some current dimensions of applied behavior analysis. *Journal of Applied Behavior Analysis, 1*, 91–97.

Baer, M., Fowler, S.A., & Carden-Smith, L. (1984). Using reinforcement and independent-grading to promote and maintain task accuracy in a mainstreamed class. *Analysis and Intervention in Developmental Disabilities, 4*, 147–189.

Bagshaw, N.B. (1978). *An acoustic analysis of fundamental frequency and temporal parameters of autistic children's speech.* Unpublished master's thesis, University of California, Santa Barbara.

Bailey, D.B. (1987). Collaborative goal-setting with families: Resolving differences in values and priorities for services. *Topics in Early Childhood Special Education, 7*(2), 59–71.

Bailey, D.B., & McWilliam, R.A. (1990). Normalizing early intervention. *Topics in Early Childhood Special Education, 10*(2), 33–47.

Bailey, D.B., & Winton, P.J. (1987). Stability and change in parents' expectations about mainstreaming. *Topics in Early Childhood Special Education, 7*(1), 73–88.

Bailey, D.B., & Winton, P.J. (1989). Friendship and acquaintance among families in a mainstreamed day care center. *Education and Training in Mental Retardation, 24*(2), 107–113.

Bailey, D.B., Jr., & McWilliams, R.A. (1990). Normalizing early intervention. *Topics in Early Childhood Special Education, 10*(2), 33–47.

Bailey, J.S., & Pyles, D.A.M. (1989). Behavioral diagnostics. In E. Cipani (Ed.), *The treatment of severe behavior disorders: Behavior analysis approaches* (pp. 85–107). Washington, DC: American Association on Mental Retardation.

Bailey, S.L. (1981). Stimulus overselectivity in learning disabled children. *Journal of Applied Behavior Analysis, 14*, 239–248.

Baker, B.L. (1983). Parents as teachers: Issues in training. In J.A. Mulick & S.M. Pueschel (Eds.), *Parent-professional participation in developmental disability services: Foundations and prospects.* (pp. 55–74). Cambridge, MA: Ware Press.

Baker, B.L. (1984). Intervention with families with young, severely handicapped children. In J.B. Blacher (Ed.), *Severely handicapped young children and their families: Research in review.* (pp. 319–375). New York: Academic Press.

Baker, B.L. (1989). *Parent training and developmental disabilities.* Washington, DC: American Association on Mental Retardation.

Baker, B.L., & Brightman, R.P. (1984). Access of handicapped children to educational services. In N.D. Reppucci, L.A. Weithorn, E.P. Mulvey, & J. Monahan (Eds.), *Children, mental health, and the law* (pp. 289–307). Beverly Hills, CA: Sage Publications.

Baker, B.L., Brightman, A.J., Heifetz, L.J., & Murphy, D.M. (1976). *Behavior problems.* Champaign, IL: Research Press.

Baker, B.L., Heifitz, L.J., & Murphy, D. (1980). Behavioral training for parents of retarded children: One-year follow-up. *American Journal of Mental Deficiency, 85*, 31–38.

Baker, B.L., Landen, S.L., & Kashima, K.J. (1989). *Family characteristics and parent training outcomes.* Unpublished manuscript, University of California, Los Angeles.

Baltaxe, C.A.M. (1984). Use of contrastive stress in normal, aphasic, and autistic children. *Journal of Speech and Hearing Research, 27*, 97–105.

Baltaxe, C.A.M., & Guthrie, D. (1987). The use of primary sentence stress by normal, aphasic, and autistic children. *Journal of Autism and Developmental Disorders, 17*, 255–271.

Baltaxe, C.A.M., & Simmons, J.Q. (1975). Language in childhood psychosis: A review. *Journal of Speech and Hearing Disorders, 40*, 439–458.

Barber, D., & Hupp, S.C. (1993). A comparison of friendship patterns of individuals with developmental disabilities. *Education and Training in Mental Retardation, 28*, 13–22.

Bartak, L., & Rutter, M. (1974). The use of personal pronouns by autistic children. *Journal of Autism and Childhood Schizophrenia, 4*, 217–222.

Baumeister, A.A., & Forehand, R. (1973). Stereotyped acts. In N.R. Ellis (Ed.), *International review of research in mental retardation* (p. 6). New York: Academic Press.

Baumgart, D., Brown, L., Pumpian, I., Nisbet, J., Ford, A., Sweet, M., Messina, R., & Schroeder, J. (1982). Principle of partial participation and individualized adaptions in education programs for severely handicapped students. *Journal of The Association for Persons with Severe Handicaps, 7*, 17–27.

Belsky, J., Spanier, F., & Rovine, M. (1983). Stability and change in marriage across the transition to parenthood. *Journal of Marriage and the Family, 45*, 567–577.

Bensky, J.M., Shaw, S.F., Gouse, A.S., Bates, H., Dixon, B., & Beane, W.E. (1980). Public Law 94-142 and stress: A problem for educators. *Exceptional Children, 47*(1), 24–29.

Benson, H.A., & Turnbull, A.P. (1986). Approaching families from an individualized perspective. In R.H. Horner, L.H. Meyer, & H.D.B. Fredericks (Eds.), *Education of learners with severe handicaps: Exemplary service strategies* (pp. 127–157). Baltimore: Paul H. Brookes Publishing Co.

Berger, E.H. (1991). *Parents as partners in education: The school and home working together* (3rd ed.). New York: Charles E. Merrill.

Berler, E.S., Gross, A.M., & Drabman, R.S. (1982). Social skills training with children: Proceed with caution. *Journal of Applied Behavior Analysis, 15*, 41–53.

Bernard-Opitz, V. (1982). Pragmatic analysis of the communicative behavior of an autistic child. *Journal of Speech and Hearing Disorders, 47*, 99–109.

Berndt, T.J. (1982). The features and effects of friendship in early adolescence. *Child Development, 53*, 1447–1460.

Bettelheim, B. (1967). *The empty fortress*. New York: Free Press.

Bickel, W.K., Stella, M.E., & Etzel, B.C. (1984). A reevaluation of stimulus overselectivity: Restricted stimulus control or stimulus control hierarchies. *Journal of Autism and Developmental Disorders, 14*, 137–157.

Bierman, K.L., & Furman, W. (1984). The effects of social skills training and peer involvement on the social adjustment of preadolescents. *Child Development, 55*, 151–162.

Bierman, K.L., Miller, C.L., & Stabb, S.D. (1987). Improving the social behavior and peer acceptance of rejected boys: Effects of social skill training with instruction and prohibitions. *Journal of Consulting and Clinical Psychology, 55*, 194–200.

Bigelow, B. (1977). Children's friendship expectations: A cognitive-developmental study. *Child Development, 48*, 246–253.

Bigelow, B.J., & La Gaipa, J.J. (1975). Children's written descriptions of friendship: A multidimensional analysis. *Developmental Psychology, 11*, 857–858.

Bijou, S.W., Peterson, R.F., & Ault, M.H. (1968). A method to integrate descriptive and experimental field studies at the level of data and empirical concepts. *Journal of Applied Behavior Analysis, 1*, 175–191.

Biklen, D., Corrigan, C., & Quick, D. (1989). Beyond obligation: Students' relations with each other in integrated classes. In D.K. Lipsky & A. Gartner (Eds.), *Beyond separate education: Quality education for all* (pp. 207–221). Baltimore: Paul H. Brookes Publishing Co.

Billingsley, F.F. (1984). Where *are* the generalized outcomes? (An examination of instructional objectives). *Journal of The Association for Persons with Severe Handicaps, 9*(3), 186–192.

Blacher, J., & Turnbull, A.P. (1983). Are parents mainstreamed? A survey of parent interactions in the mainstreamed preschool. *Education and Training of the Mentally Retarded, 18*(1), 10–16.

Bloom, L., & Lahey, M. (1978). *Language development and language disorders*. New York: John Wiley & Sons.

Borden, M.C., & Ollendick, T.H. (1994). An examination of the validity of social subtypes in autism. *Journal of Autism and Developmental Disorders, 24*, 23–37.

Bouma, R., & Schweitzer, R. (1990). The impact of chronic childhood illness on family stress: A comparison between autism and cystic fibrosis. *Journal of Clinical Psychology, 46*, 722–730.

Boyce, G., Behl, D., Mortensen, L., & Akers, J. (1991). Child characteristics, demographics, and family processes: Their effects on the stress experienced by families of children with disabilities. *Counseling Psychology Quarterly, 4*(4), 273–288.

Bradley, R.H., & Caldwell, B.M. (1979). Home observation for measurement of the environment: A revision of the preschool scale. *American Journal of Mental Deficiency, 84*(3), 235–244.

Bradley, R.H., Rock, S.L., Whiteside, L., Caldwell, B.M., & Brisby, J. (1991). Dimensions of parenting in families having children with disabilities. *Exceptionality, 2*, 41–61.

Brady, M.P., McEvoy, M.A., Gunter, P., Shores, R.E., & Fox, J.J. (1984). Considerations for socially integrated school environments for severely handicapped students. *Education and Training in Mental Retardation, 19*, 246–253.

Brady, M.P., Shores, R.E., McEvoy, M.A., Ellis, D., & Fox, J. (1987). Increasing social interactions of severely handicapped autistic children. *Journal of Autism and Developmental Disorders, 17*, 375–390.

Brantlinger, E. (1991). Home-school partnerships that benefit children with special needs. *Elementary School Journal, 91*(3), 249–259.

Breen, C., & Haring, T.G. (1991). Effects of contextual competence on social initiations. *Journal of Applied Behavior Analysis, 24*, 337–347.

Breen, C., Haring, T.G., Pitts-Conway, V., & Gaylord-Ross, R. (1985). The training and generalization of social interaction during breaktime at two job sites in the natural environment. *Journal of The Association for Persons with Severe Handicaps, 10*, 41–50.

Brewer, N., & Smith, J.M. (1989). Social acceptance of mentally retarded children in regular schools in relation to years mainstreamed. *Psychological Reports, 64*, 375–380.

Brinker, R.P. (1992). Family involvement in early intervention: Accepting the unchangeable, changing the changeable, and knowing the difference. *Topics in Early Childhood Special Education, 12*(3), 307–332.

Brinker, R.P., & Thorpe, M.F. (1984). Integration of severely handicapped students and the proportion of IEP objectives achieved. *Exceptional Children, 51*(2), 168–175.

Bristol, M.M. (1979). *Maternal coping with autistic children: The effect of child characteristics and interpersonal support.* Unpublished doctoral dissertation, University of North Carolina, Chapel Hill.

Bristol, M.M. (1985). Designing programs for young developmentally disabled children: A family systems approach to autism. *Remedial and Special Education, 6*(4), 46–53.

Bristol, M.M., & Schopler, E. (1983). Stress and coping in families of autistic adolescents. In E. Schopler & G.B. Mesibov (Eds.), *Autism in adolescents and adults* (pp. 251–278). New York: Plenum.

Bristol, M.M., & Schopler, E. (1984). A developmental perspective on stress and coping in families of autistic children. In J. Blacher (Ed.), *Severely handicapped young children and their families* (pp. 91–141). Orlando, FL: Academic Press.

Broden, M., Hall, R.V., & Mitts, B. (1971). The effect of self-recording on the classroom behavior of two eighth-grade students. *Journal of Applied Behavior Analysis, 4*(3), 191–199.

Brophy, J.E., & Good, T.L. (1970). Teachers' communication of differential expectations for children's classroom performance: Some behavioral data. *Journal of Educational Psychology, 61*, 365–374.

Brotherson, M.J., & Goldstein, B.L. (1992). Time as a resource and constraint for parents of young children with disabilities: Implications for early intervention services. *Topics in Early Childhood Special Education, 12*(4), 508–527.

Brown v. Board of Education, 347 U.S. 483 (1954).

Brown, L., Branston, M., Hamre-Nietupski, S., Johnson, F., Wilcox, B., & Gruenewald, L. (1979). A rationale for comprehensive logitudinal interactions between severely handicapped students and nonhandicapped students and other citizens. *AAESPH Review, 4*(1), 3–14.

Brown, L., Long, E., Udvari-Solner, A., Schwarz, P., VanDeventer, P., Ahlgren, C., Johnson, F., Gruenwald, L., & Jorgensen, J. (1989a). The home school: Why students with severe intellectual disabilities must attend the schools of their brothers, sisters, friends, and neighbors. *Journal of The Association for Persons with Severe Handicaps, 14*(1), 1–7.

Brown, L., Long, E., Udvari-Solner, A., Schwarz, P., VanDeventer, P., Ahlgren, C., Johnson, F., Gruenwald, L., & Jorgensen, J. (1989b). Should students with severe disabilities be based in regular or in special education classrooms in home schools? *Journal of The Association for Persons with Severe Handicaps, 14*, 8–12.

Brown, L., Nietupski, J., & Hamre-Nietupski, S. (1976). The criterion of ultimate functioning and public school services for severely handicapped students. In M.A. Thomas (Ed.), *Hey, don't forget about me: Education's investment in the severely, profoundly, and multiply handicapped* (pp. 197–209). Reston, VA: Council for Exceptional Children.

Brown, L., Schwarz, P., Udvari-Solner, A., Kampschroer, E.F., Johnson, F., Jorgensen, J., & Gruenewald, L. (1991). How much time should students with severe intellectual disabilities spend in regular education classrooms and elsewhere? *Journal of The Association for Persons with Severe Handicaps, 16*(1), 39–47.

Burke, J.C., & Cerniglia, L. (1990). Stimulus complexity and autistic children's responsivity: Assessing and training a pivotal behavior. *Journal of Autism and Developmental Disorders, 20*, 233–253.

Burke, J.C., & Koegel, R.L. (1982, May). *The relationship of stimulus overselectivity to autistic children's responsivity and incidental learning.* Paper presented at the Association for Behavior Analysis, Milwaukee, WI.

Burrello, L.C., & Wright, P. (1993) *The principle letters.* Bloomington, IN: National Academy/CASE.

Burnstein, N.D., (1986). The effects of classroom organization on mainstreamed preschool children. *Exceptional Children, 52*(5), 425–434.

Buscaglia, L.F., & Williams, E.H. (1979). *Human advocacy and P.L. 94-142.* Thorofare, NJ: Charles B. Slack.

Calhoun, G., & Elliott, R. (1977, March). Self concept and academic achievement of educable retarded and emotionally disturbed pupils. *Exceptional Children, 43*(6), 379–380.

Camarata, S.M. (in press). *The assessment and treatment of speech intelligibility disorders in children.* Nashville, TN: Bill Wilkerson Press.

Camarata, S.M., & Nelson, K.E. (1992). Treatment efficiency as a function of target selection in the remediation of child language disorders. *Clinical Linguistics and Phonetics, 6*, 167–178.

Campbell, M., Friedman, E., DeVito, E., Greenspan, L., & Collins, P.J. (1974). Blood serotonin in psychotic and brain damaged children. *Journal of Autism and Childhood Schizophrenia, 4*, 33–41.

Campbell, C.R., & Stremel-Campbell, K. (1982). Programming "loose training" as a strategy to facilitate language generalization. *Journal of Applied Behavior Analysis, 15*, 295–301.

Carden-Smith, L.K., & Fowler, S.A. (1983). An assessment of student and teacher behavior in treatment and mainstreamed classes for preschool and kindergarten. *Analysis and Intervention in Developmental Disabilities, 3*, 35–57.

Carcy, R.G., & Bucher, B. (1983). Positive practice overcorrection: The effects of duration of positive practice on acquisition and response reduction. *Journal of Applied Behavior Analysis, 16*, 101–109.

Carpenter, R.L., & Robson, D.L. (1979). P.L. 94-142: Perceived knowledge, expectations, and early implementation. *Journal of Special Education, 13*(3), 307–314.

Carr, E.G. (1980). Generalization of treatment effects following educational-intervention with autistic children and youth. In B. Wilcox & A. Thompson (Eds.), *Critical issues in educating autistic children and youth* (pp. 118–134). Washington, DC: U.S. Department of Education, Office of Special Education.

Carr, E.G. (1988). Functional equivalence as a mechanism of response generalization. In R.H. Horner, G. Dunlap, & R.L. Koegel (Eds.), *Generalization and maintenance: Life-style changes in applied settings* (pp. 221–241). Baltimore: Paul H. Brookes Publishing Co.

Carr, E.G. (1994). Emerging themes in the functional analysis of problem behavior. *Journal of Applied Behavior Analysis, 27,* 393–399.

Carr, E.G., & Carlson, J.I. (1993). Reduction of severe behavior problems in the community using a multicomponent treatment approach. *Journal of Applied Behavior Analysis, 26,* 157–172.

Carr, E.G., & Durand, V.M., (1985a). Reducing behavior problems through functional communication training. *Journal of Applied Behavior Analysis, 18,* 111–126.

Carr, E.G., & Durand, V.M., (1985b). The social-communicative basis of severe behavior problems in children. In S. Reiss & R. Bootzin (Eds.), *Theoretical issues in behavior therapy* (pp. 219–254). New York: Academic Press.

Carr, E.G., & Kologinsky, E. (1983). Acquisition of sign language by autistic children: II. Spontaneity and generalization effects. *Journal of Applied Behavior Analysis, 16,* 297–314.

Carr, E.G., & Lovaas, O.I. (1983). Contingent electric shock as a treatment for severe behavior problems. In S. Axelrod & J. Apsche (Eds.), *The effects of punishment on human behavior* (pp. 221–245). New York: Academic Press.

Carr, E.G., Newsom, C.D., & Binkoff, J.A. (1976). Stimulus control of self destructive behavior in a psychotic child. *Journal of Abnormal Child Psychology, 4,* 139–153.

Carr, E.G., Schreibman, L., & Lovaas, O.I. (1975). Control of echolalic speech in psychotic children. *Journal of Abnormal Child Psychology, 13,* 101–117.

Carr, E.G., Taylor, J., Carlson, J.I., & Robinson, S. (1989). Reinforcement and stimulus-based treatments for severe behavior problems in developmental disabilities. In *Proceedings of the Consensus Conference on the Treatment of Severe Behavior Problems in Developmental Disabilities* (pp. 173–229). Washington DC: National Institute of Health.

Cataldo, M.F. (1984). Clinical considerations in training parents of children with special problems. In R.F. Dangel & R.A. Polster (Eds.), *Parent training* (pp. 329–356). New York: Guilford Press.

Cavallaro, C.C., & Bambara, L.M. (1982). Two strategies for teaching language during free play. *Journal of The Association for Persons with Severe Handicaps, 7,* 80–91.

Chadsey-Rusch, J., Drasgow, E., Reinoehl, B., Halle, J., & Collet-Klingenberg, L. (1993). Using general-case instruction to teach spontaneous and generalized requests for assistance to learners with severe disabilities. *Journal of The Association for Persons with Severe Handicaps, 18,* 177–187.

Chan, K.S., & Keogh, B.K. (1974). Interpretation of task interruption and feelings of responsibility for failure. *Journal of Special Education, 8,* 175–178.

Chandler, L.K., Lubek, R.C., & Fowler, S.A. (1992). Generalization and maintenance of preschool children's social skills: A critical review and analysis. *Journal of Applied Behavior Analysis, 25,* 415–428.

Chapman, R.S. (1981). Exploring children's communicative intent. In J.F. Miller (Ed.), *Assessing language production in children* (pp. 111–136). Austin, TX: PRO-ED.

Chapter 766 of the Acts of 1972, The Commonwealth of Massachusetts.

Charlop, M.H. (1983). The effects of echolalia on acquisition and generalization of receptive labeling in autistic children. *Journal of Applied Behavior Analysis, 16,* 111–126.

Charlop, M.H., & Milstein, J.P. (1989). Teaching autistic children conversational speech using video modeling. *Journal of Applied Behavior Analysis, 22,* 275–285.

Charlop, M.H., Schreibman, L., & Thibodeau, M.G. (1985). Increasing spontaneous verbal responding in autistic children using a time delay procedure. *Journal of Applied Behavior Analysis, 18,* 155–166.

Charlop, M.H., & Walsh, M.E. (1986). Increasing autistic children's spontaneous verbalizations of affection: An assessment of time delay and peer modeling procedures. *Journal of Applied Behavior Analysis, 19,* 307–314.

Chen, D., Hanline, M.F., & Friedman, C.T. (1989). From play group to preschool: Facilitating early integration experiences. *Child: Care, Health & Development, 15,* 283–295.

Chess, S. (1977). Follow-up report on autism in congenital rubella. *Journal of Autism and Child-hood Schizophrenia, 7,* 69–81.

Childs, R.E. (1979). Perceptions of mainstreaming by regular classroom teachers who teach main-streamed educable mentally retarded students in the public schools. *Education and Training of the Mentally Retarded, 14,* 225–227.

Cipani, E., (1988). Providing language consultation in the natural context: A model for delivery of services. *Mental Retardation, 27,* 317–324.

Clark, H.B., Rowbury, T., Baer, A.M., & Baer, D.M. (1973). Timeout as a punishing stimulus in con-tinuous and intermittent schedules. *Journal of Applied Behavior Analysis, 6,* 443–455.

Clark, P., & Rutter, M. (1979). Task difficulty and task performance in autistic children. *Journal of Child Psychology and Psychiatry and Applied Disciplines, 20,* 271–285.

Cobb, S. (1976). Social support as a moderator of life stress. *Psychosomatic Medicine, 38,* 300–314.

Coe, D., Matson, J., Fee, V., Manikam, R., & Linarello, C. (1990). Training nonverbal and verbal play skills to mentally retarded and autistic children. *Journal of Autism and Developmental Disor-ders, 20,* 177–187.

Coie, J.D., & Dodge, K.A. (1983). Continuities and changes in children's social status: A five-year longitudinal study. *Merrill-Palmer Quarterly, 29,* 261–282.

Coie, J.D., Lochman, J.E., Terry, R., & Hyman, C. (1992). Predicting early adolescent disorder from childhood aggression and peer rejection. *Journal of Consulting and Clinical Psychology, 60,* 783–792.

Cole, D.A. (1986). Facilitating play in children's peer relationships: Are we having fun yet? *Ameri-can Education Research Journal, 23,* 201–215.

Cole, K.N., Mills, P.E., Dale, P.S., & Jenkins, J.R. (1991). Effects of preschool integration for chil-dren with disabilities. *Exceptional Children, 58*(1), 36–45.

Coleman, R.S., & Whitman, T.L. (1984). Developing, generalizing, and maintaining physical fitness in mentally retarded adults: Toward a self-directed program. *Analysis and Intervention in Devel-opmental Disabilities, 4,* 109–127.

Collins, D.T. (1965). Head banging: Its meaning and management in the severely retarded adult. *Bulletin of the Meninger Clinic, 4,* 205–211.

Comegys, A. (1989). Integration strategies for parents of students with handicaps. In R. Gaylord-Ross (Ed.), *Integration strategies for students with handicaps* (pp. 339–350). Baltimore: Paul H. Brookes Publishing Co.

Cone, J.D., Delawyer, D.D., & Wolfe, V.V. (1985). Assessing parent participation: The Parent/Fam-ily Involvement Index. *Exceptional Children, 51*(5), 417–424.

Cook, R.A., Anderson, N., & Rincover, A. (1982). Stimulus overselectivity and stimulus control: Problems and procedures. In R.L. Koegel, A. Rincover, & A.L. Egel (Eds.), *Educating and under-standing autistic children* (pp. 90–105). San Diego: College-Hill Press.

Cooper, L.J., Wacker, D.P., Thursby, D., Plagmann, L.A., Harding, J., Millard, M., & Derby, M. (1992). Analysis of the effects of task preferences, task demands, and adult attention on child behavior in out patient and classroom settings. *Journal of Applied Behavior Analysis, 25,* 823–840.

Cooper, M.R., & Wood, M.T. (1974). Effects of member participation and commitment in group decision making on influence, satisfaction, and decision riskiness. *Journal of Applied Psychology, 59*(2), 127–134.

Council for Learning Disabilities. (1993). Concerns about the full inclusion of students with learn-ing disabilities in regular education classrooms. *Learning Disability Quarterly, 16*(2), 126.

Courchesne, E., Lincoln, A.J., Yeung-Courchesne, R., Elmasian, R., & Grillon, C. (1989). Patho-physiologic findings in nonretarded autism and receptive developmental language disorder. *Jour-nal of Autism and Developmental Disorders, 19,* 1–17.

Courchesne, E., Saitoh, O., Townsend, J.P., Yeung-Courchesne, R., Press, G.A., Lincoln, A.J., Haas, R.H., & Schreibman, L. (in press). Two distinctly different cerebellar pathologies in infantile autism: Hypoplasia and hyperplasia. *Lancet.*

Cowen, E.L., Pederson, A., Babigian, H., Izzo, L.D., & Trost, M.A. (1973). Long-term follow-up of early detected vulnerable children. *Journal of Consulting and Clinical Psychology, 41*, 438–446.

Crawford, D. (1978). Parent involvement in instructional planning. *Focus on Exceptional Children, 10*(7), 1–5.

Crisler, J.R. (1979). Utilization of a team approach in implementing Public Law 94-142. *Journal of Research and Development in Education, 12*(4), 101–108.

Crnic, K., & Greenberg, M. (1987, April). *Early family predictors of developmental and social competence of risk and normal children at age five.* Paper presented at the meeting of the Society for Research in Child Development, Baltimore.

Crockett, M.S. (1984). Exploring peer relationships. *Journal of Psychosocial Nursing and Mental Health Services, 22*, 18–25.

Cullingford, C. (1984). The battle for the schools. Attitudes of parents and teachers toward education. *Educational Studies, 10*(2), 113–119.

Curcio, F., & Paccia, J. (1987). Conversations with autistic children: Contingent relationships between features of adult input and children's response adequacy. *Journal of Autism and Developmental Disorders, 17*, 81–93.

Dadds, M.R., Schwartz, S., & Sanders, M.R. (1987). Marital discord and treatment outcome in behavioral treatment of child conduct disorders. *Journal of Consulting and Clinical Psychology, 55*. 396–403.

D'Alonzo, B.J. (1982). Parent involvement in special education. *Journal for Special Educators, 18*(2), 5–13.

Damasio, A., & Maurer, R. (1978). A neurological model for childhood autism. *Archives of Neurology, 35*, 777–786.

Dangel, R.F., & Polster, R.A. (1984). WINNING! A systematic, empirical approach to parent training. In R.F. Dangel & R.A. Poster (Eds.), *Parent training: Foundations of research and practice* (pp. 162–201). New York: Guilford Press.

Daniel R. v. State Board of Education 691 F. 2d 266 (6th Circuit Court of Appeals, 1982).

Darling, R.B. (1983). Parent-professional interaction: The roots of misunderstanding. In M. Seligman (Ed.), *The family with a handicapped child: Understanding and treatment* (pp. 95–121). New York: Grune & Stratton.

Darling, R.B. (1988). Parental entrepreneurship: A consumerist response to professional dominance. *Journal of Social Issues, 44*(1), 141–158.

Dawson, G., Finley, C., Phillips, S., & Lewy, A. (1989). A comparison of hemispheric asymmetries in speech-related brain potentials of autistic and dysphasic children. *Brain and Language, 37*, 26–41.

Dawson, G.D., & Adams, A. (1984). Imitation and social responsiveness in autistic children. *Journal of Abnormal Child Psychology, 12*, 209–226.

Dawson, G.D., Hill, D., Spencer, A., Galpert, L., & Watson, L. (1990). Affective exchanges between young autistic children and their mothers. *Journal of Abnormal Child Psychology, 18*, 335–345.

Dawson, G.D., & Lewy, A. (1989). Arousal, attention, and the socioemotional impairments of individuals with autism. In G.D. Dawson (Ed.), *Autism: Nature, diagnosis, and treatment* (pp. 49–74). New York: Guilford Press.

Day, H.M., Horner, R.H., & O'Neill, R.E. (1994). Multiple functions of problem behaviors: Assessment and intervention. *Journal of Applied Behavior Analysis, 27*, 279–289.

Demchak, M., & Drinkwater, S. (1992). Preschoolers with severe disabilities: The case against segregation. *Topics in Early Childhood Special Education, 11*(4), 70–83.

DeMyer, M., & Goldberg, P. (1983). Family needs of the autistic adolescent. In E. Schopler & G.B. Mesibov (Eds.), *Autism in adolescents and adults* (pp. 225–250). New York: Plenum.

DeMyer, M.K. (1979). *Parents and children with autism.* New York: John Wiley & Sons.

Dodge, K.A. (1983). Behavioral antecedents of peer social status. *Child Development, 54*, 1386–1399.

Dodge, K.A., Coie, J.D., Pettit, G.S., & Price, J.M. (1990). Peer status and aggression in boys' groups: Developmental and contextual analysis. *Child Development, 61*, 1289–1309.

Dodge, K.A., Schlundt, D.C., Schocken, I., & Delugach, J.D. (1983). Social competence and children's sociometric status: The role of peer group entry strategies. *Merrill-Palmer Quarterly, 29,* 309–336.

Donder, D., & Nietupski, J. (1981). Nonhandicapped adolescents teaching playground skills to their mentally retarded peers: Toward a less restrictive middle school environment. *Education and Training of the Mentally Retarded, 16,* 270–276.

Donnellan, A.M., & Mirenda, P.L. (1983). A model for analyzing instructional components to facilitate generalization for severely handicapped students. *Journal of Special Education, 17,* 317–331.

Dore, J. (1974). A pragmatic description of early language development. *Journal of Psycholinguistic Research, 3,* 343–350.

Dore, J. (1975). Holophrases, speech acts and language universals. *Journal of Child Language, 2,* 21–40.

Dorsey, M.F., Iwata, B.A., Ong, P., & McSween, T.E. (1980). Treatment of self-injurious behavior using a water mist: Initial response suppression and generalization. *Journal of Applied Behavior Analysis, 13,* 343–353.

Dougherty, A.M. (1990). *Consultation: practice and perspective.* Pacific Grove, CA: Brooks/Cole.

Dougherty, B.S., Fowler, S.A., & Paine, S.C. (1985). The use of peer monitors to reduce negative interaction during recess. *Journal of Applied Behavior Analysis, 18,* 141–153.

Downing, J. (1987). Conversational skills training: Teaching adolescents with mental retardation to be verbally assertive. *Mental Retardation, 25,* 147–155.

Downing, J. (1988). Active versus passive programming: A critique of IEP objectives for students with the most severe disabilities. *Journal of The Association for Persons with Severe Handicaps, 13*(3), 197–201.

Doyle, A., Connolly, J., & Rivest, L. (1980). The effects of playmate familiarity on the social interactions of young children. *Child Development, 51,* 217–223.

Doyle, B., & Guttierrez, M. (1988). *Parent professional collaboration (A Parent/Professional Training Module).* Sacramento: California State Department of Education, Special Education Division.

Drabman, R.S., Spitalnik, R., & O'Leary, K.D. (1973). Learning and self-stimulation in mute and echolalic autistic children. *Journal of Autism and Developmental Disorders, 13,* 365–381.

Dudley-Marling, C. (1985). Perceptions of the usefulness of the IEP by teachers of learning disabled and emotionally disturbed children. *Psychology in the Schools, 22,* 65–67.

Duganne, M.A., Ferrara, M., & Justice, T. (1986). *Educators and parents working together to develop special education parent support groups.* Sacramento, CA: Resources in Special Education.

Duker, P.C., & Moonen, X.M. (1986). The effect of two procedures on spontaneous signing with Down's syndrome children. *Journal of Mental Deficiency Research, 30,* 355–364.

Duker, P.C., & van Lent, C. (1991). Inducing variability in communicative gestures used by severely retarded individuals. *Journal of Applied Behavior Analysis, 24,* 379–386.

Dumas, J.E., & Wahler, R.G. (1983). Predictors of treatment outcome in parent training: Mother insularity and socieconomic disadvantage. *Behavior Assessment, 5,* 301–313.

Dunlap, G. (1984). The influence of task variation and maintenance tasks on the learning and affect of autistic children. *Journal of Experimental Child Psychology, 37,* 41–64.

Dunlap, G., & Egel, A.L. (1982). Motivational techniques. In R.L. Koegel, A. Rincover, & A.L. Egel (Eds.), *Educating and understanding autistic children* (pp. 106–126). San Diego: College-Hill Press.

Dunlap, G., & Kern, L. (1993). Assessment and intervention for children within the instructional curriculum. In J. Reichle & D. Wacker (Eds.), *Communication and language intervention series, Vol. 3, Communicative alternatives to challenging behavior: Integrating functional assessment and intervention strategies.* (pp. 177–203). Baltimore: Paul H. Brookes Publishing Co.

Dunlap, G., Kern-Dunlap, L., Clark, S., & Robbins, F.R. (1991). Functional assessment, curricular revisions, and severe problem behavior. *Journal of Applied Behavior Analysis; 24,* 387–397.

Dunlap, G., & Koegel, R.L. (1980). Motivating autistic children through stimulus variation. *Journal of Applied Behavior Analysis, 13,* 619–627.

Dunlap, G., Koegel, R.L., & Burke, J.C. (1981). Educational implication of stimulus overselectivity in autistic children. *Exceptional Education Quarterly, 20,* 37–49.

Dunlap, G., Koegel, R.L., Johnson, J., & O'Neill, R.E. (1987). Maintaining performance of autistic clients in community settings with delayed contingencies. *Journal of Applied Behavior Analysis, 20,* 185–191.

Dunlap, G., Koegel, R.L., & Koegel, L.K. (1984). Continuity of treatment: Toilet training in multiple community settings. *Journal for The Association of Persons with Severe Handicaps, 9*(2), 134–141.

Dunlap, G., Robbins, F.R., Dollman, C., & Plienis, A.J. (1988). *Early intervention for young children with autism.* Huntington, WV: Marshall University.

Dunlap, L.K., & Dunlap, G. (1989). A self-monitoring package for teaching subtraction with regrouping to students with learning disabilities. *Journal of Applied Behavior Analysis, 22,* 309–314.

Dunlap, L.K., Dunlap, G., Koegel, L.K., & Koegel, R.L. (1991). Using self-monitoring to increase students' success and independence. *Teaching Exceptional Children, 23,* 17–22.

Dunn, L.M. (1968). Special education for the mildly retarded: Is much of it justifiable? *Exceptional Children, 34,* 5–22.

Dunst, C.J., Johanson, C., Trivette, C.M., & Hamby, D. (1991). Family-oriented early intervention policies and practices: Family-centered or not? *Exceptional Children, 58*(2), 115–126.

Dunst, C.J., & Trivette, C.M. (1986). Mediating influences of social support: Personal, family, and child outcomes. *American Journal of Mental Deficiency, 90*(4), 403–417.

Dunst, C.J., & Trivette, C.M. (1988a). Determinants of parent and child interactive behavior. In K. Marf (Ed.), *Parent-child intervention and developmental disabilities: Theory, research, and intervention* (pp. 3-31). New York: Praeger.

Dunst, C.J., & Trivette, C.M. (1988b). An enablement and empowerment perspective of case management. *Topics in Early Childhood Education, 8*(4), 87–101.

Dunst, C.J., & Trivette, C.M. (1990). Assessment of social support in early intervention programs. In S.J. Meisels & J.P. Shonkoff (Eds.), *Handbook of early childhood intervention* (pp. 326–349). New York: Cambridge University Press.

Dunst, C.J., Trivette, C.M., & Deal, A.G. (1988). *Enabling and empowering families: Principles and guidelines for practice.* Cambridge, MA: Brookline Books.

Dunst, C.J., Trivette, C.M., Hamby, D., & Pollock, B. (1990). Family systems correlates of the behavior of young children with handicaps. *Journal of Early Intervention, 14*(3), 204–218.

Durand, V.M. (1990). *Severe behavior problems: A functional communication training approach.* New York: Guilford Press.

Durand, V.M., & Carr, E.G. (1987). Social influences on "self-stimulatory" behavior: Analysis and treatment application. *Journal of Applied Behavior Analysis, 20,* 119–132.

Durand, V.M., & Crimmins, D.B. (1988). Identifying the variables maintaining self-injurious behavior. *Journal of Autism and Developmental Disorders, 18,* 99–117.

Dussault, W. (1994, March). *How to avoid due process hearings.* Paper presented at the 1994 "Strategies for Managing Challenging Behaviors in Community Settings" conference, University of California, Santa Barbara.

Dyer, K. (1987). The competition of autistic stereotyped behavior with usual and specially assessed reinforcers. *Research in Developmental Disabilities, 8,* 607–626.

Dyer, K. (1989). The effects of preference on spontaneous verbal requests in individuals with autism. *Journal of The Association for Persons with Severe Handicaps, 14,* 184–189.

Eales, M.J. (1993). Pragmatic impairments in adults with childhood diagnoses of autism or developmental receptive language disorder. *Journal of Autism and Developmental Disorders, 23,* 593–617.

Eaves, L.C., Ho, H.H., & Eaves, D.M. (1994). Subtypes of autism by cluster analysis. *Journal of Autism and Developmental Disorders, 24,* 22.

Economic Opportunity Act, PL 88-452. (August 20, 1964). Title 42, U.S.C. 2701 et seq: *U.S. Statutes at Large, 78,* 508–534.

Economic Opportunity Amendments of 1966, PL 89-794. (November 8, 1966). Title 42, U.S.C. 2781 et seq: *U.S. Statutes at Large, 80,* 1451–1477.

Education for All Handicapped Children Act of 1975, PL 94-142. (August 23, 1977). Title 20, U.S.C. 1401 et seq: *U.S. Statutes at Large, 89,* 773–796.

Education of the Handicapped Act Amendments of 1986, PL 99-457. (October 8, 1986). Title 20, U.S.C. 1400 et seq: *U.S. Statutes at Large, 100,* 1145–1177.

Epstein, J.L. (1987). Parent involvement: What research says to administrators. *Education and Urban Society, 19*(2), 119–136.

Erwin, P. (1993). *Friendship and peer relations in children.* New York: John Wiley & Sons.

Esposito, B.G., & Peach, W.J. (1983). Changing attitudes of preschool children toward handicapped persons. *Exceptional Children, 49,* 361–363.

Evans, I.M., & Meyer, L.H. (1985). *An educative approach to behavior problems: A practical decision model for interventions with severely handicapped learners.* Baltimore: Paul H. Brookes Publishing Co.

Evans, I.M., Salisbury, C.L., Palombaro, M.M., Berryman, J., & Hollowood, T.M. (1992). Peer interactions and social acceptance of elementary-age children with severe disabilities in an inclusive school. *Journal of The Association of Persons with Severe Disabilities, 17,* 205–212.

Evans, R. (1990). Making mainstreaming work through prereferral consultation. *Educational Leadership, 48*(1), 73–77.

Farkas, S. (1981). *Taking a family perspective: A principal's guide for working with families of handicapped children.* Washington, DC: Office of Special Education and Rehabilitative Services. (ERIC Document Reproduction Service No. ED 213 1971)

Favell, J.E., McGinsey, J.F., & Jones, M.L. (1978). The use of physical restraint in the treatment of self-injury and as positive reinforcement. *Journal of Applied Behavior Analysis, 11,* 225–241.

Fay, W. (1969). On the basis of autistic echolalia. *Journal of Communication Disorders, 2,* 38–47.

Fay, W. (1973). On the echolalia of the blind and of the autistic child. *Journal of Speech and Hearing Research, 16,* 478–489.

Fay, W.F., & Schuler, A.L. (1980). *Emerging language in autistic children.* Baltimore: University Park Press.

Featherstone, H. (1980). *A difference in the family: Living with a disabled child.* New York: Basic Books.

Fein, D., Waterhouse, L., Lucci, D., & Snyder, D. (1985). Cognitive subtypes in developmentally disabled children: A pilot study. *Journal of Autism and Developmental Disorders, 15,* 77–95.

Feldman, D., Gerstein, L.H., & Feldman, B. (1989). Teachers' beliefs about administrators and parents of handicapped and nonhandicapped students. *Journal of Experimental Education, 58*(1), 43–54.

Fenton, K.S., Yoshida, R.K., Maxwell, J.P., & Kaufman, M.J. (1979). Recognition of team goals: An essential step toward rational decision making. *Exceptional Children, 45,* 638–644.

Ferguson, D.L. (1984). Parent advocacy network. *The Exceptional Parent, 14*(2), 41–45.

Ferguson, D.L., & Baumgart, D. (1991). Partial participation revisited. *Journal of The Association for Persons with Severe Handicaps, 16,* 218–227.

Ferrara, D.M. (1979). Attitudes of parents of mentally retarded children toward normalization activities. *American Journal of Mental Deficiency, 84*(2), 145–151.

Fesler, J.E. (1988). *The effects on classroom practices of a comprehensive systems change to a critial skills/community-based instructional model.* Unpublished doctoral dissertation, University of California, Santa Barbara.

Fewell, R.R., & Oelwein, P.L. (1990). The relationship between time in integrated environments and developmental gains in young children with special needs. *Topics in Early Childhood Special Education, 10*(2), 104–116.

Fey, M.E., & Leonard, L.B. (1983). Pragmatic skills of children with specific language impairment. In T.M. Gallagher & C.A. Prutting (Eds.), *Pragmatic assessment and intervention issues in language* (pp. 65–82). San Diego: College-Hill.

Field, T. (1984). Play behaviors of handicapped children who have friends. In T. Field, J.L. Roopnarine, & M. Segal (Eds.), *Friendships in normal and handicapped children* (pp. 153–162). Norwood, NJ: Ablex Publishing Corporation.

Field, T., Roopnarine, J.L., & Segal, M. (1984). *Friendships in normal and handicapped children.*
New Jersey: Ablex Publishing Corporation.

Fields, L., Bruno, V., & Keller, K. (1976). The stages of acquisition in stimulus fading. *Journal of
the Experimental Analysis of Behavior, 26,* 295–300.

Fine, G.A. (1981). Friends, impression management, and preadolescent behavior. In S.R. Asher
& J.M. Gottman (Eds.), *The development of children's friendships.* New York: Cambridge
University Press.

Fleming, L.A., Wolery, M., Weinzierl, C., Venn, M.L., & Schroeder, C. (1991). Model for assessing
and adapting teachers' roles in mainstreamed preschool settings. *Topics in Early Childhood Special Education, 11*(1), 85–98.

Ford, A., & Davern, L. (1989). Moving forward with school integration: Strategies for involving students with severe handicaps in the life of the school. In R. Gaylord-Ross (Ed.), *Integration strategies for students with handicaps* (pp. 11–32). Baltimore: Paul H. Brookes Publishing Co.

Ford, A., & Mirenda, P. (1984). Community instruction: A natural cues and corrections decision
model. *Journal of The Association for Persons with Severe Handicaps, 9,* 79–87.

Forehand, R., Furey, W.M., & McMahon, R.J. (1984). The role of maternal distress in a parent training program to modify child non-compliance. *Behavioral Psychotherapy, 12,* 93–108.

Forehand, R., & McMahon, R.J. (1981). *Helping the noncompliant child: A clinician's guide to parent training.* New York: Guilford Press.

Forehand, R., Sturgis, E.T., McMahon, R.J., Aguar, D., Green, K., Wells, K.C., & Breiner, J. (1979).
Parent behavioral training to modify child noncompliance: Treatment generalization across time
and from home to school. *Behavior Modification, 3,* 3–25.

Foster, M., Berger, M., & McLean, M. (1981). Rethinking a good idea: A reassessment of parent
involvement. *Topics in Early Childhood Special Education, 1,* 55–56.

Fowler, S.A. (1984). Introductory comments: The pragmatics of self-management for the developmentally disabled. *Analysis and Intervention in Developmental Disabilities, 4,* 85–89.

Foxx, R.M., & Bechtal, D.R. (1983). Overcorrection: A review and analysis. In S. Axelrod &
J. Apsche (Eds.), *The effects of punishment on human behavior* (pp. 133–220). New York: Academic Press.

Frankel, F., Simmons, J.Q., Fichter, M., & Freeman, B.J. (1984). Stimulus overselectivity in autistic
and mentally retarded children: A research note. *Journal of Child Psychology and Psychiatry, 25,*
147–155.

Frea, W.D. (1990). *Assessing pragmatic deficits in autistic children.* Unpublished master's thesis,
University of California, Santa Barbara.

Frea, W.D., Koegel, R.L., & Koegel, L.K. (1993). *Understanding why problem behaviors occur: A
guide for assisting parents in assessing causes of behavior and designing treatment plans.* Santa
Barbara: University of California at Santa Barbara.

Frey, K.S., Fewell, R.R., & Vadasy, P.F. (1988). Parental adjustment and changes in child outcome
among families of young handicapped children. *Topics in Early Childhood Special Education,
8*(4), 38–57.

Friend, M., & Cook, L. (1993, November/December). Inclusion. *Instructor,* pp. 52–56.

Frith, U. (1969). Emphasis and meaning in recall in normal and autistic children. *Language and
Speech, 12,* 29–38.

Funk, R. (1987). Disability rights: From caste to class in the context of civil rights. In A. Gartner &
T. Joe (Eds.), *Images of the disabled, disabling images* (pp. 7–30). New York: Praeger.

Furman, W., & Buhrmester, D. (1985). Children's perceptions of the personal relationships in their
social networks. *Developmental Psychology, 21,* 1016–1024.

Gallagher, J.J. (1989). The impact of policies for handicapped children on future early education
policy. *Phi Delta Kappan, 71*(2), 121–124.

Gallagher, J.J. (1990). The family as a focus for intervention. In S.J. Meisels & J.P. Shonkoff (Eds.), *Handbook of early childhood intervention* (pp. 540–569). New York: Cambridge University Press.

Gallagher, J.J., Beckman, P., & Cross, A.H. (1983). Families of handicapped children: Sources of stress and its amelioration. *Exceptional Children, 50*(1), 10–19.

Gardner, W.I., Cole, C.L., Berry, D.L., & Nowinski, J.M. (1983). Reduction of disruptive behaviors in mentally retarded adults. *Behavior Modification, 7,* 76–96.

Gargiulo, R.M. (1985). *Working with parents of exceptional children.* Boston: Houghton Mifflin.

Gaylord-Ross, R.J., Haring, T.G., Breen, C., & Pitts-Conway, V. (1984). The training and generalization of social interaction skills with autistic youth. *Journal of Applied Behavior Analysis, 17,* 229–247.

Gee, K., Graham, N., Goetz, L., Oshima, G., & Yoshioka, K. (1991). Teaching students to request the continuation of routine activities by using time delay and decreasing physical assistance in the context of chain interruption. *Journal of The Association for Persons with Severe Handicaps, 16,* 154–167.

Gerardi, R.J., Grohe, B., Benedict, G.C., & Coolidge, P.G. (1984). IEP: More paperwork and wasted time. *Contemporary Education, 56*(1), 39–42.

Gerber, M.M. (1988). Tolerance and technology for instruction: Implications for special education reform. *Exceptional Children, 54*(4), 309–314.

Gerber, M.M., & Levine-Donnerstein, D. (1989). Educating all children: Ten years later. *Exceptional Children, 56*(1), 17–27.

Gerber, M.M., & Semmel, M.I. (1985). The microeconomics of referral and reintegration: A paradigm for evaluation of special education. *Studies in Educational Evaluation, 11*(1), 13–29.

Gerber, P.J. (1977). Awareness of handicapping conditions and sociometric status in an integrated preschool setting. *Mental Retardation, 15,* 24–25.

Gickling, E.E., & Theobald, J.T. (1975). Mainstreaming: Affect or effect. *Journal of Special Education, 9*(3), 317–328.

Gillberg, C., & Gillberg, I.C. (1983). Infantile autism: A total population study of reduced optimality in the pre, peri-, and neonatal period. *Journal of Autism and Developmental Disorders, 13,* 153–166.

Gillberg, C., Rosenhall, U., & Johansson, E. (1983). Auditory brainstem responses in childhood psychosis. *Journal of Autism and Developmental Disabilities, 13,* 181–195.

Gilliam, J.E. (1979). Contributions and status rankings of educational planning committee participants. *Exceptional Children, 45*(6), 466–468.

Gilliam, J.E., & Coleman, M.C. (1981). Who influences IEP committee decisions? *Exceptional Children, 47*(8), 642–644.

Glynn, E.L., Thomas, J.D., & Shee, S.M. (1973). Behavioral self-control of on-task behavior in an elementary classroom. *Journal of Applied Behavior Analysis, 6,* 105–113.

Gobbi, L., Cipani, E., Hudson, C., & Lapenta-Neudeck, R. (1986). Developing spontaneous requesting among children with severe mental retardation. *Mental Retardation, 24,* 357–363.

Goldberg, S.S., & Kuriloff, P.J. (1991). Evaluating the fairness of special education hearings. *Exceptional Children, 57*(6), 546–555.

Goldfarb, W., Braunstein, P., & Lorge, I. (1956). A study of speech patterns in a group of schizophrenic children. *American Journal of Orthopsychiatry, 26,* 544–555.

Goldstein, H., & Cisar, C.L. (1992). Promoting interaction during sociodramatic play: Teaching scripts to typical preschoolers and classmates with disabilities. *Journal of Applied Behavior Analysis, 25,* 265–280.

Goldstein, H., Kaczmarek, L., Pennington, R., & Shafer, K. (1992). Peer-mediated intervention: Attending to, commenting on, and acknowledging the behavior of preschoolers with autism. *Journal of Applied Behavior Analysis, 25,* 289–305.

Goldstein, H., Moss, J.W., & Jordan, L. (1982). The efficacy of special class training on the development of mentally retarded children. In K.A. Heller, W.H. Holtzman, & S. Messick (Eds.), *Placing *children in special education: A strategy for equity* (pp. 262–299). Washington, DC: National Academy Press.

Goldstein, H., Wickstrom, S., Hoyson, M., Jamieson, B., & Odom, S.L. (1988). Effects of sociodramatic script training on social and communicative interaction. *Education and Treatment of Children, 11,* 97–117.

Goldstein, S., Strickland, B., Turnbull, A.P., & Curry, L. (1980). An observational analysis of the IEP conference. *Exceptional Children, 46*(4), 278–286.

Goldstein, S., & Turnbull, A.P. (1982). Strategies to increase parent participation in IEP conferences. *Exceptional Children, 48*(4), 360–361.

Goodman, H., Gottlieb, J., & Harrison, R.N. (1972). Social acceptance of EMRs integrated into a nongraded elementary school. *American Journal of Mental Deficiency, 76,* 412–417.

Gottlieb, J., & Budoff, M. (1973). Social acceptability of retarded children in nongraded schools differing in architecture. *American Journal of Mental Deficiency, 78,* 15–19.

Gottlieb, J., & Davis, J.E. (1973). Social acceptance of EMR children during overt behavioral interactions. *American Journal of Mental Deficiency, 78,* 141–143.

Gottlieb, J., & Leyser, Y. (1981). Friendship between mentally retarded and nonretarded children. In S.R. Asher & J.M. Gottman (Eds.), *The development of children's friendships* (pp. 150–181). Cambridge, England: Cambridge University Press.

Gottlieb, J., Semmel, M.I., & Veldman, D.J. (1978). Correlates of social status among mainstreamed mentally retarded children. *Journal of Educational Psychology, 70,* 396–405.

Gottman, J.M., & Parkhurst, J.T. (1980). A developmental theory of friendship and acquaintanceship processes. In W.A. Collins (Ed.), *Development of cognition, affect, and social relations* (pp. 197–253). Hillsdale, NJ: Lawrence Erlbaum Associates.

Grace, N., Cowart, C., & Matson, J.L. (1988). Reinforcement and self-control for treating a chronic case of self-injury in Lesch-Nyhan Syndrome. *Journal of the Multihandicapped Person, 1,* 53–59.

Green, A.L., & Stoneman, Z. (1989). Attitudes of mothers and fathers on nonhandicapped children. *Journal of Early Intervention, 13*(4), 292–304.

Grenot-Scheyer, M., Coots, J., & Falvey, M.A. (1990). Developing and fostering friendships. In M.A. Falvey, *Community-based curriculum: Instructional strategies for students with severe handicaps* (2nd ed., pp. 345–358). Baltimore: Paul H. Brookes Publishing Co.

Gresham, F.M. (1982). Misguided mainstreaming: The case for social skills training with handicapped children. *Exceptional Children, 48,* 422–433.

Gresham, F.M. (1984). Social skills and self-efficacy for exceptional children. *Exceptional Children, 51,* 253–261.

Gresham, F.M., & Reschly, D.J. (1986). Social skill deficits and low peer acceptance of mainstreamed learning disabled children. *Learning Disability Quarterly, 9,* 23–32.

Gruen, G.E., Ottinger, D.R., & Ollendick, T.H. (1974). Probability learning in retarded children with differing histories of success and failure in school. *American Journal of Mental Deficiency, 79,* 417–423.

Gunter, P., Fox, J.J., Brady, M.P., Shores, R.E., & Cavenaugh, K. (1988). Nonhandicapped peers as multiple exemplars: A generalization tactic for promoting autistic students' social skills. *Behavioral Disorders, 13,* 116–126.

Guralnick, M.J. (1990a). Major accomplishments and future directions in early childhood mainstreaming. *Topics in Early Childhood Special Education, 10,* 1–17.

Guralnick, M.J. (1990b). Major accomplishments and future directions in early childhood mainstreaming. *Topics in Early Childhood Special Education, 10*(2), 1–17.

Guralnick, M.J. (1990c). Social competence and early intervention. *Journal of Early Intervention, 14*(1), 3–14.

Guralnick, M.J., & Groom, J. (1985). Correlates of peer-related social competence of developmentally delayed preschool children. *American Journal of Mental Deficiency, 90,* 140–150.

Guralnick, M.J., & Groom, J.M. (1988). Peer interaction in mainstreamed and specialized classrooms: A comparative analysis. *Exceptional Children, 5,* 415–425.

Guralnick, M.J., & Paul-Brown, D. (1984). Communicative adjustments during behavior request episodes among children at different developmental levels. *Child Development, 55,* 911–919.

Halle, J.W. (1982). Teaching functional language to the handicapped: An integrative model of natural environment teaching techniques. *Journal of The Association for Persons with Severe Handicaps, 7,* 29–37.

Halle, J.W. (1987). Teaching language in the natural environment: An analysis of spontaneity. *Journal of The Association for Persons with Severe Handicaps, 12,* 28–37.

Halle, J.W., Chadsey-Rusch, J., & Collet-Klingenberg, L. (1993). Applying contextual features of general case instruction and interactive routines to enhance communication skills. In R.A. Gable & S.F. Warren (Eds.), *Strategies for teaching students with mild to severe mental retardation* (pp. 231–268). Baltimore: Paul H. Brookes Publishing Co.

Halle, J.W., Marshall, A.M., & Spradlin, J.E. (1979). Time delay: A technique to increase language use and facilitate generalization in retarded children. *Journal of Applied Behavior Analysis, 12,* 431–439.

Halvorsen, A.T., & Sailor, W. (1990). Integrating students with severe and profound disabilities: A review of research. In R. Gaylord-Ross (Ed.), *Issues and research in special education* (Vol. 1, pp. 110–172). New York: Teachers College Press.

Hamre-Nietupski, S., Hendrickson, J., Nietupski, J., & Sasso, G. (1993). Perceptions of teachers of students with moderate, severe, or profound disabilities on facilitating friendships with nondisabled peers. *Education and Training in Mental Retardation, 28,* 111–127.

Hamre-Nietupski, S., Nietupski, J., & Strathe, M. (1992). Functional life skills, academic skills, and friendship/social relationship development: What do parents of students with moderate/severe/profound disabilities value. *Journal of The Association for Persons with Severe Handicaps, 17,* 53–58.

Handicapped Children's Early Education Assistance Act, PL 90-538. (September 30, 1968). Title 20, U.S.C. 621 et seq: *U.S. Statutes at Large, 82,* 901–902.

Hanline, M.F. (1991). Transitions and critical events in the family life cycle: Implications for providing support to families of children with disabilities. *Psychology in the Schools, 28,* 53–59.

Hanrahan, L.L., & Langlois, A. (1988). Parents as language therapists. In K. Marfo (Ed.), *Parent–child interaction and developmental disabilities: Theory, research, and intervention* (pp. 242–252). New York: Praeger.

Hanson, M.J., & Hanline, M.F. (1990). Parenting a child with a disability: A longitudinal study of parental stress and adaptation. *Journal of Early Intervention, 14*(3), 234–248.

Harasymiw, S.J., & Horne, M.D. (1976). Teacher attitudes toward handicapped children and regular class integration. *Journal of Special Education, 10*(4), 393–400.

Hargrave, E., & Swisher, L. (1975). Modifying the verbal expression of a child with autistic behaviors. *Journal of Autism and Childhood Schizophrenia, 6,* 147–154.

Haring, T. (1993). Research basis of instructional procedures to promote social interaction and integration. In R.A. Gable & S.F. Warren (Eds.), *Strategies for teaching students with mild to moderate retardation* (pp. 129–164). Baltimore: Paul H. Brookes Publishing Co.

Haring, T.G. (1985). Teaching between-class generalization of toy play behavior to handicapped children. *Journal of Applied Behavior Analysis, 18,* 127–139.

Haring, T.G. (1990). Social relationships. In L. Meyer, C.A. Peck, & L. Brown (Eds.), *Critical issues in the lives of people with disabilities* (pp. 195–216). Baltimore: Paul H. Brookes Publishing Co.

Haring, T.G., & Breen, C.G. (1992). A peer-mediated social network intervention to enhance the social integration of persons with moderate and severe disabilities. *Journal of Applied Behavior Analysis, 25,* 319–333.

Haring, T.G., & Lovinger, L. (1989). Promoting social interaction through teaching generalized play initiation responses to preschool children with autism. *Journal of The Association for Persons with Severe Handicaps, 14,* 58–67.

Haring, T.G., Roger, B., Lee, M., Breen, C., & Gaylord-Ross, R. (1986). Teaching social language to moderately handicapped students. *Journal of Applied Behavior Analysis, 19,* 159–171.

Harris, S.L. (1986). Families of children with autism: Issues for the behavior therapist. *The Behavior Therapist, 9,* 175–177.

Harris, S.L., Wolchik, S.A., & Milch, R.E. (1983). Changing the speech of autistic children and their parents. *Child and Family Behavior Therapy, 4,* 151–173.

Harris, S.L., Wolchik, S.A., & Weitz, S. (1981). The acquisition of language skill by autistic children: Can parents do the job? *Journal of Autism and Developmental Disorders, 11,* 373–384.

Harrold, M., Lutzker, J.R., Campbell, R.V., & Touchette, P.E. (1992). Improving parent-child interactions for families with developmental disabilities. *Journal of Behavior Therapy and Experimental Psychiatry, 23,* 89–100.

Hart, B., & Risley, T.R. (1974). Using preschool materials to modify the language of disadvantaged children. *Journal of Applied Behavior Analysis, 7,* 243–256.

Hart, B., & Risley, T.R. (1975). Incidental teaching of language in the preschool. *Journal of Applied Behavior Analysis, 8,* 411–420.

Hart, B.M., & Risley, T.R. (1968). Establishing the use of descriptive adjectives in the spontaneous speech of disadvantaged preschool children. *Journal of Applied Behavior Analysis, 1,* 109–120.

Hart, B.M., & Risley, T.R. (1974). Using pre-school materials to modify the language of disadvantaged children. *Journal of Applied Behavior Analysis, 7,* 243–256.

Hart, B.M., & Risley, T.R. (1978). Promoting productive language through incidental teaching. *Education and Urban Society, 10,* 407–429.

Hartup, W.W. (1975). The origins of friendships. In M. Lewis & L.A. Rosenblum (Eds.), *Friendship and peer relations* (pp. 11–26). New York: John Wiley & Sons.

Hartup, W.W., & Sancilio, M.F. (1986). Children's friendships. In E. Schopler & G.B. Mesibov (Eds.), *Social behavior in autism* (pp. 61–79). New York: Plenum.

Hawkins, N.E., & Singer, G.H.S. (1989). A skills training approach for assisting parents to cope with stress. In G.H.S. Singer & L.K. Irvin (Eds.), *Support for caregiving families: Enabling positive adaptation to disability* (pp. 71–83). Baltimore: Paul H. Brookes Publishing Co.

Hayes, D.S. (1978). Cognitive basis for liking and disliking among preschool children's unilateral and reciprocal relationships. *Child Development, 49,* 906–909.

Hayes, D.S., Gershman, E., & Bolin, L.J. (1980). Friends and enemies: Cognitive basis for preschool children's unilateral and reciprocal relationships. *Child Development, 51,* 1276–1279.

Heller, K.A. (1982). Effects of special education placement on educable mentally retarded children. In K.A. Heller, W.H. Holtzman, & S. Messick (Eds.), *Placing children in special education: A strategy for equity* (pp. 262–299). Washington, DC: National Academy Press.

Hemsley, R., Howlin, P., Berger, M., Hersov, L., Holbrook, D., Rutter, M., & Yule, W. (1978). Treating autistic children in a family context. In M. Rutter & E. Schopler (Eds.), *Autism: A reappraisal of concepts and treatment* (pp. 379–412). New York: Plenum.

Hendricks v. Gilhool, 709, F. Supp 1362 (1989).

Hewitt, F.M. (1965). Teaching speech to autistic children through operant conditioning. *American Journal of Orthopsychiatry, 34,* 927–936.

Hirshoren, A., & Burton, T. (1979). Willingness of regular teachers to participate in mainstreaming handicapped children. *Journal of Research and Development in Education, 12*(4), 93–100.

Hocutt, A., & Wiegerink, R. (1983). Perspectives on parent involvement in preschool programs for handicapped children. In R. Haskins & D. Adams (Eds.), *Parent education and public policy* (pp. 211–229). Norwood, NJ: Ablex.

Hoff, M.K., Fenton, K.S., Yoshida, R.K., & Kaufman, M.J. (1978). Notice and consent: The school's responsibility to inform parents. *Journal of School Psychology, 16*(3), 265–273.

Holland, A.L. (1975). Language therapy for children: Some thoughts on context and content. *Journal of Speech and Hearing Disorders, 40,* 514–523.

Holroyd, J., & McArthur, D. (1976). Mental retardation and stress on the parents: A contrast between Down's syndrome and childhood autism. *American Journal of Mental Deficiency, 80,* 431–438.

Honig, A.S., & McCarron, P.A. (1988). Prosocial behaviors of handicapped and typical peers in an integrated preschool. *Early Child Development and Care, 33,* 113–125.

Hops, H. (1981). Behavioral assessment of exceptional children's social development. *Exceptional Education Quarterly, 1*, 31–43.

Horne, M.D. (1985). *Attitudes toward handicapped students: Professional, peer, and parent reactions*. Hillsdale, NJ: Lawrence Erlbaum Associates.

Horner, R.H., & Brigham, T.A. (1979, February). The effects of self-management procedures on the study behavior of two retarded children. *Education and Training of the Mentally Retarded*, 18–24.

Horner, R.H., Dunlap, G., & Koegel, R.L. (Eds.). (1988). *Generalization and maintenance: Life-style changes in applied settings*. Baltimore: Paul H. Brookes Publishing Co.

Horner, R.H., Dunlap, G., Koegel, R.L., Carr, E.G., Sailor, W., Anderson, J., Albin, R.W., & O'Neill, R.W. (1990). Toward a technology of nonaversive behavior support. *Journal of The Association for People with Severe Handicaps, 15*, 125–132.

Horner, R.H., Williams, J.A., & Knobbe, C.A. (1985). The effect of "opportunity to perform" on the maintenance of skills learned by high school students with severe handicaps. *Journal for The Association for Persons with Severe Handicaps, 10*(3), 172–175.

Howes, C. (1983). Patterns of friendship. *Child Development, 54*, 1041–1053.

Howlin, P. (1986). An overview of social behavior in autism. In E. Schopler & G.B. Mesibov (Eds.), *Social behavior in autism* (pp. 103–131). New York: Plenum.

Howlin, P.A. (1981). The results of a home-based language training programme with autistic children. *British Journal of Disorders of Communication, 16*, 73–88.

Huefner, D.S. (1991). Judicial review of the special educational program requirements under the Education for All Handicapped Children Act: Where have we been and where should we go? *Harvard Journal of Law and Public Policy, 14*(2), 483–516.

Huguenin, N.H. (1985). Attention to multiple cues by severely mentally retarded adults: Effects of single-component pretraining. *Applied Research in Mental Retardation, 6*(3), 319–335.

Hunt, P., Alwell, M., & Goetz, L. (1988). Acquisition of conversation skills and the reduction of inappropriate social interaction behaviors. *Journal of The Association for Persons with Severe Handicaps, 13*, 20–27.

Hunt, P., Goetz, L., & Anderson, J. (1986). The quality of IEP objectives associated with placement on integrated versus segregated school sites. *Journal of The Association for Persons with Severe Handicaps, 11*(2), 125–130.

Hyman, I., Carroll, R., Duffey, J., Manni, J., & Winikur, D. (1973). Patterns of interprofessional conflict resolution on school child study teams. *Journal of School Psychology, 11*(3), 187–195.

Hymel, S., & Asher, S.R. (1977). *Assessment and training of isolated children's social skills*. Paper presented at the biennial meeting of the Society for Research in Child Development, New Orleans. (ERIC Document Reproduction Service No. ED 136 930)

Individuals with Disabilities Education Act of 1990 (IDEA), PL 101-476. (October 30, 1990). Title 20, U.S.C. 1400 et seq: *U.S. Statutes at Large, 104*, 1103–1151.

Ingenmey, R., & Van Houten, R. (1991). Using time delay to promote spontaneous speech in an autistic child. *Journal of Applied Behavior Analysis, 24*, 591–596.

Intagliata, J., & Doyle, N. (1984). Enhancing social support for parents of developmentally disabled children: Training in interpersonal problem solving skills. *Mental Retardation, 22*, 4–11.

Ispa, J., & Matz, R.D. (1978). Integrating handicapped preschool children within a cognitively oriented program. In M. J. Guralnick (Ed.), *Early intervention and the integration of handicapped and nonhandicapped children* (pp. 167–190). Baltimore: University Park Press.

Iwata, B.A., & Bailey, J.S. (1974). Reward versus cost token systems: An analysis of the effects on students and teacher. *Journal of Applied Behavior Analysis, 7*, 567–576.

Iwata, B.A., Dorsey, M.F., Slifer, K.J., Bauman, K.E., & Richman, G.S. (1982). Toward a functional analysis of self-injury. *Analysis and Intervention in Developmental Disabilities, 2*, 3–20.

Iwata, B.A., Pace, G.M., Kalsher, M.J., Cowdery, G.E., & Cataldo, M.F. (1990). Experimental analysis and extinction of self-injurious escape behavior. *Journal of Applied Behavior Analysis, 23*, 11–27.

Iwata, B.A., Vollmer, T.R., & Zarcone, J.R. (1990). The experimental (functional) analysis of behavior disorders: Methodology, applications, and limitations. In A.C. Repp & N.N. Singh (Eds.), *Per-*

spectives on the use of nonaversive and aversive interventions for persons with developmental disabilities (pp. 301–330). Sycamore, IL: Sycamore Publishing Co.

Janes, C.L., Hesselbrock, V.M., Myers, D.G., & Penniman, J.H. (1979). Problem boys in young adulthood: Teachers' ratings and twelve-year follow-up. *Journal of Youth and Adolescence, 8,* 453–472.

Jenkins, J.R., Odom, S.L., & Speltz, M.L. (1989). Effects of social integration on preschool children with handicaps. *Exceptional Children, 55,* 420–428.

Jenkins, J.R., Speltz, M.L., & Odom, S.L. (1985). Integrating normal and handicapped preschoolers: Effects on child development and social interaction. *Exceptional Children, 52,* 7–17.

Johnson, A.B., & Cartwright, C.A. (1979). The roles of information and experience in improving teachers' knowledge and attitudes about mainstreaming. *Journal of Special Education, 13*(4), 453–462.

Johnson, G.O. (1962). Special education for the mentally retarded: A paradox. *Exceptional Children, 29,* 62–69.

Kaczmarek, L.A. (1990). Teaching spontaneous language to individuals with severe handicaps: A matrix model. *Journal of The Association for Persons with Severe Handicaps, 15,* 160–169.

Kaiser, A.P., Yoder, P.J., & Keetz, A. (1992). Evaluating milieu teaching. In S.F. Warren & J. Reichle (Eds.), *Communication and language intervention series, Vol. 1, Causes and effects in communication and language intervention* (pp. 9–47). Baltimore: Paul H. Brookes Publishing Co.

Kamps, D.M., Leonard, B.R., Vernon, S., Dugan, E.P., Delquadri, J.C., Gershon, B., Wade, L., & Folk, L. (1992). Teaching social skills to students with autism to increase peer interactions in an integrated first-grade classroom. *Journal of Applied Behavior Analysis, 25,* 281–288.

Kanfer, F.H. (1970). Self-monitoring: Methodological limitations and clinical applications. *Journal of Consulting and Clinical Psychology, 35,* 148–152.

Kanner, L. (1943). Autistic disturbances of affective contact. *Nervous Child, 2,* 217–250.

Kanner, L. (1971). Follow-up study of eleven children originally reported in 1943. *Journal of Autism and Childhood Schizophrenia, 1,* 119–145.

Kanner, L., Rodriguez, A., & Ashenden, B. (1972). How far can autistic children go in matters of social adaptation? *Journal of Autism and Childhood Schizophrenia, 2,* 9–33.

Karnes, M.B., Linnemeyer, S.A., & Myles, G. (1983). Programs for parents of handicapped children. In R. Haskins & D. Adams (Eds.), *Parent education and public policy* (pp. 181–210). Norwood, NJ: Ablex.

Kaufman, M.J., Gottlieb, J., Agard, J.A., & Kukic, M.B. (1975). Mainstreaming: Towards an explication of the construct. *Focus on Exceptional Children, 7*(3), 1–12.

Kaye, N.L., & Aserlind, R. (1979). The IEP: The ultimate process. *Journal of Special Education, 13*(2), 137–143.

Kazdin, A.E. (1978). *History of behavior modification.* Baltimore: University Park Press.

Kehle, T.J., & Guidubaldi, J. (1980). Do too many cooks spoil the broth?: Evaluation of team placement and individual educational plans on enhancing the social competence of handicapped students. *Journal of Learning Disabilities, 13*(9), 26–30.

Kennedy, J.H. (1988). Issues in the identification of socially incompetent children. *School Psychology Review, 17,* 276–288.

Kennedy, J.H. (1990). Determinants of peer social status: Contributions of physical appearance, reputation, and behavior. *Journal of Youth and Adolescence, 19,* 233–244.

Kern, L., Koegel, R.L., & Dunlap, G. (1984). The influence of vigorous versus mild exercise on autistic stereotyped behaviors. *Journal of Autism and Developmental Disorders, 14,* 57–67.

Kern, L., Koegel, R.L., Dyer, K., Blew, P.A., & Fenton, L.R. (1982). The effects of physical exercise on self-stimulation and appropriate responding in autistic children. *Journal of Autism and Developmental Disorders, 4,* 399–419.

Kirk, S. (1964). Research in education. In H.A. Stevens & R. Heber (Eds.), *Mental retardation: A review of research* (pp. 57–59). Chicago: University of Chicago Press.

Knapczyk, D.R., & Livingston, G. (1973). Self-recording and student teacher supervision: Variables within a token economy structure. *Journal of Applied Behavior Analysis, 6,* 481–486.

Koegel, L.K. (1993). *Teaching children with autism to use a self-initiated strategy to learn expressive vocabulary.* Unpublished dissertation, University of California, Santa Barbara.

Koegel, L.K., & Koegel, R.L. (1986). The effects of interspersed maintenance tasks on academic performance and motivation in a severe childhood stroke victim. *Journal of Applied Behavior Analysis, 19,* 425–430.

Koegel, L.K., Koegel, R.L., Hurley, C., & Frea, W.D. (1992). Improving social skills and disruptive behavior in children with autism through self-management. *Journal of Applied Behavior Analysis, 25,* 341–353.

Koegel, L.K., Kocgel, R.L., & Ingham, J.C. (1986). Programming rapid generalization of correct articulation through self-monitoring procedures. *Journal of Speech and Hearing Disorders, 51,* 24–32.

Koegel, L.K., Koegel, R.L., & Parks, D.R. (1989). *How to teach self-management skills to people with severe disabilities: A training manual.* Santa Barbara: University of California.

Koegel, L.K., Koegel, R.L., & Smith, A. (1995). *Motivation and testing children with autism.* Manuscript in preparation.

Koegel, L.K., Valdez-Menchaca, M.C., & Koegel, R.L. (1994). Autism: Social communication difficulties and related behaviors. In V.B. Van Hasselt & M. Hersen (Eds.), *Advanced abnormal psychology* (pp. 165–187). New York: Plenum.

Koegel, R.L., Camarata, S.M., & Koegel, L.K. (1994). Aggression and non-compliance: Behavior modification through naturalistic language remediation. In J.L. Matson (Ed.), *Autism in children and adults: Etiology, assessment, and intervention* (pp. 165–180). Pacific Grove, CA: Brooks/Cole Publishing Co.

Koegel, R.L., & Covert, A. (1972). The relationship of self-stimulation to learning in autistic children. *Journal of Applied Behavior Analysis, 5,* 381–387.

Koegel, R.L., Dunlap, G., Richman, G., & Dyer, K. (1981). The use of specific orienting cues for teaching discrimination tasks. *Analysis and Intervention in Developmental Disabilities, 1,* 187–198.

Koegel, R.L., Dyer, K., & Bell, L.K. (1987). The influence of child preferred activities on autistic children's social behavior. *Journal of Applied Behavior Analysis, 20,* 243–252.

Koegel, R.L., & Egel, A.L. (1979). Motivating autistic children. *Journal of Abnormal Psychology, 88,* 418–426.

Koegel, R.L., Egel, A., & Williams, J.A. (1980). Behavioral contrast and generalization across settings in the treatment of autistic children. *Journal of Experimental Child Psychology, 30,* 422–437.

Koegel, R.L., Firestone, P.B., Kramme, K.W., & Dunlap, G. (1974). Increasing spontaneous play by suppressing self-stimulation in autistic children. *Journal of Applied Behavior Analysis, 7,* 521–528.

Koegel, R.L., & Frea, W.D. (1993). Treatment of social behavior in autism through the modification of pivotal social skills. *Journal of Applied Behavior Analysis, 26*(3), 369–377.

Koegel, R.L., Frea, W.D., & Surratt, A.V. (1994). Self-management of problematic social behavior. In E. Schopler & G.B. Mesibov (Eds.), *Behavioral issues in autism* (pp. 81–97). New York: Plenum.

Koegel, R.L., Glahn, T.J., & Nieminen, G.S. (1978). Generalization of parent training results. *Journal of Applied Behavior Analysis, 11,* 95–109.

Koegel, R.L., & Koegel, L.K. (1986). Promoting generalized treatment gains through direct instruction of self-monitoring skills. *Direct Instruction News, 5,* 13–15.

Koegel, R.L., & Koegel, L.K. (1988). Generalized responsivity and pivotal behaviors. In R.H. Horner, G. Dunlap, & R.L. Koegel (Eds.), *Generalization and maintenance: Life-style changes in applied settings* (pp. 41–66). Baltimore: Paul H. Brookes Publishing Co.

Koegel, R.L., & Koegel, L.K. (1990). Extended reductions in stereotypic behavior of students with autism through a self-management treatment package. *Journal of Applied Behavior Analysis, 23*(1), 119–127.

Koegel, R.L., Koegel, L.K., & O'Neill, R.E. (1989). Generalization in the treatment of autism. In L.V. McReynolds & J.E. Spradlin (Eds.), *Generalization strategies in the treatment of communication disorders* (pp. 116–131). Toronto, Ontario, Canada: B.C. Decker Publishers.

Koegel, R.L., Koegel, L.K., & Schreibman, L. (1991). Assessing and training parents in teaching pivotal behaviors. In R. Prinz (Ed.), *Advances in behavioral assessment of children and families.* London: Jessica Kingsley Publishers.

Koegel, R.L., Koegel, L.K., & Surratt, A.V. (1992). Language intervention and disruptive behavior in preschool children with autism. *Journal of Autism and Developmental Disorders, 22,* 141–153.

Koegel, R.L., & Mentis, M. (1985). Motivation in childhood autism: Can they or won't they? *Journal of Child Psychology & Psychiatry, 26,* 185–191.

Koegel, R.L., O'Dell, M.C., & Dunlap, G. (1988). Producing speech use in nonverbal autistic children by reinforcing attempts. *Journal of Autism and Developmental Disorders, 18*(4), 525–538.

Koegel, R.L., O'Dell, M.C., & Koegel, L.K. (1987). A natural language paradigm for teaching nonverbal autistic children. *Journal of Autism and Developmental Disabilities, 17,* 187–199.

Koegel, R.L., & Rincover, A. (1974). Treatment of psychotic children in a classroom environment: I. Learning in a large group. *Journal of Applied Behavior Analysis, 7,* 49–55.

Koegel, R.L., & Rincover, A. (1976). Some detrimental effects of using extra stimuli to guide learning in normal and autistic children. *Journal of Abnormal Child Psychology, 4,* 59–71.

Koegel, R.L., & Schreibman, L. (1977). Teaching autistic children to respond to simultaneous multiple cues. *Journal of Experimental Child Psychology, 24,* 299–311.

Koegel, R.L., & Schreibman, L. (Eds.). (1982). *How to teach autistic and other severely handicapped children.* Lawrence, KS: H & H Enterprises.

Koegel, R.L., Schreibman, L., Britten, K.R., Burke, J.C., & O'Neill, R.E. (1982). A comparison of parent training to direct clinic treatment. In R.L. Koegel, A. Rincover, & A.L. Egel (Eds.), *Educating and understanding autistic children* (pp. 260–279). San Diego: College-Hill Press.

Koegel, R.L., Schreibman, L., Britten, K., & Laitinen, R. (1979). The effects of schedule of reinforcement on stimulus overselectivity in autistic children. *Journal of Autism and Developmental Disorders, 9,* 383–397.

Koegel, R.L., Schreibman, L., Good, A., Cerniglia, L., Murphy, C., & Koegel, L.K. (1989). *How to teach pivotal behaviors to children with autism: A training manual.* Unpublished manuscript, University of California, Santa Barbara.

Koegel, R.L., Shreibman, L., Johnson, J., O'Neill, R.E., & Dunlap, G. (1984). Collateral effects of parent training on families with autistic children. In R.F. Dangel & R.A. Polster (Eds.), *Parent training: Foundations of research and practice* (pp. 358–378). New York: Guilford Press.

Koegel, R.L., Schreibman, L., Loos, L.M., Dirlich-Wilhelm, H., Dunlap, G., Robbins, F.R., & Plienis, A.J. (1992). Consistent stress profiles in mothers of children with autism. *Journal of Autism and Developmental Disorders, 22,* 205–216.

Koegel, R.L., & Wilhelm, H. (1973). Selective responding to the components of multiple visual cues by autistic children. *Journal of Experimental Child Psychology, 15,* 442–453.

Koegel, R.L., & Williams, J.A. (1980). Direct vs. indirect response–reinforcer relationships in teaching autistic children. *Journal of Abnormal Child Psychology, 8,* 537–547.

Kohler, F.W., Strain, P.S., & Shearer, D.D. (1992). The overtures of preschool social skill intervention agents: Differential rates, forms and functions. *Behavior Modification, 16,* 525–542.

Kolvin, I. (1971). Studies in the childhood psychoses: I. Diagnostic criteria and classification. *British Journal of Psychiatry, 118*(545), 381–384.

Kouri, T. (1989). How manual sign acquisition relates to the development of spoken languages: A case study. *Language, Speech, and Hearing Services in Schools, 20,* 50–62.

Kovattana, P.M., & Kraemer, H.C. (1974). Response to multiple visual cues of color, size, and form by autistic children. *Journal of Autism and Childhood Schizophrenia, 4,* 251–261.

Kozloff, M.A. (1973). *Reaching the autistic child: A parent training program.* Champaign, IL: Research Press.

Krahn, G.L. (1993). Conceptualizing social support in families of children with special health needs. *Family Process, 32,* 235–248.

Krauss, M.W., & Jacobs, F. (1990). Family assessment: Purposes and techniques. In S.J. Meisels & J.P. Shonkoff (Eds.), *Handbook of early childhood intervention* (pp. 303–325). New York: Cambridge University Press.

Krauss, M.W., Upshur, C.C., Shonkoff, J.P., & Hauser-Cram, P. (1993). The impact of parent groups on mothers of infants with disabilities. *Journal of Early Intervention, 17*(1), 8–20.

Kroth, R., & Otteni, H. (1983). Parent education programs that work: A model. *Focus on Exceptional Children, 15*(8), 1–16.

Kurtz, L.F. (1990). The self help movement: Review of the past decade of research. *Social Work with Groups, 13*(3), 101–115.

Ladd, G.W. (1983). Social networks of popular, average, and rejected children in school settings. *Merrill-Palmer Quarterly, 29*, 283–307.

Lamorey, S., & Bricker, D.D. (1993). Integrated programs: Effects on young children and their parents. In C.A. Peck, S.L. Odom, & D.D. Bricker (Eds.), *Integrating young children with disabilities into community programs: Ecological perspectives on research and implementation* (pp. 249–270). Baltimore: Paul H. Brookes Publishing Co.

Lancioni, G.E. (1982). Normal children as tutors to teach social responses to withdrawn mentally retarded schoolmates: Training, maintenance, and generalization. *Journal of Applied Behavior Analysis, 15*, 17–40.

Larrivee, B., & Cook, L. (1979). Mainstreaming: A study of the variables affecting teacher attitude. *Journal of Special Education, 13*(3), 315–324.

Laski, K.E., Charlop, M.H., & Schreibman, L. (1988). Training parents to use the natural language paradigm to increase their autistic children's speech. *Journal of Applied Behavior Analysis, 21*, 391–400.

Lave, J., & Wenger, E. (1991). *Situated learning: Legitimate peripheral participation.* Cambridge, England: Cambridge University Press.

Layton, T.L. (1988). Language training with autistic children using four different modes of presentation. *Journal of Communication Disorders, 21*, 333–350.

Learning Disabilities Association of America. (1993). Position paper on full inclusion for all students with learning disabilities in the regular education classroom. *Learning Disabilities Association Newsbrief, 28*(2), 3.

Leinhardt, G. (1980). Transition rooms: Promoting maturation or reducing education? *Journal of Educational Psychology, 72*(1), 55–61.

LeLaurin, K. (1992). Infant and toddler models of service delivery: Are they detrimental for some children and families? *Topics in Early Childhood Special Education, 12*(1), 82–104.

Lewinsohn, P.M., Larson, D.W., & Munoz, R.F. (1982). Measurement of expectancies and other cognitions in depressed individuals. *Cognitive Therapy and Research, 6*, 437–446.

Lewis, E. (1994). *Children's experiences in a full inclusion setting.* Unpublished doctoral dissertation, University of California, Santa Barbara.

Leyser, Y. (1988). Let's listen to the consumer: The voice of parents of exceptional children. *School Counselor, 35*(5), 363–369.

Lillie, D. (1975). The parent in early childhood education. *Journal of Research and Development in Education, 8*(2), 7–13.

Litrownik, A.J., Freitas, J.L., & Franzini, L.R. (1978). Self-regulation in mentally retarded children: Assessment and training of self-monitoring skills. *American Journal of Mental Deficiency, 82*, 499–506.

Litrownik, A.J., McInnis, E.T., Wetzel-Pritchard, A.M., & Filipelli, D.L. (1978). Restricted stimulus control and inferred attentional deficits in autistic and retarded children. *Journal of Abnormal Psychology, 87*, 554–562.

Lovaas, O.I. (1977). *The autistic child: Language development through behavior modification.* New York: Irvington.

Lovaas, O.I., Freitag, G., Gold, V.J., & Kassorla, I.C. (1965). Experimental studies in childhood schizophrenia: Analysis of self-destructive behavior. *Journal of Experimental Child Psychology, 2*, 67–84.

Lovaas, O.I., Koegel, R.L., & Schreibman, L. (1979). Stimulus overselectivity in autism: A review of research. *Psychological Bulletin, 86*(6), 1236–1254.

Lovaas, O.I., Koegel, R.L., Simmons, J.Q., & Long, J. (1973). Some generalization and follow-up measures on autistic children in behavior therapy. *Journal of Applied Behavior Analysis, 6*, 131–136.

Lovaas, O.I., Litrownik, A., & Mann, R. (1971). Response latencies to auditory stimuli in autistic children engaged in self-stimulatory behavior. *Behavior Research and Therapy, 9*, 39–49.

Lovaas, O.I., & Newsom, C.D. (1976). Behavior modification with psychotic children. In H. Leiten-berg (Ed.), *Handbook of behavior modification and behavior therapy* (pp. 303–360). Englewood Cliffs, NJ: Prentice Hall.

Lovaas, O.I., & Schreibman, L. (1971). Stimulus overselectivity of autistic children in a two stimu-lus situation. *Behavior Research and Therapy, 9,* 305–310.

Lovaas, O.I., Schreibman, L., Koegel, R.L., & Rehm, R. (1971). Selective responding by autistic children to multiple sensory input. *Journal of Abnormal Psychology, 77,* 211–222.

Lovaas, O.I., Varni, J., Koegel, R.L., & Lorsch, N.L. (1977). Some observations on the non-extin-guishability of children's speech. *Child Development, 48,* 1121–1127.

Lowry, M.A., & Whitman, T.L. (1989). Generalization of parenting skills: An early intervention pro-gram. *Child & Family Behavior Therapy, 11,* 45–65.

Lusthaus, C.S., Lusthaus, E.W., & Gibbs, H. (1981). Parents' role in the decision process. *Excep-tional Children, 48*(3), 256–257.

Lutfiyya, Z.M. (1988). Reflections on relationships between people with disabilities and typical people. In Z.M. Lutfiyya (Ed.), *Materials on relationships from the Center on Human Policy* (pp. 1–17). Syracuse, NY: Syracuse University.

Lynch, E.W., & Stein, R. (1982). Perspectives on parent participation in special education. *Excep-tional Education Quarterly, 3*(2), 56–63.

Mace, F.C., & Lalli, J.S. (1991). Linking descriptive and experimental analyses in the treatment of bizarre speech. *Journal of Applied Behavior Analysis, 24,* 553–562.

Mace, F.C., Lalli, J.S., & Pinter-Lalli, E. (1991). Functional analysis and treatment of aberrant behavior. *Research in Developmental Disabilities, 12,* 155–180.

Mace, F.C., & Roberts, M.L. (1993). Factors affecting selection of behavioral interventions. In J. Reichle & D. Wacker (Eds.), *Communication and language intervention series, Vol. 3, Commu-nicative alternatives to challenging behavior: Integrating functional assessment and intervention strategies* (pp. 113–133). Baltimore: Paul H. Brookes Publishing Co.

MacAndrew, C., & Edgerton, R.B. (1966). On the possibility of friendship. *American Journal of Mental Deficiency, 70,* 612–621.

MacMillan, D.L. (1971). The problem of motivation in the education of the mentally retarded. *Exceptional Children, 37,* 579–586.

MacMillan, D.L., & Hendrick, I.G. (1993). Evolutions and legacies. In J.I. Goodlad & T.C. Lovitt (Eds.), *Integrating general and special education* (pp. 23–48). New York: Macmillan.

Madden, N.A., & Slavin, R.E. (1983). Mainstreaming students with mild handicaps: Academic and social outcomes. *Review of Educational Research, 53*(4), 519–569.

Mahoney, G. (1988a). Communication patterns: Mothers and mentally retarded infants. *First Lan-guage, 8,* 157–172.

Mahoney, G. (1988b). Enhancing the developmental competence of handicapped infants. In K. Marfo (Ed.), *Parent-child intervention and developmental disabilities: Theory, research, and interven-tion* (pp. 203–219). New York: Praeger.

Mahoney, G., Powell, A., Finnegan, C., Fors, S., & Wood, S. (1986). The transactional intervention program. In D. Gentry, J. Olson, & M. Veltman (Eds.), *Individualizing for families* (pp. 1–16). Moscow: University of Idaho.

Mahoney, G., Robinson, C., & Powell, A. (1992). Focusing on parent-child interaction: The bridge to developmentally appropriate practices. *Topics in Early Childhood Special Education, 12*(1), 105–120.

Malmberg, P.A. (1984). *Development of field tested special education placement committee parent education materials.* Unpublished doctoral dissertation, Virginia Polytechnic Institute and State University, Blacksburg.

Marcus, L.M. (1977). Patterns of coping in families of psychotic children. *American Journal of Orthopsychiatry, 47,* 383–399.

Marcus, L.M., & Schopler, E. (1989). Parents as co-therapist with autistic children. In C.E. Schaefer & J.M. Briesmeister (Eds.), *Handbook of parent training: Parents as co-therapists for children's behavior problems.* New York: John Wiley & Sons.

Masten, A.S., Morrison, P., & Pellegrini, D.S. (1985). A revised class play method of peer assessment. *Developmental Psychology, 21*, 523–533.

Matson, J.L., & Marchetti, A. (1988). *Developmental disabilities: A life-span perspective.* New York: Grune & Stratton.

McAfee, J.K., & Vergason, G.A. (1979). Parent involvement in the process of special education: Establishing the new partnership. *Focus on Exceptional Children, 11*, 1–15.

McBride, B.A. (1989). Stress and fathers' parental competence: Implications for family life and parent educators. *Family Relations, 38*, 385–389.

McClannahan, L.E., Krantz, P.J., & McGee, G.G. (1982). Parents as therapists for autistic children: A model for effective parent training. *Analysis and Intervention in Developmental Disabilities, 2*, 223–252.

McConnell, S.R., Sisson, L.A., Cort, C.A., & Strain, P.S. (1991). Effects of social skills training and contingency management on reciprocal interaction of preschool children with behavioral handicaps. *Journal of Special Education, 24*, 473–495.

McCubbin, H.I., & McCubbin, M.A. (1987). Family stress theory and assessment: The T-Double ABCX Model of Family Adjustments and Adaptation. In H.I. McCubbin & A.I. Thompson (Eds.), *Family assessment inventories for research and practice* (pp. 3–34). Madison: University of Wisconsin–Madison.

McCubbin, H.I., & Patterson, J.M. (1983). Family transitions: Adaption to stress. In H.I. McCubbin & C. Figley (Eds.), *Social stress and the family: Advances and development in family stress theory and research* (pp. 1–6). New York: Haworth Press.

McEvoy, M.A., Nordquist, V.M., Twardosz, S., Heckman, K.A., Wehby, J.H., & Denny, R.K. (1988). Promoting autistic children's peer interaction in an integrated early childhood setting using affection activities. *Journal of Applied Behavior Analysis, 21*, 193–200.

McFall, R.M. (1970). The effects of self-monitoring on normal smoking behavior. *Journal of Consulting and Clinical Psychology, 35*, 135–142.

McFall, R.M., & Hammen, C.L. (1971). Motivation structure and self-monitoring: The role of nonspecific factors in smoking reduction. *Journal of Consulting and Clinical Psychology, 37*, 80–86.

McGee, G.B., Krantz, P.J., & McClannahan, L.E. (1984). Conversational skills for autistic adolescents: Teaching assertiveness in naturalistic game settings. *Journal of Autism and Developmental Disorders, 14*, 319–330.

McHale, S.M. (1983). Social interactions of autistic and nonhandicapped children during free play. *American Journal of Orthopsychiatry, 53*, 81–91.

McHale, S.M., Olley, J., & Marcus, L. (1981, March). *Variations across settings in autistic children's play.* Paper presented at the Biannual Meetings of the Society for Research in Child Development, Boston.

McHale, S.M., Olley, J., Marcus, L., & Simeonsson, R. (1981). Nonhandicapped peers as tutors for autistic children. *Exceptional Children, 48*, 263–265.

McHale, S.M., & Simeonsson, R.J. (1980). Effects of interaction on nonhandicapped children's attitudes toward autistic children. *American Journal of Mental Deficiency, 85*, 18–24.

McHale, S.M., Simeonsson, R.J., Marcus, L.M., & Olley, J.G. (1980). The social and symbolic quality of autistic children's communication. *Journal of Autism and Developmental Disorders, 10*, 299–310.

McKinney, J.D., & Hocutt, A.M. (1982). Public school involvement of parents of learning-disabled children and average achievers. *Exceptional Education Quarterly, 3*(2), 64–73.

McLean, M., & Hanline, M.F. (1990). Providing early intervention services in integrated environments: Challenges and opportunities for the future. *Topics in Early Childhood Special Education, 10*(2), 62–77.

McManis, C., Stollenwerk, D., & Zheng-Sheng, Z. (Eds.). (1987). *Language files: Materials for an introduction to language.* Reynoldsburg, OH: Advocate Publishing Group.

McNally, R.J., Kompik, J.J., & Sherman, G. (1984). Increasing the productivity of mentally retarded workers through self-management. *Analysis and Intervention in Development Disabilities, 4*, 129–135.

McNamara, B.E. (1986). Parents as partners in the IEP process. *Academic Therapy, 21*(3), 309–319.

Meisel, C.J. (1981). Stimulus overselectivity by mentally retarded adolescents: Effects of pretraining on cue identification. *American Journal of Mental Deficiency, 86,* 317–322.

Meisels, J., & Shonkoff, J.P. (1990). *Handbook of early intervention.* New York: Cambridge University Press.

Mesibov, G.B., & Dawson, G.D. (1986). Pervasive developmental disorders and schizophrenia. In J.M. Reisman (Ed.), *Behavior disorders in infants, children, and adolescents* (pp. 117–152). New York: Random House.

Meyers, C.E., MacMillan, D.L., & Yoshida, R.K. (1975). *Correlates of success in transition of MR to regular class. Final report* Grant no. OEG-0-73-5263. Prepared for the U.S. Dept. of Health, Education and Welfare.

Michael, J. (1982). Distinguishing between discriminative and motivational functions of stimuli. *Journal of the Experimental Analysis of Behavior, 37,* 142–155.

Milgram, N.A., & Atzil, M. (1988). Parenting stress in raising autistic children. *Journal of Autism and Developmental Disorders, 18,* 415–424.

Miller, B., & Solbie, D. (1980). Normal stresses during the transition to parenthood. *Family Relations, 29,* 459–465.

Miller, C.T., Clarke, R.T., Malcarne, V.L., Lobato, D., Fitzgerald, M.D., & Brand, P.A. (1991). Expectations and social interactions of children with and without mental retardation. *Journal of Special Education, 24,* 454–472.

Miller, K.L. (1980). *Principles of everyday behavior analysis.* Monterey, CA: Brooks/Cole.

Miller, P.S. (1991). Linking theory to intervention practices with preschoolers and their families: Building program integrity. *Journal of Early Intervention, 15*(4), 315–325.

Miller, S.J., & Sloane, H.N. (1976). The generalization of effects of parent training across stimulus settings. *Journal of Applied Behavior Analysis, 9*(3), 355–370.

Minuchin, S. (1974). *Families and family therapy.* Cambridge, MA: Harvard University Press.

Mirenda, P.L., & Donnellan, A.M. (1986). Effects of adult interaction style on conversational behavior in students with severe communication problems. *Language, Speech, and Hearing Services in Schools, 17,*126–141.

Mlynek, S., Hannah, M.E., & Hamlin, M.A. (1982). Mainstreaming: Parent perspectives. *Psychology in the Schools, 19,* 354–359.

Moes, D., Koegel, R.L., Schreibman, L., & Loos, L.M. (1992). Stress profiles for mothers and fathers of children with autism. *Psychological Reports, 71,* 1272–1274.

Monroe, J.D., & Howe, C.E. (1971). The effects of integration and social class on the acceptance of retarded adolescents. *Education and Training in Mental Retardation, 6,* 20–24.

Moore, J., & Fine, M.J. (1978). Regular and special class teachers' perceptions of normal and exceptional children and their attitudes toward mainstreaming. *Psychology in the Schools, 15*(2), 253–259.

Morgan, D.P., & Rhode, G. (1983). Teachers' attitudes toward IEPs: A two-year follow-up. *Exceptional Children, 50*(1), 64–67.

Morgan, S.B. (1988). The autistic child and family functioning: A developmental-family systems perspective. *Journal of Autism and Developmental Disorders, 18,* 263–280.

Mori, A.A. (1983). *Families of children with special needs: Early intervention techniques for the practitioner.* Rockville, MD: Aspen.

Muma, J.R. (1977). Language intervention strategies. *Language, Speech, and Hearing Services in School, 8,* 107–125.

Mundy, P., & Sigman, M. (1989). Specifying the nature of the social impairment in autism. In G. Dawson (Ed.), *Autism: New perspectives on diagnosis, nature, and treatment* (pp. 3–21). New York: Guilford Press.

Mundy, P., Sigman, M., & Kasari, C. (1990). A longitudinal study of joint attention and language development in autistic children. *Journal of Autism and Development Disorders, 20,* 115–128.

Murphy, L., & Della Corte, S. (1988). Parent and teacher relationships. *Special Parent/Special Child, 4*(1), 1–8. (ERIC Document Reproduction Service No. ED 294 353)

National Education Association of the United States. (1978). *Education for all handicapped children: Consensus, conflict, and challenge.* Washington, DC: National Education Association.

National Joint Committee on Learning Disabilities. (1993). *A reaction to full inclusion: A reaffirmation of the right of students with learning disabilities to a continuum of services.* Position paper.

Nelson, J., & Aboud, F.E. (1985). The resolution of social conflict between friends. *Child Development, 56,* 1009–1017.

Nelson, R.O., & Hayes, S.C. (1981). Theoretical explanations for reactivity in self-monitoring. *Behavior Modification, 5,* 3–14.

Nelson, R.O., Lipinski, D.P., & Boykin, R.A. (1978). The effects of self-recorders training and the obtrusiveness of the self-recording device on the accuracy and reactivity of self-monitoring. *Behavior Therapy, 9,* 200–208.

Nevin, A., Semmel, M.I., & McCann, S. (1983). What administrators can do to facilitate the regular classroom teacher's role in implementing individual educational plans: An empirical analysis. *Planning and Changing, 14*(3), 150–169.

Nientimp, E.G., & Cole, C.L. (1992). Teaching socially valid social interaction responses to students with severe disabilities in an integrated school setting. *Journal of School Psychology, 30,* 343–354.

Nirje, B. (1980). The normalization principle. In R.J. Flynn & K.E. Nitsch (Eds.), *Normalization, social integration and community services* (p. 31–49). Baltimore: University Park Press.

Nixon, H.L., II. (1988). Reassessing support groups for parents of visually impaired children. *Journal of Visual Impairment and Blindness, 82*(7), 271–278.

Notari, A., & Cole, K. (1993). Language intervention: Research and implication for service delivery. In C.A. Peck, S.L. Odom, & D.D. Bricker (Eds.), *Integrating young children with disabilities into community programs: Ecological perspectives on research and implementation* (pp. 17–38). Baltimore: Paul H. Brookes Publishing Co.

O'Brien, T.P., Riner, L.S., & Budd, K. (1983). The effects of a child's self-evaluation program on compliance with parental instructions in the home. *Journal of Applied Behavior Analysis, 16,* 69–79.

O'Dell, M.C. (1974). *The effect of an attempt contingency and an approximation contingency or speech acquisition and motivation by severely communicationally delayed children.* Unpublished master's thesis, University of California, Santa Barbara.

O'Dell, S.L. (1984). Progress in parent training. In M. Hersen, R.M. Eisler, & P.M. Miller (Eds.), *Progress in behavior modification* (Vol. 19, pp. 57–108). New York: Academic Press.

Oden, S., & Asher, S.R. (1977). Coaching children in social skills for friendship making. *Child Development, 48,* 495–506.

Odom, S.L., Hoyson, M., Jamieson, B., & Strain, P.S. (1985). Increasing handicapped preschoolers' peer social interactions: Cross-setting and component analysis. *Journal of Applied Behavior Analysis, 18,* 3–16.

Odom, S.L., & McEvoy, M.A. (1988). Integration of young children with handicaps and normally developing children. In S.L. Odom & M.B. Karnes (Eds.), *Early intervention for infants and children with handicaps: An empirical base* (pp. 241–268). Baltimore: Paul H. Brookes Publishing Co.

Odom, S.L., & Strain, P.S. (1986). A comparison of peer-initiation and teacher-antecedent interventions for promoting reciprocal social interaction of autistic preschoolers. *Journal of Applied Behavior Analysis, 19,* 59–71.

Odom, S.L., Yoder, P., & Hill, G. (1988). Developmental intervention for infants with handicaps: Purposes and programs. *Journal of Special Education, 22*(1), 11–24.

Oke, N.J., & Schreibman, L. (1990). Training social initiations to a high-functioning autistic child: Assessment of collateral behavior change and generalization in a case study. *Journal of Autism and Developmental Disorders, 20,* 479–497.

Oldfield, R.C. (1966). Things, words and the brain. *Quarterly Journal of Experimental Psychology, 18,* 340–355.

Ollendick, T.H., Green, R.W., Francis, G., & Braum, C.G. (1991). Sociometric status: Its stability and validity among neglected, rejected, and popular children. *Journal of Child Psychology and Psychiatry, 32,* 525–534.

Ollendick, T.H., Weist, M.D., Borden, M.C., & Green, R.W. (1992). Sociometric status and academic, behavioral, and psychological adjustment. A five-year longitudinal study. *Journal of Consulting and Clinical Psychology, 60,* 80–87.

O'Neill, R.E., & Reichle, J. (1993). Addressing socially motivated challenging behaviors by establishing communicative alternatives: Basics of a general-case approach. In J. Reichle & D. Wacker (Eds.), *Communication and language intervention series. Vol. 3, Communicative alternatives to challenging behavior: Integrating functional assessment and intervention strategies* (pp. 205–235). Baltimore: Paul H. Brookes Publishing Co.

O'Neill, R.F., Horner, R.H., Albin, R.W., Storey, K., & Sprague, J.K. (1990). *Functional analysis of problem behavior: A practical assessment guide.* Sycamore, IL: Sycamore Publishing Co.

Orelove, F.P., & Sobsey, D. (1991). *Educating children with multiple disabilities: A transdisciplinary approach* (2nd ed.). Baltimore: Paul H. Brookes Publishing Co.

Paget, K.D. (1992). Proactive family-school partnerships in early intervention. In M.J. Fine & C. Carlson (Eds.), *The handbook of family-school intervention* (pp. 119–133). Needham Heights, MA: Allyn & Bacon.

Parker, J.G., & Asher, S.R. (1987). Peer relations and later personal adjustment: Are low-accepted children at risk? *Psychological Bulletin, 102,* 357–389.

Parker, J.G., & Gottman, J.M. (1989). Social and emotional development in a relational context. In T.J. Berndt & G.W. Ladd (Eds.), *Peer relationships in child development* (pp. 96–131). New York: John Wiley & Sons.

Parrish, J.M., Cataldo, M.F., Kolko, D.J., Neef, N.A., & Egel, A.L. (1986). Experimental analysis of response covariation among compliant and inappropriate behaviors. *Journal of Applied Behavior Analysis, 19,* 241–254.

Patterson, J.M. (1988). Chronic illness in children and the impact on families. In C.E. Chilman, Nunnally, & F. Cox (Eds.), *Chronic illness and disability* (pp. 69–107). Newbury Park, CA: Sage Publications.

Patterson, J.M. (1989). A family stress model: The Family Adjustment and Adaptation Response. In C. Ramsey (Ed.), *The science of family medicine* (pp. 95–117). New York: Guilford Press.

Patterson, J.M. (1993). The role of family meanings in adaptation to chronic illness and disability. In A.P. Turnbull, J.M. Patterson, S.K. Behr, D.L. Murphy, J.G. Marquis, & M.J. Blue-Banning (Eds.), *Cognitive coping, families, and disability* (pp. 221–238). Baltimore: Paul H. Brookes Publishing Co.

Patterson, J.M., & McCubbin, H.I. (1983). The impact of family life events and changes on the health of a chronically ill child. *Family Relations: Journal of Applied Family and Child Studies, 32,* 255–264.

Paul, R., & Shiffer, M.E. (1991). Communicative initiations in normal and late-talking toddlers. *Applied Psycholinguists, 12*(4), 419–431.

Peck, C.A. (1985). Increasing opportunities for social control by children with autism and severe handicaps: Effects on student behavior and perceived classroom climate. *Journal of The Association for Persons with Severe Handicaps, 10,* 183–193.

Peck, C.A. (1993). Ecological perspectives on the implementation of integrated early childhood programs. In C.A. Peck, S.L. Odom, & D.D. Bricker (Eds.), *Integrating young children with disabilities into community programs: Ecological perspectives on research and implementation* (pp. 3–16). Baltimore: Paul H. Brookes Publishing Co.

Peck, C.A., Carlson, P., & Helmstetter, E. (1992). Parent and teacher perceptions of outcomes for typically developing children enrolled in integrated early childhood programs: A statewide survey. *Journal of Early Intervention, 16*(1), 53–63.

Peck, C.A., Donaldson, J., & Pezzoli, M. (1990). Some benefits nonhandicapped adolescents perceive for themselves from their soical relationships with peers who have severe handicaps. *Journal of The Association for Persons with Severe Handicaps, 15,* 241–249.

Peck, C.A., Hayden, L., Wandschneider, M., Peterson, K., & Richarz, S. (1989). Development of integrated preschools: A qualitative inquiry into sources of resistance among parents, administrators, and teachers. *Journal of Early Intervention, 13*(4), 353–364.

Peck, C.A., Killen, C.C., & Baumgart, D. (1989). Increasing implementation of special education instruction in mainstream preschools: Direct and generalized effects of nondirective consultation. *Journal of Applied Behavior Analysis, 22*(2), 197–210.

Peck, C.A., Odom, S.L., & Bricker, D.D. (Eds.). (1993). *Integrating young children with disabilities into community programs: Ecological perspectives on research and implementation.* Baltimore: Paul H. Brookes Publishing Co.

Peck, C.A., & Semmel, M.I. (1982). Identifying the least restrictive environment (LRE) for children with severe handicaps: Toward an empirical analysis. *Journal of The Association for Persons with Severe Handicaps, 7,* 56–63.

Perry, D.G., & Bussey, K. (1984). *Social development* (p. 295). Englewood Cliffs, NJ: Prentice-Hall.

Pfeiffer, S.I. (1980). The school-based interprofessional team: Recurring problems and some possible solutions. *Journal of School Psychology, 18*(4), 388–394.

Plienis, A.J., Robbins, F.R., & Dunlap, G. (1988). Parent adjustment and family stress as factors in behavioral parent training for young autistic children. *Journal of the Multihandicapped Person, 1,* 31–52.

Powell, T.H., & Ogle, P.A. (1985). *Brothers and sisters: A special part of exceptional families.* Baltimore: Paul H. Brookes Publishing Co.

Power, T.J., & Bartholomew, K.L. (1987). Family-school relationship patterns: An ecological perspective. *School Psychology Review, 16*(4), 498–512.

Powers, M.D. (1991). Intervening with families of young children with severe handicaps: Contributions of a family systems approach. *School Psychology Quarterly, 6*(2), 131–146.

Powers, M.D., & Handleman, J.S. (1984). *Behavioral assessment of severe developmental disabilities.* Rockville, MD: Aspen.

Pray, B.R., Jr., Hall, C.W., & Markley, R.P. (1992). Social skills training: An analysis of social behaviors selected for individualized education programs. *Remedial and Special Education, 13,* 43–49.

Price, J.M., & Dodge, K.A. (1989). Peers' contributions to children's social maladjustment. In T.J. Berndt & G.W. Ladd (Eds.), *Peer relationships in child development* (pp. 340–370). New York: John Wiley & Sons.

Price, M., & Goodman, L. (1980). Individualized education programs: A cost study. *Exceptional Children, 46*(6), 446–454.

Price-Bonham, S., & Addison, S. (1978). Families and mentally retarded children: Emphasis on the father. *Family Coordinator, 27,* 221–230.

Prizant, B.M. (1983). Echolalia in autism: Assessment and intervention. *Seminars in Speech and Language, 4,* 63–77.

Prizant, B.M. (1983). Language acquisition and communicative behavior in autism: Toward an understanding of the "whole" of it. *Journal of Speech and Hearing Disorders, 48,* 296–307.

Prizant, B.M., & Wetherby, A.M. (1989). Enhancing language and communication in autism: From theory to practice. In G. Dawson (Ed.), *Autism: Nature, diagnosis, and treatment* (pp. 282–309). New York: Guilford Press.

Pronvost, W., Wakstein, M., & Wakstein, D. (1966). A longitudinal study of the speech behavior and language comprehension of fourteen children diagnosed atypical or autistic. *Exceptional Child, 33,* 19–26.

Prutting, C.A., & Kirchner, D. (1987). A clinical appraisal of the pragmatic aspects of language. *Journal of Speech and Hearing Disorders, 52,* 105–119.

Pugach, M.C. (1982). Regular classroom teacher involvement in the development and utilization of IEPs. *Exceptional Children, 48*(4), 371–374.

Pugach, M.C., & Johnson, L.J. (1989a). The challenge of implementing collaboration between general and special education. *Exceptional Children, 56*(3), 232–235.

Pugach, M.C., & Johnson, L.J. (1989b). Prereferral interventions: Progress, problems, and challenges. *Exceptional Children, 56*(3), 217–226.

Pyecha, J.N., Cox, J.L., Dewitt, D., Drummond, D., Jaffe, J., Kalt, M., Lane, C., & Pelosi, J. (1980). *A national survey of individualized education programs (IEPs) for handicapped children* (Vol. 1). Durham, NC: Research Triangle Institute. (ERIC Document Reproduction Service No. ED 199 9700)

Quay, L.C., & Jarrett, O.S. (1984). Predictors of social acceptance in preschool children. *Developmental Psychology, 20,* 793–796.

Quilitch, H.R., & Risley, T.R. (1973). The effects of play materials on social play. *Journal of Applied Behavior Analysis, 6,* 573–578.

Rachlin, H. (1974). Self-control. *Behaviorism, 2,* 94–107.

Rainforth, B., York, J., & Macdonald, C. (1992). *Collaborative teams for students with severe disabilities: Integrating therapy and educational services.* Baltimore: Paul H. Brookes Publishing Co.

Rapport, M.J.K., & Thomas, S.B. (1993). Extended school year: Legal issues and implications. *Journal of The Association for Persons with Severe Handicaps, 18,* 16–27.

Ray, B.M. (1985). Measuring the social position of the mainstreamed handicapped child. *Exceptional Children, 52*(1), 57–62.

Reese, R.M., Sherman, J.A., & Sheldon, J. (1984). Reducing agitated-disruptive behavior of mentally retarded residents of community group homes: The role of self-recording and peer prompted self-recording. *Analysis and Intervention in Developmental Disabilities, 4,* 91–107.

Reich, R. (1978). Gestural facilitation of expressive language in moderately/severely retarded preschoolers. *Mental Retardation, 16,* 113–117.

Reynolds, B.J., Martin-Reynolds, J., & Mark, F.D. (1982). Elementary teachers' attitudes toward mainstreaming educable mentally retarded students. *Education and Training of the Mentally Retarded, 17*(3), 171–176.

Reynolds, B.S., Newsom, C.D., & Lovaas, O.I. (1974). Auditory overselectivity in autistic children. *Journal of Abnormal Child Psychology, 2,* 253–263.

Ricks, D.M., & Wing, L. (1975). Language, communication, and the use of symbols in normal and autistic children. *Journal of Autism and Childhood Schizophrenia, 5,* 191–222.

Rimland, B. (1964). *Infantile autism.* New York: Appleton-Century-Crofts.

Rimland, B. (1994). The modern history of autism: A personal perspective. In J. Matson (Ed.), *Autism in children and adults: Etiology, assessment and intervention* (pp. 1–11). Pacific Grove, CA: Brooks/Cole.

Rincover, A., & Koegel, R.L. (1975). Setting generality and stimulus control in autistic children. *Journal of Applied Behavior Analysis, 8,* 235–246.

Rincover, A., & Koegel, R.L. (1977). Classroom treatment of autistic children: II. Individualized instruction in a group. *Journal of Abnormal Child Psychology, 5,* 113–126.

Ringlaben, R.P., & Price, J.R. (1981). Regular classroom teachers' perceptions of mainstreaming effects. *Exceptional Children, 47*(4), 302–304.

Ritvo, E.R., & Freeman, B.J. (1978). National Society for Autistic Children definition of the syndrome of autism. *Journal of Autism and Childhood Schizophrenia, 8,* 162–167.

Ritvo, E.R., Freeman, B.J., Geller, E., & Yuwiler, A. (1983). Effects of fenfluramine on 14 outpatients with the syndrome of autism. *Journal of the American Academy of Child Psychiatry, 22,* 549–558.

Ritvo, E.R., Ritvo, E.C., & Brothers, A.M. (1982). Genetic and immunohematologic factors in autism. *Journal of Autism and Developmental Disorders, 12,* 109–114.

Ritvo, E.R., Spence, M.A., Freeman, B.J., Mason-Brothers, A., Mo, A., & Marazita, M.L. (1985). Evidence for autosomal recessive inheritance in 46 families with multiple incidences of autism. *American Journal of Psychiatry, 142,* 187–192.

Robbins, F.R., Dunlap, G., & Plienis, A.J. (1991). Family characteristics, family training, and the progress of young children with autism. *Journal of Early Intervention, 15,* 173–184.

Robins, L. (1972). Follow-up studies of behavior disorders in children. In H. Quay & J. Werry (Eds.), *Psychopathological disorders of childhood* (pp. 414–446). New York: John Wiley & Sons.

Robins, L.N. (1966). *Deviant children grow up.* Baltimore: Williams & Wilkins.

Rodda, M. (1977). Language and language-disordered children. *Bulletin of the British Psychological Society, 30,* 139–142.

Rodrigue, J.R., Morgan, S.B., & Geffken, G. (1990). Families of autistic children: Psycho-social functioning of mothers. *Journal of Clinical Child Psychology, 19,* 371–379.

Rodrigue, J.R., Morgan, S.B., & Geffken, G. (1992). Psychosocial adaptation of fathers of children with autism, Down syndrome, and normal development. *Journal of Autism and Developmental Disorders, 22,* 249–263.

Roff, M. (1961). Childhood social interactions and young adult bad conduct. *Journal of Abnormal Social Psychology, 63,* 333–337.

Roff, M. (1970). Some life history factors in relation to various types of adult maladjustment. In M. Roff & D. Ricks (Eds.), *Life history research in psychopathology* (Vol. I) (pp. 265–287). Minneapolis: University of Minnesota Press.

Roff, M., Knight, R., & Wertheim, E. (1976). Disturbed preschizophrenics. *Journal of Nervous Mental Disorders, 162,* 274–281.

Roff, M., & Sells, S. (1968). Juvenile delinquency in relation to peer acceptance-rejection and socioeconomic status. *Psychology in the Schools, 5,* 3–18.

Roff, M., Sells, S.B., & Golden, M.M. (1972). *Social maladjustment and personality development in children.* Minneapolis: University of Minnesota Press.

Rogers, J. (1993). The inclusion revolution. *Research Bulletin, Phi Delta Kappa, 11,* 1–6.

Rooney, K.J., Hallahan, D.P., & Lloyd, J.W. (1984). Self-recording of attention by learning disabled students in the normal classroom. *Journal of Learning Disabilities, 17,* 360–364.

Roos, P. (1978). Parents of mentally retarded children: Misunderstood and mistreated. In A.P. Turnbull & H.R. Turnbull, III (Eds.), *Parents speak out* (pp. 12–27). Columbus, OH: Charles E. Merrill.

Root, J. (1977). The importance of peer groups. *Educational Research, 20,* 22–25.

Rose, E. (1990). *Parent involvement survey: Report for the seven state region.* Washington, DC: Office of Educational Research and Improvement. (ERIC Document Reproduction Service No. ED 330 179)

Rosenberg, S.A., Robinson, C.C., & Beckman, P.J. (1986). Measures of parent-infant interaction: An overview. *Topics in Early Childhood Education, 6*(2), 32–43.

Rosenberger-Debiesse, J., & Coleman, M. (1986). Brief report: Preliminary evidence for multiple etiologies in autism. *Journal of Autism and Developmental Disorders, 16,* 385–392.

Rosenthal, R., & Jacobson, L. (1968). *Pygmalion in the classroom.* New York: Holt, Rinehart & Winston.

Russo, D.C., & Koegel, R.L. (1977). A method of integrating an autistic child into a normal public school classroom. *Journal of Applied Behavior Analysis, 10,* 579–590.

Rutter, M. (1970). Autistic children: Infancy to adulthood. *Seminars in Psychiatry, 2,* 435–450.

Rutter, M. (1978a). Diagnosis and definition. In M. Rutter & E. Schopler (Eds.), *Autism: A reappraisal of concepts and treatment* (pp. 1–25). New York: Plenum.

Rutter, M. (1978b). Diagnosis and definition of childhood autism. *Journal of Autism and Childhood Schizophrenia, 8,* 139–161.

Rutter, M. (1983). Cognitive deficits in the pathogenesis of autism. *Journal of Child Psychology and Psychiatry, 24,* 513–531.

Safer, N.D., Morrissey, P.A., Kaufman, M.J., & Lewis, L. (1978). Implementation of IEPs: New teacher roles and requisite support systems. *Focus on Exceptional Children, 10*(1), 1–20.

Sagotsky, G., Patterson, C.J., & Lepper, M.R. (1978). Training children's self-control: A field experiment in self-monitoring and goal setting in the classroom. *Journal of Experimental Child Psychology, 25,* 242–253.

Sahley, T.L., & Panksepp, J. (1987). Brain opioids and autism: An updated analysis of possible linkages. *Journal of Autism and Developmental Disorders, 17,* 201–216.

Sailor, W. (1991). Special education in restructured schools. *Remedial and Special Education, 12*(6), 8–22.

Sailor, W., Anderson, J.L., Halvorsen, A.T., Doering, K., Filler, J., & Goetz, L. (1989). *The comprehensive local school: Regular education for all students with disabilities.* Baltimore: Paul H. Brookes Publishing Co.

Sailor, W., Gee, K., Goetz, L., & Graham, N. (1988). Progress in education for students with the most severe disabilities: Is there any? *Journal of The Association for Persons with Severe Handicaps, 13*(2), 87–99.

Sailor, W., Goetz, L., Anderson, J., Hunt, P., & Gee, K. (1988). Research on community intensive instruction as a model for building functional, generalized skills. In R.H. Horner, G. Dunlap, & R.L. Koegel (Eds.), *Generalization and maintenance: Life-style changes in applied settings* (pp. 67–98). Baltimore: Paul H. Brookes Publishing Co.

Sainato, D.M., Goldstein, H., & Strain, P.S. (1992). Effects of self-evaluation on preschool children's use of social interaction strategies with their classmates with autism. *Journal of Applied Behavior Analysis, 25,* 127–141.

Salisbury, C. (1992). Parents as team members: Inclusive teams, collaborative outcomes. In B. Rainforth, J. York, & C. Macdonald, *Collaborative teams for students with severe disabilities: Integrating therapy and educational services* (pp. 43–66). Baltimore: Paul H. Brookes Publishing Co.

Salisbury, C., & Evans, I.M. (1988). Comparison of parental involvement in regular and special education. *Journal of The Association for Persons with Severe Handicaps, 13*(4), 268–272.

Salvia, J., & Munson, S. (1986). Attitudes of regular education teachers toward mainstreaming mildly handicapped students. In C.J. Meisel (Ed.), *Mainstreaming handicapped children: Outcomes, controversies, and new directions* (pp. 111–128). Hillsdale, NJ: Lawrence Erlbaum Associates.

Sarason, S.B., & Doris, J. (1979). *Educational handicap, public policy, and social history: A broadened perspective on mental retardation.* New York: Free Press.

Sasso, G.M., & Reimers, T.M. (1988). Assessing the functional properties of behavior: Implications and applications for the classroom. *Focus on Autistic Behavior, 3,* 1–15.

Sasso, G.M., Reimers, T.M., Cooper, L.J., Wacker, D., Berg, W., Steege, M., Kelly, L., & Allaire, A. (1992). Use of descriptive and experimental analysis to identify the functional properties of aberrant behavior in school settings. *Journal of Applied Behavior Analysis, 25,* 809–821.

Sasso, G.M., Simpson, R.L., & Novak, C.G. (1985). Procedures for facilitating integration of autistic children in public school settings. *Analysis and Intervention in Developmental Disabilities, 5*(3), 233–246.

Saunders, R., & Sailor, W. (1979). A comparison of three strategies of reinforcement on two-choice language problems with severely retarded children. *AAESPH Review, 4,* 323–333.

Sawyer, H.W., & Sawyer, S.H. (1981). A teacher-parent communication training approach. *Exceptional Children, 47*(4), 305–306.

Say, E., McCollum, J., & Brightman, M.F. (1980, April). *A study of the IEP: Parent and school perspectives.* Paper presented at the annual meeting of the American Educational Research Association, Boston. (ERIC Document Reproduction Service No. ED 192 440)

Scanlon, C.A., Arick, J., & Phelps, N. (1981). Participation in the development of the IEP: Parents' perspective. *Exceptional Children, 47*(5), 373–374.

Schenck, S.J. (1980). The diagnostic/instructional link in individualized educational programs. *Journal of Special Education, 14*(3), 337–345.

Schenck, S.J., & Levy, W.K. (1979). *IEPs: The state of the art—1978.* Paper presented at the annual convention of the American Educational Research Association, San Francisco. (ERIC Document Reproduction Service No. ED 175 201)

Schnorr, R.F. (1990). "Peter? He comes and goes . . .": First graders' perspectives on a part-time mainstream student. *Journal of The Association for Persons with Severe Handicaps, 15*(4), 231–240.

Schopler, E., & Mesibov, G.B. (Eds.). (1984). *The effects of autism on the family.* New York: Plenum.

Schopler, E., & Mesibov, G.B. (1986). Introduction to social behavior in autism. In E. Schopler & G.B. Mesibov (Eds.), *Social behavior in autism* (pp. 1–11). New York: Plenum.

Schopler, E., Mesibov, G.B., Shigley, R.H., & Bashford, A. (1984). Helping autistic children through their parents: The TEACCH model. In E. Schopler & G.B. Mesibov (Eds.), *The effects of autism on the family* (pp. 65–81). New York: Plenum.

Schopler, E., & Reichler, R.J. (1971). Parents as co-therapists in the treatment of psychotic children. *Journal of Autism and Childhood Schizophrenia, 1,* 87–102.

Schover, L.R., & Newsom, C.D. (1976). Overselectivity, developmental level, and overtraining in autistic and normal children. *Journal of Abnormal Child Psychology, 4*, 289–298.

Schreibman, L. (1975). Effects of within-stimulus and extra-stimulus prompting on discrimination learning in autistic children. *Journal of Applied Behavior Analysis, 8*, 91–112.

Schreibman, L. (1988). *Autism*. Newbury Park, CA: Sage Publications.

Schreibman, L. (1994). Autism. In L.W. Craighead, E.W. Craighead, A.E. Kazdin, & M.J. Mahoney (Eds.), *Cognitive and behavioral interventions: An empirical approach to mental health problems* (pp. 335–358). Boston: Allyn & Bacon.

Schreibman, L., & Carr, E.G. (1978). Elimination of echolalic responding to questions through the training of a generalized verbal response. *Journal of Applied Behavior Analysis, 11*, 453–463.

Schreibman, L., & Charlop, M.H. (1987). Autism. In V.B. Van Hasselt & M. Hersen (Eds.), *Psychological evaluation of the developmentally and physically disabled* (pp. 155–177). New York: Plenum.

Schreibman, L., Charlop, M.H., & Koegel, R.L. (1982). Teaching autistic children to use extra-stimulus prompts. *Journal of Experimental Child Psychology, 33*, 475–491.

Schreibman, L., Kaneko, W.M., & Koegel, R.L. (1991). Positive affect of parents of autistic children: A comparison across two teaching techniques. *Behavior Therapy, 22*, 479–490.

Schreibman, L., & Koegel, R.L. (1982). Multiple-cue responding in autistic children. In J. Steffen & P. Karoly (Eds.), *Advances in child behavioral analysis and therapy: Volume II. Autism and severe psychopathology*. Lexington, MA: D.C. Heath.

Schreibman, L., Koegel, R.L., & Britten, K.R. (1982). *Parent intervention in the treatment of autistic children: A preliminary report*. Unpublished manuscript.

Schreibman, L., Koegel, R.L., & Craig, M.S. (1977). Reducing stimulus overselectivity in autistic children. *Journal of Abnormal Child Psychology, 5*, 425–435.

Schreibman, L., Koegel, R.L., & Koegel, L.K. (1989). Autism. In M. Hersen (Ed.), *Innovations in child behavior therapy* (pp. 395–428). New York: Springer-Verlag.

Schreibman, L., Koegel, R.L., Mills, D.L., & Burke, J.C. (1984). Training parent-child interactions. In E. Schopler & G.B. Mesibov (Eds.), *The effects of autism on the family* (pp. 187–205). New York: Plenum.

Schreibman, L., Kohlenberg, B.S., & Britten, K.B. (1986). Differential responding to content and intonation components of a complex auditory stimulus by nonverbal and echolalic autistic children. *Analysis and Intervention in Developmental Disabilities, 6*, 109–125.

Schreibman, L., & Lovaas, O.I. (1973). Overselective response to social stimuli by autistic children. *Journal of Abnormal Child Psychology, 1*, 152–168.

Schreibman, L., & Mills, J.I. (1983). Infantile autism. In T.J. Ollendick & M. Hersen (Eds.), *Handbook of child psychopathology*. New York: Plenum.

Seligman, M.E.P., Klein, D.C., & Miller, W.R. (1976). Depression. In H. Leitenberg (Ed.), *Handbook of behavior modification* (pp. 168–210). New York: Appleton-Century-Crofts.

Seligman, M.E.P., & Maier, S.F. (1967). Failure to escape traumatic shock. *Journal of Experimental Psychology, 74*, 1–9.

Semmel, M.I., Abernathy, T.V., Butera, G., & Lesar, S. (1991, September). Teacher perceptions of the regular education initiative. *Exceptional Children, 58*(1), 9–24.

Semmel, M.I., & Gerber, M.M. (1990). If at first you don't succeed, buy, buy again: A response to general educators' views on the REI. *Remedial and Special Education, 11*(4), 53–59.

Semmel, M.I., Lieber, J., & Peck, C.A. (1986). Effects of special education environments: Beyond mainstreaming. In C.J. Meisel (Ed.), *Mainstreaming handicapped children: Outcomes, controversies, and new directions* (pp. 165–192). Hillsdale, NJ: Lawrence Erlbaum Associates.

Semmel, M.I., & Peck, C.A. (1986). Effects of special education environments: Beyond mainstreaming. In C.J. Meisel (Ed.), *Mainstreaming handicapped children: Outcomes, controversies, and new directions* (pp. 165–192). Hillsdale, NJ: Lawrence Erlbaum Associates.

Shafer, J., Egel, A., & Nccf, N. (1984). Training mildly handicapped peers to facilitate changes in the social interaction skills of autistic children. *Journal of Applied Behavior Analysis, 17*, 461–476.

Shapiro, E.S., Browder, D.M., & D'Huyvetters, K.K. (1984). Increasing academic productivity of severely multi-handicapped children with self-management: Idiosyncratic effects. *Analysis and*

Intervention in Developmental Disabilities, 4, 171–188.

Shapiro, E.S., & Klein, R.D. (1980). Self-management of classroom behavior with retarded/disturbed children. *Behavior Modification, 4,* 83–97.

Shapiro, E.S., McGonigle, J.J., & Ollendick, T.H. (1980). An analysis of self-assessment and self-reinforcement in a self-managed token economy with mentally retarded children. *Applied Research in Mental Retardation, 1,* 227–240.

Shea, T.M., & Bauer, A.M. (1991). *Parents and teachers of children with exceptionalities: A handbook for collaboration.* Needham Heights, MA: Allyn & Bacon.

Shore, K. (1986). *The special education handbook: A comprehensive guide for parents and educators.* New York: Teachers College Press.

Shortridge, S.D. (1982). Facilitating attitude change towards the handicapped. *The American Journal of Occupational Therapy, 36,* 456–460.

Siegel, B., Anders, T.F., Ciaranello, R.D., Bienenstock, B., & Kraemer, H.C. (1986). Empirically derived subclassification of the autistic syndrome. *Journal of Autism and Developmental Disorders, 16,* 275–293.

Sigman, M., Mundy, P., Sherman, T., & Ungerer, J. (1986). Social interactions of autistic, mentally retarded and normal children and their caregivers. *Journal of Child Psychology and Psychiatry, 27,* 647–656.

Sigman, M., Ungerer, J., Mundy, P., & Sherman, T. (1987). Cognitive functioning in autistic children. In D. Cohen, A. Donnelan, & R. Paul (Eds.), *Handbook of autism and pervasive developmental disorders* (pp. 103–120). New York: John Wiley & Sons.

Silber, S. (1988). Family influences on early development. *Topics in Early Childhood Special Education, 8*(4), 1–23.

Simeonsson, R.J., & Bailey, D.B. (1990). Family dimensions in early intervention. In S.J. Meisels & D.B. Bailey (Eds.), *Handbooks of early childhood intervention* (pp. 428–444). Cambridge, England: Cambridge University Press.

Simon, N. (1975). Echolalic speech in childhood autism: Consideration of underlying loci of brain damage. *Archives of General Psychiatry, 32,* 1439–1446.

Simpson, R.L. (1980). Modifying the attitudes of regular class students toward the handicapped. *Focus on Exceptional Children, 13,* 1–11.

Simpson, R.L. (1990). *Conferencing parents of exceptional children* (2nd ed.). Austin, TX: PRO-ED.

Simpson, R.L., & Sasso, G.M. (1992). Full inclusion of students with autism in general education settings: Values versus science. *Focus on Autistic Behavior, 7*(13), 1–13.

Singer, G.H.S., & Irvin, L.K. (1989a). Family caregiving, stress, and support. In G.H.S. Singer & L.K. Irvin (Eds.), *Support for caregiving families: Enabling positive adaptation to disability* (pp. 1–25). Baltimore: Paul H. Brookes Publishing Co.

Singer, G.H.S., & Irvin, L.K. (Eds.). (1989b). *Support for caregiving families: Enabling positive adaptation to disability.* Baltimore: Paul H. Brookes Publishing Co.

Singer, G.H.S., Irvine, A.B., & Irvin, L.K. (1989). Expanding the focus of behavioral parent training: A contextual approach. In G.H.S. Singer & L.K. Irvin (Eds.), *Support for caregiving families: Enabling positive adaptation to disability* (pp. 85–102). Baltimore: Paul H. Brookes Publishing Co.

Singer, G.H.S., Singer, J., & Horner, R.H. (1987). Using pretask request to increase the probability of compliance for students with severe disabilities. *Journal of The Association for Persons with Severe Handicaps, 12,* 287–291.

Singer, J., Bossard, M., & Watkins, M. (1977). Effects of parental presence on attendance and input of interdisciplinary teams in an institutional setting. *Psychological Reports, 41,* 1031–1034.

Singh, N.N., Watson, J.E., & Winton, A.S.W. (1986). Treating self-injury: Water mist spray versus facial screening or forced arm exercise. *Journal of Applied Behavior Analysis, 19,* 403–410.

Singleton, L.C., & Asher, S.R. (1977). Peer preferences and social interaction among third-grade children in an integrated school district. *Journal of Educational Psychology, 69,* 330–336.

Siperstein, G.N., & Chatillon, A.C. (1982). Importance of perceived similarity in improving children's attitudes toward mentally retarded children. *American Journal of Mental Deficiency, 86,* 453–458.

Skinner, B.F. (1989). The behavior of the listener. In S.C. Hayes (Ed.), *Rule-governed behavior: Cognition, contingencies, and instructional control* (pp. 85–96). New York: Plenum.

Smith, S.W. (1990a). Comparison of individualized education programs (IEPs) of students with behavioral disorders and learning disabilities. *Journal of Special Education, 24*(1), 85–100.

Smith, S.W. (1990b). Individualized education programs (IEPs) in special education: From intent to acquiescence. *Exceptional Children, 57*(1), 6–14.

Smith, S.W., & Simpson, R.L. (1989). An analysis of individualized education programs (IEPs) for students with behavioral disorders. *Behavioral Disorders, 14*(2), 107–116.

Snell, M. (1987). *Systematic instruction of persons with severe handicaps.* Columbus, OH: Charles E. Merrill.

Soffer, R.M. (1982). IEP decisions in which parents desire greater participation. *Education and Training of the Mentally Retarded, 17*(1), 67–70.

Sonnenschein, P. (1984). Parents and professionals: An uneasy relationship. In M.L. Henniger & E.M. Nesselroad (Eds.), *Working with parents of handicapped children* (pp. 129–139). New York: University Press of America.

Spekman, N.L., & Roth, F.P. (1984). Intervention strategies for learning disabled children with oral communication disorders. *Learning Disability Quarterly, 7*, 7–18.

Spiegle-Mariska, J. (1990). *Common ground: A series of essays for professionals and families who unite to help young children with special needs.* Washington, DC: Special Education Programs. (ERIC Document Reproduction Service No. ED 342 166)

Stahmer, A.C., & Schreibman, L. (1992). Teaching children with autism appropriate play in unsupervised environments using a self-management treatment package. *Journal of Applied Behavior Analysis, 25*(2), 447–459.

Stainback, S., & Stainback, W. (1982). Influencing the attitudes of regular class teachers about the education of severely retarded students. *Education and Training of the Mentally Retarded, 17*(2), 88–92.

Stainback, S., Stainback, W., & Forest, M. (Eds.). (1989). *Educating all students in the mainstream of regular education.* Baltimore: Paul H. Brookes Publishing Co.

Stainback, W., & Stainback, S. (1982). Preparing regular class teachers for the integration of severely retarded students. *Education and Training of the Mentally Retarded, 17*(4), 273–277.

Stainback, W., & Stainback, S. (1984). A rationale for the merger of regular and special education. *Exceptional Children, 51*(2), 102–111.

Stainback, W., & Stainback, S. (1985). *Integration of students with severe handicaps into regular schools.* Reston, VA: Council for Exceptional Children.

Stainback, W., & Stainback, S. (1987). Facilitating friendships. *Education and Training in Mental Retardation, 22*, 18–25.

Stainback, W., Stainback, S., Courtnage, L., & Jaben, T. (1985). Facilitating mainstreaming by modifying the mainstream. *Exceptional Children, 52*(2), 144–152.

Stephens, T.M., & Braun, B.L. (1980). Measures of regular classroom teachers' attitudes toward handicapped children. *Exceptional Children, 46*(4), 292–294.

Stewart, D.M., & Hamilton, M.L. (1976). Imitation as a learning strategy in the acquisition of vocabulary. *Journal of Experimental Child Psychology, 21*, 380–392.

Stewart, M.J. (1990). Expanding theoretical conceptualizations of self-help groups. *Social Science Medicine, 31*(9), 1057–1066.

Stokes, T.F., & Baer, D.M. (1977). An implicit technology of generalization. *Journal of Applied Behavior Analysis, 10*, 349–368.

Stokes, T.F., Baer, D.M., & Jackson, R.L. (1974). Programming the generalization of a greeting response in four retarded children. *Journal of Applied Behavior Analysis, 7*, 599–610.

Stokes, T.F., & Osnes, P.G. (1986). Generalization of children's social behavior. In P.S. Strain, M.J. Guralnick, & H.M. Walker (Eds.), *Children's social behavior: Development, assessment, and modification* (pp. 407–443). Orlando, FL: Academic Press.

Stoneman, Z. (1993). The effects of attitude on preschool integration. In C.A. Peck, S.L. Odom, & D.D. Bricker (Eds.), *Integrating young children with disabilities into community programs: Eco-*

logical perspectives on research and implementation (pp. 223–248). Baltimore: Paul H. Brookes Publishing Co.

Strain, P.S. (1981). Peer-mediated treatment of exceptional children's social withdrawal. *Exceptional Education Quarterly, 1,* 93–105.

Strain, P.S. (1983). Generalization of autistic children's social behavior change: Effects of developmentally integrated and segregated settings. *Analysis and Intervention in Developmental Disabilities, 3,* 23–34.

Strain, P.S. (1984). Social behavior patterns of nonhandicapped and developmentally disabled friend pairs in mainstream preschools. *Analysis and Intervention in Developmental Disabilities, 4,* 15–28.

Strain, P.S., & Fox, J. (1981). Peer social initiations and the modification of social withdrawal: A review and future perspectives. *Journal of Pediatric Psychology, 6,* 417–433.

Strain, P.S., Kerr, M.M., & Ragland, E.U. (1979). Effects of peer-mediated social initiations and prompting/reinforcement procedures on the social behavior of autistic children. *Journal of Autism and Developmental Disorders, 9,* 41–54.

Strain, P.S., & Odom, S.L. (1986). Peer social initiations: Effective intervention for social skill development of exceptional children. *Exceptional Children, 52,* 543–552.

Strain, P.S., Odom, S.L., & McConnell, S. (1984). Promoting social reciprocity of exceptional children: Identification, target behavior selection, and intervention. *Remedial and Special Education, 5,* 21–28.

Strain, P.S., & Shores, R.E. (1977). Social reciprocity: A review of research and educational implications. *Exceptional Children, 43,* 526–530.

Strain, P.S., Shores, R.E., & Kerr, M.M. (1976). An experimental analysis of "spillover" effects on the social interaction of behaviorally handicapped preschool children. *Journal of Applied Behavior Analysis, 9,* 31–40.

Strain, P.S., Shores, R.E., & Timm, M.A. (1977). Effects of peer social initiations on the behavior of withdrawn preschool children. *Journal of Applied Behavior Analysis, 10,* 289–298.

Strain, P.S., & Timm, M.A. (1974). An experimental analysis of social interaction between a behaviorally disordered preschool child and her classroom peers. *Journal of Applied Behavior Analysis, 7,* 583–590.

Strayhorn, J.M., & Strain, P.S. (1986). Social and language skills for preventative mental health: What, how, who, and when. In P.S. Strain, M.J. Guralnick, & H.M. Walker (Eds.), *Children's social behavior: Development, assessment, and modification* (pp. 287–330). London: Academic Press.

Strickland, B.B., & Turnbull, A.P. (1990). *Developing and implementing individualized education programs* (3rd ed.). Columbus, OH: Charles E. Merrill.

Strully, J., & Strully, C. (1985). Friendship and our children. *Journal of The Association for Persons with Severe Handicaps, 10,* 224–227.

Strully, J., & Strully, C. (1989). Friendship as an educational goal. In S. Stainback, W. Stainback, & M. Forest (Eds.), *Educating all students in the mainstream of regular education* (pp. 59–68). Baltimore: Paul H. Brookes Publishing Co.

Sugai, G., & Rowe, D. (1984). The effect of self-recording on out-of-seat behavior of an EMR student. *Education and Training of the Mentally Retarded, 19,* 23–28.

Tager-Flusberg, H. (1994). Dissociations in form and function in the acquisition of language by autistic children. In H. Tager-Flusberg (Ed.), *Constraints on language acquisition: Studies of atypical children* (pp. 175–194). Hillsdale, NJ: Lawrence Erlbaum Associates.

Tager-Flusberg, H., Calkins, S., Nolin, T., Baumberger, T., Anderson, M., & Chadwick,-A. (1990). A longitudinal study of language acquisition in autistic and Down syndrome children. *Journal of Autism and Developmental Disorders, 20*(1), 1–21.

Taras, M.E., Matson, J.L., & Leary, C. (1988). Training social interpersonal skills in two autistic children. *Journal of Behavior Therapy and Experimental Psychiatry, 19,* 275–280.

Tate, B.G., & Baroff, G.S. (1966). Aversive control of self-injurious behavior in a psychotic boy. *Behavior Research and Therapy, 4,* 281–287.

Taylor, S.J. (1988). Caught in a continuum: A critical analysis of the principle of least restrictive environment. *Journal of The Association for Persons with Severe Handicaps, 13*(1), 41–53.

Taylor, S.J., & Bogdan, R. (1989). On accepting relationships between people with mental retardation and nondisabled people: Towards an understanding of acceptance. *Disability, Handicap, and Society, 4,* 21–36.

Taylor, S.J., & Knoll, J.A. (1989). Community living and the education of students with severe disabilities. In R. Gaylord-Ross (Ed.), *Integration strategies for students with handicaps* (pp. 321–338). Baltimore: Paul H. Brookes Publishing Co.

Tesch, S.A. (1983). Review of friendship development across the life span. *Human Development, 26,* 266–276.

Tesser, A., Campbell, J., & Smith, M. (1984). Friendship choice and performance: Self-evaluation maintenance in children. *Journal of Personality and Social Psychology, 46,* 561–574.

The Association for Persons with Severe Handicaps (TASH). (1992, November). Placement of students with disabilities in regular classrooms. *TASH Newsletter.*

Touchette, P.E., MacDonald, R.F., & Langer, S.N. (1985). A scatter plot for identifying stimulus control of problem behavior. *Journal of Applied Behavior Analysis, 18,* 343–351.

Tracy, E.M., & Whittaker, J.K. (1987). The evidence base for social support interventions in child and family practice: Emerging issues for research and practice. *Children and Youth Services Review, 9,* 249–270.

Tremblay, A., Strain, P.S., Hendrickson, J.M., & Shores, R.E. (1981). Social interactions of normally developing preschool children: Using normative data for subject and target behavior selection. *Behavior Modification, 5,* 237–253.

Tremblay, P., & Vanaman, V. (1979). The constitutional and statutory right of handicapped children to a free, appropriate education. In L.F. Buscaglia & E.H. Williams (Eds.), *Human advocacy and P.L. 94-142* (pp. 13–24). Thorofare, NJ: Charles B. Slack.

Turnbull, A. (1994, March). *Action groups.* Paper presented at the 1994 "Strategies for Managing Challenging Behaviors in Community Settings" conference, University of California, Santa Barbara.

Turnbull, A.P. (1978). Moving from being a professional to being a parent: A startling experience. In A.P. Turnbull & H.R. Turnbull, III (Eds.), *Parents speak out: Views from the other side of the two-way mirror* (pp. 130–140). Columbus, OH: Charles E. Merrill.

Turnbull, A.P., & Leonard, J. (1981). Parent involvement in special education: Emerging advocacy roles. *School Psychology Review, 10*(1), 37–44.

Turnbull, A.P., & Summers, J.A. (1987). From parent involvement to family support: Evolution to revolution. In S.M. Pueschel, C. Tingey, J.E. Rynders, A.C. Crocker, & D.M. Crutcher (Eds.), *New perspectives on Down syndrome* (pp. 289–305). Baltimore: Paul H. Brookes Publishing Co.

Turnbull, A.P., Summers, J.A., & Brotherson, M.J. (1986). Family life cycle: Theoretical and empirical implications and future directions for families with mentally retarded members. In J.J. Gallagher & P.M. Vietze (Eds.), *Families of handicapped persons: Research, programs, and policy issues* (pp. 45–65). Baltimore: Paul H. Brookes Publishing Co.

Turnbull, A.P., & Turnbull, H.R. (1982). Parent involvement in the education of handicapped children: A critique. *Mental Retardation, 20,* 115–122.

Turnbull, A.P., & Turnbull, H.R. (1986). *Families, professionals, and exceptionality: A special partnership.* Columbus, OH: Charles E. Merrill.

Turnbull, A.P., & Winton, P.J. (1983). A comparison of specialized and mainstreamed preschools from the perspectives of parents of handicapped children. *Journal of Pediatric Psychology, 8*(1), 57–71.

Turnbull, A.P., & Winton, P.J. (1984). Parent involvement policy and practice: Current research and implications for families of young, severely handicapped children. In J. Blacher (Ed.), *Severely handicapped young children and their families* (pp. 377–397). Orlando, FL: Academic Press.

Turnbull, A.P., Winton, P.J., Blacher, J., & Salkind, N. (1983). Mainstreaming in the kindergarten classroom: Perspectives of parents of handicapped and nonhandicapped children. *Journal of the Division for Early Childhood, 6,* 14–20.

Turnbull, H.R. (1993). *Free appropriate public education: The law and children with disabilities* (4th ed.). Denver, CO: Love Publishing Co.

Turnbull, H.R., III, & Turnbull, A.P. (1990). The unfulfilled promise of integration: Does Part H ensure different rights and results than part B of the education of the handicapped act? *Topics in Early Childhood Education, 10*(2), 18–32.

Turnbull, H.R., Turnbull, A.P., & Wheat, M.J. (1982). Assumptions about parental participation: A legislative history. *Exceptional Education Quarterly, 3*(2), 1–8.

Uhlman, W.F., & Shook, C.L. (1976). A method for maintaining high rates of performance in an open classroom setting. In T. Brigham, R. Hawkins, J.W. Scott, & T.F. McLaughlin (Eds.), *Behavior analysis in education: Self-control and reading.* Dubuque, IA: Kendall Hunt.

Ungerer, J., & Sigman, M. (1981). Symbolic play and language comprehension in autistic children. *Journal of the American Academy of Child Psychiatry, 20,* 318–337.

Van Hasselt, V.B., Sisson, L.A., & Aach, S.R. (1987). Parent training to increase compliance in a young multihandicapped child. *Journal of Behavior Therapy & Experimental Psychiatry, 18,* 275–283.

Varni, J., Lovaas, O.I., Koegel, R.L., & Everett, M.L. (1979). An analysis of observational learning in autistic and normal children. *Journal of Abnormal Child Psychology, 7,* 31–43.

Ventura, J.N. (1987). The stresses of parenthood re-examined. *Family Relations, 36,* 26–29.

Vincent, L.J., Laten, S., Salisbury, C., Brown, P., & Baumgart, D. (1981). Family involvement in the educational processes of severely handicapped students: State of the art and directions for the future. In B. Wilcox & P. York (Eds.), *Quality educational services for the severely handicapped* (pp. 164–179). Washington, DC: Division of Innovation and Development, Department of Education.

Voeltz, L.M. (1982). Effects of structured interactions with severely handicapped peers on children's attitudes. *American Journal of Mental Deficiency, 86,* 380–390.

Wacker, F., Steege, M., Northup, J., Sasso, G., Berg, W., Reimers, T., Cooper, L., Cigrand, K., & Donn, L. (1990). A component analysis of functional communication training across three topographies of severe behavior problems. *Journal of Applied Behavior Analysis, 23,* 331–343.

Wahler, R.G. (1980). The insular mothers: Her problems in parent-child treatment. *Journal of Applied Behavior Analysis, 13,* 207–219.

Walker, H.M. (1977). *The acting-out child: Coping with classroom disruption.* Needham Heights, MA: Allyn & Bacon.

Wang, M., & Baker, E. (1986). Mainstreaming program: Design features and effects. *Journal of Special Education, 19*(4), 503–521.

Wang, M.C., & Birch, J.W. (1984a). Comparison of a full-time mainstreaming program and a resource room approach. *Exceptional Children, 51*(1), 33–40.

Wang, M.C., & Birch, J.W. (1984b). Effective special education in regular classes. *Exceptional Children, 50*(5), 391–398.

Ward, A.J. (1970). Early infantile autism: Diagnosis, etiology, and treatment. *Psychological Bulletin, 73,* 350–362.

Warren, S.F., & Bambara, L.M. (1989). An experimental analysis of milieu language intervention: Teaching the action-object form. *Journal of Speech and Hearing Disorders, 54,* 448–461.

Warren, S.F., & Kaiser, A.P. (1986). Incidental language teaching: A critical review. *Journal of Speech and Hearing Disorders, 51,* 291–299.

Warren, S.F., McQuarter, R.J., & Rogers-Warren, A.K. (1984). The effects of teacher mands and models on the speech of unresponsive language-delayed children. *Journal of Speech and Hearing Research, 49,* 43–52.

Warren, S.F., & Reichle, J. (Eds.). (1992). *Communication and language intervention series. Vol. 1, Causes and effects in communication and language intervention.* Baltimore: Paul H. Brookes Publishing Co.

Waterhouse, L., & Fein, D. (1978). Patterns of kinesic synchrony in autistic and schizophrenic children. In F.C.C. Peng & W. von Raffler-Engel (Eds.), *Language acquisition and developmental kinesics* (pp. 113–119). Hiroshima: Bunka Hyoron.

Waterhouse, L., Fein, D., Nath, J., & Snyder, D. (1987). Pervasive developmental disorders and schizophrenia occurring in childhood: A review of critical commentary. In G.L. Tischler (Ed.), *Diagnosis and classification in psychiatry: A critical appraisal of DSM-III* (pp. 335–368). New York: Cambridge University Press.

Watt, N. (1978). Patterns of childhood social development in adult schizophrenics. *Archives of General Psychiatry, 35,* 160–165.

Weatherley, R., & Lipsky, M. (1977). Street-level bureaucrats and institutional innovation: Implementing special-education reform. *Harvard Educational Review, 47*(2), 171–197.

Werth, L.H., & Oseroff, A.B. (1987). Continual counseling intervention: Lifetime support for the family with a handicapped member. *American Journal of Family Therapy, 15,* 333–342.

Westman, J., Rice, D., & Bermann, E. (1967). Nursery school behavior and later school adjustment. *American Journal of Orthopsychiatry, 37,* 725–731.

Wetherby, A.M., & Prutting, C.A. (1984). Profiles of communicative and cognitive-social abilities in autistic children. *Journal of Speech and Hearing Research, 27,* 364–377.

White, G.D., Nielsen, H., & Johnson, S.M. (1972). Timeout duration and the suppression of deviant behavior in children. *Journal of Applied Behavior Analysis, 5,* 111–120.

Wikler, L. (1981). Chronic stresses of families of mentally retarded children. *Family Relations, 30,* 281–288.

Will, M.C. (1989). Foreword. In W. Sailor, J.L. Anderson, A.T. Halvorsen, K. Doering, J. Filler, & L. Goetz, *The comprehensive local school: Regular education for all students with disabilities* (pp. vi–viii). Baltimore: Paul H. Brookes Publishing Co.

Williams, J.A., Koegel, R.L., & Egel, A.L. (1981). Response-reinforcer relationships and improved learning in autistic children. *Journal of Applied Behavior Analysis, 14,* 53–60.

Wilson, W.C. (1989). Administrative strategies for integration. In R. Gaylord-Ross (Ed.), *Integration strategies for students with handicaps* (pp. 299–319). Baltimore: Paul H. Brookes Publishing Co.

Winborne, D.G. (1991). Early intervention: In consideration of medicine, education, and changing demographics. In J. Harris (Ed.), *The state of education in pluralistic America* (pp. 97–111). Bloomington: Indiana University Press.

Wing, L. (1972). *Autistic children: A guide for parents.* New York: Brunner/Mazel.

Wing, L., & Gould, J. (1979). Severe impairments of social interaction and associated abnormalities in children: Epidemiology and classification. *Journal of Autism and Developmental Disabilities, 9,* 11–29.

Winterling, V., Dunlap, G., & O'Neill, R.E. (1987). The influence of task variation on aberrant behaviors of autistic students. *Education and Treatment of Children, 10,* 105–119.

Winton, P.J. (1986). The consequences of mainstreaming for families of young handicapped children. In C.J. Meisel (Ed.), *Mainstreaming handicapped children: Outcomes, controversies, and new directions* (pp. 129–148). Hillsdale, NJ: Lawrence Erlbaum Associates.

Winton, P.J. (1990). Promoting a normalizing approach to families: Integrating theory with practice. *Topics in Early Childhood Special Education, 10*(2), 90–103.

Winton, P.J. (1993). Providing family support in integrated settings: Research and recommendations. In C.A. Peck, S.L. Odom, & D.D. Bricker (Eds.), *Integrating young children with disabilities into community programs: Ecological perspectives on research and implementation* (pp. 65–80). Baltimore: Paul H. Brookes Publishing Co.

Winton, P.J., & Turnbull, A.P. (1981). Parent involvement as viewed by parents of preschool handicapped children. *Topics in Early Childhood Special Education, 1*(3), 11–19.

Winton, P.J., Turnbull, A.P., & Blacher, J. (1984). *Selecting a preschool: A guide for parents of handicapped children.* Baltimore: University Park Press.

Witt, J.C., Miller, C.D., McIntyre, R.M., & Smith, D. (1984). Effects of variables on parental perceptions of staffing. *Exceptional Children, 51*(1), 27–32.

Wolchik, S.A., & Harris, S.L. (1982). Language environments of autistic and normal children matched for language age: Preliminary investigation. *Journal of Autism and Developmental Disabilities, 12,* 43–55.

Wolf, L.C., Noh, S., Fisman, S.N., & Speechley, M. (1989). Brief report: Psychological effects of parenting stress on parents of autistic children. *Journal of Autism and Developmental Disorders, 19*, 157–166.

Wolfsenberger, W. (1972). *Normalization: The principle for normalization in human service.* Toronto: National Institute on Mental Retardation.

Won, K.P., Anderson, J.L., & Haring, K. (1993). *The effects of integration on the challenging behavior of students with severe disabilities.* Unpublished manuscript, California State University, Hayward.

Woolery, M. (1991). Instruction in early childhood special education: "Seeing through a glass darkly . . . knowing in part." *Exceptional Children, 58*(2), 127–135.

Woolfolk, R.L., & Lehrer, P.M. (1984). *Principles and practices of stress management.* New York: Guilford Press.

Yanok, J., & Derubertis, D. (1989). Comparative study of parental participation in regular and special education programs. *Exceptional Children, 56*(3), 195–199.

Yirmiya, N., Kasari, C., Sigman, M., & Mundy, P. (1989). Facial expressions of affect in autistic, mentally retarded, and normal children. *Journal of Child Psychology and Psychiatry, 30*, 725–735.

Yoder, P.J. (1990). The theoretical and empirical basis of early amelioration of developmental disabilities: Implications for future research. *Journal of Early Intervention, 14*(1), 27–42.

Yoder, P.J., Kaiser, A.P., Alpert, C., & Fischer, R. (1993). Following the child's lead when teaching nouns to preschoolers with mental retardation. *Journal of Speech and Hearing Research, 36*, 158–167.

York, J., Vandercook, T., MacDonald, C., & Wolff, S. (Eds.). (1989). *Strategies for full inclusion.* Minneapolis: University of Minnesota, Institute on Community Integration.

Yoshida, R.K., Fenton, K.S., Kaufman, M.J., & Maxwell, J.P. (1978). Parent involvement in the special education pupil planning process: The school's perspective. *Exceptional Children, 44*(7), 531–534.

Yoshida, R.K., Fenton, K.S., Maxwell, J.P., & Kaufman, M.J. (1978). Group decision making in the planning team: Myth or reality? *Journal of School Psychology, 16*, 237–244.

Yoshida, R.K., & Gottlieb, J. (1977). A model of parental participation in the pupil planning process. *Mental Retardation, 15*(3), 17–20.

Ysseldyke, J.E., Algozzine, B., & Allen, D. (1982). Participation of regular education teachers in special education team decision making. *Exceptional Children, 48*(4), 365–366.

Zeilberger, J., Sampen, S.E., & Sloane, H.N., Jr. (1968). Modification of a child's behavior problems in the home with the mother as therapist. *Journal of Applied Behavior Analysis, 1*, 47–53.

Zettel, J.J., & Ballard, J. (1982). The Education for All Handicapped Children Act of 1975 (P.L. 94-142): Its history, origins, and concepts. In J. Ballard, B.A. Ramirez, & F.J. Weintraub (Eds.), *Special education in America: Its legal and governmental foundations* (pp. 11–22). Reston, VA: Council for Exceptional Children.

Zigler, E., & Butterfield, E.C. (1968). Motivational aspects of changes in IQ test performance of retarded children. *Child Development, 39*, 1–14.

Index

Page numbers followed by "*f*" or "*t*" indicate figures or tables, respectively.

Positive Behavioral Support

Including People with Difficult Behavior in the Community

Edited by Lynn Kern Koegel, Ph.D.,
Robert L. Koegel, Ph.D., & Glen Dunlap, Ph.D.

People with challenging behavior can be fully included in communities—if they receive the right supports. Based on solid research, this text offers specific intervention techniques for young children, elementary or secondary students, and adults. You'll address

- **family issues** like increasing positive caregiver-child interactions and providing family education and support
- **education issues** like creating environments that support students' communication, reducing corporal punishment, and developing positive relationships between caregivers and school districts
- **social inclusion issues** like fostering relationships, integrating naturalistic language, and teaching symbolic play and social interaction skills
- **community inclusion issues** like understanding the context of behavior, educating team members to provide positive behavioral supports, and implementing "life coaching" and person-centered planning

Enhanced with compelling case studies and helpful charts and graphs, this is your research-based guide to putting nonaversive inclusion strategies to work in school, at home, and in the community.

Stock Number: 2282

Price: $37.95

1996

528 pages

6 x 9

paperback

ISBN 1-55766-228-2

Please send me

___ ***Positive Behavioral Support*** / Stock #2282 / $37.95

___ Check enclosed (payable to Brookes Publishing Co.)
___ Purchase Order attached (bill my institution)
___ Please charge my credit card: ○ American Express   ○ MasterCard   ○ Visa

Credit Card #: _____ Exp. Date: _____

Signature (required with credit card use): _____

Name: _____

Daytime Phone: _____

Street Address: _____ ❑ residential ❑ commercial
Complete street address required.

City/State/ZIP: _____ Country: _____

E-mail Address: _____
❑ Yes! I want to receive special web site discount offers! My e-mail address will not be shared with any other party.

Shipping & Handling

For pretax total of	Add*	For CAN
$0.00 - $49.99	$5.00	$7.00
$50.00 - $69.99	10%	$7.00
$70.00 - $399.99	10%	10%
$400.00 and over	8%	8%

calculate percentage on product total

Shipping rates are for UPS Ground Delivery within continental U.S.A. For other shipping options and rates, call 1-800-638-3775 (in the U.S.A. and CAN) and 410-337-9580 (worldwide).

All prices in U.S.A. dollars. Policies and prices subject to change without notice. Prices may be higher outside the U.S.A. You may return books within 30 days for a full credit of the product price. Refunds will be issued for prepaid orders. Items must be returned in resalable condition.

Subtotal $ _____
+
5% sales tax, Maryland only $ _____
+
7% business tax (GST), CAN only $ _____
+
Shipping (see chart) $ _____
=
Total (in U.S.A. dollars) $ _____

Your list code is **BA 66**